Academic Librarianship

Camila A. Alire and

G. Edward Evans

Neal-Schuman Publishers, Inc.

New York   London

Published by Neal-Schuman Publishers, Inc.
100 William St., Suite 2004
New York, NY 10038

Library of Congress Cataloging-in-Publication Data

Alire, Camila A.
   Academic librarianship / Camila A. Alire and G. Edward Evans.
      p. cm.
   Includes bibliographical references and index.
   ISBN 978-1-55570-702-6 (alk. paper)
   1. Academic libraries—United States. 2. Libraries and colleges—United States.
I. Evans, G. Edward, 1937- II. Title.

Z675.U5A427 2010
027.70973—dc22

                                                    2010017964

Contents

Don't Miss This Book's Companion Web Site!
www.neal-schuman.com/academic
21 Essays on the Future of Academic Librarianship:

Tables

Preface

Writing *Academic Librarianship* was a special pleasure for both of us as we have had long and rewarding careers in academic libraries. Between us, we have "floor" experience in all types of academic institutions and we've been directors and deans. In addition, we have had opportunities to teach courses in the field. What follows draws on our experiences, the literature, and ideas from many colleagues in academia.

After being asked by Neal-Schuman to prepare a proposal for a text on academic librarianship, we contacted a number of library directors about what they thought newly graduated librarians should know about the academy and its libraries. Their input helped guide our thinking as we prepared the proposal. Shortly after starting work on the manuscript, ACRLog (June 10, 2008) had a discussion about "What an Academic Librarianship Course Should Offer" (acrlog.org/2008/06/10). We reviewed the list of topics suggested, discussed them, and added several topics to our working outline. You now hold the result.

We wish to emphasize that this is a book about the academic library and its *environment*. While management is a significant part of academic librarianship, as it is in any type of library, this is not a management text as such. While there was no way to avoid some mention of management issues/techniques/skills at various points in the text, almost all students will take a full course that covers the basics of management; thus, we concentrate here on the academic library as an institution and its parent organization and community.

ORGANIZATION

Academic Librarianship has four major sections.

Part I, "Background and Historic Context," lays the foundation for the remainder of the book by looking at higher education in general and the role of "the academy" in both a historical and environmental sense.

Part II, "Higher Education Today," examines the basic components of colleges and universities—faculty, students, curriculum, and governance—and how they impact the library.

Part III, "Campus and Library Commonalities," provides a basic introduction to campuswide concerns—facilities, technology, financing, accreditation, and accountability—that library managers need to understand both holistically and regarding how they affect the library individually.

Part IV, "The Academic Library Today," is devoted to in-depth coverage of staffing, services, collections, repositories, collaboration, and career paths. The final chapter in this part summarizes the thoughts of 21 academic library directors, representing a cross-section of all academic library types, regarding the future of the field. They were asked to write about where they think the field is going and what it may look like in 15 to 20 years. We also encourage you to read the full text of each of these academic leaders' essays at www.neal-schuman.com/academic.

A few comments about usage and format are also appropriate. To provide some textual variation, we employed several terms when referring to the broad topic of higher education: higher education, colleges and universities, the academy, academia, and post-secondary education. Because both authors have taught courses relating to management and academic librarianship, we have included examples from our personal experiences in higher education and librarianship because we know students enjoy learning of firsthand experiences. We know that those experiences do not always reflect universals; however, they reflect what can, has, and does take place in the real world of academic librarianship. These experiences are incorporated into sidebars indicating they are from the authors' personal experiences. A final note on style: we attempted to create a text that is informal, as if we were talking with the reader, rather than the usual stiff formal style of many textbooks.

It is our deep desire that our readers both learn from the pages that follow and have as rewarding a career in academic librarianship as we have.

Acknowledgments

Our list of those we must acknowledge is long and varied. The four members of our editorial advisory board deserve special recognition and our profound thanks for reading and commenting on all chapters, sometimes more than once:

- Trudi Bellardo Hahn, Professor, University of Maryland College of Information Studies
- Carol Sinwell, Dean of Educational Support Services, Northern Virginia Community College, Annandale Campus
- Margaret Saponaro, Librarian III, Social Sciences Team, University of Maryland Libraries
- John Stemmer, Director of the Library, Bellarmine University

We wish to also thank Dr. Joseph Tiedemann, a professor of history at Loyola Marymount University and longtime chair of the Faculty Library Advisory Committee and chair of the university's Core Curriculum Committee for insightful comments on various chapters. A special thank you must go to Fr. Michael Engh, SJ, President of Santa Clara University for taking the time to read the chapter on governance. Last and certainly far from least are our 22 colleagues who contributed the 21 essays about the future of academic librarianship:

- Barbara Bintliff, Director, William A. Wise Law Library, University of Colorado at Boulder School of Law
- Holly Shipp Buchanan, Associate Vice President for Knowledge Management and Information Technology, Health Sciences Center, University of New Mexico
- Brian Bunnett, Director of Library and Education Services Health Sciences Library and Informatics Center, University of New Mexico
- Rick Burke, Executive Director, Statewide California Electronic Library Consortium
- Theresa Byrd, Director of Libraries, Ohio Wesleyan University
- Thomas Carter, Dean for Academic Resources, Saint Mary's College of California
- Susan C. Curzon, Dean, University Library, California State University, Northridge
- Joan Giesecke, Dean of Libraries, University of Nebraska–Lincoln
- Cynthia L. Henderson, Library Director, Morehouse School of Medicine
- Peter Hernon, Professor, Graduate School of Library and Information Science, Simmons College
- Michael Kelly, Associate Dean, Scholarly Resources, Special Collections, and the Center for Southwest Research, University of New Mexico Libraries
- Lynne King, Director of Library Services, Schenectady County Community College State University of New York

- John Murray, Director, Library and Information Services, Westmont College
- Catherine Murray-Rust, Dean and Director, Georgia Institute of Technology Library and Information Center
- James G. Neal, Vice President for Information Services and University Librarian, Columbia University
- Steve O'Connor, University Librarian, Hong Kong Polytechnic University
- Loretta Parham, CEO and Library Director, Robert W. Woodruff Library of the Atlanta University Center
- Carol A. Parker, Law Library Director and Keleher Professor of Law, University of New Mexico School of Law
- Carol Sinwell, Acting Director of Learning Resource Services, Northern Virginia Community College, Annandale Campus, Annandale, Virginia
- Glenda Thornton, Director, University Library, Cleveland State University
- Ninfa A. Trejo, Retired Library Director and President, Trejo Foster Foundation for Hispanic Library Education
- Patricia A. Wand, Dean, Library and Learning Resources, Zayed University, United Arab Emirates

Part I

Background and Historic Context

Chapter 1, "Background," provides an overview of the size and complexity of U.S. higher education and some of its twenty-first-century challenges. Chapter 2, "Historic Context," describes the linkages between what happened in the higher education's past which are shown in later chapters to still exert an influence on the present.

Chapter 1

Background

Considering the extraordinary pace with which knowledge is moving to the Web, it is equally difficult to imagine what an academic library will be and do in another decade.

—Jerry D. Campbell (2006, p. 30)

Early in the digital revolution when campuses became wired and libraries began acquiring licenses for campus distribution of databases and electronic journals, many people believed that libraries as physical entities would decrease in importance. The opposite effect has occurred.

—Miriam Drake (2007, p. 9)

Educating a society's youth to carry on into the future has always been a challenge. As societies became increasingly complex, so did the process of educating the next generation, as did the time it took to produce the next generation of community leaders. What we call "higher education" in the United States and most of the world has been a part of many societies for a long time. The earliest universities in Europe date from the beginning of the thirteenth century. Oxford, Paris, and Bologna each apparently started independently, within ten years of one another, around the year 1200. Over time, higher education has responded to changing social needs and technological developments. We will very briefly review the history of the colleges and universities and their libraries in Chapter 2 as well as look for long-term threads/issues in higher education.

From their earliest beginnings, libraries and learning have been intertwined. As such, libraries have been a component of society for thousands of years. Over the millennia libraries have become increasingly accessible to all members of society. The earliest libraries were available only to a small number of the ruling class. (One of the earliest recorded libraries is one that archaeologists uncovered in the city of Ur, dating to about 2850 BC. It was probably accessible only to senior religious leaders and select members of the royal household.) Thus, libraries have almost a 5,000-year history of not only providing access to information but also handling change and adapting to new technologies and circumstances.

Obviously, the fact that libraries have been cultural icons for the better part of 5,000 years means they have changed with their societies and responded effectively to new technologies. Despite popular press and some professional commentators' suggestions (e.g., Ross and Sennyey, 2008), it would seem that such a long-standing component of society will not be jettisoned easily nor without long and careful thought. It also seems highly unlikely that the linkage between libraries and learning will disappear. Just what form that linkage will take over the coming years is unclear; however, we firmly believe it will remain strong.

FUTURE OF HIGHER EDUCATION AND ITS LIBRARIES

Given the electronic world of today, why is there a need for physical institutions of higher learning, and in particular academic libraries and librarians? With the Web, people can and do take courses without setting foot on a campus, much less a campus library. Full-text databases and services such as Google's Book Search and Google Scholar lead some people, especially academic institutions' chief financial officers, to argue that there is no need for a library, and that everything a student needs is on the Web. Needless to say, the authors of this book and a great many others vigorously disagree with such assessments. We know that "everything needed" is *not* on the Web and that reliable information often is not always free on the Web.

There are pointed and valid concerns about academia's viability, just as there are about libraries. Tom Abeles (2006) wrote, "The direction of the university today must be seen, first as an enterprise that is different from the idea of university as seen by Newman, Kant and von Humboldt. Secondly, it must be seen as a problem for faculty and not that of the institution" (p. 36). The technological challenges facing the academy appear to be just as great as those facing libraries. Abeles also suggested that "the time has come for institutions and the academics to understand that the caterpillar must transform into a butterfly" (p. 42). A few years earlier, Snyder and Edwards (2003), in writing about the context of education in the United States in the year 2020, wrote, "We found little evidence of significant innovation or change in the social technologies by which we formally organize and deliver education. Nor did we find any serious movement to assess alternatives to teacher mediated classroom-based learning" (p. 5). One fact is crystal clear: higher education and its libraries must change together. Without a joint process, there is little chance of long-term viability for either entity.

Academic libraries provide open and generally free access to the entire world of knowledge, not just to some segment of it. Furthermore, we agree with the following quotation from an article about e-government and print versus electronic distribution of information:

> Reports of the death of paper, rampant in the 1990s, were evidently greatly exaggerated. The paperless office never materialized; nor, yet, have e-books. People still print letters and flip through pages of magazines. ("Flat Prospects," 2007, p. 72)

A few years ago, Okerson (2003) offered her thoughts about the digital library. Her view was that eight "eternal verities" about library collections and services remain valid today and will continue to do so into the future. Most of the truths relate to services in some manner. These truths were the following:

- Content is selectable.
- Content is collectable.
- Libraries retain information for the long term.
- Collections grow and require some type of space.
- Long-term retention requires preservation of some type.
- Libraries expect to be around for a very long time.
- Libraries exist to meet users' information needs.
- Today's information is worldwide and so are libraries, helping ensure worldwide preservation of information/knowledge.

She concluded by writing, "May we all go boldly together where no libraries have gone before" (p. 285). We believe her views are accurate and to the point—libraries will indeed go successfully and boldly forward into the future.

We also agree with Lewis's (2007) assumptions about twenty-first-century academic libraries:

- Libraries are a means not an end.
- Disruptive technologies can and will disrupt libraries.
- A small change here and there will not result in real change.
- There is time to make effective changes, if we do not wait too long. (pp. 419–420)

We think a fifth assumption is necessary to complete the picture: If libraries do not change, they will join the dinosaurs.

Everyone is in agreement that academic institutions, libraries, and librarians have changed, dramatically so when looking back over just the past 20 years. Even a cursory look at the history of the academy makes it clear that the institution and its various components are adaptable to changing circumstances and societal needs. Admittedly, the pace of change has often been rather slow, but it does change.

Successful organizational transformations are seldom neither quick nor painless. Thinking back to discussions in basic management courses about change and the change process—at its most basic level the process of unfreezing, change, freezing (Lewin, 1951)—it is clear that time is a key factor in moving from one organizational state to another. Another factor is that some organizations change more quickly than others. The agile ones tend to be the most successful in the long term.

Carbo (2008) wrote about the future of academic libraries, the Web, and change, exploring some of the negative views some librarians and students hold about profit-oriented competitors such as Google. In particular, she expressed concern about attitudes such as for-profit information services being "money-grubbing," about a cavalier dismissal of "techies" in such organizations, and about over-simplifying complex ethical and policy issues. One of her central points was that thinking of information service competitors (the for-profits) as potential partners and seeking such partnerships will be more productive for everyone concerned. She mentioned the Open Content Alliance (www.opencontentalliance.org) as an example of a collaborative project. Two ventures she did not mention are Scholarly Publishing and Academic Resources Coalition (SPARC) and Coalition for Networked Information (CNI). Her concluding comment was, "Sharing experiences, knowledge, and ideas and building a 'Bigger Us' can only help all of us prepare our future colleagues for tomorrow's academic libraries" (p. 100).

> **Check This Out**
>
> An excellent book on change management is Susan Curzon's *Managing Change* (New York: Neal-Schuman, 2006).

The Association of College and Research Libraries (ACRL) Research and Scholarship Committee conducted a study of assumptions about the future of academic libraries and their staff (Mullins, Allen, and Hufford, 2007). The authors pointed out that their purpose was not to predict but rather to formulate statements intended to "encourage ACRL librarians to embrace changes and opportunities that are *already occurring* and to build into their libraries a culture that will continue to embrace change and opportunities that the future will bring" (p. 240). The ten assumptions, in a summary form, were the following:

- Digitization of print materials will accelerate, as will efforts to preserve digital archives/collections; likewise there will be ever better methods of retrieval.
- Required staffing skills will adjust to changing demands of the service population (faculty, students, and others).
- End users will demand ever greater delivery speed and access.
- Intellectual property will be an ever more important issue for academic institutions and their libraries.
- Technological demands will require ever greater funding, likely at the expense of some services and collections.
- Colleges and universities will more and more approach their operations using "business" models.
- End users, especially students, will view themselves as customers of the institution and its library as tuition and fees increase. As a result, they will expect and demand the highest level of quality service.
- Virtual course work and degrees will represent a major component of academia's programs if not the dominant aspect.
- Publicly funded research will be increasingly available to users on a no-cost basis.
- Privacy issues will be increasingly important and a challenge to handle.

Tennant (2006) made many of the same points as the ACRL study when he wrote:

> We must again become indispensable to the teaching and research missions of our institutions.... We need people who are not afraid of jettisoning traditional activities in favor of new ones.... We need new tools that many library vendors are not even considering.... Libraries... have a window of opportunity to leap into the future... But that window may already be in the process of slamming shut. (p. 34)

Although we cannot predict the future of higher education, some trends appear likely to grow in importance over the next 15 to 20 years. Should they indeed continue, a type of "postindustrial academy" may emerge, one that is sleeker, smaller in size (at least on a campus), more technology oriented, and with an almost global scope. The concept of "lifelong learning" will take on a much greater meaning as fields grow and transform as a result of technology. The process of learning will call for "certified" practitioners to have ever greater depth of knowledge. (Perhaps the PhD will no longer be the terminal degree.)

We see some hints of this in Massachusetts Institute of Technology's OpenCourseWare (OCW) project, which has published MIT course materials since 2002 and plans to have all of its 2,000 courses publicly available (free of charge with no registration required) by sometime in 2010–2011. Each course includes class presentations, syllabi, exams, streaming video, etc. MIT does not think this diminishes the value of the MIT campus experience and thus will continue to have a student body on the campus (especially since access to these materials does not constitute an MIT education, nor does OCW grant degrees, certificates, or access to faculty). For enrolled students, the firsthand interaction between faculty and other students outside of the classroom (and of course the earning of a degree) will outweigh the convenience of just securing a virtual education.

Check These Out

OpenCourseWare (ocw.mit.edu/OcwWeb/web/home/home/index.htm) for just what MIT is currently offering.
Universitas 21 (www.universitas21.com) to explore its programs.

An example of the trend for global higher education programs is Universitas 21. This is an international network of 21 leading research-focused institutions in 13 countries. They offer graduate work, undergraduate summer schools, and much more. For example, their summer schools have been hosted by National University of Singapore, Lund University, University of Hong Kong, University of Virginia, University of Birmingham, University of Queensland, and the 2010 summer school will be held at the University of Nottingham, Ningbo Campus. Themes have included: "Global Technology Entrepreneurship," "Asia as the Global Future," "Leadership in a Global Society," and "Climate Change Adaptation" (www.universitas21.com/summer). We believe such programs, even full undergraduate degrees from international networks of like-oriented colleges, will be more or less commonplace in the future.

We end this section with an optimistic statement in a popular press article about academic libraries. The editorial statement at the beginning of a special supplement on academic libraries in the *Guardian* newspaper (Hoare, 2008) stated, "Academic libraries are changing faster than at anytime in their history. Information technology, online databases, and catalogues and digitized archives have put the library back at the heart of teaching, learning, and academic research on the campus" (p. 1).

FUTURE OF ACADEMIC LIBRARIANS

Significant changes also will be necessary in the roles libraries will play in higher education. Newly graduated professionals will play a key role in reshaping the profession of academic librarianship. One way to approach thinking about what the future may hold is to think in terms of SWOT (strengths, weakness, opportunities, and threats) analysis, which provides a structure for thinking about where one is and what challenges exist. SWOT is commonly used in the strategic planning process.

Thinking in very broad terms about the information profession, some of the *strengths* are the following:

- An ability to organize information for retrieval and long-term preservation
- A long history of providing effective free service to users
- A broad understanding of the nature and structure of knowledge
- A powerful service orientation
- A strong commitment to creating and maintaining a balance for everyone in terms of intellectual property rights

In terms of *weakness*, one might list the following:

- A general lack of in-depth knowledge of multiple subjects on an individual basis
- A limited number of individuals with in-depth technology skills
- A relatively short tradition of "selling" the value library services to the public
- A modest priority level for funding library services
- A high cost of materials for collections and long-term preservation
- An unwillingness of some individuals to change

Some of the *opportunities* would include the following:

- Providing better control and organize the daily flood of "new" information
- Creating new/better ways to access information

- Declining cost of technology in terms of capability such as storage and speed
- Establishing long-term durability of digital material and its retrieval
- Assuring long-term free access to needed information for every individual
- Rethinking and reinventing the library as "place"
- Reshaping our information profession

Threats might include the following:

- An ever-growing volume of information on the Web
- A changing set of views about the nature of information rights by users
- A decline in library gate counts and usage of print-based collections
- An ever increasing rate of change, especially in technology, and the need to respond quickly and effectively
- A lack of funding to respond quickly and effectively

What might the future hold for academic librarians? One clear trend will be a continuation of the blurring of the role between public and technical services. Position descriptions are likely to contain a variety of duties that in the past were often stand-alone jobs. An example would be a combination of reference and cataloging. The essential requirement to understand and address user needs may lead to some librarians having their offices outside of the library, serving as liaisons to departments, schools, or colleges, for example. This is already taking place in some academic library settings, and we expect increased growth in this area. Teams and teamwork will become essential to providing the highest quality service. Providing service to distant learners will become more complex. Working with faculty and other stakeholders in developing appropriate information literacy skill sets will be another important activity.

> ### Try This and Something to Explore
> Do you agree with our SWOT list? If not, why not? Can you list at least two more items to each of the of the SWOT elements?
> Another method for looking toward the future is the Preferred Library Scenario. See our Launching Pad section for some starting points for your exploration.

Certainly all of the staff, but especially the librarians, will need to have higher level technological skills. The process of selecting, processing, organizing, and servicing collections, whatever their form, will remain, but they likely will be in a different form than the activities we engage in today. One area of probable collection building will be "institutional repositories"—institutionally generated scholarly information. More and more of the work will be akin to that of information brokers, facilitating access to and management of the *accurate* and specific information required for learning, teaching, and research. Much of the work will be one on one and frequently outside of the place called library.

On a personal level, individuals will need to engage in ongoing professional development, especially in areas related to technology such as Web 2.0 resources. Much of the learning is likely to be web-based and via tele- or webconferencing rather than traveling for face-to-face learning. Individuals will need to develop proactive skills with users as well as when thinking about work-related activities. Essentially all librarians and support staff must become active in marketing and promoting information services, both overtly through talking directly to users about the value of information services and via indirect/covert activities that also promote services through providing the highest quality of service.

Two information profession educators, Youngok Choi and Edie Rasmussen (2006), conducted a survey of the 123 Association of Research Libraries (ARL) directors. The purposes of the study were to gain insight into staffing for digital library activities, to identify critical digital library activities, to determine skills and knowledge required for such activities, and to solicit thoughts about educational needs for such work.

We firmly believe in the future of the digital library, even if we do not know just what it will look like. Therefore, we believe Choi and Rasmussen's (2006) skills and knowledge list is a sound starting point for thinking about roles and professional development. The researchers organized their knowledge needs into three broad categories: technology, library, and other related. Their top five items under technology were: a knowledge of digital library architecture and software, technical and quality standards, web markup languages, database development and management systems, and web design skills. The top five library-related knowledges were: understanding users and institutional information needs, digital archiving and preservation, cataloging and metadata, indexing, and collection development. "Other related" areas were primarily management skills: communication and interpersonal skills, project management and leadership, legal issues, grant writing, and teaching/group presentation skills. Choi and Rasmussen (2006) concluded their essay by saying, "Clearly, digital libraries are the future of academic and research institutions, and digital professionals will be required to have both more breath and depth of knowledge and skills across the dimensions of traditional library knowledge, technology, and human relations" (p. 7).

WHY BOTHER STUDYING THE SUBJECT IF EVERYTHING WILL CHANGE?

It may seem counterintuitive to spend time studying a subject when it is a "moving target" of sorts and always evolving. First and foremost, the answer to the question is everything changes, and one needs to understand what is good and what is not so good when deciding what to change. We firmly believe that it is by attending to the background (the past and present) that individuals and society are most likely to achieve new insights into what adjustments are necessary and desirable.

Another reason is that you will be more effective in working with others in higher education when you have a broad understanding of its components. For example, it is easier to develop good working relationships with faculty when you understand most of the pressures under which they operate. Understanding the components of the institution and its fiscal requirements can help make your efforts to gain the financial support necessary for your service to be more successful. A library exists to provide services to its community of users, and having a knowledge of the "whats and hows" of that community allows you to identify and to implement the most useful and desired services. This knowledge will also assist you in establishing efficient policies and procedures from both the library and user perspective—something that is very important when funding is tight, as it almost always is.

WHAT MAKES AN ACADEMIC LIBRARY ACADEMIC?

A book many managers have found useful at times is Sun-Tzu's (also called Sunzi) *The Art of War*. We certainly do not subscribe to the notion that the book can be a basic management guide; however, it does contain useful ideas. One of the more useful of these concepts appears in the first chapter: "Warfare is a great matter to a nation...it is the way of survival and of destruction and must be examined" (Sun-Tzu, accessed 2008). If you substitute *environment* for *warfare* and *organization* for *nation*, you have a key concept of this book—a library's operating environment is the fundamental factor in what it does and how it does its work.

The answer to this section's heading is, it is the organization of which the library is a part that makes it what it is. That answer applies to almost all libraries—there are very few stand-alone libraries. Libraries are normally part of some larger organization, be it government, business, school district, academic institution. They all perform, in some manner, the same fundamental functions: selection, acquisition, organization, storage/preservation, and service/access. What differentiates the types is the library's "parent" organization's mission and goals. These factors are the key environment within which the fundamental library functions are developed and put into operation. Without a sound understanding of this environment one cannot consistently create and maintain appropriate information services for the parent group. Although it is always beneficial to understand the nature of the parent organizational environment and its culture regardless of library type, such an understanding is essential in order to have a successful academic library career.

Libraries exist in a tripartite environment. First, the library has an internal environment, over which it has or should have reasonably good control and influence. Second, there is the environment within the parent organization, over which the librarians may have some, if small, influence. And, finally, there is the environment beyond the parent institution over which there is no control. All three environments require monitoring and responding to if the library is to be successful. A good article that explores the reason for examining the environment of a nonprofit organization is by Andrews, Boyne, and Walker (2006).

Another element in becoming a successful librarian is learning the organizational culture. Every organization has a culture that its members learn, or should learn, in order to be an effective member. That culture plays a very significant role in how the organization operates. Typically staff members are unaware of its influence on their behavior and actions except when someone acts in a contrary manner. Essentially, "learning" the culture is an informal process where a newcomer picks up bits and pieces through observation. Both the library and its parent institution have a culture, and it is necessary to understand both. Often these cultures have significant differences, so being aware of which culture you are currently operating in is a key to successful interactions with people and other units.

Just what is "organizational culture"? As Kell and Carrott (2005) noted, "Corporate culture, like personal character, is an amorphous quality that exerts a powerful influence" (p. 22). They go on to note both the positive and negative aspects of organizational culture. Although we acknowledge that the concept is rather amorphous, some elements are generally agreed on. One such element is that it is shared (consciously or not) by members of the organization. What they share are a set of values, assumptions, and expectations regarding what the organization is "about," how things should be done,

---

Check This Out

A good article that address some of the challenges faced by librarians new to academic libraries is Joanne Oud's "Adjusting to the Workplace: Transitions Faced by New Academic Librarians" in *College & Research Libraries* 69, no. 5 (2008): 252–285.

what is important and acceptable. People act on these views even though the culture is rarely articulated much less recorded. One learns it, as we learn social culture, through observation and the mistakes we make. Although it is an internal "environment," it can and does evolve as result of changes in the external environment. Individuals who ignore this internal environment do so at their peril—understanding the culture can make all of the difference when it comes time for the organization to make changes due to external factors.

HIGHER EDUCATION VARIATIONS

What constitutes U.S. academia? There is no short answer to this question. It exists in a bewildering array of public and private institutions. They are embedded in various political arrangements and governance structures of remarkable diversity. Some are multicampus operations, in some cases with each campus functioning as more or less autonomous institutions with its own curriculum and admission standards. Others operate as a single entity, even if geographically dispersed. There are single purpose institutions— law schools, for example—while others offer a wide range of subjects and degrees.

In light of the great diversity within U.S. postsecondary education, it is not surprising that academic libraries are equally diverse. Perhaps the U.S. Department of Education's National Center for Education Statistics' (Institute of Education Services, 2008) definition of an academic library is the most comprehensive:

> An academic library is defined as an entity in a postsecondary institution that provides all of the following: An organized collection of printed or other materials, or combination thereof; a staff trained to provide and interpret such materials as required to meet the informational, cultural, recreational, or educational needs of the clientele; an established schedule in which services of the staff are available to clientele, and the physical facilities necessary to support such collections, staff, and schedule (p. 1)

The center's 2004 survey of academic libraries, published in 2006, identified 3,617 libraries that met this definition. Public institution libraries represented 1,570 of the total. The breakdown for libraries serving institutions offering four year and above degree programs was 2,283 (p. 4).

The center's survey employs both its own "level" categories and the "Carnegie Classification" for grouping institutions. The Carnegie Classification is a widely used method of grouping "like" institutions. (Like is in quotation marks because it is difficult to identify two completely identical institutions; if nothing more, the enrollment demographics will differ.) Nevertheless the classification is better than any other and is therefore widely employed when attempting to bring some structure to the diversity of U.S. colleges and universities.

As the classification system is dynamic and subject to change as circumstances change, we based the following discussion on information available on the Carnegie Foundation for Advancement of Teaching's (2008) website (www.carnegiefoundation .org/classifications). Currently, there are six broad categories in the system: associate colleges, doctorate-granting universities, master's colleges and universities, baccalaureate colleges, special-focus institutions, and tribal colleges.

Associate colleges (often referred to as community colleges by the public) are those institutions whose highest degree is the two-year associate degree or who grant less than

10 percent of their total degrees as four-year bachelor's degrees. The majority of associate institutions are publicly funded.

Baccalaureate colleges offer more than 10 percent of their degrees as bachelor's and less than 50 master's degrees per year. The majority of institutions in this category are privately funded.

Master's colleges and universities award at least 50 master's degrees per year and fewer than 20 doctorates in addition to offering bachelor degree programs. This grouping is a mix of public and private institutions.

Doctorate-granting universities grant 20 or more doctoral degrees per year—this does not count "first professional" degrees such as law or medicine. The doctorates must be research based (PhDs). Like master's institutions, there is a mix of public and private universities in this category.

Special-focus institutions are primarily private and offer undergraduate and graduate degrees in a single field; sometimes the "field" can be rather broad such as art, design, or music. A single focus does not always mean just one type of degree—an art school might have a dozen or more degrees, such as a bachelor's of painting, another in ceramics, etc., as well offer a master of fine arts degree.

The final category is *tribal colleges*. Institutions in this category must be members of the American Indian Higher Education Consortium. These institutions have funding from tribal, private, and federal sources. They generally offer only bachelor's degrees, although some have vocational programs, and a few grant a master's degree on a limited number of subjects.

Another way that the authors of this text have structured their academic library courses is through a simplified Carnegie approach: research universities, universities, colleges, and community colleges. Research universities and their libraries (members of ARL) are the giants of U.S. higher education. They are considered giants in terms of staffing, enrollments, degrees granted (both in number and variety of subjects), funding, and public prestige. These institutions have programs for undergraduate, graduate, and postgraduate work. They normally have a variety of professional graduate schools—education, law, library and information science, and medicine, for example—that offer both first professional degrees as well as higher degrees. Often they are the "flagship" in a state's public higher education system. Their alumni are numerous and influential in public affairs. As giants, they also dominate the direction and issues in higher education as well as basic practices, including librarianship.

Universities are, in many instances, striving to achieve research university status. (One of this book's authors retired from a university that was striving "to become the Georgetown of the West.") Research status is, in part, a function of numbers (such as degrees and overall size), but it is more complex than pure numbers, as we will discuss in later chapters. The primary difference between the two categories (universities and research universities) is the research emphasis and the lack of postgraduate programs. They also offer fewer professional degrees and generally have fewer prize winning faculty members. (In some state higher education systems there may be both types of universities, such as in California, New York, and Texas.)

Colleges offer the greatest range in size and degree programs. Enrollments vary from a few hundred to thousands; a few are still single-sex institutions. They are undergraduate focused, although some offer a few master's level programs. In terms of sheer numbers they are the most numerous. Many are or were religious in origin, as we will discuss in the next chapter. Funding is always an issue, but for colleges the matter is often critical. Perhaps as many colleges in United States have been created and failed as there are existing colleges and universities. Generally the vast majority of their funding comes from the current tuition and fees of enrolled students. A shortfall in expected enrollment may lead to serious cutbacks in the current year's operations. Long-term low enrollments also result in low graduation numbers, which in turn means there are fewer alumni to turn to when fiscal problems arise.

Community colleges (Carnegie class "associate" and in the past referred to as junior colleges) provide a variety of two-year programs. They offer two broad categories of programs: "transfer" (articulated programs) and vocational degrees. Most of the community colleges (CCs) offer a two-year program that represents the equivalent of the freshmen and sophomore level work (lower division) at colleges and universities. To be effective as a transfer program (that is, allowing the student to receive academic "credit" for those courses at a four-year institution), such programs *must* engage in a high level of collaboration with at least local if not statewide four year institutions; that is, making certain that English 101 at the community college is the equivalent of English 101 at four year institutions. In the best case, a student will receive an associate degree from a community college and be able to enroll in a local four-year institution as a junior. Such a level of cooperation takes time and effort on both sides but truly benefits the students. In the past, such programs primarily benefited students whose high school academic record did not achieve the level necessary for direct admission to a four-year program. Today, with the very high cost of higher education, many students opt for the lower cost community college lower division program to cover their first two years of higher education. Needless to say, this requires careful review by the student and parents to make certain their transfer goals are fully realized.

The community colleges' vocational programs may be, along with high school programs, the key to the economic future of local economies. CCs by their nature can be more agile in responding to changing economic conditions, which allows them to adjust—add or drop—programs more quickly than four-year institutions. (A legal fact is a student who enters a four-year program has the right to complete that program, as outlined in the institution's bulletin for the year of entry. This means a two-year program can change more rapidly than one with a four-year commitment to a cohort of students.) The range of vocational programs is limited only by the current economy and projections of short-term needs (perhaps no more than two years ahead) and perhaps by accreditation standards.

Clearly U.S. higher education is highly diverse and in some ways the most diverse in the world. Opportunities in academic librarianship are equally diverse. We firmly believe the future is bright, if challenging, as the chapter has identified at various points, for those who chose this career path. We wish you the very best and know you will be wonderful colleagues in the future.

KEY POINTS TO REMEMBER

- Both higher education and its libraries face new and serious challenges in the Internet Age.
- Both have a long history of successfully responding to changing circumstances.

- Academic librarians have an equally bright future, assuming they take on the responsibility for developing the necessary skills for the digital library.
- Understanding the tripartite environment of an academic library is essential for success.
- Understanding both the library's and parent institution's organizational culture is a key element in developing sound working relationships.
- U.S. higher education is highly diverse, as are its libraries.
- The Carnegie Classification is the most widely employed system for grouping U.S. postsecondary institutions.

REFERENCES

Abeles, Tom P. 2006. Do we know the future of the university? *On the Horizon* 14, no. 2: 35–42.

Andrews, Rhys, George Boyne, and Richard Walker. 2006. Strategy content and organizational performance. *Public Administration Review* 66, no.1: 52–64.

Campbell, Jerry D. 2006. Changing a cultural icon. *EDUCAUSE Review* 41, no. 1: 16–30.

Carbo, Toni. 2008. Them and us, or a bigger and better us. *Journal of Academic Librarianship* 34, no. 2: 99–100.

Carnegie Foundation for the Advancement of Teaching. 2008. Classification. Available: www.carnegiefoundation.org/classifications (accessed June 7, 2008).

Choi, Youngok, and Edie Rasmussen. 2006. What is needed to educate future digital librarians. *D-Lib Magazine* 12, no. 9. Available: www.dlib.org/dlib/september06/choi/09choi.html (accessed June 7, 2008).

Drake, Miriam. 2007. Academic libraries are alive and thriving. *Searcher* 15, no. 1: 8–12.

Flat prospects. 2007. *Economist* 382, no. 8520: 72–73.

Hoare, Stephen. 2008. Libraries unleashed. *The Guardian*. Suppl. (April): 1–22.

Institute of Education Sciences, National Center for Education Statistics. 2008. *Academic libraries: 2006: First look*. Washington, DC: U.S. Department of Education. Available: nces.ed.gov/pubs2008/2008337.pdf.

Kell, Thomas, and Gregory Carrott. 2005. Culture matters most. *Harvard Business Review* 83, no. 5: 22

Lewin, Kurt. 1951. *Field theory in social sciences*. New York: Harper & Row.

Lewis, David. 2007. A strategy for academic libraries in the first quarter of the 21st century. *College & Research Libraries* 68, no. 5: 418–434.

Mullins, James L., Frank R. Allen, and Jon R. Hufford. 2007. Ten top assumptions for the future of academic libraries and librarians. *College & Research Library News* 68, no. 4: 240–246.

Okerson, Ann. 2003. Asteroids, Moore's Law, and the Star Alliance. *Journal of Academic Librarianship* 29, no. 5: 280–285.

Ross, Lyman, and Pongracz Sennyey. 2008. The library is dead, long live the library. *Journal of Academic Librarianship* 34, no. 2: 145–152.

Snyder, David Pearce, and Gregg Edwards. 2003. The strategic context of education in America—2000 to 2020. *On the Horizon* 11, no. 2: 5–18.

Sun-Tzu. n.d. *The art of war*. Available: www.gutenberg.org/etext/132 (accessed June 7, 2008).

Tennant, Roy. 2006. Academic library futures. *Library Journal* 131, no. 20: 34.

LAUNCHING PAD

Castronova, Edward. 2005. *Synthetic worlds*. Chicago, IL: University of Chicago Press.

Chowdhury, G. G., and Sudatta Chowdhury. 2003. *Introduction to digital libraries*. London: Facet Publishing.

Ehrenberg, Ronald G. 2006. Perfect storm and the privatization of public higher education. *Change* 38, no. 1: 46–53.

Evans, G. Edward. 1986. Research libraries in 2010. In *Research libraries—The past 25 years, the next 25 years*, ed.Terry Hubbard. Boulder, CO: Colorado State University Press.

Gayton, Jeffrey. 2008. Academic libraries: "Social" or "communal?" *Journal of Academic Librarianship* 34, no. 1: 60–66.

Koohang, Alex, and James Ondracek. 2005. User's views about the usability of digital libraries. *British Journal of Educational Technology* 36, no. 3: 407–423.

Kotter, John P. 1996. *Leading change.* Cambridge, MA: Harvard Business School Press.

Kurzweil, Raymond. 2005. *The singularity is near.* New York: Viking Press.

Lynch, Beverly P., et al. 2007. Attitudes of presidents and provosts on the university library. *College & Research Libraries* 68, no. 3: 213–227.

Magrath, C. Peter. 2008. America's secret educational weapon: Community colleges. *Phi Delta Kappan* 89, no. 9: 640–642.

Martell, Charles. 2007. The elusive user: Changing use patterns in academic libraries. *College & Research Libraries* 68, no. 5: 435–444.

Raggett, Peter. 2006. Librarians in the 21st century. *OECD Observer* 257: 32–33.

Rizzo, Michael J. 2004. The public interest in higher education. Cornell Higher Education Research Institute Working Paper no. 55. Available: www.ilr.cornell.edu/cheri/wp/cheri_wp55 .pdf (accessed June 7, 2008).

Ozaki, C. Casey, Marilyn J. Amey, and Jesse S. Watson. 2007. Strategies for the future. *New Directions for Community Colleges* no. 139: 105–113.

Sapp, Gregg, and Ron Gilmore. 2002. A brief history of the future of academic libraries: Predications and speculations from the literature of the profession, 1975 to 2000—part one, 1975 to 1989. *portal: Libraries and the Academy* 2, no. 4: 553–569.

———. 2003. A brief history of the future of academic libraries: Predications and speculations from the literature of the profession—part two, 1990 to 2000. *portal: Libraries and the Academy* 3, no. 1: 13–34.

Shuler, John A. 2007. The civic value of academic libraries and the open source university. *Journal of Academic Librarianship* 33, no. 2: 301–303.

Snelson, Pamela. 2006. Communicating the value of academic libraries. *College & Research Libraries News* 67, no. 8: 490–492.

Stoffle, Carla, et al. 2003. Continuing to build the future: Academic libraries and their challenges. *portal: Libraries and the Academy* 3, no. 3: 363–380.

Townsend, Barbara K. 2007. Interpreting the influence of community college attendance upon baccalaureate attainment. *Community College Review* 35, no. 2: 128–136.

U.S. Department of Education. 2006. A test of leadership: Charting the future of U.S. higher education. Washington, DC: U.S. Department of Education. Available: www.ed.gov/about/ bdscomm/list/hiedfuture/reports/pre-pub-report.pdf (accessed June 7, 2008).

Chapter 2

Historic Context

Those who control the present then control the past. Those who control the past, control the future.

—Anonymous

Reflecting on the forces that produced the first universities 800 years ago provokes consideration of today's universities at the start of the new millennium.

—Barton Kunstler (2006)

Today's higher education institutions in the United States, and in most of the rest of the world, owe more to the past than many people inside and outside higher education realize. Much of the structure, culture, basic purposes, and ceremonies have roots in the first days of university development in Europe. Although one reviewer of the proposal for this book suggested we drop any mention of history because the reviewer had never needed such information to administer an academic library, we have decided to retain a short chapter on the historical context of academia and its libraries. We agree that one can operate an academic library without any thought to how we arrived at where we are; however, given the pervasive historic roots we believe that some understanding of the past can be helpful and, on occasions, useful in planning for the future.

What, if any, lessons can the new millennial academy and libraries learn from spending a few moments pondering the past? If nothing else, such consideration may provide a strong sense of hope for the future. That hope can arise from seeing how higher education has managed to adapt to a changing world, times of high social stress, variable economic conditions, and new technologies. Higher education has its roots in the arrival of a new millennium (1000 AD) when there was a general fear and great uncertainty that the world would survive the arrival date. (Those worries remind one somewhat of the widespread Y2K stress in the late 1990s and the possible challenges for technology-dependent societies.) Once 1000 came and went, European societies became optimistic about the future, and economic development rapidly increased. As the need for more and more people with some education grew, cathedral schools expanded. By 1200, these had transformed into the beginnings of what we think of today as higher education.

Looking at the past also demonstrates that some issues, at their most basic level, are enduring. They play a role in today's world just as they did in 1200, 1300, 1400, and onward. Certainly there is no guarantee they will remain so forever; however, it seems highly probable they will continue to play a role for the foreseeable future, given their existence over the past 800 plus years. Before listing those basics issues, we will briefly explore the development of higher education and its libraries.

WHERE IT ALL BEGAN

As we stated, the roots of U.S. higher education lie in Western Europe. The four most influential countries in order of development of universities are Italy, France, England, and Germany. Each country contributed something to today's universities, just as they influenced one another during their developmental phases.

During the first 100 plus years the university was a not a "place." Rather, students and teachers/masters were international in character and highly mobile. Instruction was in Latin, the language of the church and learned nobility. The two groups sought communities that were teacher and student friendly and quickly moved on when they thought they could do better elsewhere. Thus, developments in one country were carried to other countries by the peripatetic students and teachers.

What we know as universities today grew out of the training process the Catholic Church had developed to educate those individuals who would prepare documents and help maintain the Church's business. Parish priests provided some basic instruction for the local boys of nobility. A few boys went on to a secondary education at cathedrals where, at least in theory, they were educated in the seven "liberal arts": grammar, rhetoric, logic, arithmetic, geometry, astronomy, and music. These arts reflected the skills needed by the church to carry out its administrative and some religious activities—individuals who could prepare logical and grammatically correct documents, who could calculate dates for movable feasts and help provide music for services.

Instruction in all of the subjects was "in theory," because few cathedrals had individuals who were fully competent or interested in all the subjects. The differing interests and/or knowledge led to different cathedrals developing reputations for excellence in a few of the arts that in turn attracted a few students who had a strong interest in the area(s) of strength. Learning was a matter of memorization, as there were few books. Certainly no library was accessible to the students. Those books that were available were costly and kept under tight control. An instructional day would generally have a lecture and discussion of the lecture, repetition of the lecture's content, writing practice, and students' reciting the previous day's lecture. That pattern, at least the lecture and memorization, remained the standard for centuries (some critics of higher education might say it still has not changed all that much).

The mechanics of higher education—instruction by faculty in a formal course of study, examinations, commencements, and degrees—were established by the thirteenth century. Higher education remained the territory of the well-to-do male student for the better part of six centuries.

Italian Influence

Italy had the first institutions we can identify as universities (Salerno and Bologna), and they served as the seed beds for the rest of European higher education. Salerno was perhaps the earliest (circa 1050), but its focus on medicine restricted its influence on the schools with a broader focus. Had the Carnegie classification existed at the time it would have been classed a "special-focus institution."

It is Bologna that most scholars consider the site of the development of higher education. It was also much larger than Salerno in terms of students and masters. Bologna gave rise to the term *university* (universitas). "University" has nothing to do with the universe of knowledge or universality of learning, rather it referred to an organized group that existed to establish standards/rules of behavior/activity and to protect the group's rights (a guild)—for example, the rights of groups such as merchants, blacksmiths, weavers, masons, or students. Students in Bologna created their guild (universitas) to protect themselves from the townspeople (town and gown issues go back to the beginning), and later they added instructional rights (Hyde, 1988, pp. 18–19). Initially, student activism focused on the most immediate needs—setting room rents, the cost of food, and other services provided by the city's people. There were no dormitories, food services, laundry facilities, or other amenities that today's students expect and consider due them, if they think much about such issues.

Once the universitas was established (it was a document that magistrates first looked to when handling a student–town person dispute) the students turned their attention to instructional expectations. Until there was a corporate institution of higher education, teachers/masters earned their income from fees they collected directly from individual students. Bologna student guilds created an employment contract that they could use to assure some measure of learning opportunities. The contract covered such issues as how often a teacher might be absent from the lecture room and still receive a fee, the structure and length of instruction, and the quality of the instruction.

Clearly today's concern for the need to listen to and attend to students' voices as well as the students' desire to have a seat at the table grew out the efforts of the Bologna student universitas. Many academic libraries today have advisory committees that include student representatives, an outgrowth of this early involvement of students. Students' evaluations of teaching that are commonplace today have their roots in the student–masters contracts.

French Influence

The leading French university during the early years was in Paris. "In" is an important word during the developmental period. We noted earlier that students and teachers were highly mobile. So, it was a university *in* Paris not the university *of* Paris. Several times in the 1200s and 1300s the Paris students and masters left the city for a variety of reasons, only to return later (Ferruolo, 1988, p. 23).

Teachers in Paris were among the first to form their own universitas in order to gain some protection and rights. Initially the masters' guild was a loose confederation of individuals who looked solely to their personal interests. However, relatively quickly they thought of themselves as a formal group (a faculty) and secured faculty rights such as establishing student admission standards/qualifications, timing of examinations, and approving the granting of a degree. Often the prospective student had to pass an entrance exam before being allowed to attend lectures. The faculty's granting of a degree/license served to prove that the holder had the knowledge to teach others. Faculty reserved for themselves the right to decide what courses they would offer as well as when. (Faculty workloads and when they will teach at what time issues remain with us.)

About 1231, the university in Paris had four faculties, each with a dean and the beginnings of a sense of place. The four faculties were liberal arts, canon law, medicine, and theology. They, the faculties, elected a person to serve as rector—a person who represented the interests of all the faculties both internally and to the outside world. Later, the four groups (colleges) began to act like a corporation (university) that could hold property and control money for the good of all the students and faculties. Up until then, lectures took place wherever a teacher could rent a room large enough for his class. Students and faculty rented living accommodations and took their meals wherever they could for the money they had. The college as physical place arose from the need for faculty to find reasonable accommodations. What started as a place to live and take meals soon grew into a gathering place for faculty and students. It was not too long before space was added or adjacent space rented to provide classrooms. Thus, the concept of *campus* began to form. At this time, the universities did not have libraries and depended on access to religious order collections for what little access the teachers required.

Check This Out

A comprehensive book on early libraries is James Westfall Thompson's monumental *The Medieval Library* (Chicago: University of Chicago Press, 1939).

French influence on higher education is seen in the structure of today's postsecondary campuses, faculties and their attendant rights, deans, rectors, and other administrators. It also led to a corporate institution. What started as a means of limiting local jurisdiction (the guild) soon led to a royal charter that protected the institution from local and papal interference or a papal charter that protected against local and royal requirements. The first higher education institution anywhere in the world to receive a legislative charter was Harvard in 1650 (Kivinen and Poikus, 2006).

English Influence

Oxford and Cambridge (both of which were Puritan in orientation) developed the concept of campus and college beyond that of most continental universities. (A number of scholars of the history of higher education, at least in the United States, refer to them as Oxbridge to save space and emphasize their dual influence on each other and other institutions.) For the United States, they were, and to some degree still are, highly influential in terms the symbols, forms, and vocabulary for undergraduate education. Essentially they represented the "ideal" institution for the United States until late in the nineteenth century; for some they still represent what undergraduate education is, or should be, about.

What are some of the elements of that ideal? Having a residential educational experience with tutorial instruction in the liberal arts is the starting point, selective admission, honors program, the "quad," attention to campus grounds, and the "gentleman scholar" (the gentleman's C grade) are all legacies of Oxford and Cambridge. Other elements such as elaborate extracurricular activities, sports (especially crew racing), pipe smoking, and tweed jackets with leather patches on the sleeves when combined with the first list brings to mind Hollywood B movies about college life before the 1960s. Stereotypical or not, much of the forgoing is still what many people think of as a college or university (an ivory tower isolated from the real world).

In some ways that ideal influenced individuals like Clark Kerr when he formulated a master plan for California higher education in the mid-twentieth century. (One of his goals was to make a highly complex and large system appear less so by having a sequence or levels from community college to research university.) As late as 1970 the ideal served as the inspiration of St. Mary's College of Maryland's attempt to create a quality, public, and residential liberal arts education.

Not everyone believed the Oxford/Cambridge model was appropriate for the U.S. environment. Their selective admission of primarily the sons of rich and influential families for an education in the liberal arts did not seem useful in a country that needed a population of workers and entrepreneurs. (The original meaning of the liberal arts was non–money making.) Johnson (1958), in writing about the Oxbridge model and questioning its value, wrote:

> But it is applied to the education of sons of American farmers, store-keepers, plumbers, policemen, and street car conductors who have not inherited money and have made enough to send their boys to college only by years of intensive concentration on their jobs to the exclusion of purely intellectual interests.... Secondary education...has always been and is highly selective, restricted to an extremely small class. (p. 392)

The question of the value of English model was a major issue as far as the U.S. general public was concerned. Many doubted the need for and/or the value of higher education. Nevertheless, the English model was extremely influential during several hundred years of U.S. higher education.

German Influence

To a large extent, the Black Death's impact on the region's population caused German universities to get off to a slower start than elsewhere in Europe (it was 1386 when Heidelberg University became operational). However, once started they quickly drew on what other European universities were doing and added elements of their own. They differed from their European colleagues in their heavy emphasis on scholarship. Teaching and scholarship (especially in the form of expanding knowledge) were seen as interlaced—good teachers added to sum total of knowledge; they were not just dispensers of what already existed.

German universities also created two special rights, one for students and another for faculty. Students had the right to attend lectures at any university in the process of earning a degree. (The concept of taking classes at several institutions and having the work count toward a single degree, at least in terms of a person's major, is still not widely accepted in the United States.) The faculty right is one that plays a role today, which is the right to be allowed to "seek the truth" without interference from others (academic freedom).

Another trait from the German universities was the creation of *institutes* for advanced study for a few select individuals (Thelin, 1982). Ultimately this led to the granting of higher degrees than the baccalaureate—the master's degree or doctor of philosophy or a general master's degree. Like their English counterparts, German institutions drew their students from aristocratic families. The curriculum was designed to build a cadre of men for government service. Thus, it was more overtly practical than the English model and the liberal arts curriculum that did not focus on that end result. Nevertheless, most of the English graduates engaged in some form of professional/governmental work.

From the outset, higher education faced questions about who should teach what to whom and where as well as how to pay for the process. We hardly mentioned libraries in the previous discussion of the early days of higher education. The nature of instruction (memorization) meant for students there was little need for an institutional library; even where libraries did exist, students rarely had access. You gain a sense of the limited access from the following quotation taken from the medieval Oxford library regulations:

> Since in the course of time the great number of students using the library is in many ways harmful to the books and since the laudable purpose of these desiring to profit [by reading them] is often defeated by too much disturbance of noisy people, the university has ordered and decreed that only graduates and people in religious orders who have studied philosophy for eight years shall study in the library of the university. (Lucas, 1994, p. 56)

An additional factor limiting access was the mobile character of the university. Moving a library is never fun, and one can only speculate about the challenges of trying to move the books of the thirteenth and fourteenth century. Only when the Gutenberg revolution took hold did books become relatively affordable (students today may think books are still not affordable) and the prospect of real college/university libraries become necessary. Also, until about 1300 there were few new books written, new in the sense of new content. Prior to that time, "new" books were basically copies of older works.

This brief review of early higher education in Europe merely highlights some of the antecedents of the form and function of today's postsecondary institutions. As you might expect, when the Europeans arrived in other parts of the world (especially in the western hemisphere), established colonies, and desired to have local higher education, the institutions they created were full transplants of what existed in the home country.

HOW THE TRANSPLANTS TOOK ROOT
IN THE UNITED STATES, 1636–1770

U.S. higher education, until the 1820s, was essentially a full transplant of the English/Scottish colleges whose classical curriculum was packaged in a theological framework. Between 1636 (Harvard) and 1769, nine colleges were established by several religious denominations (see Table 2.1). Although there were strong theological differences, even within the same group (one Puritan group established Harvard and other group founded Yale), they all shared the same basic challenges: enrollments were low, it was hard to find teachers, physical facilities were minimal, who should control what was

Table 2.1. Early College Transplants to the United States			
Founding Name	Founding Date	Current Name	Church Affiliation
Harvard	1636	Harvard	Puritan
William & Mary	1693	William & Mary	Anglican
Yale	1701	Yale	Puritan
Philadelphia College	1740	University of Pennsylvania	Quaker
College of New Jersey	1746	Princeton	Presbyterian
King College	1754	Columbia	Anglican
Rhode Island College	1765	Brown	Baptist
Queens College	1766	Rutgers	Dutch Reform
Moor's Indian Charity School	1769	Dartmouth	Congregational

to be taught was a frequent issue, and town and gown relations were unpredictable, especially if money was involved, and funding was always touch and go.

You gain a sense of the low enrollments from the fact that by 1770 (134 years after the establishment of the first college) there had been only 3,000 graduates (Vinton, 1878, p. 102). This should not be too surprising given that the course of study was not about making money, unless one wished to become a minister. At that time, what most people were concerned with was making it to tomorrow in a rather hostile country. What was socially important was creating settlements and a self-sustaining independent economy. Given the nature of a frontier society and its values, it is not surprising few young men knew about, much less considered, attending college. Even those few who did had to look long and hard to find a local person who could teach them the rudimentary skills necessary to be considered for college admission. The issue of practicality and relevance remains a subject of debate within academia and society.

Despite the challenges, as Table 2.1 illustrates, the early transplants took root and survived, unlike many of the colleges created in the nineteenth century. What was different and all the more impressive is that they, unlike the colleges in Spanish America, did not serve the needs of a single religious group, the government, or a substantial wealthy aristocratic community. Another factor that encouraged taking root was that the English did not, as matter of course, transplant colleges into their colonies as their empire grew. The mother country universities—Oxford, Cambridge, Dublin, and Edinburgh—had ample room for the "young men from the colonies."

Perhaps one of the biggest factors in the Puritans establishing Harvard was the high concentration of Oxford and Cambridge graduates in New England, as many as 100 by some estimates. A second factor was the desire to assure/control the availability and quality of the ministers for what they hoped would be a guiding set of moral values for the world. They also believed a college was an essential part of any good society. Other than the number of English college graduates, most of the first colleges were created for basically the same reasons. Clearly there was a desire to use higher education as a part of achieving the religious ends of a particular denomination. All the colleges listed in Table 2.1, except for what was to become Dartmouth, had as an early goal the training of ministers for a particular denomination (Stille, 1878, pp. 122–130).

Like European cities, larger communities in the United States viewed the presence of a college as a mark of prestige and status. Not that these attitudes translated into significant financial support. Staying open was always a challenge. U.S. colleges did not, at least initially, meet the same social demand that those in England, Ireland, and Scotland did, beyond graduating a few ministers. What the latter institutions had that was lacking in the United States was a "market" of landed gentry whose sons required educating to be true gentlemen. Lacking such a market, there were few places to turn to for students and donations. There were a few families with ideas/pretensions of aristocracy, but they sent their sons "home" (meaning Europe) for their education. All of this translated into funding challenges.

College presidents then, as now, were always looking for opportunities to secure funding/donations to reduce financial uncertainty. (Today fund-raising has also become a part of any academic library director's life.) Two examples from the early years illustrate this point. Harvard is Harvard because of a gift from John Harvard. He was a Cambridge graduate, and when he died in 1638 he left his library (329 books) and half of his estate (£780) to a then unnamed college (Carpenter, 1986, p. 2). Another "naming opportunity" (more about that concept in the chapter on finances) occurred when Elihu Yale, a wool merchant, donated £550 worth of cloth to another unnamed college in Connecticut (Handlin and Handlin, 1970, p. 39). Then as now, all higher education institutions were dependent on student tuition to meet current expenses. (Certainly today there are some universities with huge endowment funds that take some of the fiscal pressure off, but this does not keep them from raising tuition each year.) A different example of the financial troubles comes from what was to become the College of William & Mary. In 1619 the college had 9,000 acres to sell to raise the funds to create a college, but there were no takers. It tried again in 1660 to sell the land with the same result (Brubacher and Rudy 1997, pp. 3–23). Obviously the effort to get started was long and frustrating; however, they kept trying, and William & Mary is now the second oldest institution of higher education in the United States. As someone said about early colleges, they were short of money, faculty, and students, were searching for a public, and had befuddled policies, but they were convinced the future demanded their existence and growth. Sometimes faith can achieve surprising long lasting results.

Slowly the notion developed in the United States, as it had in England, that there were two goals for colleges: educate the clergy and "lettered gentlemen." As early as 1647, President Dunster (Harvard) talked about the possibility of having students interested in going into all of the professions (Handlin and Handlin, 1970, p. 29).

During this early history, academic libraries were small. The College of William & Mary was the first college library recorded as being authorized to buy books in 1732. Before that, donations were the way the collections grew. As is so often the case with academic firsts, Harvard had the first U.S. academic librarian (The Keeper of the Books) in the person of Solomon Stoddard (Carpenter, 1986, p. 60). Harvard library hired its first female employee in 1859 (Carpenter, 1986, p. 97), two years after the Boston Athenaeum became the first U.S. library to do so.

Not surprisingly, during this time, access to books for students was very limited, and most colleges had lists of prohibited books. Most of the works listed were deemed to be potentially dangerous to the denomination's beliefs and/or young men's minds. Other limited access items, just as today, were reference works, and no one could check them out. Not only were certain titles prohibited, but undergraduates could read a book only in the reading room while under the supervision of a tutor/teacher. As a final limitation, the libraries were open only a few hours two or three days a week, at least for students.

POST–WAR OF INDEPENDENCE TO 1860

While the basics remained unchanged during this period of development, some details were changing. First of all, there were many more colleges to choose from; between 1772 and 1802, 19 new colleges were chartered, all of which have managed to survive.

One aspect of this period was the slow but steady expansion of the curriculum beyond the liberal arts. Although Latin remained *the* language of most of texts that were taught, Greek (humanistic works) and Hebrew (as the language of the prophets) also began to be taught. "Natural history" appeared in some colleges, and overall there was a loosening of the theological requirements. As a result of French assistance in the war, some colleges added courses in French and French history. The trend was away from medieval scholarship toward a more practical/technological orientation. Perhaps the clearest indication of change was the establishment of West Point Military Academy in 1802 with its engineering curriculum and the Philadelphia College of Apothecaries in 1821.

This period was also a time when governments began to seriously view higher education as something they should support. The first "public" college/university was the University of Virginia in 1819. Certainly there had been some funds from towns and legislatures earlier—Harvard received Charles River ferry tolls, and William & Mary had sporadic income from an export tax. However, these were small supplements to operating budgets, and no one thought the state should be the primary source of funding. Today both the public and private institutions have a mix of funding sources.

The divide between public and private was not distinct. All of the colleges had to receive a charter from the legislature. A few did receive some money from the state or local government. The real question was: Who controlled the institution? It took the U.S. Supreme Court to settle the matter with a decision regarding Dartmouth College (a private school today). As is often the case today, the dispute started between the college president (John Wheelock, son of the founder) and the trustees. (We explore the issue of governance in more depth in a later chapter.) President Wheelock went public about the dispute in 1815 when he asked the New Hampshire legislature to investigate the affairs of the college. Needless to say, the trustees were less than happy with this and voted to remove Wheelock from the board, the presidency, and his professorship. Seeing a political opportunity in the situation, the Republican Party took up Wheelock's cause and managed to win the 1816 elections using the case as key element in their platform. The new governor (a Republican) and the legislature passed a law that would bring the college under state control on the grounds that the trustees perpetuated aristocratic rather than democratic values. When the court cases followed and eventually appealed to the U.S. Supreme Court, an unknown young Dartmouth graduate (Daniel Webster) presented the trustees' position. In a five to one decision (it became a landmark case), the Court ruled that Dartmouth was not a public institution because the state charter was a contract for a private venture.

That decision (*Trustees of Dartmouth College v. Woodward*, 17 U.S. 518) safeguarded private colleges from legislative interference. Another major outcome of the ruling made it clear that it was the governing board not the faculty, students, or administrators who held overall control of the institution. A major outcome of the decision was phenomenal growth in the number of colleges created over the next 30 plus years. Before the War of Independence there were 9 colleges; by the start of the Civil War there were 250. The end result was at this time there were nearly as many colleges in existence as there were elementary schools. By comparison, in 1860, England, with a population of more than 23 million, had 4 universities; Ohio, with a population of about 3 million, had 37 colleges and universities.

Most of the new schools were located in rural settings, were small and underfunded, with teenage male enrollments, a liberal arts-oriented curriculum, and were using an "in loco parentis" (in the place of the parent) concept. Acting in the place of the parent was a constant challenge for the staff. One suspects the addition of organized sports to campus life was an attempt to burn off some of the boundless energy of teenage boys and keep them from causing trouble in the local communities. A common complaint of college presidents and faculty was the amount of time they had to devote to monitoring and controlling the boys' behavior. The expectation that the staff of the institution would control students' behavior has been long-standing and, as we will show later in this chapter, can have serious consequences for an institution.

Oberlin became the first institution to go coeducational when it admitted women in 1837. Georgia chartered the first women's college (Georgia Female College, which later became Wesleyan College) in 1836.

A rural setting did not mean life was peaceful. School violence is not a late twentieth, early twenty-first-century phenomenon; medieval students had brawls, sword fights, etc. Between 1800 and 1900 there were an average of four student deaths a year from fights/duels and at least one "student rebellion" per year from 1800 to 1875 (Brubacher and Rudy, 1997, pp. 59–119).

Underfunding was a perennial problem during this time and can be illustrated by the sad story of John W. Browne, founder of Miami University of Ohio. Browne went on a yearlong trip to collect money and books for the library. At the end of his journey, he had $700 and a wagonload of books. Near the college, while crossing a river, the wagon tipped over, resulting in one dead John Browne and a load of lost books. Another example is Emory College, which "opened" on the basis of unpaid interest on unpaid pledges of support. At one point, when Bowdoin College (established in 1794) needed a classroom building, the college offered a Maine township (36 square miles of land) to anyone who would build such a building and found no takers (Handlin and Handlin, 1970, pp. 56–91).

The liberal arts curriculum never had wide popular support, which was a significant factor in low enrollments. Three primary factors were behind the low public opinion regarding a college education, all related to labor. First, the cost was too high, perhaps not in terms of today's dollars but rather in combination of the expense of the schooling and the lost labor at home. During the nineteenth century, the lost labor had the much larger impact; even if the families did not calculate an actual labor cost they understood the loss of a worker. Second, the colleges were seldom near home, resulting in substantial travel time. Often the distance was too great to return home during school holidays, meaning even those periods of potential labor were lost. Finally, there was the overriding fact that a liberal arts curriculum was not practical for the majority of people. Little if anything learned would translate into better production, less work, or improved income.

A key to the development of public higher education and an education with a practical emphasis was Morrill Act of 1862, with its provision of either land or "script" for the use in operating higher education institutions. The act, although not excluding "classical studies" or science, called for institutions to offer learning related to agricultural and mechanical arts. Although today a few universities retain "A&M" in their names, most such schools dropped that element from their name in the mid-twentieth century. Schools that started or existing schools that became recipients of land or script are known as land grant schools. In a few cases, the schools still have some of the original tracts of land; however, the bulk of the land was sold to start or support one or more state-operated institution(s). The legislation provided for 30,000 acres of public land per representative and senator or the equivalent in cash (script) for states in which there was little or no federal land. There are 68 land grant colleges and universities, almost all of them large research universities with names the reader probably knows.

What was the status of academic libraries at the time? Libraries were small and still barely accessible to students, open perhaps one or two hours a week. Library staffs, such as there was, were charged with preserving the collection from unnecessary use. Almost always the person in charge of the library was one of the most respected faculty members who could be counted on to control collection access. There was little effort to organize the small collections beyond maintaining an alphabetical author order on the shelves. As late as the 1850s, most schools depended on book donations rather than purchases to build their collections.

Students responded to the lack of library access by creating literary societies, often away from campus, where they created their own libraries to address their interests. Those interests included newspapers and magazines, not just books, as were housed in the campus libraries. Such societies were both social and intellectual. A favorite activity was debating, which called for a wide range of material. The library was open to any member anytime, and outsiders might gain access with the permission of the members. Until the late 1800s, some of these student libraries had the broadest based collections in a state. Table 2.2 summarizes the key issues associated with the development of higher education in the United States at this time.

> **From the Authors**
>
> Ironically, Alire recalls volunteering to set up an academic library in the 1970s with donated books for a University Without Walls institution.

Table 2.2. Summary of U.S. Higher Education before 1860	
	Key Issue
Student Body	Small enrollment Primarily white males 13–18 years old Families better off than the average family Tight control by the faculty and administrators Campus was the residence First coeducational institution was Oberlin, in 1836 Few higher education opportunities for women
Curriculum	Primarily liberal arts and strong religious component Fixed sequence of courses Limited, if any, electives Recitation and memorization of a few key books Shift toward practical courses late in the 1850s
Faculty	Primarily practicing or former ministers Scholarship and/or research interests of little importance High turnover due to low salary and dislike of acting as a father Few had broad knowledge beyond what they had learned in college
Governance	Board of trustees/overseers and presidential control Faculty had little say in operations Students had no say—primary factor in "student rebellions" Land grant institutions brought legislative oversight for those institutions
Facilities	Few buildings but a campus setting Libraries generally small with very limited student access—student literary societies filled the void Lack of facilities often limited what the school could do
Funding	Financial condition often so poor closure seemed likely until passage of the Morrill Act (from 1862 until after 1960) Fund-raising a constant challenge Faculty and staff wait for months for their pay
Society's View	Rather ignored the institutions during the earliest years With the beginning of practical course work interest grew

1860s TO WORLD WAR II

The post–Civil War to World War II period was a time of growth, greater stability, and a continuation of the trends of late 1850s. More coeducational opportunities existed, electives and majors became a staple, enrollments increased as the value of higher education was recognized, and the tension between the value of liberal/theoretical and practical became sharper (a tension that remains with us today). The need to assure the public and the students' families of the quality of an institution led to accreditation (the first was the New England Association of Colleges and Preparatory Schools in 1885). Social activities (especially Greek organizations) and athletics became a standard feature of college life.

One of the key developments at this time was the leading role that state universities took in expanding the subject options one could study. Two institutions, Cornell and Wisconsin, were influential in this expansion. Cornell was created to be an all-purpose university. Its seal states, "I would found an institution in which any person can find instruction in any study" (Becker, 1943, p. 88). Essentially all subjects were to be equally valued, an idea that still receives lip service at most academic institutions but when it comes to funding and support is often ignored. The "Wisconsin Idea" took shape in the early twentieth century as the idea that a college/university should address all of the needs of a democratic society. It was a reflection of what the citizens of Wisconsin demanded, and they expected that the university would improve farming and industry. They did not want an "ivory tower" institution. Both of these concepts played important roles in the expansion of the curriculum for many colleges and universities.

Another important development during this period was the movement toward the German model of faculty advancing knowledge rather than just being dispensers. Johns Hopkins University, founded in 1876, is usually credited as being the first institution to fully achieve true university status. Within a few years, many other institutions were reorganizing themselves to offer graduate work and hire faculty who understood they were to be productive scholars. Today colleges and universities still have to address this orientation/desire. The expectation that faculty will engage in research had, and has, implications for teaching loads and the number of faculty required to maintain a desired teacher-student ratio. It also, at least in larger institutions, has an implication for who teaches which level course. For example, it is common that graduate student teaching assistants teach the lower division introductory classes and full professors teach only graduate level courses. Also, the German concept of academic freedom became an issue, especially in the oldest institutions. Further research often required new buildings, especially for science and engineering activities, and overall more classrooms, offices, and dormitories were needed.

For academic libraries, the implication of the research emphasis and curriculum expansion had a profound influence on collections and collection building. Exploring new frontiers of knowledge calls for understanding what is already known as well as communicating what you have done recently. Collection depth and breath had to increase dramatically to support the new curriculum and research activities. We will explore the research and scholarly communication issues in more depth in the next chapter.

Intercollegiate athletics had its roots in this period of time. What is now viewed by many as "big time athletics" and the commercialization of college sports became an expected part of campus life. The first Rose Bowl football game took place in 1902. Today it is difficult to keep track of all the postseason bowl games on television. At the time probably few, if any, individuals would have thought these activities might one day be multimillion-dollar-a-year operations both as an expense and as income. We will explore this issue in more depth in the chapter about student affairs.

A new category of institution became part of U.S. higher education during this time—junior community colleges. During the early years, the label was junior college (JC). In the last third of the last century most had changed their names to community college (CC). As a result of economic conditions at the start of the twentieth century, there were a number of advocates for creating an institution that handled the first two years of a baccalaureate degree. As reported by Sinwell (2008), "The mission of the original junior college was to provide passage to 4-year degrees for many young people who otherwise would have been denied access to higher education" (pp. 23–24). Sinwell also noted that the first JC owed it existence, in part, to William Rainey Harper, President of the University of Chicago, who signed an agreement to allow graduates of Joliet Junior College to have advanced standing on admission to the University of Chicago. This took place in 1901, and Joliet Junior College was the first two-year public institution of the new type.

For the first 30 years of their existence, community colleges focused on an articulated-transfer curriculum; that is, they offered the equivalent of the first two years of a baccalaureate degree. Enrollment was generally low, with no more than a few hundred students. By the start of World War II, over 200 such school had been established, a substantial increase from the 25 that existed by 1910 (American Association of Community Colleges, n.d.).

Community colleges shifted their focus during the 1930s depression to offering vocational education. Initially students appeared to be equally attracted to both curriculums, but in time the vocational aspect surpassed the transfer programs in popularity.

Community college students almost always lived off campus and often lacked some of the credentials for direct admission to a four-year institution. Often, unlike four-year institution students, they held part-time jobs while attending school. Faculty focused on instruction and attempting to ensure the course quality was such that the work would meet transfer requirements.

Today the transfer program is once again coming to the forefront of CC programs. For example, after years of seeing themselves as competitors, the Coconino County Community College and the University of Northern Arizona announced in the summer of 2008 they had entered into an agreement that would allow for easy transfer. The program, CCC2NAU, is a joint admission designed to meet the needs of students seeking a bachelor's degree ("CCC2NAU," 2008).

During this time faculty status for librarians became an issue, because libraries of the time faced challenges that should seem familiar to today's academic librarians. For the first time, individuals working in the libraries thought of themselves as professionals and wanted to be treated like faculty rather than clerks. There was not enough money to acquire all the materials the faculty and students wanted and materials were not processed satisfactorily. Examples of complaints included classification of books being either inadequate or catalogers placing books in the wrong class number, acquisition of materials taking too long, and items being at the bindery for too long. Additionally, students and faculty wanted more reading space, more service hours, and additional services. Harvard did not offer reference service until the late 1930s, the attitude being that if you were intelligent enough to attend or work at Harvard you should be smart enough to find things without help. That may just be Harvard library folklore that gets passed on from one library staff to another; however, what is true is that reference service was a long time in coming—students first made a formal request for such assistance in 1914 (Carpenter, 1986, p. 142). Collection growth also created space challenges. Harvard President Charles Eliot suggested in 1901 that rather than build additional library space on campus that the University should store "dead books" away from campus (Carpenter, 1986, p. 122). It was not until 1942 that a specially designed facility for such storage was built. Table 2.3 summarizes the developments in higher education during this period.

WARS AND HIGHER EDUCATION

Wars are always disruptive to higher education. If nothing more, the young people are either in military service, preparing for such service, or preoccupied by what is and may happen. For the United States until the Civil War, these were the only issues.

Table 2.3. 1860 to 1940 Developments	
	Developments
Student Body	Dramatic increase in numbers as the range of possible studies increased Many coeducational institutions Athletic opportunities begin to play a role in school selection Family incomes closer to the national average Less control by the faculty and administrators, but still important Campus was residential in most cases Invention of the automobile led to new challenges for campus staff in terms of student control and community relations
Curriculum	Liberal arts still present but great expansion in subjects "Practical" courses come close to equaling the classical courses Electives a normal part of a course of study
Faculty	More often educated in the subjects they taught—doctorate often a requirement Scholarship and/or research became a key factor in larger institutions More stable faculty in terms of tenure of stay
Governance	Board of trustees/overseers and presidential control Faculty had more say in operations Students had little say Land grant institutions brought legislative oversight for those institutions
Facilities	New and often specialized buildings Campuses become small cities in themselves Libraries grew in size and hours of availability
Funding	Larger enrollments lead to more stable funding Broader course offerings and more students requiring more staffing and facilities Sports complexes added new financial demands
Society's View	Public institutions expected to improve life and solve problems Value in sending daughters and sons to schools with practical courses of study

Things began to change with the passage of the Morrill Act and the requirement that land grant institutions include military tactics in the curriculum and with the use of a military service draft during the Civil War. World War I brought additional issues—academic freedom became a subject of community concern; should faculty be required to actively support the war in their classrooms or be allowed to voice personal concerns? Reserve Officers Training Corps (ROTC) became a fixture at many institutions, even after the war was over. Some schools entered into contracts to provide military training as part of the degree program. Then there was the idea of exemptions from the military draft for certain classes of students, such as medical and science majors and ROTC members.

World War II had all of those elements plus another feature that would have long-term consequences: contract research for the federal government. Universities' success in scientific problem solving greatly aided the war effort, and this type of work continued during the Cold War period. Government's real, and imagined, influence on institutional priorities often generated heated debates. The impact has resulted in a sense of *haves* (scientists) and *have-nots* (humanists and to a lesser degree social scientists) in terms of having research funding sources from outside the institution.

The successes of university researchers in solving defense challenges also led to a general belief that universities could resolve any problem, including long-standing social issues. When they were much less successful in these areas, public doubts began to grow about the worth of universities in the 1970s and 1980s.

Part of the war effort research even had an influence on libraries. The military activities were taking place in parts of the world that military planners had never thought much about. Academic library collections were scoured for maps and other data about little known areas. Overall, the libraries did not have as rich collections in the lesser studied areas as was desired. A postwar consequence of this situation was the creation of the Farmington Plan wherein academic research libraries across the country made an effort to collect everything printed in a country or subject. One product of the library WWII effort still exists today, the Human Relations Area Files (www.yale.edu/hraf/). HRAF is an outgrowth of efforts during the war to dissect the contents of books (paragraph by paragraph) and devise a sound retrieval system, especially for items relating to the Pacific and Southeast Asia for the U.S. Navy.

Perhaps one of the most significant outcomes of WWII, for academic institutions, was the GI (Government Issue) Bill of Rights and the 1947 Presidential Commission report on higher education's role in society (U.S. President's Commission, 1948). Essentially these two documents helped crystallize the idea that there should be a federal program to support higher education. While the GI Bill provided federal funds for veterans for educational purposes, the commission recommended that higher educational opportunities for everyone capable of such work should have some federal support. The commission envisioned enrollment in higher education would be 4.6 million by 1960, assuming economic, racial, and geographic barriers were removed (p. 101). They also thought that free education should extend to two years beyond high school graduation. Needless to say, although the free aspect never materialized, the number of community colleges grew dramatically; 92 new institutions were founded between 1941–1950, and 497 between 1960–1970 (American Association of Community Colleges, n.d.). However, it was not until passage of the 1965 Higher Education Act that a broad permanent

From the Authors

Evans started his full-time professional career at an "instant campus"; his first office was in what had been the women's shower room in a condemned high school building. Within a year we were relocated to a new building on what was to be the new campus. Our collection-building activities involved buying entire bookstores along with the more traditional methods of acquiring collection material.

program of federal financial aid for both public and private colleges and their students was created.

Not only did CCs grow in number at this time, but all colleges and universities began to plan for expansion as the GIs began to take advantage of the educational benefits available to them. Over the next 20 years there were "instant" new colleges, including libraries, across the country, and existing institutions added staff to handle the growing workload. It was a time of great optimism about the future of the academy. The ALA publication Books for College Libraries was initially designed to help new libraries create "opening day" collections.

A summary of the issues surrounding this time appears in Table 2.4.

RETRENCHMENT AND REALIGNMENT

In some sense, the Vietnam War and the related campus protests against the conflict as well as protests about campus-based military and defense research drew an end to an era of phenomenal growth. Unlike their nineteenth-century counterparts, students during the first 60-plus years of the twentieth century did not engage in regular "student revolts." For the general public, such behavior was what one might expect from students in other countries, but certainly not from U.S. students. As a result, doubts began to surface among the public, legislators, and even parents of students about faculty and administrators' control of the students as well as concerns about what was being taught.

From the Authors

For Evans, having had firsthand experience at the University of California during this time as a faculty member, the memories of the sound of helicopters and the smell of tear gas on the campus are still sharp, as are the memories of the financial consequences for many years as a result of the general perception that the faculty and administrators had failed in being effective "in loco parentis."

There were, of course, other factors operating that led to the decline in support of higher education at this time, primarily economic conditions. Taxpayer revolts, in various guises (such as California's "Proposition 13," which passed in 1978), caused public institutions to engage in "belt tightening," such as deferring maintenance of buildings,

Table 2.4. Post–World War II Assumptions about the Academy	
Assumption	**Key Issues**
Open to all	More students, more classes, more extracurricular activities
Productive scholars	Narrow fields of interest, increased operating costs
Research justifies existence	Results now, with outside grants key to support
Exists to serve society	Extension/adult education programs, facilities opened to community use
Will be supported indefinitely	Little strategic/long-term planning

reducing program size, and encouraging senior faculty to take early retirements. For private institutions, a major issue was maintaining enrollments as it became increasingly difficult for families to pay the escalating costs of private higher education.

Libraries faced midyear budget cuts, primarily in collection funds, as institutions faced budget shortfalls. There were years when all of the available collection funds had to go to pay for journal subscriptions with nothing left for new books. Hiring "freezes" occurred at the same time that more services were demanded. At best, institutions achieved a "steady state" status rather than losing ground.

Technology started to play a greater role at this time. Libraries were actually at the forefront of technological usage and collaboration, something not always recognized outside of the profession. One significant example is Online Computer Library Center (OCLC), which was and is a highly successful library collaborative effort in the area of technology and services. When Wyman Parker was hired by the Ohio College Association in 1963 to develop a cooperative cataloging center, few people, if anyone, thought that it would in time become one of the world's largest library cooperatives. Perhaps Fredrick Kilgour had a grander vision in 1967 when he took the leadership of what then was known as the Ohio College Library Center (OCLC). At one point, the organization was known as Online Library Computer Center Inc., which indicated its technological aspects as well as a much broader membership. By the 1970s, larger academic libraries were operating homegrown computer-based systems, and it was not much later that commercial systems were marketing "library automation" packages. Academic libraries were probably one of the first campus units to fully employ technology for almost all of its daily operations.

Another area affected by technology was the development of alternative educational programs (distance education). This has had major impacts on how academic libraries provide services and resources to students and faculty working remotely. For-profit programs started and offered almost unlimited flexibility for the student in how, when, and where she or he completed a degree. Again, this had implications in terms of expectations for public-supported academic libraries to provide services and resources to students and faculty not enrolled in the respective libraries' home institutions but who are paying tax dollars to support those public colleges and universities.

Table 2.5 summarizes the issues associated with this period.

Before we end the discussion we need to mention two rather unique U.S. academic institutions: African American Colleges (historically black colleges and universities, HBCUs) and Native American Tribal Colleges. Both types of institutions play an important role in today's postsecondary educational system. Both types of institutions face(d)

Table 2.5. Post-1970s Issues	
Issues Common after 1970	
Funding decreased for institution as a whole.	Value of higher education once again questioned.
Costs increased for students and the institution.	Growing competition arose with alternative educational opportunities.
Research into social issues failed to produce real results.	Pool of potential students decreased.
General public's view of the academy shifted from neutral to skeptical.	Technology presented both opportunities and financial challenges.

the same challenges as the white institutions as well as some that are unique to their development, circumstances, and mission.

Looking back at Table 2.1, you see that the first college for Native Americans was the institution that became Dartmouth. Although its initial purpose was to educate Native American preachers and it later dropped the Native American orientation, it was a college. The gap between Moor's Indian Charity School and what are today's tribal colleges (community colleges) was several hundred years. From the time of Moor's startup until the post–Civil War period, Native American education was handled by missionaries. Almost all of that education was at the primary level, and focus was on "civilizing the savages." Although throughout U.S. history relations between native peoples and the dominant society was a federal matter, the government asked that missionaries address education on its behalf. Needless to say, the instruction always took the slant of the teacher's religious orientation in the expectation that this would lead to the students' joining that denomination. The first two higher education schools after Dartmouth changed location, name, and "Indian" orientation were Pembroke State College in 1887 (now part of the University of North Carolina system) and Bacone College in 1880 (a four-year college). Even these institutions had an acculturation goal, with little or no recognition of the students' cultural heritage.

In the 1960s, tribes began to push for tribally oriented higher education, and a series of tribal community colleges came into existence. Their curriculums are bilingual and bicultural in an effort to provide a balanced approach. "Native people, on the whole, have favored schools that teach their children non-Indian ways without forcing them to forget their Indian ways" (Reyhner and Eder, 2004, p. 330). More and more Native American students are enrolling and succeeding in all categories of higher education institutions. As of September 2008, the American Indian Higher Education Consortium had 36 members.

Black colleges had some different challenges to overcome. Without a doubt the greatest challenge was the racial issue that did and still does exist, although to a much lesser extent. No colleges for blacks in the South existed until after the Civil War because southern states made it illegal to provide such opportunities. In the North, the first black colleges were Cheyney College in 1837 (now a university as part of the Pennsylvania State System of Higher Education), Lincoln College in 1854 (now a university and part of the Pennsylvania State System of Higher Education), and Wilberforce University in 1856 (a private institution located in Ohio). With the passage of the second land grant Morrill Act (1890) the real growth in black colleges took place; today there are 106 such institutions. HBCUs help keep their issues on the public agenda.

The 1890 act's primary purpose was to create better endowments and physical facility maintenance of the white land grant schools. A secondary outcome was it provided land grant funding for African American colleges. Essentially, the 17 black colleges created after the Civil War became land institutions, and some of their funding challenges became less severe (Harris and Worthen, 2004). "Black land grant institutions continue as a subgroup of the land grant system because of the economic and political forces that denied full citizenship to Africans freed from slavery after the Civil War" (Harris and Worthen, 2004, p. 454).

Most academic libraries in these unique institutions have additional collection development requirements that include supporting their institutions' appropriate ethnic studies curriculum. This includes supporting special collections that reflect the uniqueness of their institutions' missions.

Additionally, we need to recognize that with this country's changing demographics there are a larger number of Hispanic-serving higher education institutions (210) represented by the Hispanic Association of Colleges and Universities (HACU). Unlike the HBCUs and tribal colleges, many of the Hispanic-serving institutions did not set out with that particular goal in mind. However, as their community populations continued to change from predominantly white residents to emerging Hispanic populations, so did part of the mission of the institutions change.

> **From the Authors**
>
> Alire served a library deanship at a Hispanic-serving university whose law school ranked number 1, engineering college ranked number 3, and medical school ranked number 6. Her library consisted of a significant special collections and archives department that concentrated in southwest collections reflecting both Hispanic and Native American materials.

BASIC ISSUES IN HIGHER EDUCATION

We believe that higher education and its libraries have and will continue to face seven fundamental issues. The following chapters explore each issue in more depth as well as examine how those issues relate to academic librarianship. Those issues are the following:

- Faculty—who should teach what, how does an academy attract and retain quality teachers?
- Students—who should have access, who should be admitted, how are students retained?
- Curriculum—what to teach, how to teach it, what is an "educated person"?
- Governance—who should have a say about what, what should be controlled internally or externally?
- Facilities—what is essential, what is nice, is the campus a place?
- Funding—how to pay for the process, who should pay what?
- Society—how does an academy maintain good relations, how does it prove worth?

These issues, in a variety of guises, have confronted academia through time. We see little likelihood they will go away in the future, although technology will play a major role in what the future will look like and how colleges and universities will respond to the issues.

REFERENCES

American Association of Community Colleges. n.d. *About community colleges.* Available: www .aacc.nche.edu/AboutCC (accessed July 22, 2008).

Becker, Carl L. 1943. *Cornell University: Founders and the founding.* Ithaca, NY: Cornell University Press.

Brubacher, John S., and Willis Rudy. 1997. *Higher education in transition: A history of American colleges and universities.* New Brunswick, NJ: Transaction Publishers.

Carpenter, Kenneth E. 1986. *The first 350 years of the Harvard University Library.* Cambridge, MA: Harvard University Library.

CCC2NAU: Twice the value. 2008. *Arizona Daily Sun,* August 5, p. A1.

Ferruolo, Stephen C. 1988. Parisius-Paradisus: The city, its schools, and the origin of the University of Paris. In *The university and the city*, ed. Thomas Bender, 22–41. Oxford: Oxford University Press.

Handlin, Oscar, and Mary Handlin. 1970. *The American college and American culture*. New York: McGraw-Hill.

Harris, Rosalind, and Dreamal Worthen. 2004. Working through the challenges: Struggle and resilience within historically black land grant institutions. *Education* 124, no. 3: 447–455.

Hyde, J. K. (copy editor). 1988. Universities and cities in medieval Italy. In *The university and the city*, ed. Thomas Bender, 13–21. Oxford: Oxford University Press.

Johnson, Gerald W. 1958. Should our colleges educate? In *The college years*, ed. Auguste C. Spectorsky. New York: Hawthorn Books.

Kivinen, Osmo, and Petri Poikus. 2006. Privileges of universitas magistrorum et scolarium and their justification in charters of foundation from the 13th to 21st centuries. *Higher Education* 52, no. 2: 185–213.

Kunstler, Barton. 2006. The millennium university, then and now. *On the Horizon* 14, no. 2: 62–69.

Lucas, Christopher J. 1994. *American higher education: A history*. New York: St. Martin's Press.

Reyhner, Jon, and Joanne Eder. 2004. *American Indian education: A history*. Norman, OK: University of Okalahoma Press.

Sinwell, Carol A. Pender. 2008. Post-transfer students' perception of a community college's institutional effectiveness in preparing them for persistence to baccalaureate attainment. Doctor of Education dissertation, University of Virginia Curry School of Education.

Stille, Charles J. 1878. University of Pennsylvania. In *The college book*, eds. Charles F. Richardson and Henry A. Clark, 122–130. Boston, MA: Osgood & Company.

Thelin, John R. 1982. *Higher education and its useful past*. Cambridge, MA: Schenkman Publishing.

U.S. President's Commission. 1948. *Higher education for democracy: A report*. New York: Harper & Row.

Vinton, Frederick. 1878. The College of New Jersey. In *The college book*, ed. Charles F. Richardson and Henry A. Clark. Boston, MA: Osgood & Company.

LAUNCHING PAD

Bailey, Thomas R., and Vanessa S. Morest. 2006. *Defending the community college equity agenda*. Baltimore, MD: Johns Hopkins Press.

Bender, Thomas. 1988. *The university and the city*. Oxford: Oxford University Press.

Bentinck-Smith, William. 1986. *The Harvard book: Selections from three centuries*. Cambridge, MA: Harvard University Press.

Brint, Steven, and Jerome Karabel. 1989. *The diverted dream: Community colleges and the promise of educational opportunity in America—1900–1985*. New York: Oxford University Press.

Carpenter, Kenneth E. 1986. *The first 350 years of the Harvard University Library*. Cambridge, MA: Harvard University Library.

Cobban, Alan B. 1975. *The medieval universities*. London: Methune & Company.

Cohen, Arthur M., and Florence B. Brawer. 2003. *The American community college*. San Francisco, CA: Jossey-Bass.

Cremin, Lawrence Arthur. 1980. *American education, the national experience, 1783–1876*. New York: Harper and Row.

Eisenmann, Linda. 2006. *Higher education for women in postwar America: 1945–1965*. Baltimore, MD: John Hopkins University Press.

Evans, G. Edward. 1981. Bilingual education projects. *Journal of American Indian Education* 20, no. 2: 19–21.

Geiger, Roger L., 1986. *To advance knowledge: The growth of American research universities, 1900–1940*. New York: Oxford University Press.

Haskins, Charles H. 1940. *The rise of universities*. New York: P. Smith Company.

Roy Lowe, ed. *The history of higher education: Major themes in education.* New York: Routledge 2009.

Pedersen, Olaf. 1997. *The first universities.* Cambridge: Cambridge University Press.

Perspectives on the history of higher education, annual, 2005– . New Brunswick, NJ: Transaction Publishers.

Riddle, Phyllis I. 1989. *University and the state.* Stanford, CA: Stanford University Press.

Ringenberg, William C. 2006. *The Christian college: A history of protestant higher education in America.* 2nd ed. Grand Rapids, MI: Baker Academic.

Rury, John, and Glenn Harper. 1986. The trouble with coeducation. *History of Education Quarterly* 26, no. 4: 481–502.

Thelin, John R. 1982. *Higher education and its useful past.* Cambridge, MA: Schenkman Publishing Company.

Wagner, Ralph D. 2002. *A history of the Farmington Plan.* Lanham, MD: ScarecrowPress.

Williams, Roger L. 1991. *The origins of federal support for higher education.* University Park, PA: Pennsylvania State University Press.

Woodcock, Don, and Osman Alawiye. 2001. The antecedents of failure and emerging hope: American Indians and public higher education. *Education* 121, no. 4: 810–820.

Part II

Higher Education Today

The chapters in this section address the major components of U. S. higher education. Chapter 3, "Faculty," examines the role of faculty, their responsibilities, and activities; it also touches on how these activities have linkages to an academic library's operations. Chapter 4, "Students," discusses how the students are the lifeblood of the institution and how their needs drive academic library services. Chapter 5, "Curriculum," describes the many variations that present in the curriculum of today's U.S. academy as well as the implications that such variations have for library operations. Chapter 6, "Governance," illustrates some of the complexities of how and why institutions of higher education operate the way they do.

Chapter 3

Faculty

The essence of academic life is the opportunity—indeed, the demand—for continual investment in oneself. It is a unique chance for a lifetime of building and renewing intellectual capital.

—Henry Rosovsky (1990)

Research conditions at universities have changed drastically in recent years. Calls for greater utility of research and more cost-effective oriented evaluation from the political system may not have changed the content of research, but it has changed the way research is initiated, organized, and funded.

—Finn Hansson and Mette Mønsted (2008)

How many of us have jobs that have great flexibility in the work schedule, with rarely any two days alike, where you *must* engage in lifelong learning, and it is almost always a pleasure to arrive at work? Among those with such good fortune are professors/teachers in the academy. Contrary to a widely held belief among the general public, faculty members *do* work long hours, longer than anyone other than colleagues and family members realize. Just doing a reasonably adequate job of preparing for each class session takes substantially longer than the general public believes possible. All good instructors regardless of level—preschool to postdoctorate work—devote large blocks of time just to staying current with developments in the subjects they teach. For great teachers, that time commitment is even longer.

In addition to the teaching responsibilities that necessitate a person keep up to date, there is pressure that comes from students, especially graduate students, to be "current." For some of today's students, anything older than tomorrow is out of date. Perhaps this is a function of the web. There are probably few instructors or academic librarians, at least those working in public services, who have not heard more than once some variation of the comment, "I couldn't find *anything* on the web about ____. It must not exist." We know of one academic library that due to space limitations decided to place all of its bound journals into remote storage. There was a fear on the part of public service staff that the storage would lead to a significant workload increase during student term paper times. That problem never materialized. The students had long before ceased looking at back files. If they did not find what they needed in a database or on the web, they looked no further. The only complaints about the move came from senior faculty. At the risk of sounding old fashioned, we do worry that today's students seem unaware that all our knowledge was and is built on the shoulders of past generations and that there are still a host of ideas that are still useful that someone long ago had and expressed. However, the bottom line is student pressure for "new" does keep faculty on their toes.

Another factor forcing lifelong learning has been the ever increasing cross-disciplinary nature of scholarship and the requirement for collaborative work. There has always been some degree of cross-fertilization; however, the rate of crossover research has been steadily growing for the past 50 plus years. This requires a person to have a sound understanding of one or more fields that were not the focus of one's original training. An example from our personal experience is archaeology. Fifty years ago, an archaeologist would normally excavate a site with a small crew of students and perhaps some volunteers. Today a field crew often consists not only of students and volunteers but also of several specialists (which could include a paleobotanist, perhaps a soil, a ceramic, and/or a lithics specialist) in addition to the archaeologist. A successful project requires the archaeologist to know enough about the other specialties and to understand the different agendas of each area to maintain a collaborative effort. It also calls for some managerial skills that probably were not part of the person's academic course of study.

The archaeologist is also required to stay current with the many library-related databases in the various disciplines. Given that these databases are available online, the archeologist can access them from remote sites. Additionally, the archaeologist needs to know how to access "open access" materials through various research institutional repositories, most often operated by the library. Theses repositories also provide access to data sets that may be useful when the person engages in field work.

In writing about interdisciplinary work in U.S. universities, Sá (2008) made three key points. First he noted that the concept of "interdisciplinarity has become a laudable goal for federal agencies, scientific associations, industry, and academic leaders in the U.S." (p. 537). As such, he observed that "creating adequate environments for the practice of interdisciplinary research is often viewed as a management problem that requires academic leadership" (p. 538) and that "given the deep roots of traditional academic structures, the small number of institutions that engage in the reform of core academic policies and organizational frameworks is to be expected.... They still innovate at the margin" (p. 549). No matter how few institutions innovate in terms of structure or policy for interdisciplinary activities, there are still an increasing number of faculty members who take it upon themselves to collaborate across discipline boundaries. For libraries, such collaboration expands the range of resources to which they must provide access and the type of services they offer to faculty and their students.

Faculty members are sometimes rather proud of their freedom/independence. Perhaps the clearest example of this is an incident that occurred at the University of California, Berkeley, in the early 1960s during a time when California required all state employees to sign an anticommunist loyalty oath. Grover Sales (1963) reported on a Berkeley faculty member who refused to sign the oath. The professor, E. K. Kantorowicz, who was at the time an eminent medieval scholar, is quoted as saying, "There are three professions which are entitled to wear the gown—the judge, the priest, and the scholar. This garment stands for

---

From the Authors

Alire was present when a young faculty member requested that his dean have the public safety department change the sign at the entrance of the parking lot he used from "employee parking" to "faculty parking." That incident took place in 2003.

Tip

One skill academic librarians need to develop is the ability to deal effectively with the occasional faculty member who has a rather strong sense of self-importance. At times, controlling the frustration at what seems to be, or is, a special privilege or service that no one else should receive is a challenge. We touch on this type of "diplomacy" in the chapters on library services.

its bearer's maturity of mind, his independence of judgment, and his direct responsibility to his conscience and his god" (p. 30). Dr. Kantorowicz's objection to the oath was not the loyalty aspect but rather that the document was to be signed by *employees*. The idea that faculty are *not* employees is still around and held by younger as well as senior faculty members.

FACULTY RESPONSIBILITIES

Since the late nineteenth century U.S. postsecondary institutions regardless of type have had three broad categories of faculty responsibility: teaching, research/scholarship, and service. How much emphasis is placed on each category depends on one's institutional type. As Burton Clark (1993) noted, "The academic profession is a multitude of academic tribes and territories" (p. 163). As such, "Disciplinary location and institutional locations together compose the primary matrix of induced and enforced similarities and differences among American academics" (p. 164). These factors play a role in how much emphasis the institution places on the above responsibilities.

Michelle Toews and Ani Yazedjian (2007) likened the handling of the responsibilities to that of a circus ringmaster where newcomers to the profession must master a sharp learning curve. They suggest the first two responsibilities are the main acts. Research/scholarly activities are akin to a high wire performer or acrobats providing the "wow" factor that attracts the attention of colleagues and the general public. Their suggestion that teaching is analogous to being an animal trainer may seem a tad harsh; however, anyone with teaching experience, at any level, recognizes there is an element truth in their view. Service, following their circus analogy, calls in the clowns: "They are a distraction between the main acts (research and teaching), but would be sorely missed if they were not part of the show" (p. 114). Although life in academia is not really a circus, their analogy does suggest the challenges faculty face. Having experienced these pressures firsthand, we know one often feels like a juggler trying to keep actually four balls in motion—teaching, research, service, and, if one is lucky, something of a personal life.

A faculty member in a doctorate granting institution experiences heavy pressure to be equally effective in the entire triumvirate, but research had better be top-notch. Anything less will lead to an early departure. Masters institutions come closest to having a balance between the three obligations. Baccalaureate schools place their emphasis on teaching and service, with scholarly activity as an added bonus; it may even carry some institutional rewards. Associate degree organizations focus almost exclusively on teaching and service; any research performed is unexpected and not required.

The following discussion is not just background information about the academic environment. When academic librarians have academic status, they face the same or similar performance expectations. We will explore this issue in more depth in the chapter on library staffing.

> **Keep in Mind**
>
> Faculty status, or something similar to that status, for academic librarians carries with it all or almost all of the same requirements as for teaching faculty. Sometimes there is a tendency to think only of what are perceived to be faculty "perks" during efforts for librarians to achieve a status similar to that of teaching faculty. A Chinese proverb goes something like "Be careful what you wish for because you might get it."

SERVICE

We start our coverage of faculty responsibilities with the concept of service, because it is probably the least understood outside of higher education and because it receives the least credit within institutions. While a necessary element in shared governance, when it comes to promotion or compensation, service rarely carries much weight. As the title of Audrey Jaeger and Courtney Thornton's (2006) article aptly stated, "Neither Honor nor Compensation: Faculty and Public Service."

> **Keep In Mind**
>
> By service, we mean the activities that faculty and staff including librarians engage in outside of their primary job responsibilities. Service activities that are of interest to the academy and which may carry modest weight when it comes to performance appraisal time tend to fall into two broad categories: institutional service and public/community service. Institutional service generally involves campus governance, a topic we explore in more depth in Chapter 6. Community service takes many forms, which we'll discuss.

What is acceptable service from a college or university perspective? There is no simple answer to this question. There are both internal and external aspects to service that may or may not count.

In terms of external service, one can trace the expectation that university employees provide service to the community back to its roots in the land grant institutions and the Wisconsin Idea we mentioned in Chapter 2. In the case of land grant institutions, service to state citizens was mandated by the Morrill Act. Dan Butin (2007) stated that in terms of service at land grant institutions, "The boundaries of the university are contiguous with the boundaries of the state" (p. 34). He went on to note that while the boundaries are state lines, until rather recently even land grant schools had been rather lax in providing much in the way of new community services. Certainly extension programs were created shortly after the institution was founded, but not too much more was done.

> **From the Authors**
>
> Evans had a staff member who wanted the fact he engaged in recycling listed as one of his services to the university. Needless to say, this did not happen. However, what if he had said he was a Boy Scout troop leader or he had served as a Community Chest volunteer? That might have warranted a notation in his personnel file, but it would not have been likely to impact his compensation or promotion prospects.

It seems the recent general emphasis on volunteerism has given rise to more community service. Some colleges and universities now require their students to engage in some volunteer work prior to graduation. One now also sees community service mentioned on institutional homepages and on the covers of alumni magazines. However, in terms of compensation and promotion of faculty, this type of community service would probably not count for much.

One gray area when it comes to service is "consulting," which some faculty engage in on a fairly regular basis. Is it a service (free) or a second job (fee)? Even a fee-based consultancy can, at times, be a service in the sense intended by the institution's community relations goals. Libby Morris (2007) identified some of the significant questions to think about when making a decision about what is and is not community service:

> [D]o our students sense our respect for the clients and collaborators? . . . Do they see reciprocity in our service, who benefits and who gains? Do we take more than we give in community partnerships and applied research? . . . are we enacting ethical behaviors from which our students learn?. (pp. 248–249)

Morris's questions suggest that some faculty and administrators view service/consulting as enhancing the learning experience as it brings "real world" issues into their classrooms.

A person might well ask what impact service could have on a library. There are a number of impacts, but two will serve as examples. First there is the question of how much support the library should give service activities of individual faculty members. Another impact is additional library services and resources required when faculty members engage in institutionally sponsored activities (a small business assistance program, for example) that may call for both library services and resources.

Internal service is, in some ways, more important than external. As we will explore in the chapter on governance, internal service is a critical element in shared governance. The most common form internal service takes is committee work. Committee work is often viewed as one the major banes of the workplace in general; within academia it is a part of the culture, like it or not. A significant problem is, especially in doctorate granting institutions, as Jaeger and Thornton (2006) stated, "Increased prominence of research enterprise and lack of rewards for public service leads to a socialization of faculty away from public service.... For these reasons, faculty at land grant institutions may receive mixed messages about their role in fulfilling the institution's articulated public service mission" (p. 346). Although Jaeger and Thornton were writing about "public" service rather than institutional service, their point applies to either type of service.

Anyone spending any time in an academic institution will hear, with some regularity, complaints about having to serve on yet "another committee." (This applies to almost all full-time staff, not just teaching faculty, including librarians.) This is a common complaint of junior (untenured) faculty who often appear to be given more than an average committee workload. The problem is the junior faculty are, at least at doctoral institutions, facing serious time challenges when dealing with the "up or out" aspect of tenure. (We will explore this concept and its time limits later in this chapter.)

> **From the Authors**
>
> Both of us saw a surprising number of junior teaching faculty members on our library advisory committees over the years. Generally it took the better part of a year before they understood the campus and library to become effective committee members.

Women and faculty of color also apparently get tapped more often than their white male colleagues (Adams, 2002; Baez, 2000; Laden and Hagedorn, 2000; Turner and Myers, 2000). Some researchers consider the level of involvement is excessive given their other tenure requirements. Porter (2007) suggested two possible reasons for this phenomenon. One reason may be an institutional desire to have diverse committee membership, and with a relatively small pool of possible appointees, the requests are more frequent. Another reason may be that, at least in some cases, it is a matter of choice by individuals who believe they can advance the interests of their group through actively

> **Keep In Mind**
>
> All categories of library staff may be called on to serve on institutional committees from time to time. When librarians have something similar to faculty status, they will be called for even greater service. Committee work takes time, and if the library does not factor such time consideration into planning workloads, especially for library faculty who have to staff reference desks, timely virtual reference, or reference by appointment, then library service performance problems may result.

working to change the environment, such as increasing the number of women and faculty of color at the institution.

TEACHING

Teaching, like service, is complex. It is more than just time spent in the classroom. Classroom time is a fraction of the total effort that goes into effective teaching at any educational level. Earlier in this chapter we noted the preparation time that any good teacher must engage in as well as the need to keep current with developments in his or her teaching areas. Further time demands include office hours (often a mandated amount based on classroom hours), advising, mentoring, preparing tests, and, last but not least, grading students' work.

Certainly it is possible to do some of this during one's office hours when no students are waiting. However, the good teachers usually have a steady flow of students whose needs often exceed posted office hours and the teachers schedule sessions with individuals at mutually acceptable times.

Another time commitment, especially at institutions offering graduate degrees, is working one on one with students on what might be broadly thought of as independent projects. An independent study course number may be in the course catalog; again the best teachers usually have a number of independent study requests every term. Rarely is this work thought of as part of the teaching load. Certainly such work is taken into account in terms of promotion and compensation; however, given its unpredictable frequency, it normally would not reduce a person's formal course load. Most baccalaureate institutions have honors or capstone requirements that may also call for one-on-one teaching. Thesis and dissertation advising/committee chair activities, which most often revolves around teaching research methods and analysis, likewise are not generally considered as part of the teaching load. Again, the best professors tend to have the greatest number of requests to serve as thesis advisor.

These factors should suggest that teaching load is a perennial issue at most institutions. Part of the problem lies in the fact there is no national standard for "contact hours" for any type of institution or discipline. Overall an institution may have some general guidelines, but there will be variations across disciplines. Another factor is, as we have mentioned several times, that some professors are viewed by the students as more willing to take on independent student work. The process is similar to how students' informally evaluate teaching and make efforts to avoid taking classes from teachers they believe are ineffective. Such factors play a role in departmental politics and can make a department chairperson's work of preparing balanced and effective teaching schedules more complex and frustrating. (Perhaps the least favorite activity of any department head, library or teaching, after conducting performance appraisals is scheduling courses or night and weekend duties in the case of the library.) One has to strive for balance while recognizing that there will be performance differences that may impact end consumers' assessment of departmental quality and staff resentment about workloads.

> **Keep In Mind**
>
> For libraries, the teaching of information literacy courses can raise some of the same workload issues. We will discuss this topic in the chapter on library services.

The foregoing suggests that not all faculty members are good much less great when it comes to teaching, both in and out of the classroom. Perhaps one reason is that there are number of methods for handling a course—lecture, discussion, laboratory, case, fieldwork, small group, and workshop to mention a few—and some teachers are better at one or two options. Often no assistance is available to help a person determine which methods would work best for the course content and for the particular skills the person possesses. Some institutions do offer services to individual faculty members to help individuals assess and improve their teaching styles (one such example is at the University of Maryland, where the Center for Teaching Excellence exists to support faculty teaching). Both authors worked at institutions where these centers were available to teaching faculty. However, it is up to an individual to take advantage of such services.

For some individuals, the idea that they might benefit from such services never crosses their minds; for others it may be something akin to losing face by admitting they could use some assistance. More often than not, there is only some mentoring effort within a department. A senior faculty member works with a junior member who is having trouble, but often even the best teachers do not realize just what makes their teaching special. Another reality is that few graduate programs, especially at the doctoral level, offer, much less require, courses in how to teach. This is a rather interesting fact given that elementary and secondary school teachers (and library media specialists) receive extensive training in how to plan and present course material. This may account for the fact that the lecture is still the predominant teaching method, still rather like its medieval beginnings. Julia Hughes (2008) in writing about the teaching-research pressures made the following point:

> If demonstrated competence as a researcher is the predominant requirement of university faculty, then it should not be surprising that the lecture has remained the dominant pedagogical form. Within the traditional lecture, the speaker is expected to present his or her knowledge to those listening, something that most people with a Ph.D. should be more or less competent at doing. . . . Based on this assumption, the preparation of faculty for their teaching roles may be adequate. But is lecturing necessarily synonymous with teaching? (p. 52)

Understanding what method will work best for what group of individuals is essential for high quality of teaching. However, at graduate institutions the research component tends to dominate the situation with almost no regard for teaching skills. Holding a teaching assignment while a graduate student does not necessarily translate into knowing how to be an effective teacher.

Some critics of higher education teaching methods have a saying, "A teacher should be a guide at the side rather than a sage on the stage." This jingle is rather insulting to the vast majority of academic teachers. Certainly anyone who has spent time in higher education has encountered the egotistic, self-important blowhard who does in fact act like the sage on the stage. However, for every egotist, there are hundreds of teaching faculty who do act the part of guide; these nonsages are the individuals who understand the linkage between teaching and learning. Mary Burgan (2006) makes the point that "the opposition of saging and staging to teaching and learning derives from a set of pressing concerns in an age of rapid changing higher education. Among the most critical of these concerns are student diversity and the uses and possibilities of technology, each of which has played a part in re-centering higher education pedagogy from teachers to students" (p. 31).

In the past, a teacher used overhead slides to supplement lectures, perhaps to show details/data that enhanced the content of the presentation. Because such slides were extremely time-consuming to prepare, if they were to look even halfway professional the person thought about what to spend time on preparing. Today, most of us who teach or give talks use presentation software packages to provide some graphic relief to our lectures. Such packages make it easy to create slides quickly.

Unfortunately, few of us realize that such packages are presenter rather than audience oriented. As a result, our slides tend to help us stay on track (a form of lecture notes) rather than to enhance the *content* of the presentation. We may have some color graphics and even a touch of animation, but have we added real information/value to the presentation? (An example of what not to do can be found at norvig.com/Gettysburg/sld006.htm; in a way it is humorous and sad at the same time.) In their article "Death by PowerPoint?" Eves and Davis (2008) stress that lecturers should "develop presentations that are engaging and easy to understand. Don't get caught up in the technology" (p. 9).

Check This Out

A good source for assistance in use of presentation software as a teaching tool is E. R. Tufte's *Cognitive Style of PowerPoint* (Cheshire, CT: Graphic Press, 2006).

Technology has changed teaching in significant ways over the past 20 years. First, it opened up the way in which institutions could think about and deliver courses to distant learners. Second, it has been changing classes on campus. Thus, technology has once again played a role again allowing higher education to become less "place" oriented and more virtual in nature, somewhat like its earliest phases when "place" was transient.

Looking at the campus situation first, "smart classrooms" with a wide range of technological capabilities are becoming more common. They represent a significant expense both to install and maintain; sometimes one has to wonder if the expense did/does actually enhance learning. For all of their benefits, such classrooms often cause frustrations to everybody involved in the following ways:

- Senior faculty who are not technology oriented may view the equipment as an impediment to their teaching methods.
- Junior faculty may want more sophisticated technology than what is available and, of course, upgrades for existing equipment on a regular basis.
- Students may expect more sophisticated use of the existing technologies as well as more effective use.
- Those who must acquire and support the technologies when usage is very uneven and are on the receiving end of the frustrations of the first three groups suffer.

From a virtual point of view, technology has opened up new audiences for institutions as well as new revenue streams. A person can earn a degree from a number of fully accredited institutions by successfully completing all or almost all the class work online. Being able to do the work whenever and from wherever one desires has increased higher education opportunities for many individuals who might never have done so had they been required to go to a campus and handle the institution's schedule. It also has meant that institutions do not need as extensive night and weekend programs they had instituted to meet the needs of local students who had to work full time.

One factor that has been overlooked but now is being recognized is the time commitment when using technology to teach a course. This applies equally to online and smart classroom courses, assuming one uses the classroom equipment. Joseph Cavanaugh ("Comparing Online Time to Offline Time," 2006) is one of the few to report, with sound data, on the time commitment in teaching the *same* course in the *same* term in an online and classroom format. Cavanaugh tracked his time for both courses (Introduction to Economics) and found that his preparation time was ten times greater for the online version and overall the online course took a total of 93 more hours than the face-to-face class. Perhaps the time variation would be greater or lesser depending on the subject, but

> **Keep In Mind**
>
> Distance education programs, whatever their format, as well as night and weekend degree programs do present some service challenges for academic libraries. Online degree programs make the concept of 24/7 library service just a tad more complex. Accrediting agencies do look closely at how effectively the library serves the distant learner.

his data gives solid credence to the widely held view that online courses require more time. Clearly such time differences should have an impact on faculty workloads.

Online courses also raise the interesting question of intellectual property—who "owns" the course? No one worried about this question when a professor taught a face-to-face course. If you, as instructor, spend long hours putting together what turns out to be a highly successful online course, do you own the rights and could you make it available to other institutions, for a fee that would not be shared by your home institution? Different institutions have different answers, but they tend to expect at least some ownership of the course material.

Successful teaching takes time that far exceeds the class time. Good instructors understand the linkage between teaching and learning, share their enthusiasm for their subject, mentor the learners, and make themselves available to their students as much as possible. These points apply to any classroom teaching, including courses offered by the library.

> **Check These Out**
>
> An excellent book that any teacher should read is Kenneth Bain's *What the Best College Teachers Do* (Cambridge, MA: Harvard University Press, 2004).
>
> Two good articles that address online teaching are Cathy Galyon Keramides and colleagues' "Saving Your Sanity When Teaching in an Online Environment," *Rural Special Education Quarterly* 26, no. 1 (2007): 28–29, and Lawrence Tomei's "The Impact of Online Teaching on Faculty Load," *Journal of Technology and Teacher Education* 14, no. 3 (2006): 531–541.

RESEARCH

Without question, the German academic model has played a major role in the development of U.S. higher education since the end of the nineteenth century. A rather unkind saying about academic research, but one containing more than one grain of truth, is that research leads to fewer and fewer people knowing more and more about less and less. The grains of truth have implications for academic libraries—more about this later in this chapter.

Today there is a generally accepted belief that research and teaching are complementary activities, the basic concept from early German universities. Research (new insights) inform teaching and can lead to valuable developments for society in general. Teaching is what generates interest in some students to become the next generation of researchers, thus starting another cycle of research. Rosovsky (1990) discussed the need for both activities and why students should seek teachers who engage in research as well as those who are good teachers. He contended that this type of situation (the good teacher/researcher) leads to the greatest learning opportunities—essentially they are the best "guides" because they demonstrate the potential of research for the long-term benefit of society.

At its most basic academic meaning, research is a process that either brings to light new information/knowledge or revises a generally accepted conclusion. Note: most "research," as the public thinks about the term, done worldwide is conducted by profit-oriented organizations and focuses on developing new products rather than advancing knowledge. Research, in conjunction with new ways of thinking, is a special characteristic of academia. It is what attracts and keeps people in it and working hard to contribute something in return.

By now the reader probably realizes that few, if any, simple concepts exist in academia. (The Alire-Evans law of higher education is, if it is simple, rest assured academics can and will make it complex.) So, no surprise, research is both complex to carry out successfully and the manner of thinking about the activity is complicated. This is not the book to explore the hundreds if not thousands of variations in research methodology. However, there is a widespread, if informal, accepted matrix that broadly categorizes academic research—pure, applied, hard, and soft. Table 3.1 provides an overview of the matrix.

Table 3.1. Research Matrix		
	Pure	**Applied**
Hard	Chemistry Physics	Medicine Geology
Soft	Computer Science Engineering	Education Library Science

Although one can think of how something "hard and pure" has applications for society, the categories do provide a broad structure for thinking about academic research from a library point of view. Hard pure research tends to be in the "hard sciences" (biology, botany for example) and tend to be journal-focused. Pure soft research tends to be in the other sciences, which are also generally journal-focused. Hard applied disciplines are a mix of sciences and social sciences; these researchers use a combination of journals and monographs in their work. Soft applied research is generally found in the humanities and draws heavily on monographs and, to a lesser degree, journals. Knowing who is doing what type of research can be helpful in not only allocating funds for library collections but also what to collect.

Keep In Mind

Although many within higher education might publicly deny it, there is an informal pecking order when assessing academic research, at least when comes to questions of promotion, compensation, and special recognition. If faced with the task of ranking research in terms of the matrix, the order would be pure-hard, applied hard, pure-soft, and applied-soft among faculty at most institutions.

It is one thing to come up with new insights from one's research and another to have them accepted by one's peers. Until the late nineteenth century, the process of acceptance was slow and depended on many face-to-face discussions with one's peers. (We see a remnant of this process in the thesis and dissertation defense.) Although the "public lecture" and responding to questions from the audience rarely still occurs in the United States, a final "defense" of one's thesis with the advisory committee is typical. Also typical is that anyone knowing about the time and place of the examination may attend and ask the candidate questions about the research. This defense is the first step in what we now label "scholarly communication."

Keep In Mind

There are many definitions of scholarly communication. At its most basic meaning, it is the process by which scholars let one another know about their research results. A sound definition comes from American Library Association's Association of College and Research Libraries division:

New knowledge builds on old, and, today, is increasingly shaped by participation in a community of scholars. A vital part of this process is the broadest possible sharing of academic publications among scholars and students worldwide. Sharing is so important to the academic process that faculty routinely contribute articles to scholarly journals and serve as peer reviewers and editors—all without compensation. (Association of College and Research Libraries, 2009)

Daniel Coit Gilman, founder of Johns Hopkins (1878) believed a major duty/responsibility of universities was to advance humankind's knowledge *and* to disseminate that knowledge. At the time, the notion of disseminating new knowledge beyond the lecture hall was a novel idea in the United States. Being a realist, Gilman knew that what was a thriving commercial publishing industry was most unlikely to undertake publishing scholarly/research findings due to the limited market for such material—risks would be too high and sales too low to generate a profitable return. His solution to the dissemination challenge was to establish the Johns Hopkins University Press to fulfill the publisher's role. The press's first two publications were journals, which were later followed by monographs. The number of such presses grew along with the number of institutions offering doctoral degrees. They stopped growing in the 1970s when institutional financial difficulties impacted their sales. Essentially, this occurred when a majority of libraries cut back on their book and journal purchases as academic libraries were the major customers of academic presses.

Since the first university presses (UPs) began operating, most research/doctoral institutions established similar operations. One special aspect of such presses is their nonprofit status. As a result they are linked to the institution's mission of serving the general good rather than generating a maximum profit. This is not to say that they do not hope that every title they publish will break even, but doing so is all that is required. Should a title do better than that, the added revenue goes toward putting out additional titles rather than increasing owner equity or shareholder dividends.

Publishing scholarly material, especially scientific items, is generally more costly than other categories, except those requiring large numbers of high quality color graphics, such as art books and textbooks for the K–12 school market, for example. Not only do many scholarly titles require high quality graphics, they often call for special characters and symbols. Scholarly publishers (UPs and professional associations) often employ a publishing subsidy fee to try to break even on their publications. A fairly common fee in the scientific journal area is a "page charge." That is, authors pay a fee to publishers based on the number of pages in their articles. The charges are rather significant; two examples as of 2008 are the *Astronomical Journal* at a cost of $105 per page for an electronic version and $150 for a print version (www.iop.org/EJ/journal/-page=extra.2/AJ) and *Astronomy & Astrophysics* at a cost of 100€, which at the time was roughly $150.

Some might wonder about this cost control approach. Is it not the same as vanity publishing? Vanity publishing requires only that a person have money enough to cover the printing and binding costs; there is no review of the manuscript by peers or the publisher and thus no quality control.

There are at least two important differences between vanity and scholarly publishing subsidies. The most significant difference is, unlike vanity publications, a scholarly manuscript undergoes a rigorous peer review process. The process is generally labeled "refereed review." Reviewers are other academics who specialize in the field that the manuscript covers. They are asked to assess the content and its accuracy as well as its overall significance and, most importantly, whether it should be published. Thus the review process provides a measure of quality control—essentially a method of acting as an "honest broker" of the information put forth in the name of higher education. The subsidy comes into play only after the manuscript has been accepted for publication.

The second difference is it is well understood that the market for scholarly material is limited and production costs are high, even when the referees are not paid a reading fee. The high costs, again, are what drive the per-page charge.

> **Keep In Mind**
>
> Having a strong collection of refereed journals in all of the fields of faculty interest is an important library service.

Serving on a scholarly publisher's editorial board is considered a form of service to higher education as well as a form of peer recognition of one's standing in the field. This suggests, and it is often the case, that reviewers are senior academics who have a track record of publishing. Refereeing does carry something of a quality stamp. However, there is a danger, given who is selected to be a reviewer, that the "old boy network" will impact the flow of new/contradictory research. The typical way publishers attempt to control such influence is to employ an anonymous (double blind) process—the author(s) name(s) and institutional information is redacted from the manuscript and the reviewers comments/feedback go to the author(s) without the name(s) of the reviewer(s). Overall, the process works well when dealing with broad topics, such as personnel management, academic librarianship, or information technology, for example. However, the system is not nearly as effective when it comes to very narrow topics (paleobotany in the Southwest for example). The fact that advanced research results in fewer people knowing more about less leads to a tiny pool of potential authors and reviewers. The small pool means it is relatively easy to know who wrote what, as either author or reviewer, based on the content. Regardless of its shortcomings, refereeing nonetheless provides a large measure of quality control.

An interesting article looking at faculty members' attitude about the refereeing process is by Brian Hemmings, Peter Rushbrook, and Erica Smith (2007). They analyzed 205 responses from faculty members about factors encouraging or limiting writing for refereed publications. Just over 50 percent of the respondents indicated the primary reason for doing such writing was because of promotion prospects. Another 30 percent identified institutional pressure to do so was their prime motivation. Thus, almost 80 percent indicated some form of pressure led to their engaging in such writing activities. Not too surprising, the two highest limiting factors were workload (61 percent) and lack of support (23 percent).

> **Think About This**
>
> One interesting limiting factor mentioned in the Hemmings, Rushbrook, and Smith (2007) article was the availability of library resources and services (13 percent). Sometimes we, academic librarians, forget just how critical our role is in scholarly communication, especially for junior faculty members.

An interesting outcome of scholarly publishers using a subsidy system was that a few commercial publishers saw an opportunity to enter the field, especially by working with professional associations in producing journals, memoirs, and conference proceedings. The examples of page charges indicate why they might see a potential opportunity in the area. Academic libraries' materials budgets were rather quickly impacted by the change of publishers as the cost of the publications escalated. Journal subscription prices became at least dual in nature, with one price charged for the individual and another much higher institutional/library price. Today, this is complicated by the fact that, in many cases, libraries have to deal with the institutional print price and another fee for a digital version.

Today, the scholarly communication process is undergoing significant changes due to technology, primarily the Internet. It is clear that scholarly publishing, at least UPs, face serious financial challenges. Sarah Gold (2007) reported that 70 percent of the UPs acknowledged that they were operating in the red, despite underwriting fees. It is important to note that most of today's UPs are publishing primarily monographs, and few of those publications have any underwriting of costs.

If anything, technology is making it harder for UPs to get back into the black. Competition from Open Access projects and institutional repositories (more about this in Part III) are likely to grow in scope and reduce the amount of potential titles for the UPs to publish. Furthermore, academic libraries face increasing difficulty in allocating limited funds for collection building as all of the formats escalate in cost faster than budgets increase.

Technology makes it possible to disseminate information quickly at a relatively modest cost. (Remember an early primary purpose of the Internet was to enhance and speed up scholarly communication.) In today's web environment, it takes a reasonably sophisticated person to sort out the good, the bad, the ugly, and the irrelevant material. The lack of anything like the refereeing process for web postings means a great deal of useless material floats around and is findable in virtual space.

> **Keep In Mind**
>
> University presses' primary market is academic libraries. Without that market most UPs would fold as there would be too few personal buyers to generate the necessary income.

> **Check This Out**
>
> For a brief overview of the history of the Open Access movement visit www.earlham.edu/~peters/fos/overview.htm.

A question that has not been explored to any great extent is whether the Web has enhanced scholarship. One study suggests that it may have a limiting effect. James A. Evans (2008) published some data in *Science* that suggested there has been a narrowing of focus and possible limiting of thinking due to the digital availability of scholarly material online. He used Thompson Scientific citation indexes and Fulltext Sources Online to generate a data set of 26,002,796 articles online by 2006. Thus, his data set cannot be considered too small to be representative of what is happening among scholars. One of his findings was that as more material became available there was a decline in the number and age (published date of the article cited) of articles cited in a paper. He went on to state:

> This research ironically intimates that one of the chief values of print library research is poor indexing. Poor indexing—indexing by titles and authors, primarily within core journals— likely had unintended consequences that assisted the integration of science and scholarship. By drawing researchers through unrelated articles, print browsing and perusal may have facilitated broader comparisons and led researchers into the past. Modern graduate education parallels this shift in publication—shorter in years, more specialized in scope, culminating less frequently in true dissertation than an album of articles. (p. 398)

We believe his research should be followed up as it has implications for scholarship in general and academic librarianship in particular.

THE LADDER AND TENURE

Being a tenured faculty member has some benefits not often found in other fields of endeavor, such as a degree of job security, frequently an opportunity to have a paid leave to engage in research (sabbatical), and flexible working hours. In the not too distant past it was a good career choice for the academically inclined. Today, the situation is rather different as additional pressures (seeking grant funding for example) have generally become almost equal to the benefits.

There are few individuals outside of higher education who fully understand the concept of tenure. In fact, most of the public is highly suspicious of the practice. The suspicions are largely based on a lack of understanding of the concept. Some of the negative ideas that are widely held are tenured faculty are accountable to no one, are lazy and overpaid, are guaranteed a lifetime job, are getting away with *something* even if we do not know what that something is, and their teaching performance is almost always bad. Among college students, there is a belief that their favorite teachers are almost always denied tenure. Some junior faculty (untenured) harbor suspicions that they are brighter and better teachers than some of their tenured colleagues who may or may not grant them tenure.

None of the above ideas are true, at least not 95 percent of the time. So what is tenure? It does provide some degree of job security, at least from indiscriminate dismissal. However, as many faculty members have learned, large numbers can and have been dismissed when the institution declares a financial exigency. Entire departments can be and have been closed down, and in such cases tenure will do nothing to protect one's position.

Originally, tenure was intended to help preserve academic freedom and the German university notion that a professor should be free to explore ideas without outside interference. Thus, a professor may structure and present course content as he or she sees fit. Over the past 15 years or so there have been efforts by individuals and groups outside of the academy to redress what they believe are unwarranted liberal biases in the classroom. Tenure will help with such challenges but not keep the matter from, on rare occasions, ending up in civil court in an attempt to force the dismissal or resignation of a targeted faculty member.

> **From the Authors**
>
> While a doctoral student and working on her dissertation, Alire had all of the tenured faculty in her major's department released/dismissed due to financial exigencies. Both authors shared an experience in which their school was closed for the same reason. None of the tenured faculty members were even given the opportunity to apply for positions in the institution's library.

Other, less well-known factors supporting the use of tenure are: the process does provide a measure of quality control—the period of time before one gains tenure allows the institution to assess the individual's academic performance; it provides a measure of stability in the core faculty—most people are disinclined to undergo a second tenure process, so they tend to stay at the institution that granted the tenure; and, to some degree, it helps balance out the higher income a person might earn in the nonacademic sector by offering a measure of job security.

A general assumption on the part of the public is that anyone teaching at an academic institution is a "professor." Depending on what type of academic institution the teacher is from, this assumption has a greater or lesser chance of being correct. If the person is from a baccalaureate institution, there is a good chance the individual has a "ladder appointment" and has a job title with the word *professor* in it. (There are three levels to the ladder/tenure process: assistant professor, associate professor, and professor, sometimes called a full professor.) At either graduate or associate level institutions (community colleges) there is a chance the person does not have a job title containing the word *professor* (or if they do hold the title it may be without a similar tenure process seen at doctorate institutions).

Graduate degree schools employ a number of job titles for those who engage in teaching. There are teaching assistants (TAs) at the lowest level of responsibility; they may assist only by reading and grading student assignments or, at a slightly higher level of responsibility, monitor/run one or more "lab" sessions for a course. TAs are often first- or second-year graduate students, and their positions help cover some of their educational expenses. A more responsible teaching position is "instructor," held often by an advanced level graduate student. Instructors have full responsibility for planning and teaching one or more courses. Another category is "adjunct professor." Such individuals usually are doctorate degree holders who do not have a full-time appointment (generally adjuncts have contracts for one or two academic terms at best even though they are reappointed year after year). Finally, there are specialists from outside of higher education who may have a terminal degree in the field they are teaching—for example, a master of fine arts. Such appointments are often multiyear contracts and carry the title of lecturer. In addition to these standardized categories, some institutions have the additional category of faculty emeritus. The emeritus/emerita title is for the most part honorific and is intended to acknowledge outstanding service to the institution for a retired faculty member.

Associate degree institutions (community colleges) usually do not have the TA category as they do not have a pool of graduate students to draw on. They may however have a ladder similar to that of baccalaureate institutions that starts at the instructor rank and ends at professor. Associate degree institutions vary from their counterparts in two other ways: first, it may be possible for a faculty member to achieve the rank of professor without holding a doctorate in the field, and second, as mentioned previously, there likely will not be the same tenure requirements or procedures in place. These institutions may make more use of lecturer and adjunct teachers than other institutions but generally require lecturers and adjuncts to have the same qualifications as their full-time counterparts.

PART-TIME/ADJUNCT FACULTY

The part-time/adjunct category needs some fuller discussion as the usage has been increasing as institutions attempt to control personnel costs. Recent doctoral graduates often have to turn to the adjunct or postdoctoral research appointments, something of a holding pattern, as they seek a tenure track appointment. In the not too distant past, some institutions employed the adjunct category as a means of offering multiple course offerings without taking on more full-time teachers. Generally an adjunct position is part time and provides no benefits beyond the course fee. Even the course fee is tenuous as it is paid only if the course "makes"—that is, it has a predetermined number of enrollees. Lacking the minimum number of enrollees, the class is cancelled. Accreditation bodies tend to take a dim view of what they consider excessive use of part-time appointments.

There are good reasons to worry about the overuse of part-time appointments. First and foremost are quality concerns. Although well-planned programs for part-time teachers can address many of the quality concerns, few institutions have well-planned operations. Part-timers are generally on their own. They seldom get to meet full-time faculty who may have taught the same course. At best the part-timer gets a copy of the course syllabus as the course was organized at some point in time. Mentoring is rarely in place, and the institution really only assesses course quality on the basis of student evaluation. No full-time staff sit in on a few class sessions of an adjunct or other part-timer's course to assess the quality of the instruction. Adjuncts rarely are integrated into the department much less asked to take part in curriculum discussions. They often know little or nothing about the content of other courses and certainly are in no position to advise students. Today, many adjuncts are trying to make a living by teaching several courses at several institutions in same term. Thus, they are rushing in and out of the classroom as they try to get through traffic from one institution to another.

From a library point of view, adjunct and other part-time appointments present several challenges, at least based on the authors' experiences. The first question is, while the adjuncts must receive access to library collections and services, just how much access? Should they have the same privileges as full-time faculty? Probably two of the thornier areas are number of collection items the individual may have at any one time and what level of access he or she has to document delivery services , at least those that require returning the items.

From the Authors

Evans had a situation in which the library was a member of a statewide network—Link+California—that offered a feature of being able to request an item at one library and have it delivered to another then returned at a third institution. This proved to be enough of a challenge when it came to one's own full-time professor pushed to have the same service because she taught at two member institutions, we gave her the privileges, much to our sorrow in the long run.

There are no "best" answers for how many and at what level of service the adjunct should receive. What one must keep in mind when thinking about the various questions is the library has little leverage with part-time instructors, unlike full-time staff. They can be temporary, and the library rarely knows when their appointments end. Often the library learns that the person is no longer a part-time instructor only several months after the individual has departed along with 20 items from the collection. Ninety-nine percent of these individuals are not problematic—they seldom have much time to engage in library research at any of the institutions they teach at (often what they ask for is remote access to the online databases and services). However, what services to offer them does require thoughtful planning. One good way to explore the issues and options is to discuss them with the library advisory committee.

Turning to ladder/tenure appointees, the issues for the institution and library are different. While a tenure track/ladder appointment is full time, it does not imply that one has job security. At best, it means one may earn it, if all goes well. The first rung on the ladder is assistant professor. The second rung is associate professor; when one achieves this level one normally has tenure. (A person may be appointed as an associate professor when coming from another institution without tenure but in the expectation it will be granted rather quickly. This approach provides the department and institution an opportunity to see if there is a "fit.")

The final rung is professor (or full professor); at some institutions this rank may have some additional levels, as does the associate rank, such as professor 1, 2, 3, 4, and 5. Promotion to such additional levels involves an assessment of performance rather similar to that of moving from assistant to associate and associate to full professor. This type of system provides an additional level of quality control, motivation, and protection against a person becoming the "lazy faculty member" so popular in the public mind. It is also a system that most of the general public does not realize exists. Some states require a post-tenure review of all levels of the professoriate. Usually the institution determines the process for the post-tenure review with the faculty governing body leading the effort.

An assistant professor must prove her or his academic worth to the tenured faculty in the department in order to gain tenure. Having a ladder appointment as an assistant professor has some added performance pressures over and above the triad of faculty responsibilities. One added pressure in today's environment and especially in some fields such as the sciences is the expectation that the person will be able to secure research grants from outside of the institution. (Outside grants usually carry an overhead charge, which is money going to the institution; more about overhead in the chapter on finances.) The process is pressure-filled because one does not have an unlimited amount of time in which to prove one's worthiness. Generally the maximum time frame allowed is seven years. At the end of that time, one either gets tenure or has to leave the institution. A number of assistant professors do not gain tenure.

Earlier we mentioned that the juggling of obligations and tasks that many faculty members engage in for newcomers can almost be overwhelming. By their third year, the time limit seems to be looming large, and worries something along the lines of "Will I get tenure? What will I do if I don't? What will family and friends think/say if I fail to get it?" begin to creep into their thoughts. We believe that the assistant professors, if one

---

From the Authors

Evans worked at an institution that made no secret of the fact that less than 10 percent of the assistants had a real chance at becoming an associate, at least in that institution. Young PhDs chose to accept an assistant position knowing they would probably have to move on but believed that having the institution's name on their curriculum vitae was well worth the time and effort.

As the authors can attest to from personal experience as ladder appointees and from experiences of library staff members who had faculty status, seven years seems generous at the time the "clock" starts ticking. However, the time seems to flash by at lightning speed, especially when one is a new PhD and really teaching for the first time. The first year is almost entirely devoted to trying to get one's courses structured.

As an example from Evans's first year teaching experience and with what the department called a "light" teaching load, the fall term the assignment consisted of two sections of one course, two courses for winter term, and two more courses for spring term, one of which the department had never before offered. Needless to say, many late nights were spent trying to get the next morning's class material organized. There was precious little time for putting the final touches on the dissertation and getting something ready to submit for publication (naturally in a refereed journal). Certainly there was no time to engage in new research or think about submitting a grant proposal. This experience is not atypical of what new assistant professors encounter in their first year of a ladder appointment.

must prioritize library service to faculty—and this is necessary more often than librarians would like—are the ones that should get the greatest assistance.

DIVERSITY

We cannot conclude a chapter about faculty and ignore the important issue of faculty diversity. Students need mentors and role models, especially for those inclined toward an academic lifestyle. Although women and nonwhite male students have been a growing part of the academic scene for more than 150 years, they make up a small percentage of faculty, tenure track, or part time (Turner and Myers, 2000). Jennifer White and Jessica Meendering (2008) noted that women account for 38 percent of faculty at U.S. institutions of higher education, and 30 percent of those are in non-tenure-track positions. The percentage of faculty of color is about 13.4 percent (Stanley, 2006), which of course includes women of color, so the overall picture is that white males continue to make up more than 50 percent of today's faculty members.

Given the preponderance of white males at the senior tenured level, most women and faculty of color do face some additional challenges in their efforts to achieve tenure, at least at white colleges and universities. There appear to be four broad significant factors that are especially challenging—campus life and climate, tenure and promotion, discrimination, and teaching. As Stanley (2006) wrote, "Some of us believe that the academy is truly a meritocracy and culturally neutral. However, critical race theory shows that understanding truth and merit means challenging concepts that are socially constructed to reflect and benefit the majority" (pp. 724–725). Stanley's article contains seven and a half pages of recommendations to address the challenges, divided between what faculty members might do and what administrators might do. As the demographics of the country changes, higher education must do more than just enroll a more diverse student body.

One of every three residents of the United States is a member of a racial/ethnic group, which should translate into a need for more aggressive recruitment and retention of students of color (more about this in the next chapter). As the demographics of the country continue to change, higher education must do more than just enroll an increasingly diverse student body. It needs more faculty of color to serve as role models for students. This also holds for the recruitment of academic librarians.

KEY POINTS TO REMEMBER

- Faculty members have three broad responsibilities: teaching, research, and service.
- Institutional service (committee work) is a requirement if there is to be shared governance.
- At some institutions—for example, land grant—there is a legal requirement to provide service to the community.
- Teaching loads vary substantially within an institution and by the type of institution.
- Research/scholarly activity is a major responsibility at graduate level institutions and is considered important, but not required, at lower degree institutions.
- Scholarly work requires having access to large bodies of information about the area of interest as well as disseminating the results of one's own work.

- Research/scholarly activity is a key factor in planning, developing, and paying for academic library services.
- The issues covered in this chapter may well apply to academic librarians in institutions where they have a status identical or similar to teaching faculty.

REFERENCES

Association of College and Research Libraries. 2009. Integrating scholarly communication into your library. Available: acrl.ala.org/scholcomm (accessed March 20, 2010).

Adams, Kathrynn A. 2002. *What colleges and universities want in new faculty.* Washington, DC: Association of American Colleges and Universities. Available: www.aacu.org/pff/pdfs/Pff_Adams.PDF.

Baez, Benjamin. 2000. Race-related service and faculty of color: Conceptualizing critical agency in academe. *Higher Education* 39, no 3: 363–391.

Burgan, Mary. 2006. In defense of lecturing. *Change* 38, no. 6: 30–34.

Butin, Dan W. 2007. Focusing our aim: Strengthening faculty commitment to community engagement. *Change* 39, no. 6: 34–37

Cavanaugh, Joseph. 2006. Comparing online time to offline time: The shocking truth. *Distance Education Report* 10, no. 9: 8–9.

Clark, Burton R. 1993. Faculty differentiation and dispersion. In *Higher education in America*, ed. Arthur Levine, 163–177. Baltimore, MD: Johns Hopkins University Press.

Evans, James A. 2008. Electronic publication and the narrowing of science and scholarship. *Science* 321 (July): 395–399.

Eves, Robert, L., and Larry E. Davis. 2008. Death by PowerPoint? *Journal of College Science Teaching* 37, no. 5: 8–9.

Gold, Sarah. 2007. University presses need to change to survive. *Publisher's Weekly* 254, no. 30: 13–14.

Hansson, Finn, and Mette Mønsted. 2008. Research leadership as entrepreneurial organizing for research. *Higher Education* 55, no. 6: 651–670.

Hemmings, Brian, Peter Rushbrook, and Erica Smith. 2007. Academics views on publishing refereed works: A content analysis. *Higher Education* 54, no. 2: 307–332.

Hughes, Julia C. 2008. Challenging the research teaching divide. *Education Canada* 48, no. 1: 52–57.

Jaeger, Audrey, and Courtney Thornton. 2006. Neither honor nor compensation: Faculty and public service. *Educational Policy* 20, no. 2: 345–366.

Laden, Berta V., and Linda S. Hagedorn. 2000. Job satisfaction among faculty of color. In *What contributes to job satisfaction among faculty and staff*, ed. Linda S. Hagedorn, 69–78. San Francisco, CA: Jossey-Bass.

Morris, Libby. 2007. Faculty power and responsibility. *Innovative Higher Education* 31, no. 5: 247–249.

Porter, Stephen R. 2007. A closer look at faculty service. *Journal of Higher Education* 78, no. 5: 523–541.

Rosovsky, Henry. 1990. *The university: An owner's manual.* New York: W. W. Norton Company.

Sá, Creso M. 2008. Interdisciplinary strategies in U.S. research universities. *Higher Education* 55, no. 5: 537–552.

Sales, Grover. 1963. The scholar and the loyalty oath. *San Francisco Chronicle*, December 8, pp. 27–30.

Stanley, Christine A. 2006. Coloring the academic landscape. *American Educational Research Journal* 43, no. 4: 701–736.

Toews, Michelle, and Ani Yazedjian. 2007. The three-ring circus of academia: How to become the ringmaster. *Innovative Higher Education* 32, no. 2: 113–122.

Turner, Caroline S., and Samuel L. Myers. 2000. *Faculty of color in academe: Bittersweet success.* Boston, MA: Allyn and Bacon.

White, Jennifer, and Jessica Meendering. 2008. Four basic strategies for success in the early years in higher education. *Delta Kappa Gamma Bulletin* 74, no. 3: 32–34.

LAUNCHING PAD

Abel, Richard, and Lyman Newlin. 2002. *Scholarly publishing.* New York: John Wiley & Sons.

Green, Robert G. 1998. Faculty rank, effort, and success. *Journal of Social Work* 34, no. 3: 415–426.

Johnson, W. Brad. 2007. *On being a mentor: A guide for higher education faculty.* Mahwah, NJ: Lawrence Erlbaum.

Kassiola, Joel J. 2007. The erroneous accusation of research "Mission Creep" at Mater's Institutions: Why teaching in the 21st century must be research-based. *College Teaching* 55, no. 4: 139–143.

Laudel, Grit, and Jochen Gläser. 2008. From apprentice to colleague: The metamorphous of early career researchers. *Higher Education* 55, no. 3: 387–406.

Marcus, Jon. 2007. Helping academics have families and tenure too. *Change* 39, no. 2: 27–32.

Mello, Jeffery A. 2007. Adjuncts: Groomed for success. *BizEd* 6, no. 6: 42–44.

Mitchell, W. Bede, and Bruce Morton, 1992. On becoming faculty librarians: Acculturation problems and remedies. *College and Research Libraries* 53: 379–392.

Mruck, Katja, and Günter Mey. 2002. Between printed past and digital future. *Research in Science Education* 32, no. 2: 257–268.

Mulligan, Bern, Kate Bouman, Susan Currie, Sean McKitrick, and Sharon Fellows. 2008. Critical research practices at Binghamton University. *College & Research Library News* 69, no. 7: 382–385.

Oud, Joanne. 2008. Adjusting to the workplace: Transitions faced by new academic librarians. *C&RL* 69, no. 3: 252–266.

Roth, Wolff-Michael. 2002. Editorial power/authorial suffering. *Research in Science Education* 32, no. 2: 215–240.

Simonson, Michael, Sharon E. Smaldino, Michael Albright, and Susan Zvacek. 2008. *Teaching and learning at a distance: Foundations of distance education.* Upper Saddle River, NJ: Prentice Hall

Tierney, William, and Estela M. Bensimon. 1996. *Promotion and tenure: Community and socialization in academe.* New York: State University of New York Press.

Tomei, Lawrence A. 2006. The impact of online teaching on faculty load. Journal of Technology and Teacher Education 14, no. 3: 531–541.

Chapter 4

Students

University success requires mastery of the "college student" role. Mastering the college student role enables young people to understand their instructor's expectations and apply their existing skills to meet those expectations successfully.
—Peter Collier and David Morgan (2008)

Today's students are far more experienced with advanced technologies than those who arrived just five years ago.
—Christelyn Karazin (2008)

When academicians discuss higher education issues, you are more likely to hear them talking in terms of faculty–student concerns rather than the other way around. This also applies to the order in which we have presented the material in this book. Does this imply that students are a secondary factor rather than the reason that higher education exists? We do not believe this is the case. Rather, it is a function of time. The vast majority of students are in residence for four to five years while the core faculty members are there for perhaps a lifetime career. Because a student is, in some sense, transitory, and as a group their issues are often short-term, the faculty's long-term concerns tend to carry greater weight. For all that, students are *the* primary concern.

We noted in Chapter 2 how the post–World War II era radically changed U.S. higher education. The concept of "open to all" enlarged the pool of potential postsecondary students; the concept is particularly appropriate in terms of community colleges. (Note: community colleges enroll well over 40 percent of all students in higher education.) The concept raised the expectation that the academy would in fact increase the student body diversity. It also brought about the first broad scale, government-based support for baccalaureate students. The effects of the concept have been significant. Today's student body demographics are almost the polar opposite of the homogenous, largely male, and overwhelming white and Protestant composition of pre–World War II student bodies.

As we prepared this chapter, the United States was officially in a recession, and with students experiencing tremendous challenges in securing funding to continue or begin their academic careers as U.S. and world markets were in financial crisis. If the library is the heart of the campus (a debatable point), there is no question that students are the life blood of the institution. They are why postsecondary institutions exist; and, equally important, they are the primary source of most institutions' operating budget.

The open-to-all concept, at least in urban schools, created a larger and more diverse student body, many of whom lacked some of the necessary skills to have successful academic careers without additional institutional assistance. This diversity also led to new degree programs, creation of special academic units such as ethnic study centers/institutes, and the development of new student organizations such as an African

61

American Student Association. All of these factors added to the institutions' operational complexity and costs.

Other changes have included an increase in the average age of the students; students tend to have to commit more time to working at outside jobs to pay their educational fees. Many are independent from their parents, and an increasing number have dependents of their own. Some institutions have opened child care centers for students and institutional staff to help address a challenging issue. Certainly the shift in demographics has led to a loss of a sense of community for the students, at least in the large urban universities.

Academia, at least in the public sector, has a social contract with today's society, which means enrolling all eligible students regardless of socioeconomic status, partnering with secondary schools to ensure they understand the academic skills their graduates will need to succeed at the next level, and offering academic programs relevant to society. (More often it appears a person ought to have a bachelor's degree to be competitive in a technology-based workplace and an emerging global economy.) These three elements raise some interesting challenges for "selective" public institutions. Selectivity will be further discussed later in this chapter.

Needless to say, not everyone agrees with the new openness. Questions are raised about attempts to have the student body composition more closely reflect the makeup of the local/regional population. Some people, often from outside of higher education, have made efforts to correct what they believe are undue liberal biases in the classroom; more about these issues will be discussed in a later chapter. Often they are the individuals who seek the dismissal of faculty for alleged liberal biases, as we mentioned in the previous chapter.

Think About This

How many academic libraries operating in institutions with strong teacher education programs and child care centers see these preschool children as potential students? How many of them have thought of partnering with these child care centers to establish simple programs for these young children utilizing the libraries' children's literature collection? How many have thought of partnering with schools of education enlisting students enrolled in these teacher education programs as interns in their libraries? Are such programs expected only of public libraries?

Something to Consider

An example of just how diverse higher education has become since the days of a student body consisting primarily of teenage white males is the California State University system, consisting of 23 campuses statewide. Its enrollment in 2007 was just over 450,000. The average age of the students was 24 years old, and 44 percent were independent of parental support. Many had dependents of their own, and more than one-third had full-time jobs. About 20 percent were the first person in their family to attend college, and 40 percent came from households where English was the second language. Over 55 percent were students of color (Reed, 2007, p. 28).

STUDENT ATTITUDES REGARDING HIGHER EDUCATION

Although the student body has become increasingly diverse, students' long-term objectives have remained fairly constant. Given the widespread belief that college graduates have substantially higher lifetime incomes than those who have no college degree, it is no surprise that the primary stated reason for attending college is some variation of securing a good/high-paying job. As Charles Reed (2007) noted, "People with a baccalaureate degree make about $1.3 million more than a high-school graduate over their lifetime"

(p. 28). Economic gain is a far cry from the original purpose (no economic interest) of the liberal arts degree. Two other frequently mentioned reasons are becoming an authority in a subject field (perhaps closely related to being able to command a higher salary) and being able to help others. Nancy Herther (2008) noted that nationally 80 percent of the entering first-year students indicated that they had or did engage in volunteer work of some type.

CIRP has been conducting surveys of entering freshmen since 1966. As of 2007, more than 13 million freshmen have completed the survey. The data comes from 1,900 baccalaureate institutions, so one has a highly accurate sense of freshmen attitudes and behaviors. The 2007 survey added some questions related to "habits of the mind,"

> **Check This Out**
>
> The University of California, Los Angeles, Higher Education Research Institute and its Cooperative Institutional Research Program (CIRP) (www.icpsr .umich.edu/cocoon/IAED/SERIES/00021.XML) conducts regular surveys of student attitudes and reasons for attending college. Periodically reviewing its findings can provide many insights about a changing student landscape. Such information can be highly useful in planning or adjusting library services. Doing so is an element in the environmental scanning process, an important part of the planning process.

essentially factors that one might consider part of the "college role" mentioned in one of this chapter's opening quotations. A worrisome finding, which could be an opportunity for academic libraries relative to information literacy, was that only 35 percent of the freshmen indicated that they bothered to check the quality or reliability of the information they took from Internet sites. Another somewhat surprising finding was that less than 37 percent of the men took the time to revise/edit their assignment submissions; in comparison, almost 55 percent of the women took the time to improve their assignments before submitting the paper (Higher Education Research Institute, 2007).

Philip Altbach (1993) looked at U.S. students' attitudes/culture and how it reflected a worldwide higher education student culture. He noted that students are important not just to their institutions but to society at large as they are the leaders of the future and their attitudes will play a major role in the direction society is likely to take. While U.S. student political attitudes do vary, Altbach found the views "are fairly stable over time" (p. 210). By *stable* he meant that there is a pendulum effect, swinging between left and right. Over time the average political position is close to the center point.

> **Check This Out**
>
> Each fall, Beloit College in Beloit, Wisconsin, releases its "College Mindset Listing" (www .beloit.edu/mindset/2012.php) for incoming freshmen. It is well worth a look.

The notion that U.S. students are slightly left leaning, when viewed from a global point-of-view, is incorrect. From a worldwide perspective they are right leaning.

TODAY'S POTENTIAL STUDENTS

What does today's pool of prospective students look like? Starting in 2008, the number of high school graduates will decline until at least 2015 (Ashburn, 2008, p. A24). This will mean even more competition for suitable candidates for admission and perhaps declining enrollments and fiscal stress for some institutions. By 2022, almost 50 percent of high school graduates will be "minority," with Hispanics making up almost 25 percent of that total. Ashburn noted, "A growing number of would-be college students will be exactly those whom colleges have historically struggled to serve" (p. A24).

Another given for the pool of prospective students is they will be even more technologically savvy than today's students. Marc Prensky (2001a) noted that "today's students have not just changed incrementally from those in the past. . . . A really big discontinuity has taken place" (p. 1). The difference lies in the fact the students grew up in a technology-centered world—it was not something new to learn; it was just part of their environment. Because it is a basic component of their worldview, they tend to think about and process information in ways that are fundamentally different from their predecessors. Prensky suggested the rest of us are digital immigrants who may have adopted some of the technology skills and language but who retain what he calls a strong accent from the past. As he put it, "our Digital Immigrant instructors, who speak an outdated language (that of the predigital age) are struggling to teach a population that speaks an entirely new language" (p. 3).

> **Keep In Mind**
>
> Prensky's articles are important for academic librarians to read and ponder as they think about how to best reach today's students and how they design their information literacy program. Another key reading is Susan Gibbons' *The Academic Library and the Net Gen Student* (Chicago, IL: American Library Association, 2007).

In his follow-up article Prensky (2001b) discussed neurobiological research that appears to demonstrate that long-term stimulation actually changes brain structures, which in turn impacts how one thinks. His view is that hours of watching television, playing video games, using text messaging, and similar activities have changed the way today's youth think and process information. He noted that "Digital Natives crave interactivity . . . an immediate response to their each and every action. Higher education courses don't generally provide much satisfaction to such cravings" (p. 5).

RECRUITMENT, ADMISSION, AND RETENTION

John Douglass (2007) in his book *The Conditions of Admission: Access, Equality, and the Social Contract of Public Universities* suggested that the admission history of an institution plays a particularly powerful role in debates about admission policies and practices. Although his focus was on the University of California system and in particular the two flagship campuses—Berkeley and UCLA—his book has useful insights for any public institution.

Postsecondary institutions engage in an annual recruitment ritual that has become increasingly complex and costly. Admission staffs fan out over the areas where the institution has traditionally been most successful in recruiting students—visiting high schools, holding receptions, and inviting large numbers of students to come to the campus. A few have elaborate, weeklong visits for one or two groups of potential students who they most wish to enroll (for example, merit scholars).

> **Keep In Mind**
>
> Getting the library involved in some aspect of these recruiting activities helps raise the awareness in the prospective students about the value of the library to their academic careers. Even if this involvement is nothing more than one of the stops on a campus tour there is an awareness value, especially for those students who may graduate from a high schools that have no library. (Unfortunately, there more of such high schools than one might expect.)

For some individuals within academia, the notion that the institution must market itself is repulsive, inappropriate, the wrong metaphor, etc., just as the notion that libraries ought to market themselves sounds wrong to some librarians. In either case, like it or not, in today's environment, institutions need to prove their worth to society at large as well as attract clients, customers, or users. Call that process what you will. Academic institutions compete with one another to at least maintain current enrollments; and as the pool of prospects declines, the competition becomes stronger. Essentially, students equal revenue, and adequate revenue allows an institution to have greater control over its future.

> ### Check This Out
>
> See Camila Alire's "Word-of-Mouth Marketing: Abandoning the Academic Library Ivory Tower," *New Library World* 106, no.11/12 (2007): 545–551. This article dispels the perception that academic libraries do not need to market their services and resources. It also acquaints readers with the concept of word-of-mouth marketing and its potential for academic libraries as well as provides an academic library marketing success story.

Recruitment, admission, retention, and fiscal health are interrelated. (We will explore some of the historical background of the interrelationship in the chapter on finance.) Zemsky, Shaman, and Shapiro (2001), in looking at recent historic data on postsecondary institutions, reported that, even during the retrenchment period from the 1970s to mid-1990s, the "core revenues" (tuition and fees, federal funds, state and local grants, private gifts and grants, and endowment income) had real growth (that is, they increased faster than the

> ### Keep In Mind
>
> At many publicly funded institutions, the library's funding is a function, to a significant degree, of enrollment. Very often it takes the form of so many dollars per full-time equivalent (FTE) student. One FTE student represents a person who is taking the number of credits per term that constitutes a full-time course load at that institution. Almost always, the FTE number is lower than "head count" because there are students who sign up for fewer credits than what constitutes a full load. We will explore this issue in the chapter on library services. (As a long-time library director friend once said, "A half-time student never occupies half a chair in the library.")

annual inflation rate). What has happened over that timeframe (1970–1990) is tuition and student fees provided almost all of the real growth in institutional income.

At the risk of offending some friends working in enrollment management (the current umbrella label for those units that handle recruitment, admissions, and financial aid), we suggest that the financial side of acquiring a degree is somewhat akin to buying a car. Both have a sticker price, but no one expects that to be the final cost. College and universities advertise an official tuition price; however, many students receive a financial aid package that includes some amount of institutional funds, such as a scholarship or grant. Thus, the tuition is "discounted" by some amount, similar to the trade-in amount when buying an automobile. Also, like a trade-in, the discount a student receives varies due to individual considerations; nevertheless the institution has an average "discount rate." (Those involved in institutional fiscal management and admissions have frequent discussions about what that rate should be.) Student fees that are part of each term's bill are the "taxes and license" that accompany the purchase of a car. Last but not least, there is "cash price" for the educational package, which is the long-term costs that comes from borrowing some or all of the funds to pay the up-front costs. Today's current and former students are or will be repaying student loans for many, many years after they graduate. They may not think of the process as a "cash price," but they experience it. As

Zemsky, Shaman, and Shapiro (2001) noted, "A college education today is best understood as a private, even a consumer, good available to nearly everyone—although at radically different prices" (p. 13).

Some in higher education suggest that dependency on student revenue as well as the issue of attracting students is somehow new and worrisome. Is this dependency new? Not at all. Is it worrisome? Almost always. From day one, student fees have been central to the survival of higher education. As we noted in Chapter 2, teachers initially collected their income directly from the students; and throughout its history, higher education has been dependent on such income. Lack of student income is a serious issue. For some institutions with little in the way of endowments or alumni able or willing to donate to operating funds, insufficient enrollment and student tuition means closing. Often institutions develop the coming year's budget on the basis of a projected enrollment number. Failure to achieve that enrollment target can/does cause stress and cuts in unit's operating budgets.

From the Authors

Evans worked at an institution that assigned a $1 million budgeting figure for each entering first-year student. Thus, a five student swing, up or down, was a $5 million swing in terms of budgeting.

Because salaries are a large part of any operating budget and few institutions want to reduce staff, the first place budget officers look to cut are those areas that appear less critical to the year's operations. One favorite area and one that is easy to cut is the library's acquisitions allocations. A one-year reduction in acquisitions is rarely disastrous, but a series of years of such actions can cause a significant problem for the quality of education the students receive.

The institutions are not only the ones worrying about the admission process. The applicants and their families are often in an even higher state of anxiety. Tensions can last for months—from January (early notification of admission) until April when the final letters go out.

A topic that has had some discussion in the popular media is student body diversity and "legacy" students. Legacies are applicants who have a parent, grandparent, or relative who graduated from the institution and who receive special consideration in the admission process. Gasman and Vultaggio (2008) put it, "Yale has the Bushes, Basses and Whitneys, Harvard has the Astors, Roosevelts, and Kennedys. Throughout the history of American higher education, the nation's most prestigious colleges and universities have employed legacy policies that prefer children of alumni" (p. 24). They noted that a legacy applicant, on average, enjoys a 25 percent advantage over other applicants. In addition, they suggest such advantages work against diversity goals, that legacies create "a potentially negative impact on students of color, they also diminish the chances of admission for low-income and first-generation students" (p. 24).

One can easily guess the primary reason for having a legacy admission program: keeping alumni and potential donors happy with the institution. It is easier to accept that notion for small institutions that have difficulty meeting their enrollment targets and need all of the alumni support they can get in order survive. It is not so easy to accept it in the case of institutions that have billions of dollars in endowments. An interesting study that Peter Schmidt (2007) reported on indicated that legacy students were substantially more likely to have academic trouble than the average student. They are also more likely to drop out.

FINANCIAL AID

"Aid packages" are often the deciding factor that determines matriculation; that is actually becoming a student in classes. The first choice institution's package may leave too much of a financial burden for the applicant/family to absorb. Some applicants are unable to attend any college as the aid packages are too low to allow enrolling at any school.

—Porter (2006)

The issue of how aid packages are put together is complex and well beyond the scope of this book; however, we listed a solid book on the topic in the Launching Pad section of this chapter (Wilkinson, 2005). One aspect of most financial aid offers that we believe does requires some discussion is work study, as it plays a major role in library operations.

Like some other elements of student aid programs (such as Pell Grants and Guaranteed Student Direct Loans), work study is a federal program. Although the local financial aid office may allocate the funds the institution receives as well as the rate of pay, federal guidelines, such as the requirement to meet the federal minimum wage, do limit choices.

Work study is a cost-sharing program wherein the institution contributes 25 percent of the hourly salary, with the balance coming from the federal government. As federal funding for the program has fallen (Lipka, 2007), more students are seeking employment opportunities off campus. This in turn has created some serious challenges for campus units such as the library that are highly dependent on work study students in performing their daily operations. Another challenge is that as federal minimum wage increases, the decline in federal dollars further reduces the number of hours an institution has available to allocate. (Some states have higher minimum wage rates than the federal rate, and although the institution can use the federal rate, doing so just pushes more students off campus where they can earn more per hour.)

Even in the best of funding circumstances, there is a competition between on and off campus jobs at the lower wage rates. Businesses often offer some benefits that campus units cannot match, such as employee discounts and the potential for much higher pay for either outstanding performance or longevity. From the student's point of view, the only plus for work study positions is that there is no impact on the financial aid package because it is part of that package. In the case of off campus work income, 50 percent of that income must be counted as covering educational expenses under federal guidelines. This in turn can lead to a reduction in institutional aid in the following academic terms.

Students are limited on the number of work study hours they can work per week in order to keep the focus on the study side of the program. Also, at most institutions, the allocation is to the student not the academic unit. Thus, the student can "shop" for jobs, seek positions that have ample opportunities to study and get paid when things are slow. This circumstance can present a challenge for the library where there is a never-ending stream of tasks to do. Finally, there are usually some pay

> **Keep In Mind**
>
> From a library point of view, student employment is a major factor in daily operations. Summer session library operations can present some significant challenges as the pool of students is substantially lower. Most academic libraries would be hard pressed to offer the variety and quality of service they do without either a major increase in permanent staff or maintaining the level of work study students. This is why work study employees are so critical to academic libraries. The libraries can stretch their student employment budgets by hiring more work study students than hourly students.

differentials on campus, so students tend to seek the highest possible pay in order to use up either their hourly or dollar allocation (depending on how the institution handles the allocation) as quickly as possible.

KEEPING STUDENTS

Getting the students enrolled is one issue; keeping them is a different matter. A key institutional unit in the retention process is "student affairs," "student life," or some other variant label. First-time college students have many adjustments to make in order to succeed, and the institution does all it can to help the individuals make those adjustments. There are two broad categories of adjustment: academic and social integration. Both are important to retention and graduation. The library can play a role in these processes.

> **Check This Out**
>
> An excellent book to read outlining the library's critical role in keeping students is *The Role of the Library in the First College Year* edited by Larry Hardesty (First-Year Experience Monograph Series, no 45. Columbia, SC: University of South Carolina, 2007). The first 170-plus pages consist of essays about the role the library can play in the retention process and is followed by 13 case studies detailing activities that libraries have undertaken.

On the academic side are several components to retention, including students learning the "academic role," getting assistance with basic academic skills, and receiving assistance in handling a particular subject area. For social integration, opportunities are available to get to know other students who share an interest in a topic/activity (clubs), to get involved in the institution's governance (student government), and to participate in intramural and intercollegiate sports.

Student affairs is the unit that handles many, if not all, of these activities. It also handles another less pleasant activity, student discipline. In fact, student discipline (in loco parentis) of the early days of higher education remains at the root of today's student affairs divisions. However, formalization/bringing together of the student-related roles only took place the early 1930s (Rentz, 1996). The ultimate base of student affairs goes back to the medieval German concept of student freedom. It also draws on the U.S. colleges' effort to maintain order among the teenage boys. Additionally during the nineteenth century, when colleges had a perceived need to provide more student guidance as degree programs became more numerous and electives more commonplace, the concept of student affairs flourished. By the late nineteenth century, another layer of institutional administration was added in the form of one or more deans—dean of men, dean of women, or dean of students, for example. This is not the place to explore the many facets of student affairs work; we will, however, touch on some of the academic and social integration activities.

Why do some students graduate and others do not? One key factor is their success in learning the academic role. To do so requires an understanding of and accepting that role by grasping what their instructors' expectations are and what instructors will and will not do. It also means applying existing academic skills to meet and address the professors' approach to learning. Furthermore, students must learn to recognize the lack of an academic skill and to seek assistance in learning that skill. Perhaps the biggest change is to realize no one is going to be asking, "Are you doing your readings? How are you doing?" Students have great freedom, and it is incumbent on them to study and keep up to date with coursework. This can be a challenge for students living in dormitories with plenty of distractions and no parents asking questions every day about "homework."

Certainly professors and advisors are willing to assist students, but students must ask for the assistance. In higher education, there is an expectation of a certain level of maturity and commitment to succeed on the students' part. Good professors have a fine sense of who is trying to succeed and who is "skating." The student who is trying is likely to have the professor take the lead in asking if assistance would be acceptable. Almost all institutions of higher education have one or more offices that provide various types of student assistance, from remedial skills to the psychological adjustments necessary for academic life.

The students who experience the highest degree of difficulty in learning the academic role are the first-generation students—those who are the first in their family of parents/grandparents, etc., to attend college. Many come from lower socioeconomic backgrounds, and many are minorities. The National Center for Education Statistics (NCES, 2005) data indicates that students who do not have a relative who graduated from college are less likely to succeed. Engstrom and Tinto (2008), using NCES data, noted that 56 percent of the high-income students completed a four-year baccalaureate in six years or less, while only 26 percent of low-income students completed their degree in the same timeframe. The vast majority of first-generation students come from lower income backgrounds. Vincent Tinto (1993) provided a general framework for understanding the basic elements of retention—the academic and social integration we mentioned earlier.

Perhaps the one area that all students, regardless of family income status or prior college experience, can benefit from is learning higher education study skills and time management. Going from a situation in which every school hour is scheduled by someone other than the students to one in which there are large blocks of unscheduled time can be a challenge when it comes to making effective use of their free time." Some schools, especially community colleges have a mandatory study skills course—"College 101"—while some four-year schools have a similar "University 100" course designed to help new students successfully transition from high school to college or back into college life in the case of individuals returning to school, so called "nontraditional" students.

Vincent Tinto (1993) suggested that one cure for attrition was to create a mixture of academic and social interaction by creating learning communities/collaborative learning groups. Such groups of students share with one another tips for succeeding in particular academic subject or campus interaction. How these groups differ from the informal study groups that probably existed since higher education started is that institutions are encouraging their formation. For most of higher education's history, professors often thought of study groups as slightly dishonest—learning was an independent activity not a group endeavor. Learning communities are initially formed by the institution in the full knowledge and encouragement for students to move from group to group until they find a comfortable match.

Engstrom and Tinto (2008) found there was at least a 10 percent higher persistence rate for students in learning communities than for students on their own. (Persistence rate is a term used to denote students staying enrolled in their academic program

Something to Ponder

Think about ways in which the library might help address the transition challenges of entering students. What might be done in collaboration with local high schools that have agreements for their advance placement students to have library access? Might it be possible for learning communities to reserve group study rooms rather than have to "find somewhere" to get together? What other possibilities exist?

From the Authors

Alire has been at several different higher education institutions where precollegiate programs were in place for high school students from lower socio-economic backgrounds (mostly minority students) to help them prepare for college life academically and socially. At one of these institutions, the library was involved in providing information literacy programs for the precollegiate program. This provided a head start in familiarity with an academic library and its services, resources, and librarians for these high school students who later on enrolled in a college or university.

until they successfully graduate with their baccalaureate degrees.) Some of the factors they identified as contributing to better retention were safety, support, and belonging. Students felt safer in sharing ideas in the group and knew there would be support when they encountered problems. They also felt they belonged to both the group and the institution and could succeed. The lack of support is a major issue for minority students and first generation student retention.

Once the student makes a successful transition to higher education life there is still more for the institution to do. Encouraging lifelong learning is a basic goal of higher education. Another goal is to recruit the next generation of scholars, if not to one's own field then to somewhere within the academy. A key to both endeavors is faculty–student interaction outside of the classroom (such activities also assist with student persistence). As Ullah and Wilson (2007) wrote, "The quality of students' relationship with faculty was an important predictor of students' academic achievement. Encouraging faculty to explore opportunities in which students' active involvement can be fostered for service learning, collaborative assignments, integrative learning, and even enhance classroom participation, should be continued" (p. 1200).

Faculty–student research projects are one of the highly effective methods for encouraging lifelong learning and gaining an appreciation of the value of academic research. At some institutions the process is informal and in others it is highly structured. One example of the structured approach is a capstone experience for all seniors at the College of Wooster (Crawford, Garg, and Nuehoff, 2008). A common way for the collaborative process to work is the student becomes a research assistant who helps with a faculty member's projects. What role can the academic librarians play in capstone projects? The library can be assertive in marketing its personnel, services, and resources particularly to capstone students, such as offering access to document delivery services that might not be available to other students.

One rather unusual student–faculty engagement is a program at Brigham Young University called Students Consulting on Teaching (SCOT), which is a program involving 25 paid students per year who "give professors a piece of their minds" (Wasley, 2008, p. 51). The program assists approximately 80 faculty members per year in looking at their courses from a student perspective. Unlike traditional course evaluations, the SCOT is one on one with a student who has received training in assessment and consulting and who is not or has not been enrolled in any of the courses the professor teaches. Professors request the process, and many have used the program several times. The basic concept is that the student consultant, who sits in on the course, brings a special knowledge to the activity—"what it is like to be a student in your class from a student's perspective" (p. 51)—from someone who has nothing to gain or lose from being completely honest.

> **Tip**
>
> The library can play a role in encouraging lifelong learning and student research through various competitions such as best honors paper, best collaborative research paper, best publication, or best book collection.

Rona Wilensky (2007) summed up the situation for first-year students when she wrote about the gaps between students and professors from the professorial point of view:

> First, between what we value and what they value; second, between what we are good at and what the majority of them are good at; and third, between what we as professors thought students needed to know and what they might actually need in order to function well in the world that is not school.... The fundamental contradiction of college and university life is that professors want good students, while most of their students want good jobs. (p. B19)

SOCIAL SIDE

Student affairs units oversee a variety of programs that relate to social integration and developing a sense of belonging. One such activity that exists at almost every academic institution is student government.

Student government and the institution's administration have a complex relationship. Just what is the role of student government in institutional affairs? At least in the United States, the role is modest—student government is to function as the voice of the student body. It does not decide or govern in terms of the institution. It provides a mechanism for collecting student views about institutional matters and conveying that information to the administration. Student views do matter, but ultimately the board of trustees govern the institution (think back to the Dartmouth decision we mentioned in Chapter 2), which is something that few students understand and even some faculty forget from time to time. We will explore campus governance in a later chapter.

Being the voice of the student body is not a meaningless role. That voice is listened to and thoughtfully considered in almost all circumstances as long as it is a constructive and mature voice. Beyond serving as a feedback mechanism, student government does formulate student behavior policies, with guidance of a student affairs advisor.

From a library point of view, student governments can be a useful ally or a vocal critic. Having a student government representative on the library advisory committee

> **From the Authors**
>
> Evans had good success in getting the student government to select a student who was working in the library to be a liaison. Such students brought a dual perspective to discussions that were valuable for the other committee members as well as for the student government. Alire had success in working directly with the student government leaders to help secure much-needed funding for the materials budget. The biggest challenge here is that the student government leaders change from year to year, which requires library administrators to provide library-issues orientation for student leaders on a yearly basis.

is a good idea; however, more often than not the student will be someone from the student body selected by the student government president or executive committee who reports back to that body.

Short of being open 24/7/365, the library can count on having requests from the students to increase service hours from time to time. In general, student governments can be helpful in identifying new or modifying existing services. When that body is unhappy with some aspect of library services, you can guarantee there will be articles and letters to the editor about the issue in the student newspaper (another student affairs activity). It sometimes seems as if it is easier to find negative articles in the student paper than it is to secure coverage for a new service.

The label "student organizations" incorporates a wide variety of activities/groups that range from honor societies to intramural sports. Other groups include small publishing activities operated by English majors and yearbooks, political clubs, cultural groups, and special interests such as photography and bridge, for example. They may be academic in character such as an engineering society or predominately social in nature, such as Greek letter organizations.

In large and often impersonal universities, such groups provide the anchor for student identification with the institution. Frequently the extracurricular activities are as important if not more so in influencing a student's values and attitudes, as are the professors and courses taken. What the future will be for what have been the standard student groups is very unclear. The changing character of the student body—older, more working full time and attending classes part time, students with dependents, etc.—means the institution is less and less the focal point of a students' life. Because most student organizations receive little in the way of institutional financial support, any reduction in organizations or lessening of their activity will do almost nothing to change the cost of a degree. What funds are made available come from some form of student activity fees.

One category of student organization that gains institutional and community attention, often less than favorable, are Greek letter groups. (Note: there are Greek letter organizations that are academic in character such as Phi Beta Kappa and Beta Phi Mu, the librarians' honorary society. These are not the focus of this discussion.) Society, higher education, and fraternities and sororities themselves have debated the value of social Greek letter groups almost from the time when, in the nineteenth century, literary societies morphed into fraternities. Critics have a long list of reasons why such groups are detrimental to academic performance and why they are contrary to the goal of "open to all." Supporters have equally long lists of way the groups are beneficial, such as community service, developing lifelong friends/networks, and a much-needed source of peer support while in school.

More often than not, it is fraternities that draw the negative publicity for the group and its host institution. They often engage in behavior that many people regard as at least demeaning if not dangerous (on rare occasions even fatal). Perhaps the most common issue is the degree to which such groups encourage substance abuse and the attendant problems generated by such behavior. The specific issue of alcohol use by students is a broader issue than fraternities and sororities to be sure and is one that all academic institutions must address; however, Greek letter groups are seen as one major focal point of the issue.

Many faculty view Greek organizations as being anti-intellectual and encouraging academic dishonesty. This view is probably a little strong, but there is no question that members do discuss what Professor X's course is like and especially what the examinations consist of and what this professor looks for in papers. Are there files of tests and term papers in the organization's "house?" Perhaps in some instances, but some non-Greek students also engage in such behavior. The only real difference is they do not have a central location in which to do so. In reality, it is the professors' fault if they have such problems; they can control such activities through a variety of mechanisms such as updating their course content and not using old exams.

What appears clear is Greek letter organizations do emphasize the social over the academic side of the college experience. A reasonably balanced review of the pros and cons of Greek letter groups is Edward Whipple's and Eileen Sullivan's (1998) essay "Greek Letter Organizations: Communities of Learners?" A later essay (Mathiasen, 2005) explored many of the same issues in reference to fraternities but with an emphasis on moral development, or its lack thereof.

SPORTS AND THE ACADEMY

As we noted earlier, student affairs is the usual unit to be responsible for sports activities, both intramural and intercollegiate. In Chapter 2, we speculated that perhaps sports became an element in U.S. higher education as a means of burning off the excess energy of teenage boys. Whatever the reason(s) were at the outset, one cannot deny that now sports are surprisingly important within higher education. Sometimes, especially if you watch television on a fall weekend, you come away with the impression that collegiate sports are the *only* reason schools exists. This impression may intensify upon learning that some of the schools receive $1 million each time their football teams appear on national television or that a collegiate coach has a multimillion dollar employment contract as well as bonuses for "post-season" success.

Students undertook organizing sports on campus in the mid-1800s, first among themselves (intramural) and soon after that with nearby schools (intercollegiate). There was no institutional involvement, no coaches, no special training or facilities, just a few young men in a vacant field competing for the right to say "our team is better than yours." Things began to change when, in the 1850s, Rutgers played Princeton in football (today the game they played is called soccer in the United States), and there were coaches directing the game. From such a humble beginning, collegiate sports and their associated costs have mushroomed into multimillion dollar enterprises.

Money is the primary reason for where U.S. collegiate sports are today. Although most of the money is associated with two of the sports, football and men's basketball, many of the other sports are gaining ground. Women's basketball, men and women's soccer, baseball, volleyball, men's ice hockey, and even lacrosse all have professional leagues

> **From the Authors**
>
> We must put in a disclaimer here. We are both fans of collegiate sports. That said, it does not change the fact that the role of collegiate sports and their associated costs require serious debate, something that is lacking at some institutions.

> **Keep In Mind**
>
> Intercollegiate sports and all the attendant features are a U.S. phenomenon. European higher education institutions view their business as just education. In other parts of the world, most of the institutions face enough financial challenges just to stay operational and cannot think about spending funds on sports. Most do have sports, but at what people in the United States would consider no more than intramural or "club" level at best. There is no institutional involvement.

that are partially dependent on "college farm teams" to develop professional skills. No one has yet come up with a completely satisfactory explanation of what the higher education value is for intercollegiate sports. There is a high cost to fielding competitive teams; however, the revenue generated by successful teams is also large. (Even schools who are less successful but who are in leagues that are successful realize some revenue from the league's success.) One must wonder at times if the revenue outperforms the costs.

Another reason for participating is also ultimately related to money. Having teams mentioned in newspapers or appearing on television keeps the institution in the minds of alumni, especially after a successful season. Even if not all alumni are donors, many take pleasure from seeing their alma mater playing on television. Winning a national championship makes a significant difference in sports-related income and increases alumni donations.

One example of the revenue and expense comes from the University of Texas, Austin (UTA). In 2006, the University of Texas, Austin, football team won the national championship in the Rose Bowl. According to a quotation in Thomas Palaima's (2006) article the university's athletic program made "collegiate licensing history by generating the most royalties ever by a college or university" (p. B12). This income led to an annual income for UTA athletic programs of more than $90 million. The football coach saw his employment contract increase to $2.55 million (that would pay for many new professors or greatly improve library services). The football stadium, which had 62 private luxury suites renting for $50,000 to $85,000 each, was to be expanded by 20 more luxury suites and 10,000 "ordinary" seats to its already 85,000 plus seating capacity, no small construction cost. Even the university's credit union joined in the celebration by pledging $13.1 million, over five years, to renovate the university's baseball field. (The Credit Union annually donates $50,000 to the library system.) Palaima, a classics professor at UTA, concluded his article by writing, "Either way, the values we see at the University of Texas, Austin, and elsewhere in big-time college sports are values faculty committees helped set. We can't exempt ourselves from blame" (p. B12).

Is there a professional sports issue involved? The National Collegiate Athletic Association (NCAA) puts out occasional advertisements on television trying to make the case that "most NCAA athletes turn pro in something other than sports." The ad is factual— most athletes do go "pro" in something other than their chosen sport after they graduate or leave school. What it fails to note is that a great many of those had aspirations of a "pro" career when they entered school. It is also true many do go on to sign contracts for large sums of money. What some people do not realize is that every athlete who receives a grant-in-aid, and the majority do, must sign an NCAA form stating that sports are only an avocation. This, of course, does not stop the highly successful athlete from turning professional after one or two years in college. Sometimes the signing contract is for several million dollars. One cannot but wonder how many millions of that amount is due to national exposure on television by the school's team and the special coaching and training the individual received at institutional expense. A few, such as Shaquille O'Neill, give something back to their alma maters; however, this seems to be the exception rather than the rule, based on popular press reports. (It is doubtful that the NCAA would miss opportunities to get the word out when that does happen.) It is rare for coaches, who often earn much more than campus presidents, to give back something to the institution where they are employed. A notable exception is Joe Paterno, Pennsylvania State University football coach, who is a major donor to the university, in particular to the library system. Two other exceptions are Gary Williams, University of Maryland basketball coach, and Bobby Knight, another basketball coach, when he was at Indiana University.

Are college sports a problem for U.S. higher education? The answer is a qualified yes; at least there are times when they seem to skew institutional funding priorities. The scholarship athletes, at least in the major sports, often have much higher expectations for actually going on to play professionally and may seem less committed to the academic side of the college experience.

Keep In Mind

Our discussion to a large degree focuses on NCAA Division I institutions. However, some of it is drawn from lower division institutions. Also, in doing research for this section we encountered articles expressing concern about the "trickle down" effect from the big time collegiate sports to community colleges and even high school. The Budig (2007) reference in the Launching Pad section is one example.

NCAA employs a three division approach to its membership. Division I is "big time" level. To be a member an institution must field at least 14 sports—7 each for men and women. Division I schools must meet minimum financial aid awards for their athletics program, and Division I schools cannot exceed maximum financial aid awards for each sport. Division II institutions have to sponsor at least 5 sports for men and 5 for women (or 4 for men and 6 for women), with 2 team sports for each gender and each playing season represented by each gender and have a limit on the number of scholarship they may be awarded. Division II athletic programs are financed in the institution's budget like other academic departments on campus. Division III institutions also have to sponsor at least 5 sports for men and 5 for women, with 2 team sports for each gender, and each playing seasons represented by each gender. Division III athletics features student-athletes who receive no financial aid related to their athletic ability, and athletic departments are staffed and funded like any other department in the university.

We cannot end a discussion of collegiate sports without some mention of "Title IX," which as of 2008 was 36 years old. Title IX of the Education Amendments of 1972—its full title (20 U.S.C. §§ 1681-1688)—is legislation that prohibits discrimination by gender in any federally funded education activity. What the law has done is greatly expand opportunities for women to participate in collegiate sports. As Vest and Masterson (2007) wrote regarding the law, "It has forever changed budgeting and participation numbers between males and females and opened up many opportunities for women" (p. 60). Anderson, Cheslock, and Ehrenberg (2006) noted that by academic year 2001–2002 the female share of college athletes was 42 percent, a significant increase from the 15 percent in 1972, the year Title IX started. While the increase in participation is good, it also further increases the total cost of collegiate sports, and the question is, where does the funding come from? Vest and Masterson wrote that, based on their feedback back from athletic directors, "the colleges viewed Title IX as a way to recruit athletes with a charisma to put people in the seats" (p. 61). One would have to fill a great many paid seats to recover all the costs.

The reasonable goal for collegiate sports would seem to be achieving a balance of income and expense such that the cost of a degree for the nonathlete student is not underwriting the sports program. With tuition costs escalating faster than general inflation, having costly sports programs as part of the total cost mix seems inappropriate. However, with the reality of institutions devoting so much time, energy, and funds to athletics, it is doubtful intercollegiate sports will disappear from the academic scene any time soon.

STUDENT DISCIPLINE

Our final topic takes us back to origins of student affairs—maintaining some degree of order on campus. We mentioned in Chapter 2 that there were frequent student revolts in the nineteenth century. The colleges also had to worry about town and gown relations when the student body was almost completely teenage boys who generally had only pranks on their minds. However, occasionally the pranks escalated into significant property damage. The what and the how of controlling student behavior has changed over the years—no more corporal punishment, for example. There is no doubt that nineteenth-century professors and college presidents had their hands full with a student body of teenage boys. However, their challenges were small in number compared to a twenty-first-century campus.

There are some common issues between then and now; however, even the similar issues have become more complex. Three of the common issues today are alcohol consumption (which has broadened to substance abuse), intellectual honesty, and interpersonal conflicts.

Intellectual honesty is more complex as a result of the Internet and the ability to "copy and paste." Part of the challenge in this area is how young people view web content and the general lack of understanding of copyright and how that concept was/is intended to function. Their attitude seems to be, "If I find it on the web I can use it however I wish." A short conversation with a teenager about file sharing will likewise show the difference in attitude. The web has also expanded the opportunity for acquiring a term paper for a fee to submit as the student's own work.

> **From the Authors**
>
> A real-life example arose in August 2008 as we were preparing this text. Two students participating in a Semester at Sea program through the University of Virginia were expelled for honor code violations stemming from submitting papers with incomplete citations of material pulled from the Web (Kinzie, 2008, p. C01).

> **Tip**
>
> The library can help address the copyright/plagiarism concerns in its information literacy programs. Some libraries provide faculty members access to software programs that help in identifying material in a paper that came from a website or a database of sold term papers. Minimally, instruction efforts can address academic integrity issues.

When it comes to student–student or student–institution conflict, the changing demographics—older, more diverse culturally, and a growing number of student parents for example—add several levels of complexity to maintaining campus civility. If the federal government enacts legislation similar to the post–World War II GI Bill, Iraq and Afghanistan veterans will change the tone on campus and have rather different views about acceptable behavior.

Today's student affairs professionals usually view discipline as development rather than punishment. In part, this approach arises from the fact that society now views the issue as laying on the boundary between community needs and individual liberties. Furthermore, many aspects of the activity involve legal requirements. Of major significance is the concept of due process and its application. The legalistic nature of much of the work has led some institutions to label the unit handling such matters as judicial affairs.

From the Authors

Evans had an experience that involved a felony level theft (at least in terms of the state's criminal code) from the library's special collections department. The young man was a work study student assigned to sorting through a donation of four "banker boxes" of baseball trading cards. The cards had been accumulated over 60 years, and the donor believed some could be rather valuable. One day a department staff member came to the director's office to say she believed the young man was taking cards. (As we learned, "star" cards often bring hundreds of dollars each.) After further inquiry, the chief of campus public safety became part of the discussion. An undercover officer was in the department when the young man next came to work. The officer observed the student pocketing cards. This led to officers searching his dorm room where they found 2,000 cards. The library was asked to get an appraisal of what was taken and what was left. The appraiser reported that the library had 10,000 cards worth an average of $.65 each. Cards in the dorm room were valued at $3 to $4 each. Furthermore, the appraiser noted that it was strange that given the number of cards involved there were *no* star cards and that he had heard that several hundred such cards had appeared in the local market recently. One can imagine how upset the department staff was to see the young man still on campus a year later. We never learned what the outcome was due to student privacy concerns, but questions were raised about how the process was handled.

At least some of the library staff must understand how the institution handles due process. There are at least two reasons for the staff needing such knowledge. First, it is inevitable that there will be instances when the library staff will have to deal with unacceptable student behavior. Three of the most common occurrences are mutilation of library property, such as collection items, furniture, and graffiti on the walls; verbal confrontations that often occur at the circulation or reserve desk; and harassment. Handling the situation in accordance with the institution's due process procedures is important.

A second reason is staff members who understand the procedures and due process can explain the issues to other staff who are upset when they see the offender back in the library and sometimes engaging in the same behavior that triggered the first complaint. Understanding the process helps, at least a little.

> **Tip**
>
> It is critical that staff understand what the institution's policy is regarding calling in the campus public safety/police and when to call the community's police department. Sometimes it matters whether the problem is a student, staff, or general public issue. This is particularly critical if offenses are committed in the evening or weekends when there are no library administrators or department heads on duty.

KEY POINTS TO REMEMBER

- Students are the lifeblood of higher education, both in terms of purpose and financially.
- Each passing year brings an increasingly diverse pool of potential applicants.
- With an increase in diversity comes a changing demographic makeup of the student body, such as an older, more independent, somewhat less academically prepared body, with students often the first in their family to attend college.
- Today's students come with different attitudes and priorities.
- Changing demographics brings with it changes in the institution's programs and services.

- Although current students have different attitudes and priorities than those of the past, their basic reason for wanting a college degree has not changed: a better lifetime earning potential.
- Attracting and retaining students is critical for institutions, if for no other reason than financial stability.
- Faculty–student interaction outside of the classroom and its character is a key to student persistence.
- Libraries can play a role in the recruitment and retention process.
- Libraries benefit from engaging students in their planning and activities.
- Collegiate athletics play a role in higher education and its overall cost.
- Student discipline is a complex matter and often legalistic in character.

REFERENCES

Altbach, Philip G. 1993. Students: Interests, culture, and activism. In *Higher education in America: 1980–2000*, ed. Arthur Levine, 203–221. Baltimore, MD: Johns Hopkins University Press.

Anderson, Deborah J., John Cheslock, and Ronald Ehrenberg. 2006. Gender equity in intercollegiate athletics: Determinants of Title IX compliance. *Journal of Higher Education* 77, no. 2: 225–250.

Ashburn, Elyse. 2008. Student pool expected to dip and diversify. *Chronicle of Higher Education* 54, no. 29: A1, A24–A25.

Collier, Peter, and David L. Morgan. 2008. Is the paper really due today? *Higher Education* 55, no. 3: 425–446.

Crawford, Iain, Shelia Garg, and John Nuehoff. 2008. Undergraduate research as faculty development: The College of Wooster experience. *Council on Undergraduate Research* 29, no. 1: 14–17.

Douglass, John Aubrey. 2007. *The conditions of admission: Access, equality, and the social contract of public universities.* Palo Alto, CA: Stanford University Press.

Engstrom, Cathy, and Vincent Tinto. 2008. Access without support is not opportunity. *Change* 40, no. 1: 46–50.

Gasman, Marybeth, and Julie Vultaggio. 2008. A legacy of racial injustice in American higher education. *Diverse: Issues in Higher Education* 24, no. 25: 24.

Herther, Nancy K. 2008. Service learning and engagement in the academic library. *College & Research Libraries News* 69, no. 7: 386–389.

Higher Education Research Institute. 2007. The American freshmen: National norms for fall 2007. *HERI Research Briefs.* Los Angeles, CA: Higher Education Research Institute.

Karazin, Christelyn. 2008. Digital learners. *Vistas* 11, no. 2: 25–27.

Kinzie, Susan. 2008. An education in the pitfalls of online research: Expelled students ran afoul of U-Va. honor system by inadequately citing sources in their papers. *Washington Post*, Suburban Edition, August 10, C01.

Lipka, Sara. 2007. More students seek off campus jobs as work study positions dwindle. *Chronicle of Higher Education* 53, no. 2: A40.

Mathiasen, Robert E. 2005. Moral development in fraternity members. *College Student Journal* 39, no. 2: 242–252.

National Center for Education Statistics. 2005. *First-generation students in post-secondary education: A look at their college transcripts.* Washington, DC: NCES. Available: nces.ed.gov/pubs 2005/2005171.pdf.

Palaima, Thomas G. 2006. The real price of college sports. *Chronicle of Higher Education* 53, no. 13: B12.

Porter, Jane R. 2006. Financial strains keep millions out of college. *Chronicle of Higher Education* 53, no. 5: A25.

Prensky, Marc. 2001a. Digital natives, digital immigrants: Part 1. *On the Horizon* 9, no. 5: 1, 3–6.

———. 2001b. Digital natives, digital immigrants: Part 2—Do they really think differently? *On the Horizon* 9, no. 6: 1, 3–6.

Reed, Charles B. 2007. The future cannot wait. *Change* 39, no. 6: 28–32.

Rentz, Audrey L. 1996. A history of student affairs. In *Student affairs practices in higher education*, 2nd ed., ed. Audrey L. Rentz, 28–53. Springfield, IL: Charles C Thomas.

Schmidt, Peter. 2007. Children of alumni are uniquely harmed by admission preferences. *Chronicle of Higher Education* 53, no. 31: A1.

Tinto, Vincent. 1993. *Leaving college: Rethinking the causes and cures for student attrition*. Chicago, IL: University of Chicago Press.

Ullah, Hafeez, and Mardell Wilson. 2007. Students' academic success and its association to student involvement with learning and faculty and peers. *College Student Journal* 41, no. 4: 1192–1202.

Vest, Becky, and Gerald Masterson. 2007. Title IX and its effect on sports programs in high school and collegiate athletics. *Coach and Athletic Director* 77, no. 5: 60–62.

Wasley, Paula. 2008. How am I doing. *Education Digest* 73, no. 5: 51–53.

Whipple, Edward G., and Eileen G. Sullivan. 1998. Greek letter organizations: Communities of learners? *New Directions for Student Services* 81: 7–17.

Wilensky, Rona. 2007. For some high-school students, going to college isn't the answer. *Chronicle of Higher Education* 23, no. 34: B18–B19.

Zemsky, Robert, Susan Shaman, and Daniel B. Shapiro. 2001. Revenue. *New Directions in Educational Research* no. 111: 9–20.

LAUNCHING PAD

Artinger, Lori, Lisa Clapman, Carla Hunt, Matthew Meigs, Nadia Milord, Bryan Sampson, and Scott Forrester. 2006. The social benefit of intramural sports. *NASPA Journal* 43, no. 1: 69–86.

Ashburn, Elyse. 2007. To increase enrollment, community colleges add more sports. *Education Digest* 73, no. 2: 58–60.

Budig, Gene A. 2007. An athletic arms race. *Phi Delta Kappan* 89, no. 4: 283–284.

Burk, Nanci M. 2007. Conceptualizing American Indian/Alaskan Native college students' classroom experiences: Negotiating cultural identity between faculty and students. *Journal of American Indian Education* 46, no. 2: 1–18.

Drinan, Patrick M., and Tricia Bertram Gallant. 2008. Plagiarism and academic integrity systems. *Journal of Library Administration* 47, no. 3/4: 125–140.

Eberhardt, David, N. Dewaine Rice, and Lisa D. Smith. 2003. Effects of Greek membership on academic integrity, alcohol abuse and risky sexual behavior at a college. *NASPA Journal* 41, no. 1: 135–146.

Farrell, Elizabeth F. 2007. When legacies are a college's lifeblood. *Chronicle of Higher Education* 53, no. 20: A1.

Fisher, Celia B., Adam L. Fried, and Andrea Anushko. 2007. Development and validation of college drinking influences survey. *Journal of American College Health* 56, no. 3: 217–230.

Guerra, Patricia, and Leonard Valverde. 2008. Latino communities and schools: Tapping assets for student success. *Education Digest* 73, no. 6: 4–7.

Holsendolph, Ernest. 2006. When academics and athletics collide. *Diverse: Issues in Higher Education* 23, no. 4: 22–23.

Hord, Shirley M. 2008. Evolution of the professional learning community. *National Staff Development Council* 29, no. 3: 10–13,

Horwedel, Dina M. 2008. Putting first-generation students first. *Diverse: Issues in Higher Education* 25, no. 5: 10–12.

Kim, Kyung-Sun, and Sei-Ching Joanna Sin. 2006. Recruiting and retaining students of color in LIS programs. *Journal of Education for Library and Information Science* 47. no. 2: 81–95.

Kovacs, Patty R. 2008. Effects of the college admission process on adolescent development. *Journal of College Admission* no. 198: 15–18.

Lowen, J. Trout. 2008. From combat to campus. *Minnesota* 108, no. 1: 16–21.

McCook, Kathleen de la Peña. 2003. Transformations of librarianship in support of learning communities. *Reference User Services Quarterly* 43, no. 2: 120–123.

O'Donnell, Victoria L., and Jane Tobbell. 2007. The transition of adult students to higher education. *Adult Education Quarterly* 57, no. 4: 312–328.

Shaman, Susan, and Robert Zemsky. 2003. On markets and other matters: A price model for public two-year colleges. *New Direction for Community Colleges* no. 122: 63–75.

Tinto, Vincent. 1997. Classrooms as communities. *Journal of Higher Education* 68, no. 6: 599–623.

Wilkinson, Rupert. 2005. *Aiding students, buying students: Financial aid in America.* Nashville, TN: Vanderbilt University Press.

Chapter 5

Curriculum

Before the end of this century demographers expect Euro-descended Americans to make up less than half of the U.S. population.... This change is reflected world-wide.... To be effective in this environment, colleges and universities must ensure that their curriculums provide opportunities for students to learn how to function effectively in an increasingly diverse multi-cultural global environment.

—James L. Morrison (2003)

If one looks at educational problems without historical perspective, he is likely to start with the assumption the current social scene is new.

—Henry Wriston (1939)

U.S. higher education did not debate what the curriculum should be until the early nineteenth century. Up until then it was based on the liberal arts. Every graduate from every college was exposed to the same subjects and taught in almost the same manner. The only exception was in the area of theology, which was the reason various denominations established their own colleges—to ensure a steady stream of "properly" trained ministers for their faith. When college graduates met, they had a shared college experience. The commonality also meant that the library's collection was highly uniform in content from one college to another. That commonality began to fade in the early part of the nineteenth century as colleges expanded the topics and degrees they offered.

By the end of the nineteenth century, after adding a host of different practical degree programs and even more electives, institutional commonality was gone. Kenneth Boning (2007) noted that, at the height of elective course growth, student options "were so varied that students earning the same degree at the same institution may not have any of the same classes.... Overall, the emphasis on individualized education fragmented the academic community and brought dubiousness to the value of the baccalaureate degree" (p. 5).

As a result of the situation Boning described, there was pressure to bring back some of the old commonality. What that commonality ought to consist of and what its goals ought to be have been debated since the early twentieth century. (This was also the period in which community colleges started, with the goal of educating students to transfer to four-year institutions. This development made it even more important that there be greater consistency in what was required to graduate from a four-year school.) However, people in and out of the academy are presently questioning the need for "general ed" courses, as our opening quotation from Morrison shows. Where the debate will lead is anyone's guess; however, there is little doubt that the outcome will impact libraries and their resources.

WHAT IS GENERAL EDUCATION?

Our opening quotation from Henry Wriston relates to the first section of this chapter, general education. His essay explored what he thought general education's goal ought to be. Many others have grappled with the issue—probably more faculty committee hours have been devoted to debating this concept than any other topic.

A very simple definition of general education might be: a general education program is one in which students learn how to assess facts, make connections, and integrate knowledge. From the library perspective, assessing facts and information is a major contribution to a person's lifelong learning and ability to successfully handle changing circumstances. That may be a reasonable goal, but it does not suggest how one would go about doing it, what the content of the courses would be, and how many general versus specialized courses should be part of a baccalaureate degree. These are the areas that generate the heated debates. Another fact is the set of "general ed" courses varies over time at a single institution. Thus, there is no true commonality even within the institution, much less countrywide.

Almost all U.S. institutions of higher education have some form of general education. The larger and more complex the institution (especially doctoral granting institutions), the more difficult it is to put together a meaningful core for all the undergraduates. A very common approach is to employ a "distributive core." The size of the core varies but is generally between 46 and 52 semester hours of required courses. In the distributive approach, a student has a list of broad areas and a list of "acceptable" courses under each topic. It is reminiscent of a restaurant menu from which a person selects two from column A, three from B, and so on until the meal/degree requirements are met. Is there articulation among the courses? Sometimes yes and sometimes no, depending on the institution's interest in the core. Even when the interest is high, linkages between core courses may be weak. Most of the courses are "lower division" or introductory in character and thus make it difficult to create a coherent whole. Finally, at larger schools, the courses are taught by teaching assistants whose primary objective is a paycheck rather than developing meaningful linkages between the core courses.

The lack of commonality has generated federal government interest/concern over the years. Most recently, the federal government framed its concerns in terms of accountability and assessment rather than general education as such. Its interest is a reflection of societywide concerns about the cost and value of higher education as well as just what, if anything, the student has learned. We mentioned the "Spellings Report" in Chapter 1 (U.S. Department of Education, 2006; the Spellings in the popular title refers to Margaret Spellings, the former Secretary of Education who appointed the commission). Although the report did not specify a core curriculum, it did recommend national testing of certain skills:

> Higher education institutions should measure student learning using quality-assessment data from instruments such as, for example, the Collegiate Learning Assessment, which measures the growth of student learning taking place in colleges, and the Measure of Academic Proficiency and Progress, which was designed to assess general education outcomes for undergraduates in order to improve the quality of instruction and learning (p. 23).

Just how influential the report and its recommendations will be is difficult to predict. What does seem likely is that colleges and universities will consider some type of general ed outcome assessment, if for no other reason than accreditation. (We will explore accreditation later in this chapter as well as in other chapters.)

The two tests mentioned in the quotation are very different in character. Collegiate Learning Assessment (CLA) is a commercial product developed by the Council for Aid to Education and the RAND Corporation. CLA employs a written test intended to "test reasoning and communication skills that most agree should be one outcome of a college education" (www.cae.org/content). The test covers four areas—critical thinking, analytic reasoning, written communication, and problem solving. The Measure of Academic Proficiency and Progress (MAPP) is an Educational Testing Service (ETS) product that follows the traditional ETS multiple choice format. MAPP has been used by over 380 colleges and universities since it became available (www.ets.org). This number is likely to be much larger by the time you read this chapter as the pressure on institutions to demonstrate outcomes is unlikely to fade in the near future.

Before we go further, we should note another phrase that some people employ by which they more or less mean general education: liberal education. Are the two terms synonymous? Only in the very broadest sense. Gary Miller (1988) in his book *The Meaning of General Education* drew a number of distinctions between the two concepts, which we summarize in Table 5.1.

Table 5.1. General Education and Liberal Education Differences	
General Education	Liberal Education

Instrumentalist
    problem solving
    acquisition of skills
	Rationalist
	    life of the mind
	    mental process

Psychological
    individual
    social change
	Logical/essentialist
	    societal
	    seeks universals

Some other differences distinguish the two curricula. It is generally accepted that general education has six broad approaches: heritage, counterpoint, instrumental, developmental/empowerment, social agenda, and valuing. As you would expect, "heritage" cores focus on enhancing a student's appreciation of cultural heritage, generally by taking Western civilization classes, at least until fairly recently. "Counterpoint" packages are efforts to expand a student's exposure to subjects outside of the major that enrich the major at the same time. "Instrumental" is almost a synonym for liberal arts, as such programs concentrate on writing, speaking, and analytical thinking skills. "Development" or "empowerment" packages emphasize skills that should lead a person to becoming a lifelong learner. "Social agenda" purposed cores contain a set of courses that are topical and societal in nature such as global warming, responsibilities of citizens in a democratic society, and worldwide health

> **Try This**
>
> Think of at least three issues that each of the core types would have for an academic library and note how each type varies from one another. Think in terms of collections and services.

and hunger. "Valuing," as the name suggests, centers on setting values, assessing what values exist in a situation, and, at some institutions, even inculcating a specific set of values in the students.

Virginia Smith (1993) noted that in reality a person ought not to refer to general education as a "program." She pointed out that, from an organizational point of view, general education is "accorded far less importance than the lowest discipline-based department... even the smallest discipline-based unit has someone designated as chair" (p. 248). (By small/lowest discipline, she means the number of faculty and student majors, not the content of the discipline.) Based on her research, she indicated that less than 3 percent of the institutions with a general education component had a full time faculty member in charge of the operation, and, furthermore, that even fewer have something like a departmental budget. Rather than a program, she suggests one should think of general ed as a "catalog construct— a listing of required courses/areas that the student must have on her or his transcript in order to graduate. It becomes the students' and advisors' responsibilities to make certain the requirements are met. Finally, Smith made a key point about general education at any institution: its shape "is determined by putting together pieces of a curriculum usually designed for some other purpose" (p. 248).

DEBATING THE CURRICULUM

Some people liken curriculum reform to a "black hole" that swallows up enormous amounts of faculty time with very little coming out of the effort. As noted by Pittendrigh (2007), "The process of changing a general education curriculum has been compared to moving a graveyard" (p. 34). Along the same lines, Rhodes (2001) noted that "eyes glaze over; tempers shorten; people of generosity and goodwill become intolerant and those of sound judgment and thoughtful balance become rigid, hard line advocates" (p. B7). Such are some thoughts regarding debating... much less changing, the core. From the library point of view, the difficulties of making such changes is a plus as it gives staff more time to plan for what adjustments will be required to meet new requirements.

> **From the Authors**
>
> As an example later in this chapter will illustrate, delays in getting approval can allow the library staff time to begin the process of identifying potentially useful resources for a new program. In the latter example of the long period of time to get an education doctorate program approved, the stretch of time provided invaluable lead time for the library as well as time to begin working with the department faculty on their priorities for acquisitions.

Why is it so difficult to reach a consensus on what all students should be exposed to and hopefully learn by the time they graduate, even within an institution much less nationally? The answer is that multiple factors come into play, and their weight varies through time. Moreover, circumstances change within the institution.

Some people frame the debate as a battle between practicality (career) and theory (whole person). Opponents to broad general ed programs claim, with a degree of truth behind their argument, that each passing year adds more and more complexity to a subject field and students need more courses in that field to succeed. Thus, general ed classes mean either they do not serve the long-term career interests of students because they limit the number of specialized courses a student may take or they lengthen the overall degree program and increase students' costs. Supporters of general ed argue that true long-term interests are better served by having a breadth of knowledge and knowing how to think effectively rather than by having a narrow subject focus.

What will constitute the core, at most institutions, is a complex political process. (At some schools, such as St. John's College of Annapolis and Santa Fe and Thomas Aquinas College in Santa Paula, California, the core is basically the entire curriculum.) Seven significant factors affect the final composition of the core—history, institutional issues, career/whole person beliefs, accreditation bodies, societal issues/pressures, students "voting" with their feet, and departmental power/strength. The latter factor is often expressed in the form of departmental turf wars, as often the departments with one or more core courses also get additional faculty positions to handle the additional workload.

Obviously, institutional history and issues underlie the final decision. What the traditional curricular approach at a school acts as a significant brake on radical reform efforts. Senior faculty and alumni tend to resist more than minor changes in the core curriculum. The institution's definition of its purpose also serves as a brake on reform/reformulation. Trustees rarely redefine an institution's mission unless they are facing a serious fiscal crisis. Trustees have few problems in considering expansions of purpose over time, but narrowing the scope is a different matter. There is no question that the "push–pull" of educating the whole person versus the career aspirations of students and parents play a role in determining core size and its content. We will come back to this point shortly.

Accreditation bodies can also influence curriculum decisions. There are two broad types of accreditation organizations. One type looks at the entire institution, sometimes referred to as regional agencies—for example, Middle States Association of Colleges and Schools, North Central Association of Colleges and Schools, and Western Association of Colleges and Schools. The second type, such as the National Association of Schools of Music and the American Library Association, addresses discipline/subject issues. Both types can play a role in how big the core may be and how many specialized courses are required. Institutional and programmatic accreditations are important to parents and students as well as to the community at large, especially in the case of publicly funded schools. Accreditation matters to an institution if for no other reason than being fully accredited makes it easier to attract students. Essentially accreditation is a stamp of approval that the institution/program, based on an assessment by an outside agency, is in compliance with professional and community expectations.

Today both types of accreditation groups reflect a society-wide concern with assessment and accountability. The visiting team will ask pointed questions about the relationship

---

Keep In Mind

A fact of academic library life, at least in the more comprehensive institutions, is that accreditation activities seem to be never ending. It is a given that institutional-wide accreditation visits will look into library operations. The same is almost always true for programmatic visits. No matter which type of visit is coming up, the library will be asked to provide information about its operations for the self-study document that is sent to the accrediting agency and its visiting team members.

In a medium or large college or university, there is likely to be at least one programmatic accreditation visit a year. Library staff members either gather the requested self-study data or meet with a visiting team to address any concerns they may have that were not satisfactorily covered in the self-study. Consequently, the role of the library subject specialist/bibliographers must know the collections in their specific subject assignments. This not only helps in the self-study but also in the external team's campus visit. As important, their role often solidifies a strong relationship with the program/department's faculty.

between various courses and the institutional/programmatic mission and evidence of outcomes. The library's information literacy program staff can expect similar questions about their activities.

Sometimes the accrediting agency's expectations can create a major tension for those planning the curriculum when it comes to balancing core and specialized courses. Some programmatic agencies specify that a certain percentage (60 to 70 percent for example) of the total courses taken be in the programmatic area. That, of course, heightens the tensions between those focused on career interests and those who believe in lifelong skills. The argument of those in the latter group has been strengthened by data that show that people are now likely to change their career orientation several times during their working life as employers rapidly expand and contract their workforces due to changing economic circumstances.

Check This Out

An interesting book that explores the issues confronting today's and tomorrow's workforce is by Louis Uchitelle, *The Disposable Americans: Layoffs and Their Consequences* (New York: Knopf, 2006).

We noted earlier that the process of determining curricula is complex, especially in publicly funded institutions. To the mix of institutional history, philosophical differences, and accreditation agencies you must add societal/political pressure. Starting in the 1980s (roughly from the elections of President Reagan and Prime Minister Margaret Thatcher in the United Kingdom) neoconservatives' interest in and influence on higher education and its curricula has grown. As Dan Smith (2005) wrote regarding neoconservative views and the push–pull between the core and discipline-oriented degrees: "This dichotomy between the more humanistic approach to university education and the desire to 'create functional skills' expresses a debate in the university that meshes well with the neoconservative agenda," which is one of "commodification and privatization" (p. 114). As a result, there is a widely held view that higher education does or should play a significant role in the "new economy" and that it ought to focus on meeting that role. (Other issues affecting higher education include immigrant or international student populations, more high school graduates with developmental needs, and students with disabilities seeking access to higher education and then needing special support services.) An editorial about accountability and postsecondary institutions in *Change* magazine noted that institutions should have "better performance on outcomes that the political process has deemed important and success in the labor market" ("When the Customer Is Right," 2000, p. 6). The article went on to propose that this should be the focus of reforming the curriculum. Sarah Turner (2002) likewise suggested, "One rationale for state investment in colleges and university education is that states should enjoy the returns of such investments in the form of a more skilled workforce" (p. 33). Although none of this directly suggests that liberal education is inappropriate, those wishing for more specialized/ applied components in the baccalaureate degree use such arguments in their debate. (Note: community colleges with their dual role—transfer and vocational—do not face pressures that are as strong, for they have a defined role in educating what Bragg labeled a "midskilled" workforce [Bragg, 2001, p. 5]. This role is significant as between 70 and 80 percent of the workforce is in the category described by Bragg.)

Bernard Shapiro (2003) disagreed with the strong shift to a "labor market oriented" curriculum for colleges and universities. He wrote:

Having responded—perhaps too quickly and all too well—to demands of the marketplace, these institutions are now filled with students more focused on the vocational and financial prospects of their graduation than with the larger, more civilizing mission of higher education. I believe this concern is legitimate. Indeed, I am convinced this is the case, not only for many students, but also for many faculty whose desire and apparent capacity to understand much about higher education outside their own particular specialties is very limited indeed. (p. 15)

Although Shapiro's interest was in the Canadian situation, his views resonate in the United States. They also suggest that the debate is far from finished.

Certainly students and their parents vote with their feet and dollars when it comes to what type of curriculum they believe is most appropriate in today's environment. However, one wonders if they fully appreciate the value of broad-based/lifelong learning focused education when it comes to a lifetime of work. Balancing the need to recover/pay for the cost of degree reasonably quickly and meeting lifetime needs is difficult even for those who have an appreciation of long-term factors.

The reality is that three undergraduate degree models are now in play: general/liberal education with no specialty (bachelor of the arts), applied (e.g., bachelor of recreational studies), and mixed (e.g., bachelor of applied mathematics). The last model has been growing in favor over the past 20 or so years, in part because it helps avoid coming to grips with the fundamental issue: immediate application versus being able to adjust effectively to changing life situations.

Our final element in the great curriculum debate relates to the political strength of the various departments and their discipline focus in the institution. (Note: political strength is not always a function of faculty size and majors.) Powerful departments are often able to drive final curriculum decisions. Some years ago the Carnegie Foundation for the Advancement of Teaching (1998) sponsored a study that commented on departmental power in postsecondary institutions:

We believe that research universities must be willing and able to break free of traditions.... Departments necessarily think in terms of protecting and advancing their own interests, defined in terms of number of faculty, courses, and majors. Initiatives for change coming from sources outside the department are viewed as threats rather than opportunities. (p. 14)

Although the report's focus was research universities, the statement can and does apply to any academic institution. In the authors' experience, departmental influence/power is a significant factor in the direction of curricular change and development. It is even more of an issue in our next section, adding and dropping of courses and programs.

MODIFYING THE CURRICULUM AT THE MICRO LEVEL

If an academic library can maintain close liaison with only one faculty committee, that committee should be the one that reviews changes in courses and programs. This is why library liaison assignments to that committee are important. The librarian assigned as the liaison needs to ensure that discussion and decision by the committee are made known to the other librarians and library administrators. The authors have experienced weak librarian liaisons to that committee. When there is a weak liaison the duties ought to be reassigned to someone who is a more effective communicator.

Institutions employ a variety of labels for that body, but the name almost always contains one or more of the following words: courses, programs, studies, curriculum, and review. The committee is the first level of institutional assessment of proposed curricula changes. At the most basic level, the committee usually has the power to approve new courses. When it comes to expansion of an existing program or starting a new one, the group normally only has recommendation authority with the governing board retaining approval power.

An annual ritual for many librarians at the start of a new academic year is at least one request from a newly hired faculty member for a meeting. Such meetings almost always revolve around requests for special library support for the courses the person was hired to teach as well as around subscriptions to several new journals and to provide some funding to buy books/media in the person's specialty. (Note: even when the person is to teach the same courses as the person she or he replaced, the teaching approach will vary and often employ different library resources.)

Depending on the institution, the amount of freedom the library has to meet such requests varies. In some instances, the vast majority of the materials budget is allocated to the teaching departments and studies centers leaving almost no flexibility. When funds are thus allocated, all the librarian can do is suggest that the individual discuss the requests with departmental colleagues. When the reason for the request is that the person is scheduled to teach a course not previously offered at the institution, the department is likely to make some adjustment. (Note: often the meeting is the first time the library learns of the new course. When such situations arise, the librarian shares the person's frustration and renews efforts to get information from the courses and program committee about newly approved courses in a timely fashion. The library may also now have a new faculty member who is less than happy with its service orientation. Again, this is why it is important to place an effective library liaison to the committee.)

When the library has some flexibility in the materials budget, it is normally only in the area of books and media. Subscriptions to journals, databases, and other serials are generally both a fixed and annually increasing expense component in a library's budget. Just receiving funding adequate to cover the increased cost of existing subscriptions is a challenge, and rarely is any money available for new ones. In such instances, even departmental colleagues may be unwilling to drop any subscriptions over which they may have some control. The good news is that often one of the existing databases may contain some of all of the journal(s) the person is interested in and the individual was unaware of the fact that library had access to an electronic version.

The situation is even more challenging when it is more than just one or two new courses being introduced. Both authors have experienced a new person also saying he or she was hired to develop a new specialty within the existing degree, a certificate, or even a new degree, and this was the first time the library has heard of the development. Any of these new elements in the curriculum can have a significant impact on a library's services as well as on collections.

The top library administrators also have a role to play in all this. Most of them sit on their respective provost/dean's council, where these major curricular changes/additions are placed on the agenda and discussed. It is at that time that the library administrators should be working with their subject specialists to get an idea of the implications for the library's acquisition budget and make those implications known to the council. This allows for the possibility of the library having input in more than one venue.

A new certificate program is problematic, but not as much as a full degree. Usually a certificate draws on existing programmatic strengths, and thus the library will already have some support resources in place. With existing resources in place, the library has some time to secure other desired materials and is likely not to have an unhappy faculty member, at least in terms of the support of the new program.

When blindsided by a new degree program, something both authors experienced on more than one occasion, there are significant challenges for the library. One almost certain occurrence is that no one will have thought to have library funding included in the startup budget. Another highly likely reality is that when a library "wish list" is finally developed, the list will be long and expensive. If one is lucky, there will be a year or two before students enroll in the program. With at least a year to prepare and with proper funding from some source other than existing library funds, the library can begin to build up some of the resources needed to support the new activity. Lacking such lead time, it is inevitable almost everyone involved in the program will be unhappy for as long as it takes to address the issues.

The ideal approach to the committee's review process from an academic library point of view is to have a checklist of points that each proposal addresses. One element in this list is a section asking about library resources/services that are required to support the proposed change. If new library materials are needed, the proposal should include an estimate of the cost of meeting them. Such an approach ensures that the library is not blindsided by requests. It does not ensure the funding will be available, but this approach does help maintain better relationships between new faculty and the library. It also makes clear what additional funding ought to be made available for the desired level(s) of library support for the new course/program.

> **Keep In Mind**
>
> Even when there are the best of intentions and relations among all of those involved, a few newly approved courses do not get reported to the library in a timely manner. It is much rarer for a new certificate or degree program to slip between the cracks, but it does happen. There are a number of positive reasons for library staff to "show the colors" as it were by attending various open faculty/staff activities and eating one or two meals a week in the faculty dining room and attending welcome and going-away parties and open houses. From such attendance, as long as librarians at the event do not stay together but rather talk with faculty about their research interests, courses, and departmental plans, the library can gain much-needed early warning about potential changes.

At universities lacking a doctoral program, one or two academic departments will usually have aspirations of offering a doctoral degree. A new doctoral program will not come as a surprise to the library because extensive campuswide discussion of any such program will take place long before it ever reaches the governing board for final approval. One factor in the debate over starting such a program is the high cost of such programs. We discuss the costs of programs in more depth in a later chapter, but for now it's enough to say undergraduate programs are the lowest cost per student, masters programs cost more, and doctoral programs are the most costly.

Up to this point we discussed what the general public thinks of as higher education's curricula. For many institutions, especially land grant institutions, this is only a part of the total picture of course offerings. We turn now to two of the other big components in many institutions' total curriculum: continuing/adult education and distance learning programs.

From the Authors

Evans had five experiences working with departments with hopes of implementing a doctoral program, PhD or applied. Only one of them succeeded in securing institutional approval for a degree. As a general rule, securing approval is a long-term process requiring substantial amounts of time devoted to planning. In all five instances, the department chair or the proposal's lead faculty member came to the library to explore the idea long before preparing the first draft proposal. Having had some success in shepherding an applied doctoral proposal through the approval process at a research institution, the author always recommended undertaking what he called a "dissertation feasibility" study early in the planning process.

A feasibility study draws on existing doctoral dissertations in the field(s) of the proposed degree. (Rarely does a doctoral program begin by offering work in the entire discipline but rather in just a few subfields based on existing faculty strengths and interest in directing a doctoral student's work.) Essentially the purpose of the study is to determine if the dissertation could have been completed using the institution's resources, especially library resources. Table 5.2 lists several of the most common assumptions surrounding doctoral degree proposals.

Table 5.2. Doctoral Degree Proposal Assumptions
Common Assumptions about Doctoral Degree Proposals
Only a few of the possible subfields in the discipline will be offered initially. Subfields offered reflect existing institutional resource strengths.
Any meaningful dissertation will need to draw on some off-campus resources; however, most of the necessary resources will be locally available. A less than 50 percent level of availability of necessary resources in local library holdings indicates substantial work will be required to build up appropriate resources. The number of specialties offered will expand over time.
Enrollment will be low during the start period, which will reduce pressure on library services.
Any such program will substantially increase institutional direct and indirect operating costs, including those of the library.

One factor in moving the proposal forward in one instance was that the private university's dean of the school of education had been the academic vice president during the first five years of Evans's tenure as director of the library. He had had to struggle with finding funding to allow the library to acquire resources for new certificate and degree programs that had not factored those needs into their proposals. As a result, the dean fought for and secured special funding over a five-year period for library purchases of material to support the program once it was approved. In the final approved version, the program was a stand-alone degree at the private university. What a study does is provide both the department and the library with realistic, useful data about existing collection strengths in the subfields. It also provides a basis for calculating some of the startup costs in terms of library resources as well as a sense of how much time may be required to acquire the items.

Of the five departments hoping to implement a doctoral program in this example, only one had succeeded as of 2009. Four of the PhD hopefuls had yet to demonstrate the need for a program or that adequate resources existed to support such a program should it be authorized. The successful program was an applied doctorate, an EdD (doctorate of education), and even this proposal went through a number of iterations. In its first form, it was to be a joint program with a nearby public university, with that university's library supplying all of the resources for the students. (This was a result of a feasibility study involving 16 dissertations in the subfields the schools of education wished to offer.)

The point we are making is that new degree programs require careful planning, with library involvement at the earliest developmental stages. Many faculty members and administrators do not fully appreciate the amount of time it takes for a library to identify, acquire, and process a substantial number of items in a new area of interest or how students may access information in the future. This is especially true for graduate level programs where some or many of the desired items are no longer in print.

CONTINUING/ADULT EDUCATION

Continuing/adult education is a broad concept. People employ the concept to embrace a variety of educational experiences that range from literacy programs to earning a degree through a distance education program. In between the two are other activities such as a person enrolling in noncredit courses for self-enrichment, individuals taking courses to earn a certificate or update a degree or certificate, and a person engaging in self-directed learning. Such activities are a significant part of the total U.S. educational picture. They are significant enough that profit-oriented organizations offer courses. Professional groups and academic institutions (our sole focus here) are all involved in offering workshops and programs. In the broadest sense we are looking at lifelong learning. Typically, students in such programs are older than the traditional baccalaureate student and may be returning to academia after a long break.

In a sense, adult education is about possibilities. Marsha Rossiter (2007) made this point in broad-brush terms when she wrote:

> We know that learning is a way of being in the world that describes our capacity to respond constructively to the constant change in our lives. It is the capacity to find the potential for learning in every new event and interaction with our environment. As we live, we learn our way into new possibilities for ourselves (p. 5).

Expanding one's possibilities through learning, whether in terms of leisure or work, has become a significant source of income for many higher education institutions, regardless of type. In some cases, it generates the second largest revenue stream after on-campus degree candidates' tuition and fees. Expenses for such programs are somewhat higher than for traditional degree programs (not that those costs are low), as the schools must compete against for-profit and professional organizations to attract students. (Essentially, these groups add two additional types to an institution's list of those competing for students.) All this means is greater marketing costs. Even with these added costs such programs can generate large sums of cash for the institution.

Adult education programs are relatively young in academia—little more than 100 years old. Perhaps the earliest adult education programs date from the late 1860s in the United Kingdom, as a result of efforts at Cambridge and Oxford to assist some prospective students in London qualify for admission (McLean, 2007, p. 4.) U.S. origins lie in the land grant program and the Wisconsin Idea. The programs were then viewed as an "extension" of the campus and serving the nondegree needs of citizens of the state. Most academic-institution-based programs started in the early twentieth century. The term extension shifted to "continuing" as non-land-grant schools started offering coursework/workshops and as various professional bodies mandated lifelong updating to maintain a person's license/certificate to continue to practice with the organizational "stamp of approval." Today, the most common term is "adult," as the programs are so varied in character and purpose.

Something to Ponder

How do people learn? Jay Cross (2004) provided a short paragraph outlining some thoughts on the matter. "One of the best ways to learn is social; we learn with and from other people. We learn by doing. Aristotle said, 'What we have to learn to do, we learn by doing,' and Einstein echoed, 'The only source of knowledge is experience. (Aristotle added, 'We cannot learn without pain.') Confucius said, 'I hear and I forget. I see and I remember. I do and I understand.' And I'll add that if I hear and see and do and then practice and teach I understand even better" (p. 104).

U.S. adult education looks to three major markets for its students: individuals, communities (e.g., archives, libraries, and small businesses), and professional organizations (e.g., certified public accountants and educators). Community colleges are particularly active in adult education. A rather typical breakdown of offerings at a CC are noncredit courses/workshops, corporate/business courses and workshops, and credit courses for nondegree candidates.

Spending some time looking over adult education catalogs will quickly demonstrate how wide-ranging the topics being offered are and how they vary from term to term. All of which raises the question of how much support is necessary or should be available from the library. The answer depends on several variables. One major variable is the long-term versus short-term nature of the course or workshop. Often the offering is a one-time occurrence or the instructor varies from term to term, making it almost impossible to plan library services to meet course needs. The topic also matters; a course on making holiday candies needs no support while one on world religions may require substantial support. Support for academic offerings may present no special challenges if there are similar credit courses. Where challenges do arise is long standing certificate programs for which adequate library support is an important element in the success or failure of the program. Instructors tend to vary over time more often than in similar credit courses, which results in more variations in the course requirements and resources.

Another library challenge is what privileges the adult learner should/must have. Will those privileges vary by type of course/workshop the individual enrolls in—noncredit, credit, or certificate? Does it matter if the student is on or off campus? How will the library gain this type of information? Especially challenging is the fact that the data vary from term to term. Many of the issues are not unlike those regarding part-time faculty.

From the Authors

Two examples from Evans's experience were a six-week high school debate "camp" and an eight-week talented youth program. Both programs generated significant income for the institution and were also thought to raise the awareness in the young peoples' minds of the possibilities of enrolling at the institution as an undergraduate. As these two programs approached each summer, the library staff became more anxious. The label "talented youth" was most appropriate, especially when it came to thinking up pranks. Certainly the library was not the only facility on the receiving end of the mischief. However, for the library there was a constant battle to maintain the appropriate level of access to electronic resources for all users, as one or two of the students attempted and sometime succeeded in hacking into the library system or campus network.

Debaters presented a different challenge in their use of material required to prepare for debates and general housekeeping in the photocopy areas. The library lost journal articles from bound journals as some of the young people cut or tore out material rather spend money on photocopying. As the number of online databases increased, the mutilation rate dropped. Library staff and the program coordinators held annual meetings to discuss how to handle past and potential problems. Over time issues became less severe, but the library staff always felt under siege during these programs.

Most of today's academic institutions must maximize the use of their campus and personnel. As a result, in addition to the "academic year," most schools offer "summer school" and even "intersession" (between academic year terms) programs. Where such activities lie administratively varies, but often they are part of the adult education division. Interterm courses are almost always part of the academic side of the house—these sessions almost never offer personal enrichment courses. Summer schools are often a mix of degree-related courses and typical adult education offerings. Summer school may present some special library challenges when there are annual programs that operate for almost the entire summer break period and are financially important but are not degree oriented.

DISTANCE EDUCATION

Of special importance in adult and degree program education is the issue of distance education. Like summer school, distance education administration varies from institution to institution. While not every academic institution offers distance education options for degrees, the number of schools that do not shrinks year after year. In the not too distant future, such programs may have a greater number of students enrolled than in the on-campus programs.

As information/communication technologies continue to improve, the totally virtual degree becomes more acceptable both to students and to those who later employ the graduates. Each technology has its pluses and minuses, which change through time. Peter Glowacki (2006) in commenting on changing technology noted that those offering continuing education courses must "constantly review their offerings and adjust them to capitalize on those positive traits and to develop a curriculum that educates the widest group with the most diverse adult learning requirements" (p. 543). Not only do technological developments force schools to rethink their distance degree programs, but they also must evaluate/reevaluate how much the elements of the distance degree can or should vary from the on-campus degree.

Perhaps one of the important elements of an on-campus degree program that is missing in distance education is the "social" aspect of learning that Cross mentioned. Much learning occurs in the informal social interaction between students over a cup of coffee or lunch as well as getting together to study (learning communities). Patricia Sobrero (2008) discussed some of the ways to overcome the lack of social aspects of learning and ways to create effective e-learning communities. She identified five elements involved in creating such communities:

- Leadership
- Negotiation
- Reliable technology and support
- Building trust
- Maintaining momentum

In many ways, the needs of an effective e-learning community are no different than those required for any virtual group effort. Someone must be willing to lead the process without dominating the group. Building consensus and trust are even more significant factors than when working with a co-located group (people physically together), as the nonverbal communication is lacking; for example, something that is clearly a joke in a face-to-face situation may fail in the virtual environment, even if the person has added "lol" to the message.

In Chapter 3 we noted that online teaching is significantly more time consuming than face-to-face instruction. Instructors and their institutions discovered that one cannot just use technology to deliver the former face-to-face course. To be effective, the course has to take on a new structure—it has to be redesigned. This in itself takes time to accomplish, and then the instructor must allow for more interaction time with students. As Thomas Cyrs (1997) wrote, "Anyone who says teaching at a distance is the same as traditional teaching is dead wrong" (p. 18). Barbara DuCharme-Hansen and Pamela Dupin-Bryant (2005) identified six factors that lead to successful online learning:

- Assessment (what are student needs)
- Guidance (a greater need to be a guide rather than being the "sage")
- Building community (instructors must encourage and assist in developing learning communities)
- Communication (employing multiple pathways)
- Humanization (creating a people-focused learning environment)
- Evaluation (building in more student feedback than in a face-to-face course and recognizing that technology, design, and structure must be part of that evaluation)

Distance education is an area of major concern, or should be, for academic libraries, and one that will only grow in importance. For libraries there are dual concerns: supporting coursework and its own online course offerings. The former has been a given; the latter is an area in which libraries must be more active. While face-to-face information literacy instruction will remain in place for the foreseeable future, online instruction will become ever more critical. The focus should be on the new generation of students who seem to have little regard for the accuracy of the information they find on the Web (see the student attitude section of Chapter 4).

> **Check This Out**
>
> A good, if slightly dated, article that provides an overview of distance education and academic libraries is Smithi Gandhi's "Academic Libraries and Distance Education," *Reference & User Services Quarterly* 43, no. 2 (2003): 138–154. Other articles on distance education and the library are in the Launching Pad section of this chapter.

For many academic libraries, distance education is a rather familiar issue. In the late 1970s and early 1980s, some institutions started moving into distance education. A few schools tried going nationwide with their courses but often were limited by the need to have access to a physical facility and other support services such as libraries and testing centers. Not surprisingly accreditation agencies began to question just how equal the on- and off-campus programs really were as well as the quality of the off campus support services.

Today, technology can address most distance education library support issues (reference, e-reserves, database access, etc). Nevertheless, the issues are of such importance to academic libraries that the Association of College and Research Libraries (2008) issued a set of standards for library support of distance education. The document outlines 12 principles for developing distance education services:

- Access for achievement of superior academic skills (Doing so may call for different but equivalent services/resources.)
- Direct human contact (A library must develop direct access to staff in a timely manner.)

From the Authors

Evans experienced several of the distance education quality questions as a member of accreditation teams, as a consultant, and as a head of a library with a neighboring distance education program. As an accreditation team member he found himself traveling on several occasions to a distance education site to interview students and investigate the quality of site support services. On one consulting assignment, undertaken at the request of the academic vice president because of on-campus student complaints at a school that had a major distance degree program, he found that the distance education program support needs from the library had completely distorted the balance between on- and off-campus student support. One example of the distortion was the fact that the library essentially allocated all of the collection development funds on the basis of distance education needs. A random sample of the online catalog database showed that no new books or media had been acquired in over 18 years but that the funds had gone toward databases and journals specially needed for the distance program.

The experience with a neighboring distance education program was enlightening regarding the importance of maximizing distance learning revenue. Initially, the distance program was small, and only a few students came to the private university's library; in fact, there was no contact regarding access to library services. The library learned of the program's presence through the reference process with students from the program. As the distance program grew and more of its students arrived asking for not just reference assistance but essentially all of the services available to the university's students, we undertook a user study and found that just over 20 percent of all reference transactions were with distance learners. This figure represented the equivalent of one of the university's full-time reference staff. This information led to a meeting between the university's head librarian, the university's academic vice president, and the person in charge of the local distance education site. The distance education representative refused even to put forward to her home institution the idea that some fee should be paid to the university for providing library services to its students—at the time over 200. In fact, she voiced the opinion it was not her institution's responsibility to provide library services; it would cost the program so much that it would have to close down. That situation, as well as increased use by many other non–university students/users, led the institution to initiate a closed access policy unless one had a "user's card," which was fee-based.

- Additional resources (As one of the examples illustrated, simply stretching existing resources and budget usually does not provide equal service to all students.)
- Mandated support (The originating institution must allocate additional funding to provide equivalent library services to distant learners.)
- Technological linkages (Obviously, technological issues take on greater importance for distance students, and the issue goes beyond just the library.)
- Meeting other standards, guidelines, laws, and regulations (Support of distant learners must meet or exceed all of the relevant standards for on-campus students.)
- Institutional involvement of library and other personnel (It is essential that the library "have a seat at the table" from the outset of distance education planning, development, and evaluation of such programs.)
- Written agreements (One of the earlier examples illustrated the need for contracts if there is to be support from distant libraries. This support should not substitute for the originating institution's financial responsibility.)
- Meeting needs the primary responsibility (The originating library, not a library near them, has the responsibility of addressing distance learners' needs.)
- Strategic planning (It is imperative, if effective distance support is to materialize, that the library incorporate distance education support into the overall library strategic plan.)
- Outcome assessment (As is true for all library services, ongoing assessment is critical to long-term success.)

- Information literacy (In some ways, providing distance learners with effective instruction on information literacy is more important than for on-campus students due to their greater dependence on technology.)

The foregoing principles make clear just how complex distance education support is for academic libraries.

INTERNATIONALIZING THE CURRICULUM

In a global economy, it might be reasonable to think there is a developing international curriculum, and to a degree this is correct. Certainly it is not the "international" curriculum (liberal arts) that existed at the beginning of higher education. However, English is becoming something of the lingua franca of higher education worldwide. Furthermore, more colleges and universities, regardless of country, are offering courses that address the same topic/concepts. Movement toward an internationalized curriculum has been underway for some years.

Most people would not think that something like the General Agreement on Trade in Services (GATS) would have anything to do with higher education. However, it does in fact cover higher education as one of the dozen trade-related sectors now negotiated among countries. Nelly Stromquist (2007) indicated that for the United States "education and training represents indeed its fifth largest service trade sector. Globally, education investments abroad resulted in capital flows of more than $30 billion in 2003" (p. 83). She concluded her article by writing, "This internationalization is an expression of economic and technological globalization in which university 'entrepreneurs' are not merely looking for more contracts and contacts with industry but, ultimately, are concerned with establishing regular international sites and presence" (p. 102).

> **From the Authors**
>
> Evans was a participant in such an international effort in the mid-1980s. The goal of the conference was to determine if there could be agreement on a worldwide set of core management topics that any information professional, regardless of country, ought to learn during their education. After a week of sometimes contentious debate, teachers from Asia, Africa, Europe, and South, Central, and North America did reach a consensus on 16 management topics that are central to information work. Other international professional bodies have been engaging in similar harmonization efforts related to the education of their professionals.

Nigel Healy (2008) explored the question of internationalization of the curriculum in some depth and concluded that while there was evidence of such a movement, he questioned the midterm viability of the current model(s). He noted:

> The role of universities is to create and disseminate knowledge; that is, to research and teach. Insofar as the creation of knowledge bases in major discipline areas is a collective enterprise of humankind, universities must necessarily be international in their orientation—the nature of scientific advancement is that today's research builds upon the discoveries of others, wherever in the world they may be.... It has been the internationalization of the *student* body rather than the internationalization of the faculty or research/teaching that gives rise to the perception that universities are beginning to mimic corporations in their orientation. (p. 334)

His point is well taken; however, many of the students returning home become teachers who reflect, to some degree, the education they received overseas. Also, one must consider the impact of program such as the Fulbright. One of the authors of this book returned from a Fulbright teaching assignment with a new perspective that resulted in a more internationalized approach to the courses he taught.

Perhaps sometime in the future, academic library holdings will be more homogenous, at least at the broad subject level, and perhaps there will be some of the commonality in the students' educational experiences that many in today's academy miss and wish would return.

KEY POINTS TO REMEMBER

- The debate regarding how much general and "specialized" education a graduate should experience is an ongoing one.
- The outcome of the debate has, does, and will impact academic library collections and services.
- A variety of factors influence the final composition of the curriculum, such as institutional history and issues, beliefs about the value of educating the "whole person," societal concerns, accreditation agencies, student and parental interests, and departmental strength. All of these factors vary over time, thus library support must also vary.
- The faculty committee that reviews, approves, and recommends changes in courses and programs is the body the library *must* create and maintain close ties with in order to most effectively support the institution's educational purposes.
- Continuing education plays a significant role in many institutions in terms of curriculum issues as well as revenue. This is sometimes an area of the total curriculum that does not receive adequate attention from libraries.
- Distance/online education is playing an ever greater role in higher education and in the not too distant future may be the major source of earned degrees from an institution. Library support of these programs is a complex issue and creates some challenges for balancing library services to students on and off campus.
- Internationalization of the curriculum is likely to become more important and will call for ever greater cooperative efforts among academic libraries.

REFERENCES

Association of College and Research Libraries. 2008. Standards for distance learning library services. *College & Research Library News* 69, no. 9: 555–569.

Boning, Kenneth. 2007. Coherence in general education. *Journal of General Education* 56, no. 1: 1–16.

Bragg, Debra. 2001. Opportunities and challenges for new vocationalism in American community colleges. *New Directions for Community Colleges* 115: 5–15.

Carnegie Foundation for the Advancement of Teaching. 1998. *Reinventing undergraduate education: A blueprint for America's research universities.* Modified 2001 by Melissa Bishop. Washington, DC: Carnegie Foundation for the Advancement of Teaching.

Cross, Jay. 2004. An informal history of e-learning. *On the Horizon* 12, no. 3: 103–110.

Cyrs, Thomas. 1997. Competence in teaching at a distance. *New Directions in Teaching and Learning* 71: 15–19.

DuCharme-Hansen, Barbara, and Pamela Dupin-Bryant. 2005. Course planning for adult learners. *TechTrends* 49, no. 2: 31–39.

Glowacki, Peter. 2006. Accreditation of technology-based continuing legal education. *Valparaiso University Law Review* 40, no. 2: 543–554.

Healy, Nigel. 2008. Is higher education in reality internationalizing? *Higher Education* 55, no. 3: 333–335.

McLean, Scott. 2007. University extension and social change. *Adult Education Quarterly* 58, no. 1: 3–21.

Miller, Gary. 1988. *The meaning of general education.* New York: Teachers College Press.

Morrison, James L. 2003. U.S. higher education in transition. *On the Horizon* 11, no. 1: 6–10.

Pittendrigh, Adele. 2007. Reinventing the core: Community, dialogue and change. *Journal of General Education* 56, no. 1: 34–56.

Rhodes, Frank. 2001. A battle plan for professors to recapture the curriculum. *Chronicle of Higher Education* 48, no. 3: B7–B10.

Rossiter, Marsha. 2007. Possible selves: Adult education perspective. *New Directions for Adult and Continuing Education* 114: 5–15.

Shapiro, Bernard. 2003. Canada's universities: Quantitative success, qualitative concerns. *Policy Options* 24, no. 8: 15–17.

Smith, Dan. 2005. Liberal arts vs. applied programming. *Canadian Journal of Higher Education* 35, no. 1: 111–132.

Smith, Virginia. 1993. New dimension for general education. In *Higher learning in America, 1980–2000,* ed. Arthur Levine, 243–258. Baltimore, MD: Johns Hopkins University Press.

Sobrero, Patricia. 2008. Essential components for successful virtual learning communities. *Journal of Extension* 46, no. 4: 1–11.

Stromquist, Nelly. 2007. Internationalization as a response to globalization: Radical shifts in university environments. *Higher Education* 53, no. 2: 81–105.

Turner, Sarah. 2002. Connecting higher education and the labor market. *Change* 34, no. 4: 32–39.

U.S. Department of Education. 2006. *A test of leadership: Charting the future of U.S. higher education.* Washington, DC: Department of Education.

When the customer is right: Market driven accountability in postsecondary education. 2000. *Change* 32, no. 3: 53–56.

Wriston, Henry. 1939. A critical appraisal of experiments in general education. In *The thirty-eighth yearbook of the National Society for the Study of Education,* eds. Guy Montrose Whipple and Alvin C. Eurich, 297– 321. Bloomington, IL: Public School Publishing.

LAUNCHING PAD

Arcilla, Rene. 2007. The questions of liberal education. *Liberal Education* 93, no. 2: 14–19.

Bralower, Timothy, Geoffrey Feiss, and Cathryn Manduca. 2008. Preparing a new generation to face earth's future. *Liberal Education* 94, no. 2: 30–23.

Downey, John A., Brian Pusser, and J. Kirsten Turner. 2006. Competing missions: Balancing entrepreneurialism with community responsiveness in community college continuing education divisions. *New Directions for Community Colleges* 136: 75–82.

Fenwick, Tara. 2008. Workplace learning. *New Directions for Adult and Continuing Education* 119: 17–26.

Fuller, Alison. 2007. Mid-life "transitions" to higher education. *Studies in the Education of Adults* 39, no. 2: 217–235.

Gano-Phillips, Susan, and Robert Barnett. 2008. Against all odds: Transforming institutional culture. *Liberal Education* 94, no. 2: 36–41.

Grosejean, Garnet, and Thomas Sork. 2007. Going online: Uploading the virtual classroom. *New Directions for Adult and Continuing Education* 113: 13–24.

Jacobs, Jonathan. 2008. The odd couple reflections on liberal education. *Liberal Education* 94, no. 3: 50–55.

Katz, Stanley. 2008. Assessment and general education. *Liberal Education* 94, no. 3: 30–37.

Largent, Liz, and Jon Horinek. 2008. Community colleges and adult service learner. *New Directions for Adult and Continuing Education* 118: 37–47.

McLean, Scott. 2007. University extension and social change. *Adult Education Quarterly* 38, no.1: 3–21.

Mason, Terrance, Robert Arnove, and Margaret Sutton. 2001. Credits, curriculum and control in higher education: Cross-national perspectives. *Higher Education* 42, no. 3: 107–137.

Merriam, Sharon. 2008. Adult learning theory for twenty-first century. *New Directions for Adult and Continuing Education* no. 119: 93–98.

Needham, Gill, and Kay Johnson. 2007. Ethical issues in providing library services to distance learners. *Open Learning* 22, no. 2: 117–128.

Oldham, Bonnie. 2008. Providing library services to distance education students. *Journal of Interlibrary Loan, Document Delivery & Electronic Reserves* 18, no. 2: 219–227.

Tritelli, David. 2008. Give students a compass: Can general education rise to the challenge? *Liberal Education* 94, no. 3: 6–9.

Wyss, Paul Alan. 2008. Getting started as a distance learning librarian. *College Student Journal* 42, no. 2, part A: 440–448.

Zacharakis, Jeffery. 2008. Extension and community. *New Directions for Adult and Continuing Education* 117: 13–23.

Chapter 6

Governance

On campuses throughout the United States the issue of governance is being hotly debated.

—Joseph Simplicio (2006)

One should not presume to tell a college or university what its governance structure should be. In fact, there is no *general* model of governance, shared or otherwise, that can be replicated from place to place.

—Stanley Fish (2007)

Some readers may wonder why a chapter on governance is necessary; after all, every organization has a structure that provides the means for doing things, making decisions, and designating leadership roles. This is true. However, within the academy, unlike in other organizations, a very long tradition and belief about how governance should operate exists—sometimes the concept is labeled "shared governance" and at other times "collegial governance." Whether this tradition has been fully operational in the recent past may be debatable. Nevertheless, the belief in the concept is widely held and has deep roots in today's colleges and universities.

What is shared/collegial governance? Does it really differ from other forms of organizational governance? The answer to both questions is yes. Shared/collegial governance models have several common features. First and foremost is the idea that all participants in operational activities ought to have a voice in operations. (Just because everyone has, or should have, a voice does not imply that all voices carry equal weight. It means only that there should be an opportunity to express a point of view.) Second, the decision-making process tends to be slow in comparison to most other organizations due to the need for broad input. Third, decisions will likely reflect a consensus that builds up during the discussions and rarely fully reflects any one person's or group's position. Fourth, it is assumed that the process occurs within a community of peers (again, not all "peers" are equal in the academy). Finally, the process involves a great deal of interpersonal interaction. Combined, these elements make it difficult for a newcomer to quickly sort out how the process operates.

Most of these elements can be found in other organizational structure models such as participatory management. However, not all of the elements are present in the other organizational models. Also, almost no other organizational model has a tradition going back nearly 800 years, except the Catholic Church. From the very beginnings of higher education, faculty and students played an active role in making decisions about the whats and hows of the process. The goal was a consensus that did and does take time; and although students and faculty were not full peers, the different voices were listened to respectfully. There is something to the idea that history does carry weight into the present.

Collegial governance in U.S. higher education results in a complex and, at times, frustrating decision-making process and questions about who is in charge. (The phrase "herding cats" has some application when it comes to higher education governance.) Anyone, regardless of staff category, who is new to academia may be surprised to learn how difficult it is to determine who is running the place and how. Some people, both within and outside of higher education, think that "campus governance" is an oxymoron. A published organization chart may reflect the official version of how lines of communication and control operate. However, all organizations have an informal structure in addition to the formal lines of communication. In the case of the academy, the informal structure is much more important in terms of how things actually work. Learning how the institution really operates is important for any librarian joining an academic institution. Needless to say, you must start with the formal elements and then move on to the informal side in order to begin to understand what and how it happens; the latter may take some time to sort through.

The twenty-first century has brought with it several changes that make the first opening quotation so significant. Adrianna Kezar and Peter Eckel (2004) wrote:

> Three significant changes in the environment within the last decade make governance even more problematic:...(1) the need to respond to diverse environmental issues, such as accountability and competition; (2) weak mechanisms for faculty participation, major faculty retirements with close to half of the faculty retiring in the next ten years and a more diverse group entering the professoriate; and (3) the need to respond more effectively based on shorter decision times. (p. 371)

All institutions in the academy, whether public or private, have seven broad groups that may have a voice in decision making: a governing board, a chief executive officer (usually called a president but other titles also exist), the president's cabinet (usually vice presidents/vice chancellors), "middle level" administrators (deans, department chairs, and heads of other operating units such as information services or human resources), the faculty, the students, and the staff. For public institutions, another layer that adds to the complexity of governance—the state or other funding body.

Community college governance is varied, as Pam Schuetz (1999) noted:

> **Check This Out**
> Does collegial/shared governance really matter in terms of academic library operations? Yes, and the influence does go beyond how the library structures its governance. A good article that explores the influence on a library service is Lawrence Thomas's "Tradition and Expertise in Academic Library Collection Development," *College & Research Libraries* 48, no. 6 (1987): 487–493. After reading the article, think about other library activities that might also be influenced in similar ways.

> Public community college governance stands quite apart from governance systems employed by public universities....Governance in America's community colleges is virtually a state-by-state choice with some of the variations being: state vs. local elected vs. appointed, state appointed vs. locally appointed, tax authority vs. no taxing authority, voluntary shared governance vs. mandated shared governance, and various combinations. (p. 1)

ROLE OF THE STATE

The state also has a role, if even a minor one, in every academic institution within its borders. Its role in private institutions is primarily limited to issuing the charter that allows for the establishment of the school. Clearly, as a significant source of funds for the public institutions, the state has some say in the governance of those institutions. You may recall that in Chapter 2 we mentioned that Harvard was the first school in the world to receive a charter from a legislative body. This pattern of legislative authority for U.S. higher education institutions is one of its distinguishing features.

During the nineteenth century, state legislatures were liberal in handing out charters with little regard for how sound the institution might be. They also took little interest in overseeing the institutions after granting the charter—there was no quality control beyond that exercised by the institution. Part of the reason for the lack of oversight of private schools was the Dartmouth decision by the U.S. Supreme Court indicating the trustees should be in control (see the section "Post–War of Independence to 1860" in Chapter 2). In some cases, state legislatures delegated the granting of charters to an ex officio agent who had no interest in higher education beyond collecting the appropriate fee for a charter. By the start of the twentieth century, states began to worry about the quality of higher education within institutions they had chartered, and the movement toward accreditation gained momentum.

Michael R. Mills (2007) summarized the role of states in public higher education as follows: "states seem to stagger in different directions; some opt for more centralized organizations while others attempt to decentralize their systems" (p. 162). In broad terms, there are three state models:

- A statewide governing board responsible for all operations of public institutions
- A statewide coordinating board
- A statewide planning board, but lacking coordinating authority

A few institutions (University of Michigan, University of California, and University of Colorado, for example) exist as a state constitutional entity. That is, the university is established through the state constitution as are the legislator, judiciary, and executive branches.

As far as academic library operations go, the state's role is generally minimal. That is not to say that state rules and regulations do not intrude from time to time, especially when it comes to major purchases or statewide budget cuts. In the past, some states imposed rules on public academic library acquisitions practices for books and journals that treated them the same as buying office supplies and/or requiring the library to annually go out for bids for its journal subscriptions. Such practices disrupted subscriptions to the delays in awarding a contract, even when the former vendor's won the bid.

> **An Interesting Fact**
>
> New York had a statewide Board of Regents for all chartered academic institutions. Melvil Dewey, of Dewey Decimal fame, served as Secretary of the State Board of Regents from 1888 through 1899. Under his stewardship the board required annual reports from the institutions from which Dewey then compiled a list of institutions in "good standing." The list was a forerunner of today's accreditation. ("Prof. Melvil Dewey Resigns," 1899)

THOSE WHO ESTABLISH GUIDELINES

In any type of organization, all of their activities are being done by one of three categories of individuals—those who do the work, those who administer the work, and those who set guidelines for doing the work. Within academia, some of those roles are blurred as we noted in the opening sections of this chapter. However, in theory, the institution's governing board is the body that establishes guidelines and policy. Although individuals debate where the responsibility for academic leadership ought to reside, how influential certain voices should be in determining institutional direction, or a host of other policy issues, no one argues that the governing board doesn't have the final legal authority when it comes to the institution.

Governing boards have several different titles depending on the history and nature of the school. Generally private institutions employ the term *trustees*. A large percentage of the public institutions use *regents*. Some of the oldest schools have labels such as *overseers*, *visitors*, and even *curators* for their board members.

Composition of the governing board has varied through time. At the start of the nineteenth century, schools were caught up in a struggle between sectarian and secular control of their boards. As you will recall, all of the early colleges started as church-related institutions. As you might guess, the early boards consisted of clergy of the denomination that established the college (similar to the pattern in northern Europe). A few followed the English model of "collegial control" with occasional visitations by selected laypersons. Today, many such schools have only nominal connections with their founding denomination. Others, such as Catholic colleges and universities, have remained steadfast to their religious roots. However, even these institutions have changed their board compositions over time. A governing board made up of unpaid laypeople is a distinguishing feature of U.S. higher education.

> ### From the Authors
>
> Evans once had the title "The Librarian" and worked with a subcommittee of the "Visitors Board" as part of his duties. At least once a year, several committee members made an appointment to meet with "The Librarian" to discuss library operations. All but one of those meetings were friendly and pleasant and revolved around what the committee might do to help move the library's activities forward. They were of enormous help in raising funds for special projects. However, Evans's decision to switch to the Library of Congress Classification system, after 120 years of using a homegrown system, triggered a "visit" from the entire committee and other interested institutional staff. The visit lasted a full day, but with the assistance of the central library personnel the library gained the approval of the committee to move ahead with the change. Certainly it is unusual to have even a subcommittee of the governing board take such an interest in the library operational details, but it does happen.

Until the late nineteenth century, boards did in fact control the institutions, especially after the Dartmouth decision. However, many college presidents engaged in major struggles with their boards over the degree of control each had. By the late nineteenth century, presidents began to gain the ascendancy in terms of overall leadership. Several factors led to this, including the growing complexity of programs and institutional size. Part-time lay board members simply lacked the detailed knowledge to do more than depend on the president for information and recommendations. Another factor was that, more and more, the presidents played the key role in selecting replacement board members.

Today, boards have an association to support their role as "overseers" of an institution, the Association of Governing Boards of Colleges and Universities (AGB). The association publishes a handbook for new board members. (This is a document well worth a librarian's time to review in order to better understand the board's role in institutional governance.) The book and seminars provided by the association have led to much greater standardization and quality of board practices across the country. It has also helped explain the academy to new members who may not have an in-depth knowledge of all that is involved in today's complex institutions. There is little doubt that governing boards are the keystone in the academy's governance structure and that they play a critical role in interpreting the institution to society, as well as in providing the mechanism for society's voice being heard within higher education.

What is the keystone role? It is the governing board's power, authority, and responsibility to establish policies and serve as the last "court of appeal" for the institution. (Our earlier example, relating to the changing of the library's classification system, is an example of both the final authority of the board as well as the tensions that can arise when the board becomes involved in institutional operational issues. Although the library system staff supported the move, several faculty members had objected to the change and voiced their concern to the overseers.)

Some years ago, James L. Fisher (1991), a retired university president, outlined the following 13 board responsibilities that still apply to today's boards:

- Appointing the president (perhaps its most important obligation)
- Evaluating the institution (this is in addition to any accreditation evaluations)
- Assessing board policies (this should occur every four to five years)
- Supporting the president (an important but delicate task, as the board's duty is to the institution as a whole)
- Reviewing the president's performance (second only to their appointing powers)
- Reviewing the institutional mission (boards should direct this be done every four to five years)
- Reviewing and approving long-range plans (review, adjust, approve)
- Overseeing educational programs (guide but do not direct)
- Ensuring financial solvency (make the final hard fiscal decisions, set tuition rates, monitor endowment)
- Preserving institutional independence (help resist undue outside influence)
- Representing both the institution and the public (a difficult balancing process at times)
- Serving as a court of appeal (the last stop before the civil legal system)
- Assessing its performance (hire an outside agent to assess the board's performance) (pp. 93–105)

Thinking about this list, you can imagine just how often boards are caught in the middle, sometimes between the school and society, sometimes between the president and the faculty, sometimes between students and their parents and the institution, and sometimes between any of these groups and stakeholders. Boards of public institutions probably have the greatest difficulty in being the bridge between the institution and state/society. Often they are asked or expected to reflect the current "political will" rather than sound educational practice. Obviously shifting political wills can cause serious challenges for degree programs.

One example of the complexity in a state system in terms of governing boards is California. Within the state are three separate multicampus institutions of higher education, each with their own governing structure. First are the regents of the University of California (UC), who oversee 10 campuses. The board consists of 26 members, 18 of whom are gubernatorial appointees serving terms of 12 years:

- 18 regents are appointed by the governor for 12-year terms.
- 1 is a student appointed by the regents to a one-year term.
- 7 are ex officio members—the governor, lieutenant governor, speaker of the assembly, superintendent of public instruction, president and vice president of the alumni associations of UC, and the UC president.
- In addition, 2 faculty members—the chair and vice chair of the academic council— sit on the board as nonvoting members. (Regents of the University of California, 2009)

Second are the trustees of the California State Universities (CSU). They have 23 campuses under their purview. CSU's governing body has 25 members and meets 7 times a year. "Board meetings allow for communication among the trustees, chancellor, campus presidents, executive committee members of the statewide Academic Senate, representatives of the California State Student Association, and officers of the statewide Alumni Council" (California State University, 2009).

Last is the board of governors of the California Community Colleges, which has 72 community college districts (each with a board of trustees) and 110 campuses. The following statement directly addresses governance:

> The 17-member Board, appointed by the state's Governor, formally interacts with state and federal officials and other state organizations. The Board of Governors selects a Chancellor for the system. The Chancellor, through a formal process of consultation, brings recommendations to the Board, which has the legislatively granted authority to develop and implement policy for the colleges. Additionally, each of the 72 community college districts in the state has a locally elected Board of Trustees, responsive to local community needs and charged with the operations of the local colleges. The governance system of the California Community Colleges is one which uses processes of "shared governance." (California Community Colleges Chancellor's Office, 2010)

These examples illustrate just how complex governance is and how the "political will" might become a major factor for public higher education institutions. It probably is also a clear reason why decision-making times tend to be long, as the examples describe only the top level of the total process.

One of the ongoing criticisms or concerns about governing boards is their membership. Earlier, we mentioned that the first U.S. boards were members of the clergy, then laypeople (alumni and other professionals), and now it is not uncommon for the majority of members to be businesspeople. Two significant advantages of having businesspeople on the board are that such people often, either personally or through their contacts, provide financial support for the institution as well as much-needed political support. They can also assist in decisions regarding the curriculum when it comes to understanding what the labor markets are seeking in new employees.

As the emphasis on becoming a diverse institution has grown, so has the pressure to diversify board membership. This brings with it the challenge for such new members to achieve a balance between the expectations of serving as advocates on certain issues and the broad needs of the institution and its mission.

The growth in the number of businesspeople on the boards also has generated complaints, especially from faculty and staff, that these members try to impose a "corporate model" on the institution that is counter to shared governance. Finding the correct balance between being cost aware and cost efficient is a challenge. Also, business-dominated boards can fall into practicing micromanagement. Some examples of micromanaging that arise fairly often are the following:

- Appointments and promotions (overriding faculty recommendations)
- Student recruiting strategies and tactics (second-guessing professionals, pushing to change the mix—more males, less this or that)
- Course approval (rejecting a course approved by the faculty committee)
- Approval of public programs (rejecting a speaker or group based on disapproval of the presumed message/orientation)
- Rejecting institutionally generated reallocation plans
- Changing salary adjustments (overriding distribution plans made the administration)

> **From the Authors**
>
> One of Alire's former institutions experienced a quasi-vote of no confidence from the university faculty regarding one of the board of regents who happened to be a businessman. The faculty maintained that this particular board member tried to micromanage and displayed an overt disdain for faculty and disregard for faculty governance. What the faculty voted on was a resolution asking the governor to withdraw his nomination of the regent to another term on the board.

Most boards find the middle ground and provide the help/guidance/voice that keeps the institution moving forward without unduly influencing operations. Furthermore, most boards understand that effective governance and management of an institution represent a means to an end and are not ends in themselves. They know that the central purpose is scholarship and learning. Evidence of satisfactory progress/achievement is satisfaction enough for the vast majority of boards.

THOSE WHO ADMINISTER

The list of those who administer within the institution is long and somewhat complex and is an area where governance can become muddled. There is, of course, the chief executive officer or president to whom several vice presidents—of academic affairs, student affairs, or business affairs, for example—may report to assist in the daily operations. Below this level on the academic side are deans, department chairs, and directors of centers or institutes, for example. Also located at this level are directors of various support services such as financial aid, admissions, and facilities. The academic library can fall into various levels depending on the organizational structure of the institution. Some heads of libraries hold associate vice provost or associate vice chancellor positions within academic affairs where they and their faculty maintain full faculty status. Similar to these titles are library heads, who serve as academic deans with library faculty, also holding full faculty status. Usually, positions such as university librarian or library director oversee librarians who have professional rank and not faculty status.

Until the late nineteenth century, college presidents acted as the interpreters and justifiers of governing board actions to their faculties and students. That role reversed in the twentieth century and continued that way until just before the twenty-first century began. Today, most presidents are being asked to fill both roles as boards appear to be more activist, and institutional personnel see this as counter to collegial governance.

During the first hundred plus years of U.S. higher education, there was little concern about institutional governance. The reason was, more often than not, that there were just the governing board and the president, who was also the sole instructor, governing the school. In many ways the early college president was *the* college. His character became a reflection of the college. However, as the student body grew so did the number of teachers, which in turn made administration and governance more complex. The two groups also began to assert their traditional roles in campus governance (more about this later in this chapter).

After the U.S. Civil War, new administrators began to appear on campus, adding another layer of complexity. In the mid-1870s, Harvard's President Eliot appointed a faculty member "dean." This appointment opened a floodgate of new deans and department chairs—deans of faculty, deans of colleges, deans of student affairs, and deans of libraries, for example.

From the Authors

As you might expect, more administrators leads to increased personnel costs, as many of these individuals did/do not teach and, in some cases, are not qualified to teach but can administer a campus program. The growth of this practice during the past century has not diminished; for example, when Evans started working at a university in 1988 there were 45 full-time administrators not counting department chairs. Upon his retirement in 2005, that number had grown to 68. Such growth is one of the factors that lead to the tuition increases that always seem to exceed the general inflation rate for the country.

For much of the nineteenth and first half of the twentieth centuries some of the presidents gained a reputation of being "giants" in higher education, at least by their peers and society at large. (Not many of those who had that reputation were popular with the faculty, staff, and students at their institutions as they tended to be highly autocratic and made little effort to even appear to consult on decision making or policy issues.) Starting in the early 1900s, faculty began to reassert a little of their traditional role after the American Association of University Professors (AAUP) became active. Today, for many presidents, their primary role is to serve as a mediator between the many stakeholders in higher education. The major stakeholders are the following:

- Governing board members
- Faculty
- Students
- Staff
- Parents of students
- Alumni
- Society at large (including the local community)
- Government bodies (local, state, and national)
- Accreditation agencies
- Business interests
- Donors
- Other higher education institutions

Certainly these groups overlap somewhat, but you can imagine where a president might encounter very different views on the part of two or more of these groups on an important institutional issue.

As mediators, presidents seek to maintain peace between the factions (or at least not have open warfare) and foster progress. Of the two, progress is more essential, so eventually a side will be taken, at least in the view of those who do not like the decision, even when the president's position is actually some compromise between the various views. The faculty's ultimate option for expressing their unhappiness is voting no confidence in the president. Other stakeholders have various modes for voicing their displeasure. What presidents need, and sometimes do not have, is ready access to each group; a fair opportunity to present his or her views in each forum; a chance to contrast reality with illusion(s); and, on occasions, a chance to argue for the position of reason as she or he sees it. (Essentially the foregoing is a capsulated version of what all of those involved in collegial governance ought to have. These factors do not ensure winning but are generally seen as providing an evenhanded opportunity to make a case for or against something.)

In light of these pressures, you probably would not be surprised to learn presidential tenures have been decreasing in length. Until well into the twentieth century, presidents had almost lifetime tenures, assuming they wanted to stay. Certainly presidents were dismissed, but that was a rare and highly notable event. Today, the average tenure is 5 years or less, and anything longer than 15 is exceptionally long. As the environment has become more complex, burnout is probably the major factor rather than board, faculty, or student displeasure with performance (Kerr, 1991).

Earlier, we noted that governments were one of the stakeholders in higher education. Although presidents are not the only individuals within the institution who must address governmental interests/concerns, as the primary administrators they are the lead persons as far as government agencies are concerned. We touched on the state role earlier, and the federal level also has a surprising amount of influence on institutional policy. First, when an institution accepts federal funding (such as research grants or student aid), it must abide by federal regulations or lose the funds, including the employment regulations that come into play.

Perhaps the most obvious area of government interest that has been in the popular press for some time is student body gender and diversity and any admission policies related to an effort to increase such diversity. One example occurred when the Department of Justice filed a suit against Virginia Military Institute because it was an all-male school. Another example was exemplified in the long-running legal actions relating to the University of Michigan's diversity efforts. The Department of Justice also filed a suit against a number of prestigious colleges and universities because of a "conspiracy" to coordinate tuition rates and financial aid packages. These are but a few examples. If you read the *Chronicle of Higher Education*, something we highly recommend that all academic librarians do on a regular basis, you will encounter fairly frequent stories about some area of an institution(s) that has become of interest to some federal agency.

If these factors are not enough to cause burnout, the list of skills, talents, and abilities that governing boards seek in their presidential candidates highlights the nearly impossible job today's college and university presidents face. The following list also reflects many of the interests or expectations other stakeholders have for the president:

- Be a distinguished scholar with classroom and research credentials.
- Have solid local and national political connections while being politically savvy and able to work with all political points of view.
- Be highly visible on campus and accessible to everyone associated with the school.
- Be in attendance at *all* institutional functions from governing board meetings to student picnics as well as have a presence at any off-campus activity that may have an institutional implication or value.
- Be able to address all alumni expectations no matter how contradictory some might be.
- Be supportive of high academic standards and keep retention rates high.
- Be an advocate of premier athletic programs.
- Be an exceptional fund-raiser.

- Be the leader in collegial governance.
- Be an advocate for research excellence while maintaining tight fiscal reins on institutional expenditures.

The list could go on and on, but this list outlines many of the expectations placed on new presidents. Is it any wonder that presidents feel pulled in all directions and know that by setting priorities, which they must do, they will likely upset some people? Also, it is not surprising that people on campus wonder from time to time why the president has not been seen on the campus recently. It also suggests why presidential tenures keep getting shorter and shorter. Today's presidents find themselves as the fulcrum between various constituencies, internal and external, with differing values, interests, priorities, and perspectives.

Sometimes the campus library is fortunate to have a president who has an interest in the library and does all she or he can to support its activities. At other times, a president has no interest in the library but does nothing to block library support. On rare occasions, there is a president who views the library as a major "black hole" that pulls in vast sums of money with no real return and blocks efforts to increase funding (and even may make efforts to reduce funds). Each situation requires a different approach from the library as well as an understanding of campus politics and governance. The head of the library has to understand not only the politics of the institution at all levels but also has to delve into those politics as the primary advocate for the library in efforts to influence decision makers, their peers, and faculty/student governance.

On the other hand, librarians can play an important advocacy role articulating the value of the campus library and their value as well. These frontline librarians have access to a multitude of campus faculty and students that the head of the library doesn't have through areas such as reference services, department liaisons, and information literacy classes. Providing new library employees with an orientation to the library and the campus can help emphasize the fact that all of the library staff are essential pieces in the library's marketing and advocacy activities, which can pay dividends in the long run.

THOSE WHO DO

At the doing level there are three primary campus groups who expect or want a voice in institutional matters: faculty, students, and staff. How loud each voice is varies from institution to institution and its philosophy regarding collegial governance. The very origin of collegial governance resides at this level. It goes back to the time when students and faculty made the decisions and there were no administrators, much less governing boards. How well they did that work, at least in laying a solid foundation for higher education, is reflected in a little known fact. If you go back to the sixteenth century in Western Europe and look at what institutions existed then and still exist in the twenty-first century, you would identify 66 organizations. Leading the list are the Catholic Church and the Lutheran Church followed by the Parliaments on the Isle of Man and Iceland and then 62 universities. This is a rather impressive record for a governance model that many people believe is most ineffective.

While the presidents, vice presidents, deans, and directors provide the institutional administrative structure, a variety of bodies (senates, councils, committees, and departments, for example) at the "doing" level that also may play a role in decision making and institutional operations. Some suggest, as did William Bergquist (1992), that there is a dual culture at most institutions—managerial and collegial. Generally speaking, those at the doing level (collegial) have a louder voice on educational (courses, requirements, etc.) matters than they do on managerial issues such as finances (managerial). Gerald Kissler (1997) noted:

> At large campuses faculty have fewer interactions with administrators. Presidents seem distant; there are fewer opportunities to build trust and mutual respect. Also, faculty governance on large campuses operates through representative bodies rather than town meetings. Even if crisis conditions cause the president to call a campus meeting, many will not attend and the nature of a large gathering will lead to more of a presentation of information than an open discussion. (p. 457)

If those who do have little influence over budgets and allocations, in what areas do their voices matter? Some of the typical areas are courses, degree requirements, admission standards, distance education, and diversity issues.

The most common forum for voicing thoughts/communicating views to the administration is the senate or council (faculty, staff, and students). As the prior paragraph stated, most of such bodies are elected representatives from the group(s) in question. (Note: This is the formal side of the process; the informal side also plays a role.) Minor and Tierney (2005) wrote:

> From time to time one hears about a president who receives a vote of no confidence from the campus senate, or a senate that is dissolved by the president. Such cases exemplify campuses with troubled governance. However, dramatic examples of this kind are rare. The larger problem pertaining to shared governance rests with the ability to make decisions intended to improve the quality of the institution that have the substantial input and support of multiple groups of rather sporadically involved or disengaged contingencies. (p. 138)

One reasonably sound method for achieving such ongoing input and support is to have representative bodies that meet on a regular basis with senior administrators. We should note that most of the literature on senates or councils focuses on the faculty; however, the process and issues apply to all such bodies, including any council(s) that exists in the library.

From the Authors

Academic libraries can and are influenced by senates or councils. One obvious way is through a library advisory committee consisting of faculty and students. Such committees are often a "standing committee" of the faculty senate. (We explore such bodies in more detail in a later chapter.)

Evans had a library committee that required that all of its actions deemed "significant" (most matters they voted on fell into that category) had to go the faculty senate for ratification. (We mention student representation on this committee in the chapter on students.) He also dealt with a request from the staff senate to have a seat on the committee. Not too surprisingly, this request took time to grant as well as requiring several appearances before the faculty senate to gain their approval. The faculty senate also granted the librarians a seat on that body, although librarians did not have faculty status. They also were allowed to run for "at large" seats. Often, the librarians held two seats. Sometimes excellent library service pays off in unexpected ways.

Relative to faculty governance, Alire's library faculty experience at the two ARL libraries she headed included librarians who held full faculty status within the university and went through a promotion and tenure process. They not only served and chaired key university faculty committees, but they also served as presidents of the university faculty senate.

James Minor (2004) published a study that identified four models of faculty senates—functional, influential, ceremonial, and subverted. Although his research focused on faculty senates, his models apply to all such academic bodies.

Functional senates, according to Minor, operate in a manner that reflects the interests of the disciplines to which its members belong. While such groups do, at times, address campuswide concerns/interests, generally they tend to concentrate on self-interest topics. As in all of Minor's models, institutional by-laws govern the group's activities, and such groups tend to have a number of standing committees, such as a courses and program committee. Often membership on such committees is a function of being a friend of a member of the senate's executive committee. Membership is tightly held to faculty only. Staff committees of this type tend to focus on salary, benefits, and working conditions, while faculty groups are particularly interested in faculty appointments, promotions and tenure, and curriculum issues. Needless to say, student groups are primarily concerned with tuition rates and fees and housing/food services. Thus, you can see groups falling into this model may reflect Minor and Tierney's sporadically and disengaged category, which adds to the difficulty of having true collegial governance. Minor (2004) wrote that such groups "are not particularly assertive and usually do not set their own agendas. Instead, they respond to the initiatives and actions of the administration or issues that arise from the environment" (p. 349).

Influential bodies have and employ real governance power. They come about through an institutional tradition/culture that legitimizes their authority. Generally no one with administrative responsibilities may be a member of the body. With their greater power, such groups tend to have a broad-based campus focus and often are initiators of discussions and debates about issues. "These senates usually maintain collaborative rather than confrontational relationships with the administration" (Minor, 2004, p. 351).

Ceremonial senates, as the name suggests, carry little weight when it comes to campus decision making. Often these bodies come into existence where there are strong senior administrators who believe that actions/decisions must be taken swiftly. They are rarely created as ceremonial but evolve into this role over time, in part due to lack of interest on the part of faculty, staff, and students in governance. As a result, the administration takes on more of the authority and power to make decisions. Occasionally a very strong president or governing board that ignores input from others generates an atmosphere that leads to ceremonial bodies. Minor wrote that such groups are "a place where the faculty go to discuss what they think is going on or talk about decisions after they have been made" (Minor, 2004, p. 351).

You might wonder why an institution would bother trying to maintain a ceremonial governance body. There are probably a number of reasons for doing so. However, one major reason is accreditation. Regional accreditation agencies all address governance in their standards. For example, the Middle States Association has, as one of its broad standards, a statement (standard 4) that reads in part:

> The Commission on Higher Education expects a climate of shared governance in which all constituencies (such as faculty, administration, staff, students, and governing boards, as determined by each institution) involved in carrying out the institution's mission and goals participate in the governance in a manner appropriate to the institution. ("Regional Accreditation Standards," 2008, p. 98)

As part of its accreditation process, the Western Association employs a series of accountability questions ("a culture of evidence") that it expects the institution to answer with data or proof of how it addresses them. One of the association's questions is, "How does the institution interpret and put into practice shared governance through appropriate faculty participation in planning and decision making in pursuit of the institution's purpose and character" ("Regional Accreditation Standards," p. 102).

Minor's final model (subverted) is the least desirable but one you may well encounter sometime during your career. A common circumstance that leads to such bodies is that the informal networks dominate the decision-making process. Essentially the formal structure, which does exist, does not carry enough weight to overcome the views of a few influential people (senior faculty and staff) who are not members of the senate/council.

> **From the Authors**
>
> Evans served on several Western Association visiting teams. He knows from two such experiences that the commission interprets the question to include staff, students, governing boards, and other interested parties although the question of shared governance mentions only faculty. Also based on such experiences, he knows that the issue of governance, including library governance, can have a negative impact on the team's assessment of the institution.

In one sense, shared governance and feedback exists, but it takes place outside of the formal structure and, often, does not reflect the majority view on the issue. As Minor (2004) noted, "Subverted senates usually suffer from negative cultural and communicative aspects that affect their role in campus decision making" (p. 353).

Regardless of where the senate/council falls on the continuum from functional to subverted, they are an integral part of campus governance. The tradition of faculty and student voices being most important when it comes educational decision making goes back to the very beginning of higher education.

CONCLUDING THOUGHTS ON CAMPUS GOVERNANCE

At the core of campus governance are three fundamental issues: decision making, resource acquisition, and resource allocation. The latter two might be subsets of decision making; however, these two can become volatile in a serious emergency, making shared governance almost a must. How to handle them in a timely and effective manner is the challenge.

"Those who do" often view administrators as generating an incredible amount of red tape, constraining creativity, being concerned only about keeping costs down. They also often think of administrators as a source of "outside" pressure(s) to alter the activities in undesirable ways. On the other hand, those who administer may from time to time view those who do as totally unconcerned about costs and where the money may come from, unwilling to respond to legitimate requests for accountability, willing to change only under the most dire of circumstances, and unable to grasp the fact the supply of money is not limitless. Is it any wonder why campus governance is contentious from time to time?

One interesting aspect of shared governance is authority. From an administrative perspective, authority is predicated on control and coordination by supervisors. Professional authority is predicated on autonomy and individual knowledge. These two types of campus authority also add to the challenges of campus governance. Thinking back to your basic management coursework you will recall five types of power in society—coercive, reward, legitimate, referent, and expert (see Evans and Ward, 2007).

A quick review of the five types of power includes the following. For senior managers in higher education, including those in libraries, any use of coercive power—except in the worst of circumstances—is likely to lead to serious problems such as votes of no confidence. Even too much use of reward power can be detrimental over time. Most faculty and staff accept a modicum of legitimate power/authority use. For example, department heads have the power to set schedules, and library directors can commit their libraries to certain obligations in a consortium. (However, the wise holder of legitimate power will consult as much as possible before making a decision.) Referent power arises from others accepting the power position because of who the holder is. Expert power resides in a person's special knowledge or skill. Referent and expert power are the stuff from which true collegial governance is made.

Another factor that confuses the governance picture is that most professionals have a dual orientation. Sometimes the orientation is described as a continuum with cosmopolitan at one end and local at the other. A professional with a strong cosmopolitan orientation is first and foremost discipline/subject committed with the institution a distant second when it comes to issues that cut across both sides. You can easily tell a professional's orientation by the manner in which they describe their employment. "I teach or work at college X" is a local response. "I'm a professor of geology at university Y" is a typical response of a cosmopolitan. Does a person's orientation matter? It matters a great deal, especially when it comes to trying to balance professional and institutional needs.

Another factor that muddles the picture is status, prestige, and rank. One example is where a Nobel Prize–winning professor has greater influence within the institution among other faculty than does the president or most members of the governing board. Thus, it is not always a matter of seniority or title that matters the most. This is rather different than what you encounter in for-profit organizations.

One closing thought on the topic is offered by J. Victor Baldridge (1971), who suggested that political models are more useful for understanding campus governance than are business decision-making models. He also debunked the myth that colleges and universities are primarily rational decision-making organizations and that a formal process or structure determines how decisions are made.

KEY POINTS TO REMEMBER

- Academic governance is a complex process with many stakeholders who wish to have a voice in that process.
- Understanding this process is a key factor in how effective the librarians and academic library are in supporting the institution's mission.
- Some of the most significant stakeholders are trustees, administrators, faculty, students and parents, staff, and society.
- Governing boards are the final authority on institutional matters.
- Boards can and do take an interest in small operational matters from time to time but generally leave such matters to faculty/staff to handle.
- Boards have some obligation to provide society's voice to the institution, which can be a challenge at times as it must also take responsibility for maintaining the institution's mission.

- A board's foremost duty is to select and evaluate the performance of the institution's president.
- Presidents have the difficult role of explaining board actions to faculty, staff, and students as well as of explaining the viewpoints, needs, and desires of those groups to the board. At times of high tension between board and people within the institution, the challenge is especially great.
- Faculty members holding a part-time administrative assignment, such as department chair, have challenges in deciding what their long-term goals are—teaching or administration.
- Senates or councils for faculty, staff, and students can play a significant role in campus governance, if they make the effort.
- Prestige, status, and rank all play a role in governance and it is not always the senior rank or title that matter.

REFERENCES

Baldridge, J. Victor. 1971. *Power and conflict in the university*. New York: John Wiley.

Bergquist, William H. 1992. *Four cultures of the academy*. San Francisco, CA: Jossey-Bass.

California Community Colleges Chancellor's Office. 2010. Board of governors. Available: www.cccco.edu/SystemOffice/BoardofGovernors/tabid/190/Default.aspx (accessed March 21, 2010).

California State University. 2009. Board of trustees. Available: www.calstate.edu/bot (accessed March 21, 2010).

Evans, G. Edward, and Patricia Layzell Ward. 2007. *Management basics for information professionals*. 2nd ed. New York: Neal-Schuman.

Fish, Stanley. 2007. Shared governance: Democracy is not an education idea. *Change* 39, no. 2: 2–13.

Fisher, James L. 1991. *The board and the president*. New York: American Council on Education/ Macmillan.

Kerr, Clark. 1991. The new race to be Harvard, or Berkeley, or Stanford. *Change* 23, no. 3: 8–15.

Kezar, Adrianna, and Peter Eckel. 2004. Meeting today's governance challenges. *Journal of Higher Education* 75, no. 4: 371–399.

Kissler, Gerald. 1997. Who decides which budgets to cut? *Journal of Higher Education* 63, no. 5: 427–459.

Mills, Michael R. 2007. Stories of politics and policy. *Journal of Higher Education* 78, no. 2: 162–187.

Minor, James T. 2004. Understanding faculty senates. *Review of Higher Education* 27, no. 3: 343–363.

Minor, James T., and William Tierney. 2005. Dangers of deference: A case of polite governance. *Teachers College Record* 107, no. 1: 137–156.

Prof. Melvil Dewey resigns. 1899. Secretary of the State Board of Regents of the university gives up his office. *New York Times*, December 23.

Regents of the University of California. 2009. About the regents. Available: www.universityofcalifornia .edu/regents/about.html (accessed March 21, 2010).

Regional accreditation standards concerning academic freedom and faculty role in governance. 2008. *Academe* 94, no. 2: 98–103.

Schuetz, Pam. 1999. *Shared governance in community colleges*. ERIC–ED–433077. Available: www.ericdigest.org/2000-2/shared.htm.

Simplicio, Joseph S. 2006. Shared governance. *Education* 126, no. 4: 763–768.

LAUNCHING PAD

Birnbaum, Robert. 1989. The latent organizational functions of the academic senate: Why senates don't work but will not go away. *Journal of Higher Education* 60, no. 4: 423–443.

Bleiklie, Ivar, and Maurice Kogan. 2007. Organization and governance of universities. *Higher Education Policy* 20, no. 4: 477–493.

Bolin, Mary K. 2008. Librarian status at U.S. research libraries. *Journal of Academic Librarianship* 34, no. 5: 416–424.

Del Favero, Marietta, and Nathaniel Bray. 2005. The faculty-administrator: Partners in prospective governance. *Scholar-Practitioner Quarterly* 3, no. 1: 53–72.

Dixon, Keith, and David Coy. 2007. University governance. *Higher Education* 54, no. 2: 267–291.

Duderstadt, James J. 2000. *A university for the 21st century*. Ann Arbor, MI: University of Michigan Press.

Gumport, Patricia. 2000. *Academic governance: New light on old issues*. Washington, DC: Association of Governing Boards of Universities and Colleges.

Hamilton, Kendra. 2001. VSU president offers olive branch to faculty. *Black Issues in Higher Education* 18, no. 14: 10, 14.

Hamilton, Neil. 2002. *Academic ethics problems and materials on professional conduct and shared governance*. Westport, CT: American Council on Education.

Honan, James, and Damtew Teferra. 2001. The U.S. academic profession. *Higher Education* 41, nos. 1/2: 183–203.

King, Roger P. 2007. Governance and accountability in higher education. *Higher Education* 53, no. 4: 411–430.

McLendon, Michael, Russ Deaton, and James Hearn. 2007. The enactment of reform in state governance of higher education. *Journal of Higher Education* 78, no. 6: 645–675.

Miles, Jennifer M., Michael T. Miller, and Daniel P. Nadler. 2008. Student governance: Toward effectiveness and the ideal. *College Student Journal* 42, no. 4: 1061–1069.

Morphew, Christopher. 1999. Challenges facing shared governance within the college. *New Directions for Higher Education* 27, no. 1: 71–79.

New Directions for Community Colleges. 2008. A special issue on governance, no. 141.

Pearce, Joshua M., and Christopher Uhl. 2003. Getting it done. *Planning for Higher Education* 31, no. 3: 53–61.

Tierney, William, and James T. Minor. 2003. *Challenges for governance*. Los Angeles, CA: University of Southern California.

Trakman, Leon. 2008. Modeling university governance. *Higher Education Quarterly* 62, nos.1/2: 63–83.

Part III

Campus and Library Commonalities

The chapters in this section cover some the major common areas of concern across a campus. Chapter 7, "Funding," addresses the general revenue and expenditure streams for an academic institution as well as the basics of budgeting with an emphasis on the library. Chapter 8, "Facilities," describes the issues of planning, maintaining, and operating a campus facility with a special emphasis on the library aspects. Chapter 9, "Technology," likewise examines the basics of planning and maintaining technology for both the campus and the library. Chapter 10, "The Academy, Accreditation, and Accountability," looks at the issue of how the institution and library must meet society's growing demand for accountability and value for the support given to higher education.

Chapter 7

Funding

Ironically, while twentieth-century citizens witnessed a democratization of higher education as it ceased to remain the prerogative of a wealthy elite, increases in the price of attaining a college degree threaten to reverse this trend.

—Joseph Losco and Brian Fife (2000)

New information technologies and the organizational efficiencies of privatization can lower the cost of producing higher education enough that for-profit schools can compete with existing nonprofit and public colleges and universities by offering students a better deal and still make a profit.

—Gordon Winston (1997)

Money, or the lack thereof, has always been an issue for higher education institutions. As we drafted this chapter, the economic news was depressing, and most nonprofit educational institutions, from elementary schools to the most prestigious universities, were facing serious financial challenges. Where does all of the money go? In the following sections, we will look at expenditures and revenues for both nonprofit and profit schools. Clearly, understanding institutional finances and how and where funds come from and are spent is important to academic libraries. We will also explore the budget process from an academic library perspective.

You might well wonder how it is that there is so much trouble for nonprofit colleges and universities while for-profit institutions don't appear to have a similar problem. In fact, one of the largest for-profit institutions, University of Phoenix, is so profitable that it has paid to have its name attached to one of the National Football League stadiums. We don't have a definitive answer; however, in this chapter we will explore some of the factors that do make a difference.

Higher education's financial activities are complex. Part of that complexity arises from the multiplicity of revenue sources. Its expenditures are equally varied, and there is only a modicum of connectivity between the income streams and expenditures categories. Needless to say, the diversity of institutional types adds another layer of intricacy to sorting through where funds come from and how they are spent. Yet another issue, mentioned previously, is the presence of for-profit and nonprofit institutions essentially producing the same "product."

Institutional finances address three major educational policy issues: quality, access, and efficiency. There is a rather widely held view within the academy, at the least on the nonprofit side, that there is a positive correlation between the level of funding and the quality of education provided. (We are not certain that this is actually proven to be the case. Certainly there is a relationship, but how strong it may be seems to be an open question.) Clearly there is a connection between cost and who may gain access to higher education. Efficiency has not always been a hallmark of academic activities. Finding a balance between effectiveness and efficiency is always a challenge; and efficiency, at least in the past, was often ignored by many institutions.

The following questions underlay an institution's financial decisions:

- What is the best ratio of students to faculty?
- What is the best ratio of faculty to other staff?
- What level of student aid/tuition discount is best?

For public institutions, there is the question of in- or out-of-state students and what, if any, difference there should in their tuition. Ultimately, the institutions must wrestle with the answer to the question of who pays or should pay, as Bruce Johnstone (2005) noted, should it be the following:

- Students and their parents?
- Taxpayers?
- Philanthropists?

Johnstone also suggested two other thorny questions related to costs—how much education should society underwrite in some manner, and at what levels of efficiency should education be delivered (p. 370)?

Justin Pope (2008b), an Associated Press educational writer, reported on a biennial survey by the National Center for Public Policy and Higher Education. He noted that the center "hands out Fs for affordability to 49 states, up from 43 two years ago" (p. A1). The survey covers both the nonprofit public and private schools in all Carnegie classifications. Even the significantly lower community college costs were not enough to make the overall state affordability rise to a D, except in the case of California. Without the lower fees at the California community colleges, all 50 states would have received a failing grade.

Pope provided two sets of figures for two states. In 1999–2000, an Illinois family with an undergraduate student paid, on average, 19 percent of the family income on higher education in a public institution; by 2007–2008 that figure had risen to 35 percent. Data from Pennsylvania were even more depressing—in 1999–2000 the percentage was 29 percent, and for 2007–2008 it was 41 percent (p. A6).

HIGHER EDUCATION FINANCES

What is it that makes higher education so expensive? The *Digest of Education Statistics* (DES; U.S. Department of Education, 2008) estimated that an undergraduate at a four-year institution faced an average annual price, just for tuition and room and board, of $11,034 at a public institution and $28,384 at a private institution. Furthermore, between 1996–1997 and 2006–2007 those prices rose 32 percent at publics and 22 percent at privates. As comparison, the consumer price index rose by 28 percent during this same period (p. 363). When you add in books, fees, and other living expenses, the percentage would be even higher.

Although educational costs escalated, the resulting increase in revenue did not keep all of the schools operational. Between 1996–1997 and 2006–2007, 52 four-year institutions closed their doors. The number for two-year colleges was even worse—94 ceased to exist (U.S. Department of Education, 2008, p. 386). Justin Pope (2008a) wrote, "For 15 years, Cascade College in Portland, Ore., struggled to find the fuels that any college needs, students to pay tuition, and donors to help build an endowment.... Late last month, the small Christian college with just 280 students and $4 million in debt announced it would have to shut down at the end of the current year" (p. A6). Although Cascade was his example, the overall story was about the deep economic downturn's potential impact on all schools.

Expenditures

According to DES, U.S. higher education expenditures in 2006–2007 totaled $373 billion (p. 3). This is a great deal of money. Johnstone (2005) provided some perspective on the size of the U.S. higher education endeavors. In 2001–2002, 15.9 million students (undergraduate and graduate) enrolled in 4,197 schools across the country (p. 373). His data suggest that education, at the postsecondary level, is rather important to a large number of individuals who find a way to pay for it.

> **Keep In Mind**
>
> As we wrote this chapter, the economic picture was bleak for everyone, including the academy. One piece of good news for those involved in higher education, in any capacity and in an otherwise dismal economic environment, was the report that college education was a plus during times of layoffs. As Christopher Leonard (2009) wrote, "For one group of workers, the recession hasn't hit quite so hard. Their unemployment rate was nearly half the overall workforce in December. When they do lose jobs, they tend to find work more quickly than others, and they typically have enough savings to survive between jobs. Yes, it still pays to get a college degree" (p. A5).

Although different agencies interested in higher education employ a variety of categories when looking at expenditures and revenue, the DES format has been around for many years, making it easier to compare results over time, thus our focus on their data. DES uses 12 broad categories of expenditure—administration, instruction, organized research, libraries, plant operations, academic support (excluding libraries), extension, scholarships, "other" general expenditures, auxiliary enterprises, and federally funded independent research and development centers.

Table 7.1 (see pp. 122–123) covers expenditures for selected years between 1929–1930 and 1995–1996. The table reveals several interesting facts. One is that in 1929–1930, only 8 percent of the total expenditures went for administration; by 1995–1996 that percentage had risen to 15 percent. During that same period the percentage of funds going to instruction dropped from 44 percent in 1929–1930 to 30 percent in 1995–1996. Furthermore, expenditures on organized research went from 4 percent to just over 9 percent. On the other hand, library funding remained constant at 2 percent. This latter figure seems too low for today's libraries as the cost of e-resources escalate. Of course, 2 percent of today's higher education expenditures is probably more than the total expenditures within U.S. higher education during 1929–1930.

When you look at public institution, data (for example, see Table 7.2, pp. 124–125) are presented slightly differently—there are no separate categories for administration or libraries. (However, a full section of DES is devoted to library data.) Administration is included in "institutional support," and library data are incorporated into "academic support" numbers. Looking at 2004–2005 data, you find that overall institutional support was 8.1 percent. Four-year institutions spent 6.9 percent on this category, while two-year schools spent 13.7 percent. In terms of instruction costs, two year colleges are far ahead of their four-year colleagues (38.7 percent compared to 25.2 percent).

The 2008 edition of DES includes some data on for-profit institutions for the first time. You would not be too surprised to learn such schools are less willing to share

Table 7.1. Academic Institutional Expenditures 1929 to 1996

Current-fund expenditures, by purpose (in thousands of current dollars)

Educational and general expenditures

	Total	Total	Adminis-tration and general expense	Instruction and depart-mental research	Organized research	Libraries	Plant operation and main-tenance	Organized activities related to instructional departments[1]
1	2	3	4	5	6	7	8	9
1929-30....	$507,142	$377,903	$42,633	$221,598	$18,007 [5]	$9,622	$61,061	([6])
1939-40....	674,688	521,990	62,827	280,248	27,266 [5]	19,487	69,612	$27,225 [7]
1949-50....	2,245,661	1,706,444	213,070	780,994	225,341 [5]	56,147	225,110	119,108 [7]
1959-60....	5,601,376	4,685,258	583,224	1,793,320	1,022,353 [5]	135,384	469,943	294,255 [7]
1969-70....	21,043,113	16,845,212	2,627,993	6,883,844	2,144,076	652,596	1,541,698	648,089
1974-75....	35,057,563	27,547,620	4,495,391	11,797,823	3,132,132	1,001,868	2,786,768	1,253,824
1979-80....	56,913,588	44,542,843	7,621,143	18,496,717	5,099,151	1,623,811	4,700,070	2,252,577
1980-81....	64,052,938	50,073,805	8,681,513	20,733,166	5,657,719	1,759,784	5,350,310	2,513,502
1981-82....	70,339,448	54,848,752	9,648,069	22,962,527	5,929,894	1,922,416	5,979,281	2,734,038
1982-83....	75,935,749	58,929,218	10,412,233	24,673,293	6,265,280	2,039,671	6,391,596	3,047,220
1983-84....	81,993,360	63,741,276	11,561,260	26,436,308	6,723,534	2,231,149	6,729,825	3,300,003
1984-85....	89,951,263	70,061,324	12,765,452	28,777,183	7,551,892	2,361,793	7,345,482	3,712,460
1985-86....	97,535,742	76,127,965	13,913,724	31,032,099	8,437,367	2,551,331	7,605,226	4,116,061
1986-87....	105,763,557	82,955,555	15,060,576	33,711,146	9,352,309	2,441,184	7,819,032	5,134,267
1987-88....	113,786,476	89,157,430	16,171,015	35,833,563	10,350,931	2,836,498	8,230,986	5,305,083
1988-89....	123,867,184	96,803,377	17,309,956	38,812,690	11,432,170	3,009,870	8,739,895	5,894,409
1989-90....	134,655,571	105,585,076	19,062,179	42,145,987	12,505,961	3,254,239	9,458,262	6,183,405
1990-91....	146,087,836	114,139,901	20,751,966	45,496,117	13,444,040	3,343,892	10,062,581	6,706,881
1991-92....	156,189,161	121,567,157	21,984,118	47,997,196	14,261,554	3,595,834	10,346,580	6,981,184
1992-93....	165,241,040	128,977,968	23,414,977	50,340,914	15,291,309	3,684,852	10,783,727	7,388,118
1993-94....	173,350.617	136,024,350	24,489,022	52,775,599	16,117,610	3,908,412	11,368,496	7,769,499
1994-95....	182,968,610	144,158,002	25,904,821	55,719,707	17,109,541	4,165,761	11,745,905	8,112,930
1995-96[9]...	190,476,163	151,445,605	27,886,345	57,810,033	17,517,887	4,293,363	12,330,885	9,003,700

—Not available.
[1]Academic support excluding expenditures for libraries.
[2]Generally includes only those expenditures associated with federally funded research and development centers (FFRDCs).
[3]Data for 1929-30 to 1945-46 are based on school-year enrollment.
[4]Constant dollars based on the Consumer Price Index, prepared by the Bureau of Labor Statistics, U.S. Department of Labor, adjusted to a school-year basis.
[5]Expenditures for federally funded research and development centers are included under "Organized research."
[6]Included under "Other current expenditures."
[7]Expenditures for hospitals included under "Organized activities related to instructional departments."
[8]Includes other sponsored programs, which are separately budgeted programs, other than research, which are supported by sponsors outside the institution.

(Columns continued on facing page.)

Table 7.1. Academic Institutional Expenditures 1929 to 1996 *(Columns Continued)*

Current-fund expenditures *(Cont'd.)* Educ. and gen. exp. *(Cont'd.)*							Educational and general expenditures per student in fall enrollment[3]	
Extension and public service	Scholar-ships and fellowships	Other general expendi-tures	Auxiliary enterprises	Independent operations[2]	Hospitals	Other current expenditures	Current dollars	Constant 2006-07 dollars[4]
10	11	12	13	14	15	16	17	18
$24,982	(6)	–	$3,127	(5)	(7)	$126,112	$343	$4,094
35,325	(6)	–	124,184	(5)	(7)	28,514	349	5,103
86,674	(6)	–	476,401	(5)	(7)	62,816	698	6,016
205,595	$172,050	$9,134	916,117	(5)	(7)	–	1,287	8,943
1,362,320 [8]	984,594	–	2,769,276	$757,388	$671,236	–	2,104	11,372
1,097,788	1,449,542	532,485	4,073,590	1,085,590	2,350,763	–	2,694	10,620
1,816,521	2,200,468	732,385	6,485,608	1,127,728	4,757,409	–	3,850	10,123
2,057,770	2,504,525	815,516	7,288,089	1,257,934	5,433,111	–	4,139	9,755
2,203,726	2,684,945	783,854	7,997,632	1,258,777	6,234,287	–	4,433	9,617
2,320,478	2,922,897	856,548	8,614,316	1,406,126	6,986,089	–	4,742	9,864
2,499,203	3,301,673	958,321	9,250,196	1,622,233	7,379,654	–	5,114	10,256
2,861,095	3,670,355	1,015,613	10,012,248	1,867,550	8,010,141	–	5,723	11,046
3,119,533	4,160,174	1,192,449	10,528,303	2,187,361	8,692,113	–	6,216	11,661
3,448,453	4,776,100	1,212,488	11,037,333	2,597,655	9,173,014	–	6,635	12,176
3,786,362	5,325,358	1,317,633	11,399,953	2,822,632	10,406,461	–	6,984	12,307
4,227,323	5,918,666	1,458,397	12,280,063	2,958,962	11,824,782	–	7,415	12,490
4,689,758	6,655,544	1,629,742	13,203,984	3,187,224	12,679,286	–	7,799	12,538
5,076,177	7,551,184	1,707,063	14,272,247	3,349,824	14,325,865	–	8,260	12,591
5,489,298	9,060,000	1,851,393	14,966,100	3,551,592	16,104,313	–	8,466	12,505
5,935,095	10,148,373	1,990,603	15,561,508	3,651,891	17,049,672	–	8,903	12,751
6,242,414	11,238,010	2,115,288	16,429,341	3,387,323	17,509,603	–	9,509	13,276
6,691,485	12,285,328	2,422,524	17,204,917	3,534,332	18,071,359	–	10,096	13,703
7,007,413	13,195,102	2,400,876	17,599,061	3,490,511	17,940,986	–	10,619	14,031

[9]Data for 1995-96 are for degree-granting institutions. The degree-granting classification is very similar to the earlier higher education classification, except that it includes some additional institutions, primarily 2-year colleges, and excludes a few higher education institutions that did not award associate's or higher degrees. (See Guide to Sources for details.)

NOTE: Institutions of higher education were accredited by an agency or association that was recognized by the U.S. Department of Education, or recognized directly by the Secretary of Education. The data in this table reflect limitations of data availability and comparability. Major changes in data collection forms in 1965-66 and 1974-75 cause significant data comparability problems among the three mostly consistent time periods, 1929-30 to 1963-64, 1965-66 to 1973-74, and 1974-75 to 1995-96. The largest problems affect Hospitals, Independent operations, Organized research, Other sponsored programs, Extension and public service, and Scholarships and fellowships. Detail may not sum to totals because of rounding.

SOURCE: U.S. Department of Education, National Center for Education Statistics, *Biennial Survey of Education in the United States,* 1929-30 through 1959-60; Higher Education General Information Survey (HEGIS), "Financial Statistics of Institutions of Higher Education," 1969-70 through 1985-86; and 1986-87 through 1995-96 Integrated Postsecondary Education Data System, "Finance Survey" (IPEDS-F:FY87-96). (This table was prepared July 2007.)

Table 7.2. Public Academic Institutions' Expenditures

Year and type of expense	Expenses (in thousands of current dollars)		
	Total	4-year	2-year
1	2	3	4
2003–04			
Total expenses	$205,068.500	$167,654,408	$37,414,092
Operating expenses	198,321,711	161,575,599	36,746,112
Instruction	56,767,947	42,287,792	14,480,155
Salaries and wages	39,431,881	29,290,396	10,141,485
Research	21,408,497	21,394,125	14,371
Public service	8,981,907	8,293,533	688,374
Academic support	13,613,774	10,904,235	2,709,539
Student services	9,426,787	6,062,776	3,364,011
Institutional support	16,849,813	11,691,429	5,158,384
Operation and maintenance of plant	12,611,040	9,469,470	3,141,570
Depreciation	8,999,651	7,586,394	1,413,258
Scholarships and fellowships[1]	8,172,682	5,123,190	3,049,492
Auxiliary enterprises	15,705,951	13,680,554	2,025,397
Hospitals	18,471,970	18,471,970	0
Independent operations	736,799	711,188	25,612
Other operating expenses and deductions	6,574,893	5,898,943	675,949
Nonoperating expenses	6,746,790	6,078,810	667,980
Interest	2,679,502	2,240,096	439,406
Other nonoperating expenses and deductions	4,067,287	3,838,714	228,574
2004–05			
Total expenses	$215,794,343	$177,191,847	$38,602,497
Operating expenses	208,488,447	170,580,039	37,908,408
Instruction	59,656,806	44,699,891	14,956,915
Salaries and wages	41,026,819	30,555,416	10,471,403
Research	22,550,836	22,528,940	21,896
Public service	9,481,391	8,819,093	662,298
Academic support	14,258,857	11,417,218	2,841,639
Student services	10,042,243	6,475,649	3,566,594
Institutional support	17,454,934	12,151,581	5,303,353
Operation and maintenance of plant	13,578,182	10,287,442	3,290,740
Depreciation	9,592,800	8,136,660	1,456,140
Scholarships and fellowships[1]	8,402,515	5,453,252	2,949,262
Auxiliary enterprises	16,664,085	14,593,314	2,070,771
Hospitals	20,104,812	20,104,812	0
Independent operations	658,166	658,166	0
Other operating expenses and deductions	6,042,819	5,254,019	788,800
Nonoperating expenses	7,305,896	6,611,808	694,089
Interest	2,989,771	2,526,222	463,549
Other nonoperating expenses and deductions	4,316,125	4,085,586	230,539

#Rounds to zero.
[1]Excludes discounts and allowances.

(Columns continued on facing page.)

Table 7.2. Public Academic Institutions' Expenditures *(Columns Continued)*

Percentage distribution of expenses			Expense per full-time-equivalent student in current dollars			Expense per full-time-equivalent student in constant 2006–07 dollars		
Total	4-year	2-year	Total	4-year	2-year	Total	4-year	2-year
5	6	7	8	9	10	11	12	13
100.0	100.0	100.0	$22,192	$30,166	$10,158	$24,344	$33,092	$11,144
96.7	96.4	98.2	21,462	29,072	9,977	23,543	31,892	10,945
27.7	25.2	38.7	6,143	7,609	3,932	6,739	8,347	4,313
19.2	17.5	27.1	4,267	5,270	2,754	4,681	5,781	3,021
10.4	12.8	#	2,317	3,849	4	2,541	4,223	4
4.4	4.9	1.8	972	1,492	187	1,066	1,637	205
6.6	6.5	7.2	1,473	1,962	736	1,616	2,152	807
4.6	3.6	9.0	1,020	1,091	913	1,119	1,197	1,002
8.2	7.0	13.8	1,823	2,104	1,401	2,000	2,308	1,536
6.1	5.6	8.4	1,365	1,704	853	1,497	1,869	936
4.4	4.5	3.8	974	1,365	384	1,068	1,497	421
4.0	3.1	8.2	884	922	828	970	1,011	908
7.7	8.2	5.4	1,700	2,462	550	1,864	2,700	603
9.0	11.0	0.0	1,999	3,324	0	2,193	3,646	0
0.4	0.4	0.1	80	128	7	87	140	8
3.2	3.5	1.8	712	1,061	184	781	1,164	201
3.3	3.6	1.8	730	1,094	181	801	1,200	199
1.3	1.3	1.2	290	403	119	318	442	131
2.0	2.3	0.6	440	691	62	483	758	68
100.0	100.0	100.0	$23,353	$31,882	$10,481	$24,869	$33,952	$11,162
96.6	96.3	98.2	22,562	30,693	10,293	24,027	32,685	10,961
27.6	25.2	38.7	6,456	8,043	4,061	6,875	8,565	4,325
19.0	17.2	27.1	4,440	5,498	2,843	4,728	5,855	3,028
10.5	12.7	0.1	2,440	4,054	6	2,599	4,317	6
4.4	5.0	1.7	1,026	1,587	180	1,093	1,690	191
6.6	6.4	7.4	1,543	2,054	772	1,643	2,188	822
4.7	3.7	9.2	1,087	1,165	968	1,157	1,241	1,031
8.1	6.9	13.7	1,889	2,186	1,440	2,012	2,328	1,533
6.3	5.8	8.5	1,469	1,851	893	1,565	1,971	951
4.4	4.6	3.8	1,038	1,464	395	1,106	1,559	421
3.9	3.1	7.6	909	981	801	968	1,045	853
7.7	8.2	5.4	1,803	2,626	562	1,920	2,796	599
9.3	11.3	0.0	2,176	3,617	0	2,317	3,852	0
0.3	0.4	0.0	71	118	0	76	126	0
2.8	3.0	2.0	654	945	214	696	1,007	228
3.4	3.7	1.8	791	1,190	188	842	1,267	201
1.4	1.4	1.2	324	455	126	345	484	134
2.0	2.3	0.6	467	735	63	497	783	67

NOTE: Degree-granting institutions grant associate's or higher degrees and participate in Title IV federal financial aid programs. Includes data for public institutions reporting data according to the Financial Accounting Standards Board (FASB) questionnaire. Detail may not sum to totals because of rounding.
SOURCE: U.S. Department of Education, National Center for Education Statistics, 2003–04 and 2004–05 Integrated Post-secondary Education Data System, Spring 2004, Spring 2005, and Spring 2006. (This table was prepared July 2007.)

much financial data beyond that required for government needs, such as information provided to the Internal Revenue Service, which is required of any for-profit organization. Data provided (U.S. Department of Education, 2008; see Table 7.3, p. 127) suggest that all such schools expended $8,830,792,000 while having an income of $10,976,154,000. As a group, in 2003–2004 they expended 26.2 percent on instruction, a drop from 35.92 percent in 1998–1999. Data for student services and academic and institutional support were lumped together and represented 64.47 percent of the total expenditures, an increase of 7 percent over the 1998–1999 period. As you would expect, the majority of income was from student tuition and fees.

A somewhat surprising figure was the level of state and local support, which rose from $59,112,000 in 2003–2004 to $63,277,000 in 2004–2005. Their investments, roughly equivalent to endowments for nonprofits, also rose, as did the category labeled "educational activities" (U.S. Department of Education, 2008; see Table 7.4, pp. 128–131).

Turning to nonprofit publics' income/revenue, data are more complex. DES divides the revenue into three broad categories: operating, non-operating, and "other" (U.S. Department of Education, 2008; see Table 7.5, pp. 132–135). Within the operating category are tuition/fees, grants/contracts, sales and services of auxiliary enterprises, sales and services of hospitals, independent operations, and "other operating revenue." Non-operating income includes appropriations from federal, state, and local governments, non-operating grants (funds that supplement non-instructional activities) from government agencies, gifts, investment income, and "other revenues and additions." Obviously, the public institutions receive the largest amounts of government appropriations; however, private schools do receive such funds, primarily for use in student aid programs. Such amounts are a small percentage of the private nonprofit schools' income—14.06 percent of the total income for 2005–2006 came from the federal government, 1.05 percent from the state, and only 0.35 percent from local jurisdictions. As you would expect, two-year institutions did much better in terms of state and local funding than did the four-year institutions. The primary reason for this is that community colleges basically are totally dependent on state and local funds.

"Other revenues and additions" income almost always relate to capital needs (generally new or renovation of buildings) and increases from endowment funds. Not surprisingly, private nonprofit programs have the largest percentage of endowment income (roughly 20 percent on average). Public universities and colleges only see about 2 percent of their income arising from endowments.

Needless to say, academic libraries have a vital interest in the health of institutional finances. Until relatively recently, approximately the past 30 years, the library was often viewed as the campus's "bottomless pit/black hole" when it came to funding. Today there is at least one other such pit at most institutions—that of computing services.

Expenditure Categories

Let's explore some of the expenditure categories. Without doubt, the largest expense category is salaries. Overall salaries and benefits account for well over half of all the institutional costs. The same is true for academic libraries. Salaries and collection development funds generally account for about 80 percent of the library's total operating budget, which leaves very little for all the other activities. At some community colleges, salaries represent 85 percent or more of the total. Frequently, people (especially young people just starting their careers) do not think of benefits as part of their compensation

Table 7.3. For-Profit Academic Institutions' Expenditures

Year and type of institution	Total	Instruction	Research and public service	Student services, academic and inst. support	Auxiliary enterprise[1]	Net grant aid to students[2]	Other
1	2	3	4	5	6	7	8
All institutions			*In thousands of current dollars*				
1998-99[3]	$3,153,591	$1,132,766	$27,060	$1,823,453	$135,398	$34,913	–
1999-2000....	3,846,246	1,171,732	24,738	2,041,594	144,305	26,278	$437,599
2000-01........	4,235,781	1,310,054	22,896	2,337,151	181,243	43,788	340,649
2001-02........	5,087,292	1,517,389	16,632	2,977,225	213,195	23,283	339,567
2002-03[4]	6,110,378	1,747,725	17,987	3,670,218	240,380	36,031	398,037
2003-04........	7,364,012	1,883,733	8,606	4,592,730	249,472	56,467	573,004
2004-05........	8,830,792	2,313,895	7,583	5,693,200	269,883	54,819	491,411
4-year							
1998-99[3]......	1,484,139	499,337	6,703	876,636	81,411	20,052	–
1999-2000....	2,022,622	595,976	4,393	1,104,001	92,071	11,805	214,377
2000-01........	2,414,655	726,328	4,878	1,385,095	113,371	18,519	166,465
2001-02........	3,046,929	883,899	3,192	1,842,373	134,740	8,229	174,495
2002-03[4]	3,754,727	1,030,470	5,339	2,337,388	153,528	14,813	213,190
2003-04........	4,821,864	1,143,050	3,705	3,108,697	168,069	32,603	365,740
2004-05........	5,989,792	1,430,196	3,513	4,110,514	180,036	38,639	226,894
2-year							
1998-99[3]	1,669,451	633,429	20,357	946,817	53,987	14,861	–
1999-2000....	1,823,624	575,756	20,345	937,593	52,234	14,473	223,223
2000-01........	1,821,126	583,727	18,019	952,056	67,872	25,269	174,184
2001-02........	2,040,363	633,490	13,440	1,134,853	78,455	15,054	165,071
2002-03[4]	2,355,650	717,255	12,648	1,332,830	86,853	21,218	184,846
2003-04........	2,542,148	740,683	4,901	1,484,033	81,403	23,864	207,264
2004-05........	2,840,999	883,699	4,070	1,582,687	89,846	16,181	264,517
All institutions			*Percentage distribution*				
1998-99[3]	100.00	35.92	0.86	57.82	4.29	1.11	–
1999-2000....	100.00	30.46	0.64	53.08	3.75	0.68	11.38
2000-01........	100.00	30.93	0.54	55.18	4.28	1.03	8.04
2001-02........	100.00	29.83	0.33	58.52	4.19	0.46	6.67
2002-03[4]	100.00	28.60	0.29	60.07	3.93	0.59	6.51
2003-04........	100.00	25.58	0.12	62.37	3.39	0.77	7.78
2004-05........	100.00	26.20	0.09	64.47	3.06	0.62	5.56
4-year							
1998-99[3]	100.00	33.64	0.45	59.07	5.49	1.35	–
1999-2000....	100.00	29.47	0.22	54.58	4.55	0.58	10.60
2000-01........	100.00	30.08	0.20	57.36	4.70	0.77	6.89
2001-02........	100.00	29.01	0.10	60.47	4.42	0.27	5.73
2002-03[4]	100.00	27.44	0.14	62.25	4.09	0.39	5.68
2003-04........	100.00	23.71	0.08	64.47	3.49	0.68	7.59
2004-05........	100.00	23.88	0.06	68.63	3.01	0.65	3.79
2-year							
1998-99[3]	100.00	37.94	1.22	56.71	3.23	0.89	–
1999-2000....	100.00	31.57	1.12	51.41	2.86	0.79	12.24
2000-01........	100.00	32.05	0.99	52.28	3.73	1.39	9.56
2001-02........	100.00	31.05	0.66	55.62	3.85	0.74	8.09
2002-03[4]	100.00	30.45	0.54	56.58	3.69	0.90	7.85
2003-04........	100.00	29.14	0.19	58.38	3.20	0.94	8.15
2004-05........	100.00	31.11	0.14	55.71	3.16	0.57	9.31

–Not available.

[1]Essentially self-supporting operations of institutions that furnish a service to students, faculty, or staff, such as residence halls and food services.
[2]Excludes tuition and fee allowances and agency transactions, such as student awards made from contributed funds or grant funds.
[3]Data imputed using alternative procedures. (See Guide to Sources for details.)

NOTE: Detail may not sum to totals because of rounding.
SOURCE: U.S. Department of Education, National Center for Education Statistics, 1998-99 through 2004-05 Integrated Postsecondary Integrated Postsecondary Education Data System, "Fall Enrollment Survey" (IPEDS-EF:98-99) and "Finance Survey" (IPED-SF:FY99), and Spring 2001 through Spring 2006. (This table was prepared July 2007.)

Table 7.4. Private For-Profit Academic Institutional Income

Year and type of institution	Total revenue and investment return, by source of funds		
	Total	Student tuition and fees (net of allowances)	Federal appropriations, grants, and contracts
1	2	3	4
	In thousands of current dollars		
2003–04			
Total	$8,989,815	$8,049,205	$397,828
4-year	6,016,415	5,489,245	196,945
Doctoral, intensive[1]	52,594	52,594	0
Master's[2]	1,799,726	1,738,389	2,038
Baccalaureate[3]	443,992	411,215	2,552
Specialized institutions[4]	3,720,104	3,287,048	192,355
Art, music, or design	800,129	722,880	22,905
Business and management	364,451	344,272	3,275
Engineering or technology.........	739,318	714,573	2,253
Medical or other health	55,484	44,907	1,406
Other specialized......................	1,760,722	1,460,417	162,516
2-year..	2,973,400	2,559,960	200,883
2004–05			
Total	10,979,154	9,566,692	673,950
4-year	7,692,472	6,864,048	345,810
Doctoral, intensive[1]	79,329	78,887	0
Master's[2]	2,551,021	2,396,116	43,374
Baccalaureate[3]	476,780	440,498	3,345
Specialized institutions[4]	4,585,342	3,948,546	299,091
Art, music, or design	827,234	706,285	54,086
Business and management	520,637	478,300	8,216
Engineering or technology.........	824,963	800,527	2,089
Medical or other health	57,884	46,728	901
Other specialized......................	2,354,624	1,916,707	233,799
2-year..	3,286,682	2,702,644	328,141

#Rounds to zero.
[1]Doctoral, intensive institutions are committed to education through the doctorate and award at least 10 doctor's degrees per year across 3 or more disciplines or at least 20 doctor's degrees overall.
[2]Master's institutions offer a full range of baccalaureate programs and are committed to education through the master's degree. They award at least 20 master's degrees per year.
[3]Baccalaureate institutions primarily emphasize undergraduate education.

(Columns continued on facing page.)

Table 7.4. Private For-Profit Academic Institutional Income *(Columns Continued)*

Total revenue and investment return, by source of funds *(Cont'd.)*

State and local appropriations, grants, and contracts	Private gifts, grants, and contracts	Investment return (gain or loss)	Educational activities	Auxilliary enterprises	Other
5	6	7	8	9	10
In thousands of current dollars *(Cont'd.)*					
$59,112	$7,079	$16,813	$139,125	$238,735	$81,918
15,076	3,696	10,931	104,314	164,260	31,948
0	0	-197	0	0	197
0	1,630	226	43,977	7,671	5,794
2,050	43	3,815	4,097	19,730	490
13,027	2,023	7,087	56,239	136,858	25,466
645	25	1,326	4,842	42,469	5,037
22	0	-46	7,884	4,812	4,232
276	139	83	5,968	9,553	6,474
465	210	36	5,452	845	2,164
11,619	1,649	5,688	32,093	79,180	7,560
44,036	3,383	5,882	34,811	74,475	49,970
63,227	7,138	24,526	231,957	252,199	159,465
21,146	4,035	17,332	173,830	201,512	64,760
0	0	442	0	0	0
0	54	-1,389	71,697	27,678	13,491
3,782	862	6,665	6,319	15,200	109
17,364	3,119	11,614	95,815	158,634	51,159
719	0	1,890	7,109	49,316	7,829
616	3	-18	14,067	7,600	11,853
276	141	151	7,890	12,759	1,130
14	178	55	5,262	1,524	3,223
15,740	2,797	9,535	61,487	87,435	27,124
42,081	3,103	7,194	58,127	50,687	94,705

[4]Specialized 4-year institutions award degrees primarily in single fields of study, such as medicine, business, fine arts, theology, and engineering. Includes some institutions that have 4-year programs, but have not reported sufficient data to identify program category. Also includes institutions classified as 4-year under the IPEDS system, which had been classified as 2-year in the Carnegie system because they primarily award associate's degrees.

(Table continued on following page.)

Table 7.4. Private For-Profit Academic Institutional Income *(Continued)*

Year and type of institution	Total revenue and investment return, by source of funds		
	Total	Student tuition and fees (net of allowances)	Federal appropriations, grants, and contracts
1	2	3	4
	Percentage distribution		
2004–05			
Total	100.00	87.14	6.14
4-year	100.00	89.23	4.50
Doctoral, intensive[1]	100.00	99.44	0.00
Master's[2]	100.00	93.93	1.70
Baccalaureate[3]	100.00	92.39	0.70
Specialized institutions[4]	100.00	86.11	6.52
Art, music, or design	100.00	85.38	6.54
Business and management	100.00	91.87	1.58
Engineering or technology.........	100.00	97.04	0.25
Medical or other health	100.00	80.73	1.56
Other specialized.....................	100.00	81.40	9.93
2-year.....................................	100.00	82.23	9.98
	Revenue per full-time-equivalent student in current dollars		
2004–05			
Total	$13,931	$12,139	$855
4-year	13,893	12,397	625
Doctoral, intensive[1]	5,333	5,304	0
Master's[2]	11,564	10,862	197
Baccalaureate[3]	12,592	11,633	88
Specialized institutions[4]	16,355	14,084	1,067
Art, music, or design	13,732	11,724	898
Business and management	12,089	11,106	191
Engineering or technology.........	17,056	16,550	43
Medical or other health	13,087	10,565	204
Other specialized.....................	18,949	15,425	1,882
2-year.....................................	14,022	11,530	1,400

#Rounds to zero.
[1]Doctoral, intensive institutions are committed to education through the doctorate and award at least 10 doctor's degrees per year across 3 or more disciplines or at least 20 doctor's degrees overall.
[2]Master's institutions offer a full range of baccalaureate programs and are committed to education through the master's degree. They award at least 20 master's degrees per year.
[3]Baccalaureate institutions primarily emphasize undergraduate education.

(Columns continued on facing page.)

Table 7.4. Private For-Profit Academic Institutional Income *(Columns Continued)*

Total revenue and investment return, by source of funds *(Cont'd.)*

State and local appropriations, grants, and contracts	Private gifts, grants, and contracts	Investment return (gain or loss)	Educational activities	Auxilliary enterprises	Other
5	6	7	8	9	10
Percentage distribution *(Cont'd.)*					
0.58	0.07	0.22	2.11	2.30	1.45
0.27	0.05	0.23	2.26	2.62	0.84
0.00	0.00	0.56	0.00	0.00	0.00
0.00	#	-0.05	2.81	1.08	0.53
0.79	0.18	1.40	1.33	3.19	0.02
0.38	0.07	0.25	2.09	3.46	1.12
0.09	0.00	0.23	0.86	5.96	0.95
0.12	#	#	2.70	1.46	2.28
0.03	0.02	0.02	0.96	1.55	0.14
0.02	0.31	0.09	9.09	2.63	5.57
0.67	0.12	0.40	2.61	3.71	1.15
1.28	0.09	0.22	1.77	1.54	2.88
Revenue per full-time-equivalent student in current dollars *(Cont'd.)*					
$80	$9	$31	$294	$320	$202
38	7	31	314	364	117
0	0	30	0	0	0
0	#	-6	325	125	61
100	23	176	167	401	3
62	11	41	342	566	182
12	0	31	118	819	130
14	#	#	327	176	275
6	3	3	163	264	23
3	40	12	1,190	345	729
127	23	77	495	704	218
180	13	31	248	216	404

[4]Specialized 4-year institutions award degrees primarily in single fields of study, such as medicine, business, fine arts, theology, and engineering. Includes some institutions that have 4-year programs, but have not reported sufficient data to identify program category. Also includes institutions classified as 4-year under the IPEDS system, which had been classified as 2-year in the Carnegie system because they primarily award associate's degrees.
NOTE: Detail may not sum to totals because of rounding.
SOURCE: U.S. Department of Education, National Center for Education Statistics, 2003-04 and 2004-05 Integrated Post-secondary Education Data System (IPEDS), Spring 2005 and Spring 2006. (This table was prepared July 2007.)

Table 7.5. Nonprofit Public Institutional Income/Revenue

Year and source of revenue	Revenues (in thousands)		
	Total	4-year	2-year
1	2	3	4
2003–04			
Total revenues	$221,921,288	$182,008,588	$39,912,699
Operating revenues	128,677,712	112,574,089	16,103,622
Tuition and fees[1]	35,150,615	28,739,354	6,411,261
Grants and contracts	42,553,845	35,501,531	7,052,314
Federal (excludes Federal Direct Student Loans)	28,881,888	24,154,274	4,727,614
State	6,585,978	4,838,356	1,747,622
Local	7,085,979	6,508,901	577,078
Sales and services of auxiliary enterprises[2]	16,989,172	15,196,430	1,792,742
Sales and services of hospitals	19,587,282	19,587,282	0
Independent operations	918,775	914,221	4,554
Other operating revenues	13,478,024	12,635,272	842,752
Nonoperating revenues	81,211,146	59,401,324	21,809,823
Federal appropriations	1,605,958	1,473,410	132,548
State appropriations	53,888.233	42,504,491	11,383,743
Local appropriations	7,707,966	230,203	7,477,762
Nonoperating grants	3,603,243	1,586,149	2,017,094
Federal	2,565,883	1,245,113	1,320,769
State	942,960	313,215	629,745
Local	94,400	27,821	66,579
Gifts	4,191,696	3,956,515	235,181
Investment income	7,164,011	6,936,235	227,777
Other nonoperating revenues	3,050,039	2,714,320	335,719
Other revenues and additions	12,032,429	10,033,175	1,999,254
Capital appropriations	4,808,048	3,438,251	1,369,797
Capital grants and gifts	3,149,016	2,672,009	477,008
Additions to permanent endowments	995,144	987,743	7,401
Other revenues and additions	3,080,221	2,935,172	145,049

#Rounds to zero.
[1]Net of allowances and discounts.
[2]After deducting discounts and allowances.

(Columns continued on facing page.)

Table 7.5. Nonprofit Public Institutional Income/Revenue (Columns Continued)

Percentage distribution of revenues			Revenue per full-time-equivalent student in current dollars			Revenue per full-time-equivalent student in constant 2006–07 dollars		
Total	4-year	2-year	Total	4-year	2-year	Total	4-year	2-year
5	6	7	8	9	10	11	12	13
100.0	100.0	100.0	$24,016	$32,749	$10,837	$26,344	$35,925	$11,888
58.0	61.9	40.3	13,925	20,256	4,372	15,275	22,220	4,796
15.8	15.8	16.1	3,804	5,171	1,741	4,173	5,673	1,910
19.2	19.5	17.7	4,605	6,388	1,915	5,052	7,007	2,100
13.0	13.3	11.8	3,126	4,346	1,284	3,429	4,768	1,408
3.0	2.7	4.4	713	871	475	782	955	521
3.2	3.6	1.4	767	1,171	157	841	1,285	172
7.7	8.3	4.5	1,839	2,734	487	2,017	2,999	534
8.8	10.8	0.0	2,120	3,524	0	2,325	3,866	0
0.4	0.5	#	99	164	1	109	180	1
6.1	6.9	2.1	1,459	2,273	229	1,600	2,494	251
36.6	32.6	54.6	8,788	10,688	5,922	9,6411	11,725	6,496
0.7	0.8	0.3	174	265	36	91	291	39
24.3	23.4	28.5	5,832	7,648	3,091	6,397	8,390	3,391
3.5	0.1	18.7	834	41	2,030	915	45	2,227
1.6	0.9	5.1	390	285	548	428	313	601
1.2	0.7	3.3	278	224	359	305	246	393
0.4	0.2	1.6	102	56	171	112	62	188
#	#	0.2	10	5	18	11	5	20
1.9	2.2	0.6	454	712	64	498	781	70
3.2	3.8	0.6	775	1,248	62	850	1,369	68
1.4	1.5	0.8	330	488	91	362	536	100
5.4	5.5	5.0	1,302	1,805	543	1,428	1,980	595
2.2	1.9	3.4	520	619	372	571	679	408
1.4	1.5	1.2	341	481	130	374	527	142
0.4	0.5	#	108	178	2	118	195	2
1.4	1.6	0.4	333	528	39	366	579	43

(Table continued on following page.)

Table 7.5. Nonprofit Public Institutional Income/Revenue *(Continued)*

Year and source of revenue	Revenues (in thousands)		
	Total	4-year	2-year
1	2	3	4
2003–04			
Total revenues	$221,841,504	$193,796,724	$41,044,779
Operating revenues	136,766.577	120,370,782	16,395,795
Tuition and fees[1]	38,525,657	31,669,001	6,856,656
Grants and contracts	44,376,325	37,319,268	7,057,057
Federal (excludes Federal Direct Student Loans)	30,070,996	25,330,597	4,740,399
State	6,818,048	5,098,257	1,719,792
Local	7,487,280	6,890,414	596,866
Sales and services of auxiliary enterprises[2]	17,672,780	15,884,386	1,788,394
Sales and services of hospitals	21,771,547	21,771,547	0
Independent operations	590,166	590,166	0
Other operating revenues	13,830,102	13,136,414	693,689
Nonoperating revenues	85,517,481	62,871,581	22,645,900
Federal appropriations	1,783,826	1,635,613	148,213
State appropriations	55,324,918	43,165,057	12,159,862
Local appropriations	7,687,161	298,771	7,388,390
Nonoperating grants	3,919,266	2,015,443	1,903,822
Federal	2,873,484	1,548,299	1,325,185
State	945,643	436,316	509,327
Local	100,139	30,828	69,311
Gifts	4,605,829	4,328,996	276,832
Investment income	9,522,937	9,105,619	417,318
Other nonoperating revenues	2,673,544	2,322,082	351,463
Other revenues and additions	12,557,446	10,554,362	2,003,084
Capital appropriations	4,693,914	3,303,568	1,390,345
Capital grants and gifts	3,169,179	2,742,551	426,627
Additions to permanent endowments	886,885	866,193	20,692
Other revenues and additions	3,807,469	3,642,049	165,419

#Rounds to zero.
[1]Net of allowances and discounts.
[2]After deducting discounts and allowances.

(Columns continued on facing page.)

Table 7.5. Nonprofit Public Institutional Income/Revenue *(Columns Continued)*

Percentage distribution of revenues			Revenue per full-time-equivalent student in current dollars			Revenue per full-time-equivalent student in constant 2006–07 dollars		
Total	4-year	2-year	Total	4-year	2-year	Total	4-year	2-year
5	6	7	8	9	10	11	12	13
100.0	100.0	100.0	$25,122	$34,357	$11,071	$26,753	$36,588	$11,790
58.2	62.1	39.9	14,360	21,340	4,422	15,580	22,725	4,710
16.4	16.3	16.7	4,121	5,614	1,849	4,389	5,979	1,970
18.9	19.3	17.2	4,747	6,616	1,903	5,055	7,046	2,027
12.8	13.1	11.5	3,217	4,491	1,279	3,426	4,782	1,362
2.9	2.6	4.2	729	904	464	777	963	494
3.2	3.6	1.5	801	1,222	161	853	1,301	171
7.5	8.2	4.4	1,891	2,816	482	2,013	2,999	514
9.3	11.2	0.0	2,329	3,860	0	2,480	4,110	0
0.3	0.3	0.0	63	105	0	67	111	0
5.9	6.8	1.7	1,479	2,329	187	1,576	2,480	199
36.4	32.4	55.2	9,148	11,146	6,108	9,742	11,870	6,505
0.8	0.8	0.4	191	290	40	203	309	43
23.6	22.3	29.6	5,918	7,652	3,280	6,303	8,149	3,493
3.3	0.2	18.0	822	53	1,993	876	56	2,122
1.7	1.0	4.6	419	357	514	446	381	547
1.2	0.8	3.2	307	274	357	327	292	381
0.4	0.2	1.2	101	77	137	108	82	146
#	#	0.2	11	5	19	11	6	20
2.0	2.2	0.7	493	767	75	525	817	80
4.1	4.7	1.0	1,019	1,614	113	1,085	1,719	120
1.1	1.2	0.9	286	412	95	305	438	101
5.3	5.4	4.9	1,343	1,871	540	1,431	1,993	575
2.0	1.7	3.4	502	586	375	535	624	399
1.3	1.4	1.0	339	486	115	361	518	123
0.4	0.4	0.1	95	154	6	101	164	6
1.6	1.9	0.4	407	646	45	434	688	48

NOTE: Degree-granting institutions grant associate's or higher degrees and participate in Title IV federal financial aid programs. Includes data for public institutions reporting data according to the Financial Accounting Standards Board (FASB) questionnaire. Some data have been revised from previously published figures. Detail may not sum to totals because of rounding.
SOURCE: U.S. Department of Education, National Center for Education Statistics, 2003-04 and 2004-05 Integrated Postsecondary Education Data System, Spring 2004, Spring 2005, and Spring 2006. (This table was prepared July 2007.)

package. (During 2004–2005, the average faculty member received almost 20 percent more in income when adding in the benefits package.)

Student financial aid, as we noted earlier, is a constant concern for most institutions. How much of the income to devote to such aid is almost always a matter of long, if not heated, debates during the budget preparation cycle. The amount is generally a significant percentage of the remaining budget after salaries and benefits are subtracted.

Another significant cost category that has been growing is energy/utilities expenditures. Institutions are spending ever larger amounts on retrofitting facilities to be more energy efficient, installing solar panels to generate some of the electricity, and designing "green" buildings.

Two of the campus units that vie for much of the remaining funds are the library and information technology. Both units have a never ending desire for additional funds to enhance their services for the institution.

Table 7.6 (see pp. 138–141) highlights the fact that salaries and collection development funds are the overwhelming percentage of academic library expenditures (87.5 percent for 2003–2004). What is of some significance is that this percentage is only 2.4 percent higher than it was in 1976–1977 (85.1 percent). During the roughly 25 intervening years, the cost of collection materials, especially journals, rose by double digit percentages in most years. The table also illustrates the fact that library operating expenses (OE) as a percentage of the overall institutional expenditures declined. Anecdotally, based on the authors' directorial experience as well as from colleagues, suggests the situation continues well into 2009. Other data from the table suggest that two other rather common views academic librarians hold are accurate: workload is increasing and there is pressure to do more with less. From 1976–1977 to 2003–2004, the ratio of students to library staff rose (1976–1977 the ratio was 146 to 1—by 2003–2004 the ratio was 184 to 1). Expenditure per student, in constant 2006–2007 dollars (the year the data were complied), dropped from $527 to $497.

GRANTS AND RESEARCH

One area of institutional budgeting that may or may not help increase funding is research grants and projects. Tables 7.1 to 7.5, illustrating income and expenditures, which had separate categories for grants/research, make it clear this is a significant source of income as well as expense for institutions offering advanced degrees. Why are they important to the institution? First is the prestige factor. The number of faculty receiving grants as well as the dollar value of those grants both play a role in how others view the institution. Grants also help attract top-quality faculty and students, which in turn adds to institutional status. (Note: this section applies to all institutional grants, including those secured by the library.)

A second factor, which in many ways is more important, is a grant provides additional income for the institution. From one point of view most grants have two financial aspects. One is the money available to a researcher to carry out the desired work. The other aspect is the "overhead" money that goes to the institution for allowing the project to take place. Overhead is a charge for such things as rent on the space the researchers use while engaged in the grant, the utilities consumed, support services such as the library, and administrative costs. Thus, when you hear that a researcher just received a $100,000 grant it usually does not mean the individual actually will have the full announced amount. The person probably will have something less based on the institution's overhead rate.

Overhead rates vary from institution to institution and by granting agency. They also vary as to what costs the rate is calculated on (e.g., salaries, total research cost, total cost less salaries). Faculty members and their departments that are extremely successful in securing grants often are able to have some of the overhead monies turned back to them for their use.

From the institutional perspective, grants and overhead are not just a source of operating funds; they also add some much-needed equipment or facilities improvement that will last well beyond the life of the grant. Overhead/grant monies also frequently support staff salaries. Such monies may supplement the researcher(s) salary, and they also may pay for research assistants (often graduate students) and other support staff. Individuals paid by such funds are often referred to as being on "soft" money, meaning the position lasts for only the length of the grant. Support staff positions may be partially funded by a number of grants rather than a single grant, which provides a slightly more stable position. Sof-funded positions do reduce some of the pressure on the host institution for allocating "hard" funds for support activities.

Earlier we stated that grants may or may not be cost-effective for an institution. A 2009 study reported on by *Inside Higher Education* suggested that, at least in some cases, getting a grant may cost the institution money ("Hidden Cost of Doing Business," 2009). The report indicated,

> Researchers at the University of Rochester School of Medicine & Dentistry found the cost of supporting newly recruited scientists costs an additional 40 cents over every dollar these new faculty generate from grants. While colleges may grow in prestige by expanding their research base, they're likely to dole out more money in start-up packages and other benefits for new faculty than they bring in through grants. ("Hidden Cost of Doing Business," 2009)

Senior faculty do indeed generate a positive cash flow from their research/grant activities; however, this may not be case for junior faculty, even those outside of the hard science fields. Regardless of the overall costs involved, advanced degree institutions will continue to require faculty members to engage in research and expect their libraries to support those endeavors.

Research, especially in the sciences—both pure and applied—does raise some challenging issues with regard to intellectual property rights. Who "owns" the research results, in particular those that have commercial value? There is also the issue of "sponsored research"—research underwritten by a commercial enterprise or private individual. Is it appropriate for the institution to allow such work, and what rights does the public have to access the results? When the research was defense-related during the cold war era, there were loud complaints against such work being conducted within the academy. Today, there are few comments about doing work for commercial entities.

When it comes to intellectual ownership of the content of a book written by a faculty or staff member, most institutions allow the author to retain full rights. (Probably the reason for this is the amount of money from royalties is too small to be of institutional interest, except perhaps in the case of a textbook such as Samuelson's *Economics* textbook, now in its 18th edition. Even in such cases, the total amount involved is spread

Table 7.6. Academic Library Operating Expenditures

Collections, staff, and operating expenditures	1976-77[1]	1978-79[1]	1981-82	1984-85	1987-88
1	2	3	4	5	6
Number of libraries	3,058	3,122	3,104	3,322	3,438
Number of circulation transactions (in thousands)	–	–	–	–	–
Total enrollment (in thousands)[2]	11,121	11,392	12,372	12,242	12,767
Full-time-equivalent enrollment[2]	8,313	8,348	9,015	8,952	9,230
Collections (in thousands)					
Number of volumes at end of year[3]...	481,442	519,895	567,826	631,727	718,504
Number of volumes added during year	22,367	21,608	19,507	20,658	21,907
Number of serial subscriptions at end of year	4,670	4,775	4,890	6,317	6,416
Microform units at end of year	–	–	–	–	–
Electronic units at end of year[5]	–	–	–	–	–
Full-time-equivalent (FTE) library staff					
Total staff in regular positions[6]	57,087	58,416	58,476	58,476	67,251
Librarians and professional staff....	23,308	23,676	23,816	21,822	25,115
Other paid staff	33,779	34,740	34,660	38,026	40,733
Contributed services	–	–	–	–	1,403
Student assistants	–	–	–	–	33,821
FTE student enrollment per FTE staff member	146	143	154	153	137
Hours of student and other assistance (in thousands)	39,950	39,552	40,068	28,360	–
Library operating expenditures[7]					
Total operating expenditures (in thousands)	$1,259,637	$1,502,158	$1,943,769	$2,404,524	$2,770,075
Salaries[8]	698,090	824,438	1,081,894	1,156,138	1,451,551
Hourly wages	68,683	79,535	100,847	–	–
Fringe benefits	–	–	–	231,209	–
Preservation	22,521	25,274	30,351	32,939	34,144
Furniture/equipment	–	–	–	–	–
Computer hardware/software	–	–	–	–	–
Utilities/networks/consortia	–	–	–	–	–
Information resources	373,699	450,180	561,199	750,282	891,281
Books and serial backfiles— paper	–	–	–	–	–
Books and serial backfiles— electronic	–	–	–	–	–

–Not available.

[1]Includes data for U.S. territories.

[2]Fall enrollment for the academic year specified.

[3]Includes data for schools newly added to the survey system, so end of year figure exceeds total of additions plus end of year value from previous year.

[4]Includes microform and electronic serials.

[5]Electronic files, formerly labeled "Computer files."

[6]Excludes student assistants.

[7]Excludes capital outlay.

[8]Includes expenditures for fringe benefits (except for 1984-85 and 1987-88), salary equivalents of contributed services staff, and hourly wages for 1996-97 and 1997-98.

(Columns continued on facing page.)

Table 7.6. Academic Library Operating Expenditures *(Columns Continued)*						
1991-92	1994-95	1996-97	1997-98	1999-2000	2001-02	2003-04
7	8	9	10	11	12	13
3,274	3,303	3,408	3,658	3,527	3,568	3,653
–	231,503	230,733	216,067	193,948	189,248	200,204
14,359	14,279	14,300	14,502	14,791	15,928	16,911
10,361	10,348	10,402	10,615	10,944	11,766	12,688
749,429	776,447	806,717	878,906	913,547	954,030	982,590
20,982	21,544	21,346	24,551	24,436	24,574	24,615
6,966	6,212	5,709	10,908[4]	7,499	9,855	12,764
–	–	–	1,062,082	1,111,389	1,143,678	1,173,287
–	465	983	3,473	–	–	–
67,166	67,433	67,581	68,337	69,123	69,526	69,047
26,341	26,726	27,268	30,041	31,001	32,053	32,280
40,421	40,381	40,022	38,026	37,893	37,473	36,767
404	326	291	270	229	–	–
29,075	28,411	27,998	28,373	26,518	25,305	25,038
154	153	154	155	158	169	184
–	–	–	–	–	–	–
$3,648,654	$4,013,333	$4,301,815	$4,592,657	$5,023,198	$5,416,716	$5,751,247
1,889,368	2,021,233	2,147,842	2,314,380	2,430,541	2,753,404	2,913,221
–	–	–	–	–	–	–
–	–	–	–	271,954	–	–
43,126	46,554	45,610	42,919	43,832	46,499	42,976
–	55,915	56,128	57,013	63,459	–	–
–	128,128	157,949	164,379	160,294	155,791	143,042
–	81,106	85,113	89,618	90,264	92,242	101,293
1,197,293	1,348,933	1,499,249	1,600,995	1,822,277	1,944,490	2,114,555
–	–	–	514,048	552,100	563,007	550,599
–	–	–	28,061	33,888	44,792	65,597

(Table continued on following page.)

Table 7.6. Academic Library Operating Expenditures

Collections, staff, and operating expenditures	1976-77[1]	1978-79[1]	1981-82	1984-85	1987-88
1	2	3	4	5	6
Current serials—paper.......	–	–	–	–	–
Current serials—electronic	–	–	–	–	–
Audiovisual materials...............	–	–	–	–	–
Document delivery/interlibrary loan...................................	–	–	–	–	–
Other collection expenditures	373,699	450,180	561,199	750,282	891,281
Other library operating expenditures......................	96,643	122,731	169,478	233,957	393,099
Operating expenditures per FTE student..................................	152	180	216	269	300
Operating expenditures per FTE student in constant 2006-07 dollars[9]...................................	527	536	468	518	529
Operating expenditures (percentage distribution)...............................	100.0	100.0	100.0	100.0	100.0
Salaries[9]..	55.4	54.9	55.7	48.1	52.4
Hourly wages..................................	5.5	5.3	5.2	–	–
Fringe benefits	–	–	–	9.6	–
Preservation...................................	1.8	1.7	1.6	1.4	1.2
Information resources	29.7	30.0	28.9	31.2	32.2
Other library operating expenditures[10]	7.7	8.2	8.7	9.7	14.2
Library operating expenditures as percent of total institutional expenditures for educational and general purposes	3.8	3.7	3.5	3.4	3.2

[9]Constant dollars based on the Consumer Price Index, prepared by the Bureau of Labor Statistics, U.S. Department of Labor, adjusted to a school-year basis.

[10]Includes furniture/equipment, computer hardware/software, and utilities/networks/consortia as well as expenditures classified as "other library operating expenditures."

(Columns continued on facing page.)

over a great many years.) A commercially viable outcome of institutional research can mean hundreds of thousands or even million of dollars in income in just a few years. In such cases, the institution becomes very interested. Because a book author and the inventor/discoverer of a commercially useful product/concept make use of institutional facilities and staff support, the results of which could not have been achieved by working at home, the institution takes the view that it should have a share in any income derived from the research.

Many of the large research universities have created a for-profit corporation (foundation) to handle patents and other such research outcomes and realize a surprising amount of income from its activities. Usually the researcher receives a share of the income, but the institution retains ownership. New scientific discoveries may lead to profitable products, while advances in electronic, material sciences, and biotechnology

Table 7.6. Academic Library Operating Expenditures *(Columns Continued)*

1991-92	1994-95	1996-97	1997-98	1999-2000	2001-02	2003-04
7	8	9	10	11	12	13
–	–	–	849,399	945,958	926,105	883,534
–	–	–	125,470	203,371	297,657	480,138
23,879	28,753	28,879	30,623	32,039	37,041	35,216
–	12,238	17,645	19,309	20,540	22,913	24,823
1,173,414	1,307,942	1,452,725	34,086	34,381	52,976	74,648
518,867	331,463	309,925	323,354	140,579	424,290	436,160
352	388	414	433	459	460	453
520	526	531	546	553	527	497
100.0	100.0	100.0	100.0	100.0	100.0	100.0
51.8	50.4	49.9	50.4	48.4	50.8	50.7
–	–	–	–	5.4	–	–
1.2	1.2	1.1	0.9	0.9	0.9	0.7
32.8	33.6	34.9	34.9	36.3	35.9	36.8
14.2	14.9	14.2	13.8	9.0	12.4	11.8
3.0	2.8	–	–	–	–	–

NOTE: Data through 1995 are for institutions of higher education, while later data are for degree-granting institutions. Degree-granting institutions grant associate's or higher degrees and participate in Title IV federal financial aid programs. The degree-granting classification is very similar to the earlier higher education classification, but it includes more 2-year colleges and excludes a few higher education institutions that did not grant degrees. (See Guide to Sources for details.) Detail may not sum to totals because of rounding.
SOURCE: U.S. Department of Education, National Center for Education Statistics, Library Statistics of Colleges and Universities, selected years, 1976–77 through 1984–85; 1987–88 through 2003-04 Integrated Postsecondary Education Data System, "Academic Libraries Survey" (IPEDS-L:88–98), "Fall Enrollment Survey" (IPEDS-EF:87–99), and Spring 2002 and Spring 2004; Academic Libraries Survey (ALS), 2000, 2002, and 2004; and Academic Libraries: 2004 (NCES 2007-301). (This table was prepared August 2007.)

can spawn entire industries. A few academic libraries also have a foundation in addition to the campus-wide foundation.

University presidents, for example Harvard University president emeritus Derek Bok, have raised concerns about how far an institution should go in the area of potentially "commercially valuable" research, especially for publicly funded institutions. They see licensing of the school's name, logo, mascot's image, etc. for use on sweatshirts, pens, and other memorabilia as in poor taste at worst and at best a very minor source of revenue. However, the commercialization of institutional research may threaten its integrity and core values. For example, some institutions, in particular those that are publicly funded, have tried to address the balancing of research needs of various types with institutional values by developing policies that address questions such as the following:

- How much right does the public have to know about institutional research when some or all the funds to support the work are from public sources?
- How much public disclosure should be required of researchers who have a financial interest in a firm that may benefit directly or indirectly from that person's research and institutional responsibilities that uses public funds?
- Should researchers be disqualified from participating in research where they have direct financial interest in the research sponsor?
- Should *exclusive* patents/licenses be granted to a corporation or private party where public/institutional funds underwrite some or all of the work?
- How much research should an institution allow when it is sponsored by an individual or corporation? When it is allowed, should that sponsor have exclusive rights to the results?

Something to Ponder

Sponsored research raises some interesting questions regarding library support for such activities. There are questions about there being support for research activities that fall outside of the core areas of institutional interest. Should this be special funding built into such projects to cover some of the support costs? Think about the bulleted questions; how would you respond to each one?

Achieving the best balance between profit-making and advancing human knowledge can be challenging.

ENDOWMENTS

Institutional endowments are something of a distinctive feature of U.S. higher education. At some schools, such as Harvard and Yale, there are relatively large departments (50 or more staff) devoted solely to managing the funds. Endowment income can be a significant component of an institution's annual revenue stream. During boom economic times, it can be wonderful to have the "extra" funds; during downtimes, there can be serious problems. The danger in good times is that the endowment income may become regarded as constant with expenditures and plans built around that underlying assumption.

When things go bad, as they have in the last part of the first decade of the twenty-first century, major problems can arise. It may mean that the number of schools closing will rise markedly over the coming years. Roger Kaufman and Geoffrey Woglan (2008) noted, "Recently, spending and fees at colleges and universities have been rising faster than family incomes. If that persists, increasing emphasis will be placed on endowments as a source of finance" (p. 196). What they had little way of knowing when they wrote the article was that institutional endowments would take a major downturn in value, thus reducing payouts and making it less and less likely that these funds would be a solution to the escalating costs.

What is, or was, the size of U.S. higher education endowments? According to the National Association of College and University Business Officers' (NACUBO, 2008) 2007 survey, the median endowment for the 785 reporting institutions was $91,135 million. (Keep in mind reporting was voluntary, so the actual number of schools with endowments is probably somewhat larger than 785.) However, the average value was $523,834,000, which reflects the distortion caused by 76 institutions that reported endowments in excess of $1 billion. Harvard University, as always, led the "league table," with an endowment of $34,634,906,000. Yale, Stanford, Princeton, and the University of Texas system rounded out the top five, all reporting double digit billion-dollar endowments. For the

76 schools with one billion plus in endowment, even a 1 percent return on investment would be significant.

Overall management of the endowment is generally a governing board's responsibility, with the assistance of institutional staff. In most cases, this assistance is from the chief financial officer, as few schools have full-time staff devoted to endowment management activities. From a fund management perspective, both the governing board and the institution take the position that the school will last forever and so should its endowment. As we suggested earlier, in bad times it is tempting to draw down the capital rather than just use with the return on investments. Managing the endowment rests on three major factors: spending rate, investment policy, and fund-raising activities for the endowment. Why these factors are important to academic libraries is that their endowments, in almost all cases, are incorporated into the overall institutional endowment, and consequently libraries have little or no control over their funds management.

Endowment spending rate (payout) is the most critical to the institution's overall annual revenue picture, and it is central to the endowment's long-term stability and growth. Two key questions need to be considered:

- How should the institution balance the need for income for annual expenses with the desire to increase the endowment for the future?
- How should it balance the needs of present faculty and students with those of future faculty and students?

Spending rates tend to be in the 4 to 5 percent range based on the value of the endowment. Many schools use some type of rolling average value (three- and four-year averages are common) in order to smooth out the swings in the investment marketplace.

BUDGET PROCESS

Fiscal management consists of three broad activities: identifying and securing funds, expending the funds, and accounting for and reporting on how you spent the funds. Kent Boese (2006) laid out some of the challenges you face in today's volatile economic environment in an editorial comment in *The Bottom Line*:

> Simply put, should inflation become a large problem in our economy, we will have weaker purchasing power with our money. Even if we are able to increase our budgets, we may be receiving fewer goods and services for our buck in the future.... Having adequate funding is a subjective view...no matter what the funding level you are at, there is never room to spend money poorly.... If we become efficient financial organizations, but fail to provide the services expected of us, we can not consider ourselves successful.

Being a good/effective steward of funds is complex regardless of the size of the academic library. It begins by assessing what needs doing (especially user needs) and the cost of the requisite activities, establishing priorities with stakeholder input, creating a plan (the budget), reflecting the costs and priorities, and presenting the plan to the campus budget committee. We know of few, if any, cases where the cost of desired activities were/are below the realistic amount of money you are likely to receive. Thus, setting priorities is a key element in fiscal planning/management, and this must be done with some understanding of the institutional circumstances.

Every library has a variety of needs, wants, and aspirations that exceed its financial means. The same is true of every other campus unit. The budget sets the limits on which of the categories the units will realize in a given year. This means some choices must be made. Decisions on what will be possible to do now and what must wait are not easy at the best of times, but lacking a solid planning process that helps set priorities makes the process all that more difficult in trying financial times. Having a process for setting priorities is of great assistance when it comes to addressing conflicting "good" options and a lack of adequate funds to handle all of them. Often colleges and universities do not have a sound process for setting the priorities.

Think About This

How would you go about setting priorities for the following? The library is requesting an 11 percent increase in funds for electronic resources. The law school dean wants an 18 percent increase in salary funds to help keep faculty from leaving to go into private practice. The vice president of facilities is requesting $2 million to install solar panels to help contain escalating energy costs. Enrollment management put forward a proposal to increase need-based financial aid by 30 percent. Also on the table is a request from the dean of students for two additional FTEs to strengthen the student retention activities. You do not have funds to grant all of the requests. What do you do?

To be a truly effective fiscal manager you should explore all possible sources of funding, not just campus resources. In the past, academic library directors faced only modest pressure to secure outside funding; when they did receive outside funding it was a nice plus but not expected. Today's library leaders are often required to engage in fund-raising not just for nice extras but for basic operating funds.

No matter where you seek funding, you must have a well crafted request/proposal. Preparing such documents takes time and effort and a fair amount of creativity, as you will be in competition with a great many other libraries as well as, in some cases, with other types of nonprofit organizations for the available funds.

BUDGET AS A CONTROL DEVICE

A budget is a plan that serves three interrelated purposes: planning, coordinating, and control. It represents choices made about alternative possible expenditures. Furthermore, it assists in coordinating work designed to achieving specific service goals. Funding authorities use the budget requests and expenditures as a means of comparing what the requested funds would accomplish against past outcomes. It is one of the institution's most powerful tools for holding units accountable.

These purposes apply to all levels of a unit; the library senior staff use budgets to monitor overall performance. Frontline budget managers use the budget to track day-to-day performance as well as over longer periods. An example of the first line use of the budget is the acquisitions unit that develops plans for handling expenditures as even as possible to ensure a reasonable work flow though out the fiscal year. Checking actual performance against the planned expenditure provides useful information for control and coordination purposes.

Higher education institutions start by projecting/estimating what its income will be from all of the sources seen in Table 7.2 as well as the incoming class size. In point of fact, all budgeting is essentially forecasting—how much you get and how much it will cost to operate over the budget cycle (such as increases in database prices).

Overly optimistic predictions (such as misjudging the size of an incoming class) lead to budget problems. You rarely know before the start of the budgetary period exactly how much you will receive. Often, the actual allocation is unknown until after the start of the academic year and final enrollment numbers are in. The authors' experience has been that a conservative forecast is the safest and least disruptive to operations, and having a contingency plan makes managerial life somewhat easier. Being in a publicly funded institution is both a blessing and a curse. During stable economic and political times, the school can make reasonably accurate projections regarding upcoming appropriations. During other times, predictability disappears making the early stages of the budget process very much a hopeful guess.

Because budgets are estimates, to be effective you must make expenditures adjustments as circumstances change. Budgets need to be flexible in order to meet rapid shifts in needs, but any major alteration requires careful thought and caution. Too many rapid changes can damage the integrity and stability of a budget as well as the organization. In most libraries, there is only a limited authority to make budget adjustments, and asking before doing is the best approach.

Financial planning and control consists of several basic steps:

- Determine ongoing and desirable programs and establish priorities.
- Estimate the costs of plans for each unit in monetary terms.
- Combine all estimates into a well-balanced program. This will require investigation of each plan's financial feasibility and a comparison of the program with institutional goals.
- Compare, for a given time, the estimates derived from step 3 with the actual results, making corrections for any significant differences.

A library's size does not materially affect the basic budgeting process, although in larger institutions each step is more complex and takes more time.

The second step of budgetary control—combining and coordinating subsidiary budgets—can be exceedingly complicated both for the library and the institution. It certainly involves more than just totaling the subsidiary requests. It must represent a total reflection of economic realities as well as institutional mission and goals. For this reason, very large libraries often have a person whose sole job it is to coordinate the budget activities.

Finally, budget officers compare the actual performance (what has been accomplished, the volume of work, and so forth) against what was expected (budget). At the same time, supervisors and top management need to look at the existing circumstances in order to decide whether a major or a minor shift in budget allotments is necessary or desirable. By doing this every few months throughout the fiscal year, the library tries to address the unpredictability of the future. This step is most important because many budgets are prepared 12 to 18 months before they are approved and thus may represent predictions that are 2 years old.

Academic library budgets normally are of two types: operating and capital. *Operating budgets* identify amounts of money the service expects to expend on its activities (operating expense, or OE) over a specific time frame, usually a 12-month fiscal year (FY). The fact that different institutions use different fiscal years (some examples are January 1 to December 31, June 1 to May 31, July 1 to June 30, and October 1 to September 30) and budget preparation cycles can cause surprising problems for information service consortiums attempting to fund cooperative projects.

Capital budgets address planned expenditures on equipment (usually items designed to last more than two or perhaps three years). Expenditures for technology (hardware and infrastructure) usually fall into the capital expense category. Preparation of capital budget requests may, or may not, follow the operating budget sequence. In some cases, the time period for the capital budget may be longer or shorter than the OE budget.

BUDGET CYCLE

There is some type of budget cycle, regardless of the time frame, and this cycle plays a role in the control aspect of budgeting. Good budget managers are normally dealing with at least four FYs at any time. Those FYs are the past year, this year, next year, and the year after that. Table 7.7 is an example of a budget cycle. Assume the library's FY is July 1 to June 30, look at the budget cycle and you see the reasons for the thinking about four different fiscal years.

Table 7.7. Sample Library Budget Cycle								
Past Fiscal Year		Current Fiscal Year		Coming Fiscal Year		Future Fiscal Year		
July	Dec	July	Dec	July	Dec	July	Dec	July
X		***X***	+++ooooo	X		X		X

*** Submit coming fiscal year budget.
+++ Defend coming fiscal budget.
ooo Plan future fiscal year budget.

For the current year, the library manager must monitor expenditures, compare what has occurred against expectations and make appropriate adjustments. A common practice requires senior managers to provide additional justifications to the funding body for the requested budget for the coming fiscal year. As part of that process, the person(s) is likely to have to respond to questions about the expenditures in the past fiscal year. (Because library budgets are estimates, funding bodies usually look at how well the requesting unit actually used its appropriated funds in prior years.) Senior management must be ready to defend past expenditures, explain how the library is doing with current funding, and justify why extra funds are necessary for the coming FY. In our example, this process most often occurs sometime between July and December.

During the latter part of the fiscal year, April or May, many organizations ask for the initial request for the future fiscal year. To develop a realistic request, the library must think about how well it handled questions about past budgets, review the status of the current budget, and make an educated guess as to what will be available in the coming year's budget. With this in mind, it then prepares the request for funding two years ahead.

BUDGET PREPARATION

A natural question arises of who is responsible for the budget. Like so many questions, there is more than one answer. From a legal point of view, the library's director is responsible, just as she or he is for everything that takes place within the library. From an operational perspective, there are a variety of possibilities. Only in the smallest library is the director solely responsible for handling the operational budget. Almost every medium- and large-size library, with several units/departments, usually has delegated some discretionary spending power to some units. Very large libraries usually have one or more full-time people handling budget activities.

The initial budget preparation should begin with library supervisors providing their estimates of their funding needs to their immediate supervisors and ultimately to senior management. Each successive management level combines and coordinates all subunit budgets and then passes its total on up. Finally, top management assesses all of this information and formulates the overall budget.

Every library hopes to have a stable or, at best, a predictable fiscal environment. To some extent, the planning cycle assists in creating such an environment. By setting up a budget/financial planning committee, senior management accomplishes several things. First, it involves more people in the monitoring activities. Second, it involves others in thinking about future needs. Third, it provides lower-level managers with solid budgetary planning and development experience. Finally, it can build a commitment to the library and its institution by generating some understanding of the restraints on budgetary freedom both have.

Having a contingency plan for possible library budget shortfalls is part of a stable environment. It will help avoid making hasty decisions that may be as harmful as the loss of funding. In cutting back, the people most affected, at least initially, are staff. Several studies have shown that cutting back adversely affects morale, job satisfaction, and staff retention; these in turn impact productivity at the time when it is most needed (Shaughnessy, 1989).

Some of the short-term tactics for dealing with fiscal distress include hiring freezes, staff reductions through attrition, furloughs, across-the-board cuts, and deferred maintenance and equipment replacement. Unfortunately, fiscal distress for a library is not always a short-term problem. In the long term, band-aid solutions will not work, and their use often severely damages support from both staff and users. An example is cutting funds for database access services.

Users are hurt in the long term, and they may leave never to return if the cutbacks are too severe. Hiring freezes are less damaging, at least initially, to users. Using a combination of cuts takes more time and effort, but, in the long run, is more likely to result in retained users and a more effective service. This is an example of where a thoughtfully developed contingency plan(s) demonstrates its value.

Glen Holt (2005) wrote an article about "getting beyond the pain" in which he reviewed the depressing list of budgetary woes at the state/provincial and national levels in Canada, UK, and United States during the early years of the twenty-first century. Although his focus was on the public library environment, his comments are well worth considering by academic librarians. He noted that the American Library Association estimated there had been $111 million in cuts in public library funding between 2004 and when he wrote the article. Holt provides some ideas for addressing the situation: demonstrate the critical nature of the service (at least some of its elements), demonstrate the service benefits, think broadly about possible funding sources, place greater emphasis on user/client-focused service, and recognize globalization does have an impact on the international marketplace for information and spend some time pondering the implications of those impacts. His concluding statement, "At the same time however, we must recognize the drastic changes that we will have to make to keep up with new ways of working and funding" (p. 189).

One of the probable "new ways" of funding is touched on in a book by John Buschman (2003) in which he suggests that, at least in North America, the public (taxpayers) have decided that some public sector services, if not all, deserve less public support than in the past.

Gitelle Seer (2004) made an important point, "Do not confuse short-term belt tightening with long-term financial strategies. It is sometimes hard to tell the difference; your organization's management may give you few, if any, meaningful clues" (p. 10). Seer's advice, as is ours, was to monitor the internal and external environment like a hawk.

Check These Out

L. S. Moyer published an article in 2005 outlining how one small public library responded to budget cuts, "Library Funding in a Budget-Cut World," *Bottom Line* 18, no. 3: 112–115. For an academic library perspective read Samuel T. Huang's 2006 article "Where There's a Will, There's a Way." *Bottom Line* 19, no. 3: 146–151.

Every academic library, regardless of the service community's size, faces four ongoing financial issues. The first involves trying to develop and maintain appropriate facilities and responsive users' services while remaining within budget. (Unfortunately, few library budgets take the volume of work into account—or, rather, few funding authorities do so.) It simply is a matter of trying to respond to changing needs while knowing there is little prospect of additional funding until the next fiscal period. The second financial issue relates to the requirement of continually building and maintaining collections. Print collection growth requires space (which requires money) and in time and staff effort (which requires money). Securing funding for collection resources is usually easy, at least in comparison to getting additional space or personnel. The third financial issue relates to the second and revolves around the rapid growth of electronic resources. Database vendors are no less shy about increasing their prices each year at rates well above general inflation than were/are their print journal publishers. Often these are one and the same, and you face a double hit for the same information or pay a premium for just one of the formats (more about this issue is discussed in the chapter on collection services). Finally there are staffing concerns. Like serials, staffing is an ongoing commitment that escalates in cost with each year, if staff members receive annual salary increases. Even when there are no salary increases there will be an increase in benefit costs, such as for health insurance. They can also erode the increasing funds for services and collections and the increasing need to invest in staff training and development to meet the challenges of continuous change.

PRESENTING AND DEFENDING THE BUDGET REQUEST

Preparing a budget request is often easier than presenting and defending it. This stems from the fact that all the campus units compete for the finite pool of funds, and each seeks to prove that its needs are the most urgent. Thus, the more care that you put into the preparation of a budget request and the reasons for requested increases, the more likely you are to secure the amount sought. Those units that do win the "battle of the budget" are usually the ones that recognize and act on the fact that budgeting is a very political process.

We drew the following material from Wildavsky (2006), but it is not a substitute for reading his entire book, which contains many good ideas. Some readers have difficulty translating his emphasis on the United States federal government into a library context. We suggest simply substituting the title of the library's campus chief executive officer for the word *president* and the title of the campus budget committee for the word *Congress.* Doing so usually makes clear why his ideas are relevant to library budgeting.

Despite all of the press given to such concepts as program and planning budgeting systems (PPBS) and zero-base budgeting (ZBB), most organizational budgets are basically line budgets. Organizations often find that when they do move to one of the "newer" budgeting modes the end result is much the same—an incremental budget, because after an initial startup, people use the past year as their starting point. An incremental budget usually increases in size each passing year, if nothing more than by an inflation figure.

> **Check This Out**
>
> All academic librarians ought to read the classic book by Aaron Wildavsky, *The New Politics of the Budgetary Process*, 5th edition (Boston: Little, Brown, 2006). Some information professionals, especially students, have difficulty accepting Wildavsky's ideas, as the text deals with the U.S. government and, to a lesser extent, state governments. They see information services as cultural havens somehow removed from the "ugliness" of politics. Most graduates who read some or all of Wildavsky as students quickly see the connection when they take their first position.

The incremental approach is present in most academic library budgets because of the long-term commitments (e.g., salaries, benefits, and collection development funds for books, media, databases, and serial subscriptions). Also, if the user base increases, there will be pressure to hire additional staff. In situations with strong collective bargaining units, a workload agreement clause can cause a significant increase in staffing costs. (Yes, there are some academic libraries with such units.) Annual salary "merit" and cost-of-living increases are difficult to control because the withholding of such increases is only temporary. Staff pressure will mount to make up for the losses they believe they suffered.

Like it or not, "lobbying" is, or should, be part of the library's budget preparation and presentation. Perhaps a label that carries a less negative connotation, at least in the United States, is advocacy. Both terms relate to the process of influencing people about the importance or value of an issue, cause, or service.

Gloria Meraz (2002) describes three areas where librarians can focus on in terms of lobbying: positioning oneself to be an effective advocate, achieving the most from advocacy sessions, and understanding the advocacy arena. One of her telling points is "decision makers tend to allocate funding to departments or agencies that are in trouble (crisis).... [W]ithout showing some sort of crisis, libraries are not likely to receive large allocations of resources" (p. 68). She notes that most libraries do not have to make up the crisis; all they need to do is show the crisis.

One element in the advocacy effort should draw on the user base, which will be as vocal or as silent as the library leads them to believe they should be. A large user base is fine; but if they are silent during budget crunches, they are not politically useful. A little extra help extended to users—especially to politically influential groups—can go a long way at budget request time. There is nothing wrong with saying, "Look, we know are doing a good job for you, but with a little help and a little more money, here is how we can better serve you!" People who are willing to speak for the library (whether or not they are actually called on) at budget hearings can have a positive effect on funding agencies. (The letter to a college dean from a happy faculty member can be very useful, especially if it occurs year-round, and can create a strong positive attitude in an influential person's mind before they begin thinking about budgets and the library as a competitor.)

Some years ago, Jennifer Cargill (1987) wrote a short but to the point article about "getting the budget message out." At that time, as it still remains today, one of the most difficult messages to convey to funding authorities as well as to users is the high rate of inflation of subscription prices (both electronic and paper). Finding a simple, accurate, and short way of explaining to non–information professionals why such price increase percentages are so large year after year is a challenge. As much as you might like one, there is no "magic formula" explaining the situation.

> **From the Authors**
>
> Alire effectively used simple charts/graphs that visually showed the rate of serials inflation being much higher than the rate of inflation for health care in the country over so many years. These graphs told the story without a lot of text needed.

Because the business office personnel do the digging, provide the reports, and make assessments and recommendations, their influence is significant. Developing a good working relationship with budget/business office (the label varies from institution to institution) staff members is an excellent idea, especially with the staff of the person who heads the committee that first hears the library's budget request. If your relationship is a year-round one, it will be easier to maintain, and your chances of success improve further. Keeping in touch, finding out what will be needed for the hearings (well in advance), identifying possible areas of concern, and offering assistance within reasonable limits are all methods of developing a good working relationship. You must be careful to keep the relationship on a professional basis so there is no hint of personal favoritism. There is nothing wrong with inviting influential funding personnel to attend special library functions (holiday parties for example) at which a number of users and other influential persons will also be present. They may or may not attend, but they will have the library in mind as something other than a bottomless pit into which to throw money.

Study the mood of the institution with an eye on adjusting your approach as moods shift. During "hold the line on spending" periods, let your request demonstrate how well you are cooperating. Do not try to paint too rosy a picture—play it straight, and do not try to "put one over" on them. You may fool people once or even twice because of all of the other matters they have to consider, but eventually they will catch up to you. And when they do, you will lose any goodwill you developed over time; and the library will probably suffer for a long time to come.

> **Check This Out**
>
> A solid article that addresses most of the fiscal issues we covered above is Peter Clayton's 2001 "Managing the Acquisitions Budget: A Practical Perspective," *Bottom Line* 14, no. 3: 145-151.

When presenting plans for new programs, be cautious in what you promise. Do not promise more than you know you can deliver, even when you think you can do much better. It is better to under-promise and overdeliver. As tempting as it may be to make promises in order to get money, resist! Funding officers' memories are long and detailed when necessary, and failure to deliver on past promises raises serious doubts about current promises.

Does all this sound too political for a library? It should not, because it reflects the unwritten rules by which governments and other funding bodies play the budget–politics game.

INCOME GENERATION

Today, few academic libraries expect to receive all of the funds they need from their institutions, or at least as not enough to operate the way they would like. James Walther (2005) makes the point about public libraries in an editorial:

> We are at such a crossroads in public libraries, as we seek funding from both public and private sources, we hone our political acumen to negotiate with city, county, state and federal officials to get the best financial resources for our readers. When those advocacy efforts don't work, we shift gears to marketing in new ways and identifying new resource sources.

His comments could just as well apply to any academic library. New sources of revenue are surprisingly diverse, at least for those who think broadly.

We include in new sources the traditional private individual donor, seeking grants and gifts from foundations, grants from various government agencies both outright and for services provided to the agency, creating a "friends" group, income generation from service activities, and partnerships with various organizations including profit oriented. At best, we can only briefly touch on these topics and must refer readers to some of the sources devoted just to these topics.

> **Check These Out**
>
> Two useful publications to read to get more in-depth information even though they may appear dated are Victoria Steele's *Becoming a Fundraiser* (Chicago, IL: American Library Association, 2000) and "Ten Principles for Successful Fundraising" by Gary Hunt and Hwa-Wei Lee, *Bottom Line* 6, no. 3/4 (1993): 111–121.

Developing and maintaining a special and positive image is important for all libraries—it becomes essential for fund-raising. There will be no opportunity for securing extra funds if the service's image is anything but positive. Having a positive image is not enough. You must communicate this image to users, the general public, and to prospective sources of new funding. Granting agencies are just as interested in the image of their grantees as are individual donors and private foundations.

This is an area where having a marketing plan linked to an active public relations program is essential in identifying special funding niches and opportunities. From an income generation point of view, this niche may need modification or amplification to fully explain what it is your library does exceptionally well. We indicated earlier that finding sources of funding other than the institution for "lightbulbs and toilet paper" is a challenge. Foundations, donors, and other grant-giving organizations are interested in funding only special projects that have a very high probability of success and that are sustainable after the funding is gone. Securing funding for this activity *may* free up general operating funds for important or special activities that are underfunded, if at all. Part of the niche aspect is using in-house expertise or doing something no other library in the area does or can do as well. There *will be* competition from other organizations seeking extra funding, and it will require an investment of time to be successful.

Fund-raising, while it may have to be a part-time activity, requires planning and leadership. It will not be effective if it is a matter of "I'll do it when I have time." Only the very large academic libraries have the luxury of a full-time fund-raiser. Most must depend on the efforts of several people who devote some of their time to fund-raising, a team approach. As with any team, there needs to be one person in charge to call meetings, set agendas, propose ideas, implement plans, push the initiative forward, and monitor outcomes—in essence, to provide the leadership. Generally, that person is the library's senior or next-most senior manager. One reason for this is because donors want to know they are working with the decision makers.

Regardless of source, income generation is a matter of the right person asking the right source for the right amount for the right project at the right time and in the right way. As you might imagine, getting all those "rights" right takes planning, practice, preparation, and practical experience. Workshops help, but only real-world experience and a few disappointments along the way will translate theory and ideas into "money in the bank."

Additional funding may be available from a variety of sources. One source is internally generated, assuming that the campus policy allows the library to keep income it generates. Some institutions don't allow for any, others allow some, and a few allow full retention. One long-standing internal revenue source for libraries is the sale of duplicate or otherwise unwanted gifts/donations. "Gifts in kind" to libraries are very common; how the unneeded items are disposed of varies. Publicly supported libraries need to be aware of any regulations regarding the disposal of "public property" and just when an item gains such status—in some instances it becomes upon acceptance; in other cases it becomes public property only when added to the collection. There may be tax implications for both the donor and recipient. Donors may receive tax deductions for donations in cash or kind to not-for-profit organizations.

Many academic libraries impose fines for rule infractions, lost or damaged items, etc., all of which generate income. How the campus treats such income can have an impact on the budget. Many public institutions require all fines go into the general operating fund, not credited to the agency collecting the fine. As you might guess, not getting monies paid for a lost or damaged item can become a drain on your budget, if you repair or replace the item. This in turn puts more pressure on you to raise monies from somewhere. A similar situation may exist for fees charged for services, although it is much more common for the service to be able to retain all or most of that income.

Check This Out

A good source for looking into the issue of internally generated income is Murry Martin and Betsy Park's 1998 *Charging and Collecting Fees and Fines* (New York: Neal-Schuman).

Another quasi–internal source is through activities undertaken by nonstaff people (support group) on behalf of the library—Friends of the Library, Library Associates, Supporters of ____, or some other title. Such groups may be no more formal than some volunteers to handle an ongoing book sale or may be a formal legal entity (foundation). There may be special types of internal funds such as endowments, wills, trusts, living trusts, etc. Such sources of funds are usually only found in larger academic libraries.

Check These Out

Good sources that address establishing a foundation are the following:

John A. Edie, *First Steps in Starting a Foundation*, 5th ed. (Washington, DC: Council on Foundations, 2002).

Bruce Hopkins, *Starting and Managing a Nonprofit Organization: A Legal Guide* (New York: John Wiley & Sons, 2001).

As libraries generate an ever greater amount of their total budget from noncampus sources, they create a foundation to handle outside funds. In the United States, such foundations are legal entities and generally have a 501(c)(3) status with the IRS. Such status means they must not engage in any type of political activity. A major reason for having a foundation is to raise funds that are generally not taken into consideration when establishing the library's share of campus funds. Another plus is that the foundation may invest the funds raised to generate still additional income. Without a doubt, such bodies can be very effective fund-raisers, as they are almost always composed of individuals who strongly support the service and its programs. Never underestimate the power of users voices when it comes to fund-raising.

Creating a strong positive relationship with the support group is essential. In many cases members pay an annual fee and expect to be approached for donations to special projects, perhaps to the acquisition of an important archive or piece of equipment for a library. In return, the library organizes special events for the members such as an annual dinner, a lecture, or series of lectures, or it offers special "behind the scenes" tours. All such events become relationship-building opportunities as well as fund-raising.

There are also some rare, and in the past over-looked, opportunities to raise some substantial amounts of money locally: wills and trusts, or "planned giving." Clearly, bequests in a will become a source of funds only at death. However, today many nonprofit groups actively work with people to be included in a will. Living trusts on the other hand come in many shapes and sizes. Some may generate income for the library only during the donor's life-time, others may generate income for both the donor and the library during the donor's lifetime, and others become effective only on the donor's death. These are likely to increase in importance for libraries over the coming years.

> **Check This Out**
>
> For academic libraries, regardless of type, a group source of information about "friends" groups is the American Library Association's www.altaff.org.

> **Check These Out**
>
> One online source of information on planned giving is Charitable Donations Through Planned Giving (www.paperglyphs.com/nporegulation/planned_giving.html).
>
> A book to consult, regardless of service type, is Amy Sherman and Matthew Leher's 2000 Legacies for Libraries: *A Practical Guide to Planned Giving* (Chicago, IL: American Library Association).

Partnerships with business are one of the newer fund-raising approaches for libraries, at least in the United States. Many libraries prefer to use the term "collaboration," as it seems less profit oriented. Glen Holt (2005) listed several reasons for seeking "corporate partnerships." His last reason, in our opinion, is the most telling: "co-funding through sponsorships can be a great way to build and share current and potential audiences between the public and private sector" (p. 35). What you need to do is think broadly/imaginatively to find spon-sorship possibilities. Partnerships with business can be extended to acquiring expertise that is not available within the service. Local radio and television stations may provide airtime, local newspaper reporters can brief staff on how to write good copy, and public relations companies may well be prepared to offer their help to not-for-profit services.

Grants and "gifts" from foundations and government agencies is our final "other funding" source category. (Our earlier section on grants outlined the basic of academic grant operations.) The art of grantsmanship is something you can develop—like any art it takes practice and then more practice before you have a degree of consistent success. Seeking grants is usually library project focused, such as for seed money for a new pro-gram, partial support of a facilities project, funds for new or replacement equipment, etc. As such it requires carefully thought out plans; in the case of facilities, it may require the existence of working drawings for the project.

An important step, in fact a key step, is to be certain you know what a foundation's or agency's current funding priorities are. Although their broad interest seldom changes over time, their annual funding priorities within the broad area may in fact vary from year to year. Do your research before making a call or sending a letter of inquiry. Most granting agencies have websites where you do a substantial amount of research about mission, priorities of the current funding cycle, what the funding cycle is, proposal guidelines, deadlines, and much more. Most grant-giving agencies are willing to talk by phone to explore projects. This can save the time of the agency and the library, if the nature of the proposed project can be outlined to see if it is within the scope of the agency. If it is, a valuable contact has been made.

If you have no prior experience in grant/proposal preparation, taking a workshop or two is well worth the time and possible expense. Some grant-giving agencies organize workshops to outline their requirements. Also, when possible seek the assistance of an experienced grant writer. Be prepared to fail to get a grant on your first few efforts; keep trying and you will succeed. The good news is that, with many foundations, once you are successful your chances of later grants go up, assuming you have delivered on the first grant.

> **Tip**
>
> Many granting agencies look very favorably on collaborative proposal. Proposal that relate to several types of information services engaging in a cooperative effort appear to be very attractive to agencies. An example of this is in the 2007 Loan Syndications and Trading Association (LSTA) grant guidelines in Arizona: "the library and partnering organization(s) develop a strategy to share and promote resources."

Even if the fund-raising is a part-time activity, there is an institutional cost. Time spent on fund-raising is time not spent on library activities. The library's position as part of the campus whole usually means that it must get approval before undertaking fund-raising activities. Campus development officers usually have the final say on such efforts. They do not want several campus units approaching the same source with different proposals—it makes the institution look bad. There also may be an existing relationship with the funding source and another campus unit that ought not be jeopardized. Another reason is to coordinate fund-raising activities as well as a sharing campus fund-raising expertise. Finally, there is an institutional need to assure the amount requested reflects actual costs as well as institutional priorities.

Cultivating relationships is a key to successful fund-raising. Major donations or modest ongoing gifts usually arise from long-term relationships based on respect and trust. For individual donors, this often means social contacts in a variety of settings, few of which relate directly to fund-raising. For foundations and granting agencies, it means successful projects that delivered the promised outcomes.

Part of developing/cultivating prospects involves making sure the work is completed as planned and on time. Sending a funding agency a final report on the project, especially if this is not a requirement, reminds the agency of your service and what good "value" their funds generate. Even more effective are the less formal contacts and communication; even just sending holiday greetings can help you keep in touch. The same idea applies to individual donors. Sending lists of items purchased for the collection using a donor's money or endowment income is a common library practice. While donors for a new building or space in the service receive invitations to attend the grand opening, they are often forgotten until the next fund-raising effort takes place. Letting such donors know about favorable reactions of customers and the general public to the new space is a way to keep in touch without "putting on the touch."

PLANNING AND BUDGETING

Linkages between planning and budgeting in higher education tend to be rather weak. Strategic, long-range, rolling plans are common, but when you look at how, or if, those plans link to annual budget cycles it is often difficult to find even indirect linkages. You will recall from your management 101 course that a budget is a plan (an estimate of what it will cost to operate over a period of time), consequently there should not be a problem with establishing linkages to other plans.

Long-term plans almost always reflect an institution's quest for more prestige, quality, and enrollment gains. This is where there should be clear links between aspirations and financial reality. Without that connection, financial and political problems are almost certain to arise. We suggest that the following five steps are essential to creating a sound system that links planning and budgeting for all campus units, not just the library:

- Have realistic estimates of what the cost would be for each action item in long-term/strategic plans.
- Estimate changes in revenues and prices for the action items over time in order to have a sense of what the costs will be in one year, two years, or longer. Keep in mind that in most cases the longer the wait the greater the cost.
- Allow for disproportionate budget shifts (unexpected gains or losses in revenues) and do not allow budget drift to occur unchecked.
- Monitor and reflect changes in institutional priorities as part of the annual budget process. This usually calls for some weighting system for the various budgetary components—will the library's first priority carry as much weight as the law school dean's first priority or within the library, will the reference department's first priority be equal to the catalog department's, etc.?
- Manage the conflicting pressures. You must understand that contenders for resources always attempt to exert as much influence as possible over decisions on how to allocate scarce resources.

No matter what method an institution employs, costs will increase over time for existing activities and at some point in time exceed available funding. When that occurs, the institution must either find additional money or cut expenses. This is when having an established system for assessing priorities proves its worth. It is also when Howard Bowen's (1980) five natural laws of higher education become most apparent:

- The dominant goals of an institution are educational excellence, prestige, and influence.
- In the quest for excellence, prestige, and influence, there is virtually no limit to the amount of money an institution could spend on seemingly fruitful educational ends.
- Each institution raises all the money it can.
- Each institution spends all the money it raises.
- The cumulative effect of the preceding four laws is toward ever increasing expenditures. (pp. 19–20)

Creating sound linkages between plans (aspirations) and fiscal reality is essential for the library and its parent institution. Without those linkages, the challenges of where to get adequate funds to maintain existing services or what to cut will become an annual painful process. Ultimately, the result will be closure, something we noted early in this chapter.

From the Authors

There are times in higher education when it seems as if, no matter what the official budgetary system is, there is an unofficial system in reality. One such system we experienced has sometimes been labeled "The King's Decree." What is probably a better label today would be "The King's Counselor's Decree." This often happens when there is an institution-wide budget committee whose membership is to reflect the various campus components and a membership that changes each year. The committee may spend months listening to unit heads pitching their budget requests and several weeks trying to sort out priorities in terms of available funds, only to have the institution vice presidents thank the group and indicate that they will be informed of what the budget will be. At best the process informs a growing number of staff, over time, about institutional income and expenses. At worst, it leads to a cynicism about the value of the presumed participatory process.

Another informal system is what has been called "Every Tub on Its Own Bottom." Harvard University does use a form of this method in that every unit is expected to draw much of its funding from its own sources. In the case of libraries, it generally means that any new activity had to find outside funding. Also, a majority of a library's collection development funds often came from endowment funds rather than from the institution. Needless to say, such an approach can lead to serious imbalances in services and collections.

A third notion, that is widely held, is that "The Squeaky Wheel Gets the Grease." Evans always started a new directorship by meeting with each staff person one on one. In one such meeting, a department head said, "You should know I'm a firm believer in the idea that the squeaky wheel gets the grease. Evans allowed as how that was sometimes the case, but it was also true that a wheel that squeaked too much could be taken off. Years later the department head said, at her retirement party, she always remembered that conversation whenever she came to request special funding for something.

KEY POINTS TO REMEMBER

- Expenditures on higher education in the United States are a significant element of the gross national product. Library expenditures are an important part of that total.
- There is somewhat of a disconnect between the fact that there are for-profit universities that do indeed make a profit and the financial problems of nonprofit colleges and universities and their libraries.
- Private institutions do in fact receive some funding from governments, usually in the form of research and student aid funding. Although not large amounts compared to public schools, the funds are important, but they rarely impact library finances.
- While overall budgets have been increasing in size, the percentage spent on direct instruction has been declining over the recent past. Library funding nationwide has maintained a surprisingly constant percentage of the total spent over the better part of 80 years.
- Personnel costs normally represent the major expense for academic institutions, including libraries. Only collection development funding comes close to matching library personnel costs.
- Benefit expenses are often overlooked by most academic employees, although those benefits may represent as much as 20 percent of their total compensation.
- Research/grants can be an important revenue stream for institutions offering advanced degrees.
- Grants can also raise some challenging issues related to balancing core institutional values and income generation as well as how much institutional support, such as libraries, is appropriate for noncore activities.
- Endowment building/management is increasingly important for higher education institutions and their libraries.

- Linkages between planning and budgeting need to be as strong as possible and are not strongly present in higher education.
- Libraries, if not their parent institutions, should spend time and effort in creating the strongest possible links between planning and budgeting.
- Fiscal management is about securing, expending, and accounting for the essential monies to operate the best possible library service.
- Budgeting is more than managing this year's allocation; it is thinking about what you will need in future as well how well you managed previous allocations.
- Budgeting is a political process and requires careful monitoring of the library's environment if you hope secure adequate funding.
- Securing funds from sources other than campus sources will become an increasingly important part of the library's fiscal management activities.

REFERENCES

Boese, Kent. 2006. Brother, can you spare another $2.6 billion? Editorial. *Bottom Line* 19, no.1: 3.

Bowen, Howard R. 1980. *The cost of higher education: How much do colleges and universities spend per student and how much should they spend?* San Francisco: Josey-Bass.

Buschman, John. 2003. *Dismantling the public sphere: Situating and sustaining librarianship in the age of the new public philosophy.* Westport, CT: Libraries Unlimited.

Cargill, Jennifer. 1987. Waiting for the auditor: Some interim advice. *Wilson Library Bulletin* 67, no. 9: 45–47.

Hidden cost of doing business. 2009. *Inside Higher Ed.* Available: insidehighered.com/layout/set/print/news/2009/01/07/rochester.

Holt, Glen. 2005. Getting beyond the pain: Understanding and dealing with declining library funding. *Bottom Line* 18, no. 4: 185–190.

Johnstone, D. Bruce. 2005. Financing higher education: Who should pay? In *American higher education in the twenty-first century*, 2nd ed., eds. Philip Altbach, Robert Berdahl, and Patricia Gumport, 369–392. Baltimore, MD: Johns Hopkins University Press.

Kaufman, Roger, and Geoffrey Woglan. 2008. Managing private college finances in an environment in which spending and revenues grow at different rates. *Journal of Educational Finance* 34, no. 2: 196–211.

Leonard, Christopher. 2009. It still pays to be a college grad. *Arizona Daily Sun*, January 11, p. A5.

Losco, Joseph, and Brian Fife. 2000. Higher education spending. In *Higher education in transition*, edited by Joseph Losco and Brian Fife, 51–82. Westport, CT: Bergin & Garvey.

Meraz, Gloria. 2002. The essentials of financial strength through sound lobbying fundamentals. *Bottom Line* 15, no. 2: 64–69.

National Association of College and University Business Officers. 2008. *NACUBO endowment survey—2007.* Washington, DC: NACUBO.

Pope, Justin. 2008a. College closings rare, but could rise in downturn. *Arizona Daily Sun*, November 17, p. A6.

———. 2008b. Study flunks 49 states in college affordability. *Arizona Daily Sun*, December 3, pp. A1, A6.

Seer, Gitelle. 2004. No pain, no gain: Stretching the library dollar. *Bottom Line* 17, no. 1: 10–14.

Shaughnessy, Thomas. 1989. Management strategies for financial crisis. *Journal of Library Administration* 11, no. 1: 67.

U.S. Department of Education. 2008. *Digest of education statistics.* NCES 2008-022. Washington, DC: Government Printing Office.

Walther, James. 2005. The more things change, the more they really change. *Bottom Line* 18, no. 3: 109.

Wildavsky, Aaron. 2006. *The new politics of the budgetary process.* Boston: Little, Brown.

Winston, Gordon C. 1997. Why can't a college be more like a firm? Williams College. Available: www.williams.edu/wpehe/DPs/DP-42.pdf.

LAUNCHING PAD

ALADN. n.d. Academic library advancement and development network. Available: www.library.arizona.edu/aladn/index.html

American Library Association. 2007. *The big book of library grant money 2007: Profiles of private and corporate foundations and direct corporate givers receptive to library grand proposals.* Chicago, IL: American Library Association.

Archibald, Robert B., and David H. Feldman. 2008. Explaining increases in higher education costs. *Journal of Higher Education* 79, no. 3: 268–295.

Blumenstyk, Goldie. 2008. The $375-billion question: Why does college cost so much? *Chronicle of Higher Education* 55, no. 6: A1–A15.

Bok, Derek C. 2003. *Universities in the marketplace: The commercialization of higher education.* Princeton, NJ: Princeton University Press.

Carpenter, Dave. 2009. Financial aid for college squeeze. *Arizona Daily Sun*, January 25, p. A1.

Ercolano, Adriana. 2007. But it's not my job…: The role librarians play in library development. *Bottom Line: Managing Library Finances* 20, no. 2: 94–96.

Guyer, Mark. 2002. *A concise guide to getting grants for nonprofit organizations.* New York: Kroshka Books.

Hallam, Arlita W., and Teresa R. Dalston. 2005. *Managing budgets and finances: A how-to-do-it manual for librarians and information professionals.* New York: Neal Schuman.

Hanamann, Henry. 1981. The rationale for exempting nonprofit organizations from corporate income taxation. *Yale Law Review* 91, no. 1: 54–100.

Hearn, James C., et al. 2006. Incentives for managed growth: A case study of incentives-based planning and budgeting in a large public research university. *Journal of Higher Education* 77, no. 2: 286–316.

Hebel, Sara. 2008. Colleges brace for cuts as state economies take a turn for the worse. *Chronicle of Higher Education* 54, no. 20: A17.

Jan, Tracy, and Andrew Ryan. 2008. Harvard's endowment plunges $8 billion. Available: www.boston.com/news/local/breaking_news/2008/12/harvards_endowm.html.

Jennings, Karlene N., and Kimberly A. Thompson. 2009. *More than a thank you note: Academic library fund raising for the dean or director.* Oxford: Chandos.

Kane, Thomas J., and Cecilia Elana Rouse. 2001. The community college: Educating students at the margin between college and work. In *ASHE reader on finance in higher education*, 2nd ed., ed. John L. Yeager et al. Boston, MA: Pearson Custom Publishing.

Rodas, Daniel. 2001. *Resource allocation in private research universities.* New York: Routlege-Falmar.

Stanley, Mary. 2008. Challenge grants: Frightening, frustrating, and fruitful. *Bottom Line: Managing Library Finances* 21, no. 1: 11–13.

Steele, Victoria, and Stephen Elder. 2000. *Becoming a fundraiser: The principles and practices of library development*, 2nd ed. Chicago: American Library Association.

Student loans: College on credit. 2009. *Economist* 390, no. 8613: 30–31.

UA provost suggests pay cuts. 2008. *Arizona Daily Sun*, December 23, p. A3.

Whalen, Edward. 1991. *Responsibility center budgeting: An approach to decentralized management for institutions of higher education.* Bloomington, IN: Indiana University Press.

Winston, Gordon C. 1999. For-profit higher education: Godzilla or chicken little. *Change* 25, no. 1: 14–19.

Chapter 8

Facilities

Aside from financial management itself the management of facilities has become what is commonly accepted as the largest of all nonacademic support functions of higher education.

—William Middleton (1989)

In the past fifty years, after a slow developmental phase, computer and information technology have truly transformed libraries.

—Norman D. Stevens (2006)

We are not abandoning our built libraries with the advent of the Internet but trying to make them more long-lasting, more environmentally sound.

—Bette-Lee Fox (2007)

Until relatively recently, every student's total higher educational experience included the "campus." An institutional goal was to make this a memorable (positive) experience—the stereotypical image of a campus was, and probably still is, a collection of large brick buildings covered with ivy, at least one of which has some type of tower, and, depending on the school's proclivity for athletics, a large football and/or basketball stadium/arena/complex. Thus, phrases such as "ivy-covered walls" and "ivory tower" remain the public's shorthand for higher education. To be sure, many such schools exist and convey a sense of collegiate life. Perhaps sometime during this millennium the "campus" will cease to be an issue beyond a few buildings to house personnel and computers. Until that day arrives, buildings and their management will be a challenging issue on most academic campuses.

At any large school there are a variety of building types—for example, administrative/office, classrooms library, laboratories/research facilities, health care facilities, gymnasium and other athletic venues, maintenance facilities, and parking lot/structure. Each type represents some special management challenges and, of course, costs to build and maintain. Managing the campus complex (in some cases the equivalent of a small town) rests on three broad functional areas: planning and acquisition, maintenance and operation, and assignment/utilization. Generally planning and acquisition functions involve the facilities staff and one or all of the expected tenants of the building. More often than not it also involves outside expertise, such as architects and telecommunications specialists.

Some campus facilities place a greater burden for their management and operation on the occupants than do others in what is called a semi-decentralized facilities management approach. Almost any building that is solely occupied by one activity is likely to fall into this category. Libraries are one of those types on most campuses. This means the library staff have a greater responsibility for the building and how it is utilized and maintained. At the simplest level, an example is on a rainy day you either call maintenance to come to the library (a centralized system) to place "Caution Wet Floor" signs in the entryway or a library staff member sets out the signs (decentralized).

Assignment and reutilization is generally one of the more centralized aspects of campus facilities management. Libraries become part of this activity at various times during the life of the campus. Collection growth over time means that libraries eventually exceed their storage capacity and must have more space. There are several options for handling such growth, as we will discuss later in this chapter; however, building a new library provides both the opportunity and the challenge of what to do with the old library. In today's economic environment, the challenges may be substantial as the institution may have exhausted donor interest during the fund-raising for the new building and little or no money is available to repurpose/remodel the vacated facility.

> **Keep In Mind**
>
> We use the library as the higher education facilities example throughout this chapter. Libraries are one of the most complex buildings on a campus in terms of operations and maintenance.

A given on almost every campus is there is never enough space to address all of the articulated needs, from parking (perhaps the most contentious issue), to classrooms, to office size, and the list could go on and on. Who gets how much space, where, for how long, and who is first in line for a new facility or major renovation brings out the worst in campus politics. Libraries are often in the forefront of such priority struggles, as they exhaust some of their collection space each year and can easily project when that space will be completely gone.

Academic libraries are atypical of most campus buildings. First, at least for the foreseeable future, their collections will continue their annual growth and will require more space. While the space needs on campus do grow over time, only libraries can accurately project, more or less, when they will exhaust their capacity. One challenge when designing new space is getting the nonlibrarian members of the planning team to fully comprehend the notion of ongoing growth. Often they say something along the lines of, "We can't have empty shelves or spaces when the building opens; people will think we've wasted space." In the past, the ideal was to plan a library that could handle at least 20 years of growth, which leaves a large amount of unused capacity on opening day.

Another factor that contributes to the library's atypical role is its hours of operation. More often than not, the library is open for service more than almost any other building type on campus. Unless the library is open 24/7, you can count on some pressure from students to expand service hours. Long hours, open at night, on weekends, and frequently on some of the minor holidays when the rest of campus is closed means that staff members have to take on some building management responsibility.

A third factor is greater wear and tear on the building and its furniture and equipment as a result of the long service hours. The only campus buildings that probably receive as much or more use and some abuse are residence halls. Even those halls have some breaks in service between terms and are periodically taken out of service during the summer so they may be refurbished. This rarely occurs for a campus library, even when such work does occur. The staff normally is expected to provide some service somewhere, perhaps having to work around the workpeople who are repairing/remodeling. One example of the wear issue is floor coverings. Floors are usually carpeted to reduce unwanted noise. Carpeting will have to be replaced on a regular basis, especially in the entryways and other high traffic areas. Replacing floor covering in high traffic areas while maintaining some level of service can be a challenge. All in all, deferring library building maintenance is a poor option as the cost of handling the work will only escalate over time. Be aware of the term *deferred building maintenance* because many institutional facilities and other campus administrators will use it to keep the yearly maintenance costs down and have the tendency to see the library as a permanent line in that category. This is discussed further in this chapter.

PLANNING FOR NEW SPACE

Planning any new or extensive renovation is a team effort between campus facilities personnel and those who will occupy the new space. Only a few academic librarians have the experience of planning a new library. However, almost everyone in the field will have to deal with major additions, remodeling, or working on plans for a remote storage facility at sometime during her or his career. If there are times when team planning is essential, not just nice, this is one such occasion. None of the projects should reside solely in the hands of senior administrators; those who have to make the space work as well as those who will use the space must be involved in order for a successful outcome.

> **Tip**
>
> If nothing else, soliciting input by bringing users and staff together in focus groups provides helpful advice and gives them a sense of ownership in the project.

Perceived needs almost always far exceed the funds available. This means there must be serious rethinking of space priorities. One sad fact is that the planning process takes time, for a new building perhaps several years. As the timeline extends, the cost of construction escalates, which often means that at the very end of the planning activity something called "value engineering" has to take place. Value engineering is a nice way of saying, "You have to reduce the cost of the project by X dollars." What usually gets cut at that point is equipment and furniture.

In an ideal situation, a new or remodeled facility should be the following:

- Flexible
- Adaptable
- Expandable
- Accessible
- Compact
- Stable in climate control
- Secure
- Attractive
- Economical to operate and maintain
- Comfortable
- Scalable

Flexibility is essential since the use of the space changes over time. For example, the nature of technical service activities has been changing over the past 20 years and is likely to continue to do so. More and more libraries are using outside services, such as PromptCat, to process their copy cataloging; this reduces the need for as many workstations. Changes in reference work means that staff members, who formerly sat at a service desk for most of their shift, now stand in the computer area assisting users (Warnement, 2003). This in turn changes the need for as much space at what was the primary workstation. A modular building with few, if any, internal weight-bearing walls is typical of a flexible design. This type of design has been the standard planning model for libraries for many years. Internal weight-bearing walls cannot be moved as needed without causing structural damage or requiring very expensive structural work.

Given the inevitable growth of archives and libraries, having a facility that can be expanded is highly desirable. Funds for an addition or remodeling are somewhat easier to raise than for an entirely new building simply because such work rarely costs as much as a new building. The designer must plan for future expansion and how it would relate to the designed structure. Very often libraries discover that the area labeled "future expansion" on the original plans turns out to be unsuitable or no longer available when the time comes to expand. This is true whether the expansion was identified within the building or as a future addition to the building.

The design also needs to take into account the needs of disabled users and staff. Retrofitting space to meet standards such as the Americans with Disabilities Act of 1990 (ADA) can be very expensive, as many libraries have learned. Such retrofits are likely to cover just about every aspect of the building from the entrance to aisle width, to handicap accessibility, to a host of other issues.

> **Tip**
>
> Professional journals such as *American Libraries* and *Library Journal* publish annual reviews of new and renovated archive and library premises, which are sources of information about trends in design and architectural practices. They also provide cost data.

Ideally, the primary planning team consists of five or more persons: architect, library representative, specialist/space planning consultant, designer, and representative of the parent institution, and in some circumstances a user. Larger teams are possible, but the larger the group, the longer the process takes. Clearly many people will need to have input to the project at different stages, but every additional person involved in every aspect of the project slows the planning activities.

The need for an architect is apparent. The library representative always will be one or more of the senior management team, if not *the* senior manager, because decisions need to be made reasonably quickly, especially in the later stages of the project. Campus representation is necessary to monitor project costs and to ensure that the design will fit into the campus building master plan.

> **Check These Out**
>
> The classic guide to planning academic libraries is Philip Leighton and David Weber's *Planning Academic and Research Library Buildings*, 3rd edition (Chicago: American Library Association, 2000).
>
> Other useful titles are *Academic Library Building Renovation Benchmarks* (New York: Primary Research, 2008); Janet McNeil Hurlbert's *Defining Relevancy: Managing the New Academic Library* (Westport, CT: Libraries Unlimited, 2008); Richard McCarthy's *Managing Your Library Construction Project: A Step-By-Step Guide* (Chicago: American Library Association, 2007); and Edward Ling's *Solid, Safe, Secure: Building Archives Repositories in Australia* (Canberra: National Archives of Australia, 1998).

A library building consultant provides expertise that is critical to achieving a successful outcome, as few of the other planning team members are likely to have much, if any, prior experience with such planning (Boone, 2003). Few librarians, or architects for that matter, have had experience with such a project, and even fewer have had that experience more than once. Planning any new building is a complex task—libraries are among the most complex buildings to design effectively. Like any construction project, it requires highly detailed data. Working drawings (the documents used during construction) specify everything down to nail and screw sizes. The consultant is usually the only person on the planning team with multiple experiences in developing effective designs for library service operations. A consultant's role will be to ensure that at least the interior design will be functional and as cost-effective to operate as possible.

A key document in the planning process is the building program. It is the outcome of the joint effort between library staff and the consultant outlining what functions take place, the space requirements for those functions, the relationship between functions, and other key issues such as projected growth. The architect uses the information to develop some alternative layouts and creates some schematic designs for the team to review. Often it, and some schematics, are used to raise funds for the project. To that end, it normally includes information about the existing services, collections, staff, and service population along with data about the campus. At the heart of the program, and essential for the architect, are data sheets for all the activities and units built in to the new facility. Data sheets cover not only the equipment and people that will occupy the space but also the relationship of that space to other spaces in the facility.

There are several stages in the design phase of the project—the conceptual drawings, the schematic drawings, and final working drawings. Each stage brings the project closer having a physical facility. The initial stage is very important to achieving a functional building as it is where various concepts may be laid out, with minimal cost, in order to gain a sense of the relationships and gross square footages for various activities. This is also where input from staff, students, faculty, and other stakeholders is most valuable. By the second stage, aspects of the building are more fixed, and essentially only one overall approach is "on the table." The final stage is when the final design elements are put into place. After this point, changes become more problematic and costly to implement.

The first stage yields conceptual drawings reflecting several different exterior designs and some blocks of interior space indicating work areas, collection space, etc., and their relationships to one another. Selection of the exterior design and shape of the facility occurs at this point, and the choice can have major implications for the project. A plain square or rectangular building is the least costly. As the exterior walls become more complex (L-shaped, curved walls, or irregular in some way) the cost of the exterior rises, possibly leaving less money for the interior. In today's world the concern about being "green" (see, for example, the Leadership in Energy and Leadership Design [LEEDS] rating system at www.usgbc.org) can present some significant cost considerations. Many of the new designs/features of LEEDS-type projects are more costly to install but over the life of the building save money. The challenge is balancing the available funds against long-term operational costs and library service needs for the present.

Another green building feature (windows) has been a challenge for some time. Users, staff and architects love windows. Librarians who care about preserving collections, however, want to avoid them. We will come back to such concerns in the chapter on services.

Some academic libraries become campus symbols or monuments. This generally translates into a dramatic architectural statement. Such statements are almost always costly and do little to help the library provide effective quality service. A simple cube or shoebox design does not usually make much of a statement. Conflicts over exterior statements versus the requirement for adequate functional interior space frequently emerge during this stage. This can be particularly trying when there is a donor involved whose name will go on the building and that person expects to have a "memorial" on campus.

The second stage yields the schematic drawings reflecting the architect's interpretation of the building program. These drawings start to reflect building and safety codes. Staff and user input are critical at this stage, as they will have to work in and use the space. The planning team should listen carefully to their comments and, whenever possible, incorporate them into the final design. It is at this stage that major adjustments in the location of this or that activity are the easiest to make since most of the detailed drafting comes later. An important consideration at this stage is the estimate of the operational costs for the facility and how they may be minimized.

Final working drawings are the last design stage. Here the drawings are complete to the last detail—which way a door opens, how wide it is, what it is made of, what color it is, etc. They reflect all aspects of the building, and they along with the specification documents become the basis for contractors to bid on the construction. There is a final review and approval process by the "owners"—the library and the institution—that in essence states, "Yes, this is actually what we want built in all its detail." The reason this is so critical is that anything forgotten in the design or inaccurately placed in the final drawings may be correctable or added, but for an additional charge. In the United States, such corrections are known as change orders; the more change orders, the less money will be available for furniture and equipment. So a thorough review of the construction documents is critical to the level of funding available to finish the project as planned.

There has been speculation that the number of visits made to academic libraries would decrease as remote use increased. Shill and Tonner (2003) surveyed over 300 U.S. academic libraries and described the types of recent building projects and the kinds of improvements made. A second paper examined the impact of changes on the use of the physical library. They found that while there was decreased collection, reference, and building usage in general, the majority of new and improved libraries had experienced sustained increases in the use of the physical facilities. Over a quarter reported an increase of over 100 percent (Shill and Tonner, 2004).

With a possible trend toward the development of joint-use services, such as at the San Jose State University library who shares a single facility with the city library, the planning of facilities raises new possibilities for collaboration beyond just the physical facility aspect. The needs of all users and staff must be taken into account, and there can be conflicting interests. But good communication, a positive approach to planning, and goodwill can overcome difficulties and produce a cost effective solution.

MANAGING THE FACILITY

Among the changing and challenging tasks for managers in all organizations in the twenty-first century is that of managing a facility. Changes in the operating environment increase the responsibility and accountability, which include:

- pressure to give more attention to environmental factors such energy efficiency;
- pressure to address health and safety issue of staff, users, and collections;
- pressure to maintain up-to-date technology while restraining technology expenses; and
- pressure to keep overall operating costs down.

Managing the facility is a responsibility of the library staff throughout their careers. Service hours are generally longer than any one staff member's workday. As we noted earlier, operational hours often cover seven days a week and sometimes they are 24/7. Inevitably some problems will arise when few, if any, senior members of staff are on duty and a high-level decision must be made.

Housekeeping Matters

Housekeeping is a critical issue, as poorly performed work can affect the health and safety of staff and users. Good housekeeping starts at ground level with questions such as who picks up litter and empties wastebaskets and how often? How often are the public and staff restrooms cleaned and provisioned? Does custodial staff have responsibility to dust the books and shelves? (The usual answer is that they do not dust books or shelves.) If not, how will the library handle the issue? Book dust can cause health problems for staff and users alike. This may seem like a small problem, but some health issues are involved, more for staff than for users. Staff can become sick from extended exposure to "collection dust," an affliction certified by medical professionals. In extreme cases, the person may be unable to return to work. The cost to vacuum the books and shelves in even a modest size academic library often runs to tens of thousands of dollars for a single cleaning.

Beyond the health issue, which is serious but not common, you must consider the health of the collection. Dust and dirt on the shelves act as a very fine abrasive, as users and staff pull them off shelves and replace the item. Over time that small damage from such cycles accumulates to the point that the item needs repair or replacement. Senior management has to balance and determine the average annual cost of such repair and replacement against the cost of having shelves cleaned. Dust also plays havoc with computers, photocopiers, and other equipment.

Other housekeeping issues include lights that burn out, temperature fluctuations, sun control, and plumbing. What happens when a user reports late on a Saturday afternoon that a water faucet in the restroom will not shut off and water is spilling over the floor? Is there someone to call? Will someone fix it before the start of the next shift? What does the staff do until the problem is resolved? Having plans and procedures in place assists in handling such issues. The library should have a disaster plan/emergency response plan in place that guides staff in determining what to do in such cases, albeit not a major disaster. At small and medium-size libraries where staff may not have formal responsibility delegated to them for housekeeping matters, all staff from the most senior professional to the work study students play a role in ensuring that the premises are maintained to the highest possible standard. At larger libraries it is possible to assign a full-time person to oversee facility and maintenance activities.

In most cases, custodial staff members are not part of the library staff or even employees of the school; the institution outsources such services. If they are full-time institutional staff, there is a high probability they are unionized and have a contract clearly delineating the

> **Tip**
>
> Assigning a staff member to do at least a daily walkabout is one way to spot housekeeping problems and have them addressed as quickly as possible.

> **Check These Out**
>
> Carmine Trotta and Marcia Trotta, *The Librarian's Facility Management Handbook* (New York: Neal-Schuman, 2001) and Cheryl Bryan, *Managing Facilities for Results: Optimizing Space for Services* (Chicago: American Library Association, 2007).

From the Authors

One small example, based on our experience, was an ongoing discussion/issue with a custodial staff supervisor regarding the vacuuming of carpets on stairways. While there was an agreement that custodians should vacuum floor carpets every day, the contract said nothing about the carpeted stairs *between floors*. The supervisor would vacuum the stairs but at an extra fee. Although it was a minor matter, it took time and generated occasional negative comments from users and staff. Who would have thought that becoming an academic librarian might entail spending time determining who cleans the stairways?

Try This

Write down four reasons why housekeeping must be considered to be of high importance to the manager of an information service.

services provided. Anything not covered or going beyond contractual limits may be available, but only at an additional charge. With tight budgets, extra charges are difficult, if not impossible, to handle.

Managing Risk and the Unexpected

Academic libraries, like any other facility on campus, must assess risks to people and library resources (collections and equipment, for example) and develop plans for handling potential problems. It is fine to have a library disaster plan for events such as water leaks or earthquakes, but if that plan is not integrated into a campuswide plan much of its value will be lost.

Risk management is a campuswide issue, as the school's equivalent of homeowners insurance is campuswide rather than by building. Like any insurance, the fewer claims filed the less costly the policy will be. Most institutional insurance firms have risk managers who are generally willing to assist in assessing the risk factors in a building (a risk audit).

Two challenging areas are how to place a value on the library's general collections for insurance purposes and what do about items in the rare book/special collections/archive areas. If a Shakespeare first folio is stolen or burned, you are not too likely to find a replacement copy. So what is the point in having funds for replacement? At least this is often the view of insurers and often senior campus managers. Insurers talk of making the insured "whole" after a claim and see little point in paying out for something that cannot be replaced. On the institutional side, having coverage for multimillion dollar items that cannot be replaced only drives up the cost of the insurance.

Check This Out

A detailed article describing the elements of a risk management plan is John McGinty's "Enhancing Building Security: Design Considerations" in *Library & Archival Security* 21, no. 2 (2008): 115–127.

A risk management program will identify risks and analyze the situation, the potential costs involved, and how they can be effectively and efficiently managed. Crisis management recognizes that there is a "golden

From the Authors

Alire was very much involved in working with university risk managers, insurance representatives, and disaster consultants in dealing with multimillion dollar insurance claims during several disasters at two universities. It is critical that a senior manager representing the library is always in the meetings when dealing with insurance claims of library materials and facilities. See Camila A. Alire (Ed.), *Library Disaster Planning and Recovery Handbook* (New York: Neal-Schuman, 2000).

hour"—the period during the earliest stages of managing a crisis when critical decisions are taken.

HEALTH, SAFETY, AND SECURITY

Health, safety, and security are critical issues for staff and users. Many hazards can emerge in managing facilities open to the public, and employers have a duty to care for staff and users. Laws enacted at either the national or local levels govern some points (for example, the number and placement of emergency exits). No insurance company will permit a policyholder to take unacceptable risks. However, some health, safety, and security issues are not addressed in building codes, national legislation (ADA for example), or insurance policies. It is up to the staff to address these potential problems. Having a team (disaster preparedness committee) of staff members who not only draw up plans for emergencies but also look for potential hazards is one method to start handling these areas.

Assuming the scientists are correct, a new challenge on the horizon is maintaining a comfortable work environment

> **Check This Out**
>
> Mary Breighner, William Payton, and Jeanne Drewes, *Risk and Insurance Management Manual for Libraries* (Chicago: American Library Association, 2005).

and collection storage conditions as the effects of global warming become stronger. For years, the issue of controlling temperature and humidity levels in libraries has been a challenging task. Probably every librarian has wondered from time to time, "Why, if they can send people into outer space and not have them freeze or burn to death, can they not design a building heating, ventilating, and air conditioning (HVAC) system for Earth that works?" One reason for user and staff complaints is variations in an individual's thermostat. Some people like cool temperatures; others prefer warmer environments. In addition to individual preferences, over time, systems break down, need to be taken out of service for maintenance, and simply wear out. As with other custodial work, the people responsible for servicing the HVAC are rarely part of the library staff. This means that issues of response time and level of service become matters of discussion and complaints. Some schools have a senior manager who is thought of as "energy tsar," in charge of managing

> **From the Authors**
>
> Mitigating a potential mold outbreak in a major special collections center was more challenging for one of us when dealing with the campus facilities staff who thought we were overreacting and didn't appreciate our disagreeing with their recommendations for temperature and humidity control. This happened during our monsoon weather season when the HVAC system was turned off for a long holiday weekend during asbestos abatement work in the library. It pays for library staff to be persistent in areas that they, too, have expertise.

institutional energy cost. There can be some heated debates with such individuals when it comes to temperature and humidity levels that are necessary for libraries. (The best option is to gain agreement on maintaining uniform levels rather than have wide swings and at something near the recommended standards.)

Another challenge is balancing concerns for people and the collections. Generally people need a warmer environment than is desirable for the collections. With this, compromises become necessary. Both staff and customers generally prefer a working temperature at or near 72 degrees Fahrenheit with 50 to 60 percent humidity. Ideal storage conditions for collections are 60 degrees Fahrenheit and 50 percent or less humidity. Intermixing people, equipment, and collections—a long-standing library planning concept—usually results in setting the desired levels in terms of people and technology preferences. Separation of collections and other elements, such as the human element, may not be feasible or affordable and probably would require two HVAC systems or modification of a single system into the equivalent of two systems.

Academic libraries, regardless of type, have some long-term preservation responsibilities. The university libraries have the greatest responsibility, but even community colleges have at least a modest amount of concern in this area. Institutions commit substantial amounts of money to acquiring materials for collections as well as equipment that must, or should, last for a great many years. The greater the preservation time frame the greater the likelihood the preservation conditions will reduce the degree of meeting people's comfort levels.

Safety is divided into three major areas: safety from physical harm, safety of belongings, and psychological safety. Senior librarians must address all of these areas and balance the needs of people, collections, and technology.

To gain an overview of safety issues, it is necessary to conduct a security audit as part of the risk management program. One way is to create a security checklist drawing on the expert advice from the campus facilities manager and then carry out the survey. If this expertise is not available from within the organization, then the local police and/or fire department and the insurance company will usually be able to provide professional advice, for they have an interest in seeing that safe conditions exist and generally welcome inquiries. These external bodies need to be aware of potential hazards before a crisis occurs.

A security audit covers all of the safety areas noted previously. Basics about existing fire protection equipment and emergency exits should be part of a survey. Unfortunately, people and "thing" safety can again come into conflict. In any academic library, there will be one or more emergency exits located in areas not visible to the staff and users. (Emergency exits are mandated by fire protection and building codes. Their location is a function of distance between exit, the number of persons in an area, and the activities in the area.) While emergency exits provide for people's safety, they also provide a means by which people may leave, taking materials with them without following borrowing procedures.

One method to control the problem of materials going "walkabout" is during the design stage, by placing service points within sight of all such exits. However, even in modest-sized buildings, this is almost impossible to accomplish. Another method is to install door alarms so that their opening sets off an alarm. Usually the best that happens in such cases is that the staff knows an unauthorized use of an exit occurred. (Most door alarm systems have an enunciator panel that has a light for each alarmed door. When an unauthorized opening occurs that door's number lights up so staff know where to check.) Usually, by the time a staff member gets to the offending door, the exiting person is no longer in sight. Higher levels of security may be necessary such as closed-circuit television cameras or designated security staff, with the benefits of these costs weighed against the installation and ongoing costs.

Collection items have a way of "growing legs" and leaving the building without benefit of being checked out. Many libraries, not just academic, install a security system similar to those employed in retail stores to help control loss rates. These systems use electronic strips ("targets") placed in collection items and an exit control unit that sounds an alarm if the item has not been properly discharged. These systems are expensive to purchase, and the annual costs for "targets" can also be substantial. Is it worth the cost? The answer is it depends on local circumstances. In making a decision about investing in a security system, managers should do the following:

- Collect data on thefts, such as:
  ◦ user complaints about mutilated materials
  ◦ number of items in the "lost or missing file"
  ◦ random sample of collection inventory
- Collect data on users "forgetting" to check out items
- Collect data on the amount of money spent annually on replacements
- Collect data on the cost of security system to install, maintain, and estimate annual cost of targets

With these data in hand, a decision can be made about the cost-benefit of installing a collection security system.

Crime

We live in a society where crime seems to increase yearly. In the workplace, as well as anywhere the public gathers, there are security issues. In the authors' experience, students have a mixed faith about the honesty of their peers. They often come to the library to study with their backpacks and laptops, work for a while before deciding to go to the restroom or to the student center for something to eat or drink, leaving behind their belongings and returning later to find something or everything missing. They become upset with the library staff about the loss while claiming they did not think anyone would take anything. They leave their things about even when there are workspace signs present warning against such behavior.

Academic libraries have had their share of criminal activities over the years, from minor vandalism to murder/suicide. No setting—rural or urban—is immune to such activity. It is the low-level problems that keep staff busy, such as items going missing from a workspace, confrontations over who should get to use a study space, and theft of collection items, to name but a few. However, anyone who stays in the profession any length of time will likely witness or experience serious antisocial behavior, including but not limited to physical violence between users or between a user and a staff member, attempted rape, indecent exposure, and occasionally gang activity. One key to providing a secure work/study atmosphere is to work with the campus public safety/police to develop guidelines for handling various behaviors ranging from the upset user to the worst type of behavior. These guidelines should cover how much or how little the staff should do to handle the situation, when to call campus security/police, when to call local police, and to whom within the library the staff member should report the incident (as a follow-up measure if an incident occurs on a night/weekend).

A security audit will assist in identifying areas with greater or lesser potential for trouble. User spaces in isolated or remote parts of the building are higher-risk areas than in large open areas that have many user spaces. Poorly lit and remote staircases are also high-risk areas. Academic library managers have several options that range from:

- doing nothing (let the individual assume all risk);
- devoting some staff time to patrolling the building (which reduces time for productive work);
- hiring security staff or a firm to patrol the building (a costly but effective option); and/or
- installing a variety of electronic surveillance equipment (costly and could carry unexpected legal consequences, such as questions of privacy).

There is no doubt that some action to protect both users and staff must take place. Often at closing time only two or three staff are on duty to close down the facility. Some academic libraries are in areas where the crime rate is high and/or are geographically isolated, making the staff vulnerable, particularly during night shifts. Many campuses provide escort services for both students and staff during night service hours.

Few people, if any, decide to work in a library because they want to be police officers. They are often surprised to find that they may have to monitor behaviors and perhaps become involved in some unpleasant encounters. Having developed guidelines as well as providing training in dealing with "difficult people" will help reduce the stress that may arise from this aspect of working in any type of library.

These are some of the day-to-day facility management issues—enough to make the point that the physical facility requires managing and monitoring just as much as people and collections do.

> **Check These Out**
>
> Pamela Cravey, *Protecting Library Staff, Users, Collections, and Facilities: A How-To-Do-It Manual for Librarians* (New York: Neal-Schuman, 2001).
> Robert O'Neill, *Management of Library and Archival Security: From the Outside Looking In* (Binghamton, NY: The Haworth Press, 1998).
> Bruce A. Shuman, *Library Security and Safety Handbook* (Chicago: American Library Association, 1999).

Disaster Management

During the course of your academic library career you are likely to have to deal with one or more facility disasters: major vandalism, leaking water pipes/roofs, wind damage and other natural disasters, fire, and possibly even terrorist acts.

One outcome of a security audit should be a comprehensive security plan. One element of a good plan addresses day-to-day problems. Another element is a disaster preparedness plan. Developing such a plan requires time and effort but is essential if the library is to successfully deal with a disaster. Every department must participate in the plan's development since it affects everyone. A steering committee with a representative from each unit is most effective when it comes to developing a plan as well as to regularly reviewing and updating the plan. Keys to developing a successful plan include the following:

- A realistic assessment of potential disasters
- Consideration of handling the differences between a service disaster and one that is part of a larger local or regional disaster
- Determination of collection salvage priorities
- Determination of insurance coverage and authority to commit funds for recovery
- Procedures to activate when a disaster or incident occurs

- Staff training to ensure that the procedures work and that staff are aware of them
- A telephone tree for emergency telephone calls, starting with the person who will direct the recovery efforts
- A list with telephone numbers of recovery resource vendors and service providers
- A schedule for regular reviews of the plan and updating the information
- Developing a partnership with local libraries to which users can be directed when a disaster strikes

> **Try This**
>
> Create a list of the types of disasters that might occur in an academic library with which you are familiar. List all of the points that should be included in a disaster management program, taking into account the disasters you have identified.

The most common disaster is water damage, and not just from major storms or firefighting efforts. Water pipes and radiators break. (They seem to have the capacity of knowing when no one is on duty and can leak for a long time before being noticed.) Even an unremarkable rain can cause damage if building maintenance has been deferred for too long; we will come back to deferred maintenance later in this chapter. Having some of the necessary recovery supplies on hand and having practiced salvaging water-soaked materials provides the best chance of saving the highest possible percentage of damaged items.

Recovery plans for various natural disasters—earthquakes, hurricanes, tornadoes, and typhoons—vary with the disaster type, expected frequency, and damage expected. Other factors to consider in writing a plan are the age of the facility (newer structures are more likely to reflect higher building standards) and what, if any, disaster recovery plans may exist campuswide.

While the probability of a natural disaster occurring can be calculated, vandalism and terrorism are less predictable, and the results can be serious. Even vandalism can be costly. Removing graffiti from a brick wall is surprisingly time consuming and therefore expensive.

Certainly, thought must go into developing a plan for handling all of today's information technology equipment in the event of a disaster. Although you can replace equipment, data recovery may be critical to returning to any level of service. Without a plan, the recovery process will take a substantial amount of time, or the data may be totally lost. Hence it is important that you have a regular backup schedule, at least once a day, and store copies off-site to minimize the possibility of loss.

One thing is certain about a major disaster: not everything will be salvageable. Some documents will be destroyed while most will have some damage, but there will not be time or money to save everything. Thus, it is essential to set collection priorities *before* the disaster strikes. What is irreplaceable (first priority), what is expensive and perhaps difficult to replace but is replaceable (second priority), and what is easy to replace (last priority) are typical academic library priorities. Setting these priorities will prove more difficult than you might imagine, as staff members will have differing views depending on their primary area of responsibility. Checking with users and perhaps other campus administrators often reveals that library staff and users have very different views about what should be the priorities. Library staff members may need to spend a substantial amount of time explaining and justifying the priorities, and, eventually, reduce the size of the first and second priority categories.

Check These Out

Deborah Halsted, Richard Jasper, and Felicia Little, *Disaster Planning: A How-To-Do-It Manual with Planning Templates on CD-ROM* (New York: Neal-Schuman, 2005).

Virginia Jones and Kris E. Keyes, *Emergency Management of Records and Information Programs* (New York: ARMA International, 2001).

Miriam Kahn, *Disaster Response and Planning for Libraries*, 2nd ed. (Chicago: American Library Association, 2003).

Johanna Wellheiser, Jude Scott, and John Barton, *An Ounce of Prevention: Integrated Disaster Planning of Archives, Libraries and Records Centers* (Lanham MD: Scarecrow and the Canadian Archives Foundation, 2003).

Professional journals provide graphic accounts of unexpected happenings (e.g., the aftermath of 9/11 or the 2005 floods in New Orleans), learning aids for managers, and case studies for staff training sessions. In addition, Conservation Online's "Disaster Preparedness and Response" page (cool-palimpsest.stanford.edu/bytopic/disasters/index.html) is a current source for information regarding disaster plans and disaster recovery supply resources.

A recovery plan must also address the financial aspects of the situation. Time is of the essence in the recovery of documents, and the time can translate into dollars. Waiting 72 hours or more to process wet paper materials means that there is little point in trying to recover them. Waiting to get approval to commit funds to handle recovery efforts after disaster strikes will probably mean missing the window of opportunity to save paper-based materials. The senior library managers will not have unlimited emergency spending authority, but having a reasonable upper-limit spending power is essential. This is why it is necessary to know the level of insurance coverage, the average salvage costs for high priority material, and where to go for advice and assistance. All are important keys to managing the recovery efforts.

The presence or absence of a trained recovery team is a key factor in saving as much as possible. Often the person responsible for library preservation activities is head of the team, assuming that the individual works well under high pressure and stress. (Whoever is team leader, this person must be able to stay calm, effectively direct team efforts, and at least give an outward appearance of being in full control of the situation.) Team members ought to have cell phones with programmed telephone numbers of all the key people likely to be involved in the salvage effort.

Having a regular practice of fire drills, building evacuation, and handling of fire-fighting equipment creates awareness of procedures to be followed in an emergency and ensures that the premises can be speedily and safely evacuated. A fire drill can identify any problems that may have been overlooked, such as hazards that temporarily block stairs or aisles.

Another aspect of disaster management is dealing with the emotional impact that the staff and users will experience (Klasson, 2002). The feelings that are generated need understanding, and it is important to have a plan in place to address those feelings. Knowing about counseling services that can be contacted if required is sensible, since the full impact of the incident may not be immediately evident.

ASSIGNING SPACE

There never seems to be enough space on a campus to meet everyone's desires. The facilities manager has the rather unenviable job of being the arbiter/tsar of space.

Libraries rank high on the list of those wanting additional space. More and more academic libraries have to house their collections remotely, not in the main library. Remote storage facilities are generally warehouse-like in order to keep costs as low as possible. There is often no user space, aisle width is as narrow as building and safety codes allow, and shelving is as high as feasible and frequently of the compact type (shelving on rails to reduce the number of access aisles). The library and facilities manager must work closely to assure space will be available when needed. One consequence of the library's constant need for more square footage is that other units on campus resent the library's apparent unlimited appetite for space.

When a library is fortunate enough to have an entirely new building constructed, the line of units wanting access to the old building is often very long. This is where the advantages of a modular building become apparent to everyone on campus. It can be relatively inexpensive to modify the structure for nonlibrary use.

DEFERRED MAINTENANCE

Before closing the discussion of campus facilities, we need to look at the issue of deferred maintenance—that is, not carrying out repairs or retrofits on existing buildings as soon as called for by the building condition(s). During periods of budget shortfalls, one of the easy places to cut expenses is in facility maintenance. One way facilities managers may try to save money is delaying something like having a roof redone or windows recaulked. Decisions to defer are relatively easy to make. Frequently, the work is not done until after a significant problem occurs when the cost is substantially higher than it would have been had the problem been corrected in the first place. This happens because repair costs escalate due to costs associated with damage done to the building's content—damage to floor coverings, furniture, and equipment in addition to the contents.

Deferring building repairs may be a standard method for reducing overall institutional expenses in tough economic times; however, the costs of eventually taking care of the issues can be very, very high. Campus facilities managers usually have three types of projects: preventive, scheduled, and deferred maintenance. Most of them probably even have a list of projects that require attention *if* funds are available. The "if" looms very large on

---

From the Authors

One example from our experience of deferring maintenance until too late took place in California (Loyola Marymount University, LMU). However, a similar issue could occur anywhere. In California, with its history of relatively frequent earthquakes, the state and cities have developed building and structural codes to improve safety during seismic "events." However, it has been a slow process of learning what does and does not work after each significant earthquake, which in turn leads to code modifications. Since the early 1980s, the codes have included the requirement that newly installed or modified library shelving be "seismically" braced. The codes do not usually require retrofitting to meet the new standards unless the library rearranges its existing, unbraced, stacks.

The LMU library identified that a major section of the periodical stacks was without such bracing and that installing the bracing would cost $32,000. For several years the library requested funds to retrofit the old shelving, but the project was deferred to the bottom of the priority list. In 1994, the Northridge Earthquake took care of the priorities. All of the unbraced shelving came down, destroying the shelves as well as the journals they housed. The cost of repairs just for the stacks came to $114,000, and the journal replacement costs added another $201,000.

most campuses. What happens is other institutional priorities push aside the ready-to-go projects, and each passing year escalates the final cost of doing even one of the projects.

KEY POINTS TO REMEMBER

- Academic facilities management rests on three pillars: planning and acquisition, maintenance and operations, and assignment and utilization.
- Academic libraries are among the most complex buildings on a campus from a design and operational point of view.
- Libraries tend to have more use and abuse than other buildings, with the exception of residence halls.
- Libraries' annual growth in collection size, at least for some time to come, means staff members are likely to be involved in some type of facility planning activities from time to time.
- When planning a new library, having an experienced library planning consultant on the planning team is a key factor in having a functional building.
- Managing a library facility is a surprisingly complex and constant activity, if service is to be of high quality and staff and users are to have a space that is safe and healthy.
- Having a plan for handling problems such as water leaks as well as having practiced recovery activities are the best strategies for keeping losses to a minimum.
- Deferring maintenance of a facility for too long almost always invites losses that are greater than what it would have cost to correct the problem earlier.
- Reassigning facility space on a campus is an ongoing issue, and libraries with their ever-growing need for additional space add to the challenge of assigning/reassigning existing areas as well as creating new spaces.

REFERENCES

Boone, Michael. 2003. Library facility planning—The consultant's view: A chat with Andrea Michaels. *Library Hi Tech* 21, no. 2: 246–252.

Fox, Bette-Lee. 2007. Going, going, green. *Library Journal* 132, no. 20: 44–58.

Klasson, M. 2002. Rhetoric and realism: Young user reactions on the Linkoping fire and its consequences for education and democracy. *Library Review* 51, nos. 3/4: 171–180.

Middleton, William D. 1989. Comprehensive facilities management. In *Planning and managing higher education facilities*, ed. Harvey H. Kaiser, 5–12. San Francisco: Jossey-Bass.

Shill, Harold B. and Shawn Tonner. 2003. Creating a better place: Physical improvements in academic libraries, 1995–2002. *College & Research Libraries* 64, no. 6: 431–466.

———. 2004. Does the building still matter? Usage patterns in new, expanded, and renovated libraries, 1995–2002. *College & Research Libraries* 65, no. 2: 123–150.

Stevens, Norman. 2006. The fully electronic academic library. *College & Research Libraries* 67, no. 1: 5–14.

Warnement, Mary. 2003. Size matters: The debate over reference desk height. *portal: Libraries and the Academy* 3, no. 1: 79–87.

LAUNCHING PAD

Bazillion, R. J. 2002. Academic library construction: Managing the design to build process. *Journal of Library Administration* 36, no. 4: 49–65.

Beagle, Donald Robert. 2006. *The information commons handbook*. New York: Neal-Schuman.

Beard, Jill, and Penny Dale. 2008. Redesigning services for the net-gen and beyond: A Holistic review of pedagogy, resource, and learning space. *New Review of Academic Librarianship* 14, nos. 1/2: 99–114.

Bisbrouck, Marie-Francoise. 2004. *Libraries as places: Buildings for the 21st century*. Munich: Saur.

Brown, William M. 2008. Future-proof design. *Library Journal* 133, no. 16: 1–10.

Campbell, Jerry D. 2006. Changing a cultural icon: The academic library as a virtual destination. *Educause Review* 41, no. 1: 16–30.

Cervone, H. Frank. 2006. Disaster recovery and continuity planning for digital library systems. *OCLC Systems & Services* 22, no. 3: 173–178.

Clareson, Tom, and Jane S. Long. 2006. Libraries in the eye of the storm: Lessons learned from Hurricane Katrina. *American Libraries* 37, no. 7: 38–41.

Duderstaedt, James, Daniel Atkins, and Douglas Von Houweling. 2002. *Higher education in the digital age*. Westport, CT: Praeger.

Eden, Brad. 2005. The UNLV Libraries: Four years after the construction of a new main library. *Library Hi Tech* 23, no. 1: 5–7.

Gardner, Susan, and Susanna Eng. 2005. What students want: Generation Y and the changing function of the academic library. *portal: Libraries and the Academy* 5, no. 3: 405–420.

Goetsch, Lori A., and Charles B. Lowry. 2001. Creating a culture of security in the University of Maryland Libraries. *portal: Libraries and the Academy* 1, no. 4: 455–464.

Jones, Calvert, and Sarai Mitnick. 2006. Open source disaster recovery: Case studies of networked collaboration. *First Monday* v. 11, no. 5. Available: firstmonday.org/htbin/cgiwrap/bin/ojs/index.php/fm/article/view/1325/1245 (accessed February 24, 2009).

Knight, Barry. 2008. Assessing new developments in collection security. *Liber Quarterly: The Journal of European Research Libraries* 18, no. 2: 65–75.

Ludwig, Logan, and Susan Starr. 2005. Library as place: Results of a Delphi study. *Journal of the Medical Library Association* 93, no. 3: 315–326.

Lushington, Nolan. 2002. *Libraries designed for users: A 21st century guide*. New York: Neal-Schuman.

McEntire, David A. 2007. *Disaster response and recovery*. Hoboken, NJ: John Wiley & Sons.

McGinty, John. 2008. Enhancing building security: Design considerations. *Library & Archival Security* 21, no. 2: 115–127.

Ritchie, Lorin, and Kathlin Ray. 2008. Incorporating information literacy into the building plan: The American University of Sharjah experience. *Reference Services Review* 36, no. 2: 167–179.

Shepherd, F. 2002. Diary of a move. *Records Management Bulletin*, no. 109: 107–109

Shuman, B. A. 2002. Personal safety in library buildings: Levels, problems, and solutions. *Reference Librarian*, nos. 75/76: 67–81.

Somerville, Mary M., and Lydia Collins. 2008. Collaborative design: A learner-centered library planning approach. *Electronic Library* 26, no. 6: 803–820.

Spencer, Mary Ellen. 2006. Evolving a new model: The information commons. *Reference Services Review* 34, no. 2: 242–247.

Chapter 9

Technology

Changing technology has been accompanied by changes in research, habits, scholarly communication patterns, campus roles, and more.

—Ross Housewright and Roger Schonfeld (2008)

Digital libraries in 100 years will face problems that stem from choices that we as librarians make today.

—Michael Seadle (2008)

Knowledge is what higher education is about in the sense that the role of colleges and universities revolves around its discovery, interpretation, transfer, and application. Information communication technology (ICT, which covers all aspects of today's technology) has and will continue to reshape how those roles are performed. To understand higher education in the twenty-first century, you must look at ICT's impact on all aspects of an institution from research to public service, from student recruitment to financial management and everything in between.

One danger is that the general public, as well as some of those who make policy, believe ICT creates knowledge—it does not. What it does change is how researchers, scholars, teachers, and students gain access to existing knowledge, data, and information. It also modifies how people collaborate in the process of developing new knowledge and understanding.

More often than not, when the public thinks about information technology and higher education, their thoughts tend to turn to how technology can or has changed instruction. Earlier (Chapter 3) we discussed how today's students are very different from those of the past, especially in their understanding and use of ICT. Their expectations regarding technology along with their learning styles have begun to change higher education's instructional styles. Furthermore, distance education has had an impact on how instructors in such programs structure and present their courses. However, there are still a fairly large number of senior faculty members who are essentially learning to use technology and have only modest interest in thinking about how to incorporate ICT into their courses. As a result, you still see a great number courses being taught with rather traditional methodologies.

Students today are still tolerating the traditional linear lecture structure, when they have little or no choice. They read what the teacher assigns, as long as it is required, write term papers, and sit for examinations, but these are not their preferred learning modes. They prefer nonlinear learning, creating peer learning groups, and developing sophisticated learning networks on the Web. Essentially, they build their own environment that allows for interactive, collaborative learning. A very real question for the academy is, for how long will they tolerate the old methods of teaching? It seems likely that they

---

From the Authors

One of the last major assignments that Evans had before retiring was to chair a committee to design and oversee the installation and operation of smart classrooms for Loyola Marymount University. A factor in having the assignment was that the library had the responsibility of supplying media to the classrooms and had been lobbying for upgrading the rooms. Sometimes one should be cautious about what one lobbies for.

The first of smart classrooms were new (36 classrooms) and contained a variety of ICT equipment—instructor's station that controlled all of the equipment, computers, video projector, document camera, media players, Internet and cable television connections, and a telephone connected to what became known as classroom management. Each room cost $54,000 just for the equipment. There were additional costs for creating the necessary integrating software to make the technology as easy as possible to use and, of course, for installation. The new rooms were very popular with the younger faculty and students. As a result, the registrar, who handled class scheduling, lobbied for having all the old classrooms upgraded. By 2003, there were 132 such classrooms, and, as you might guess, the cost per room was much higher, approximately $85,000 per room, in part due to the challenges of converting rooms designed for the 1960s.

Not surprisingly, there were several operational challenges as well. All faculty members using a smartroom for the first time required varying degrees of orientation to using the technology. Some faculty never did seem able to master the control panel, and a student worker frequently had to be dispatched to assist them. Maintaining the technology was an ongoing issue, and by the time the last classroom was converted it was time to upgrade the first rooms.

---

will profoundly change higher education, at least in terms of instruction, in the very near future.

Most colleges and universities have recognized the changes in the student body, at least to some degree. Many have modified existing classrooms or built new "smart" classrooms. By doing so they hope to provide the most "technologically savvy" faculty with appropriate ICT capability and perhaps encourage the less technologically oriented faculty to begin to incorporate it into their courses. Creating a smart classroom, whether through conversion or new construction, is not inexpensive. And, as we noted earlier, such classrooms seem to upset just about everyone. Regardless of costs and upset individuals, it is almost mandatory to create such rooms for institutional viability.

Today's World Wide Web/Internet was originally created to speed up or enhance scientists' collaborative activities. This potential of ICT has grown rapidly, especially as specialized collaborative software has come on the market in all disciplines, not just in the hard sciences. Essentially, ICT's impact on research/scholarship has been longer and greater than it has been on instruction.

One aspect of the changing landscape of collaborative research is how ICT opens up the possibilities for interdisciplinary work. Faculty can take on more roles in group research with technology making it possible to utilize research/collaborative time more effectively. Multiple roles such as team leader, team member, consultant for a team, and simply observer/learner in another group are more feasible in a networked setting.

ICT has and will continue to transform scholarly communication. As with learning, the digital world allows the creation of spontaneous communities worldwide of people with common research interests and the ability to quickly share information without the long delays so common in scholarly publishing. A researcher can maintain daily contacts with others specializing in her or his areas of interest. Certainly technology raises the potential to greatly reduce the cost of disseminating research findings—perhaps page charges will no longer be necessary. For technology to realize its scholarly communication potential there must be open, online, free repositories of high quality material that are stable in the long term.

A Council on Library and Information Resources (2008) report summed up the changing nature of scholarly communication:

> Researchers are asking new questions and are developing new methodological approaches and intellectual strategies. These methods may entail new methods of scholarly communication—for example, a greater reliance on data sets and multimedia presentations. This, in turn, has profound consequences for academic publications: it is difficult to imagine traditional printed books and journals adequately capturing these novel approaches. With the predicted rise in new forms of scholarship, the promotion-and-tenure process, which favors print publications, especially in the humanities, will need to be rethought. (p. 2)

Certainly it is true that ICT has had a significant impact on instruction, research, and scholarly communication, as evidenced in Table 9.1. In truth, ICT's impact has been even greater in other areas across the campus. Probably the campus unit most dependent on ICT is the library.

One of the more interesting technology relationships on an academic campus is the one between the library and computing services. In a real sense, although both are fully committed to technology, they have diametrically opposite views about what the goal of technology should be in an academic setting. The focus of computing services is on keeping the tightest possible security (closed system). Libraries on the other hand want the broadest possible open access as well as collaboration. Whatever their differences may be, these units must work together if the institution is to be successful long term. If they approach their working relationship as computing services providing the hardware and software needed to achieve an effective network on campus and the connectivity to the Internet, with the library providing much, if not most, of the network content everyone on the campus benefits from, there will be an effective use of technology.

Just as was the case with facilities, we will use the library as the focal point of this chapter. Again, the library is probably the campus unit—other than computing services and online education—that is most dependent on technology to carry out its daily activities in today's environment.

Table 9.1. Technology's Role in Higher Education Today	
Role	**Activities**
Information Access	Searching, screening, securing all information formats Visualization and learning interactively
Access to People	Networking for students, teachers, and scholars Networking for campus administrators Collaboration potential worldwide
Access to Services	Facilitating routine transactions, such as renewing library materials Packaging and distributing coursework Blurring the distinction between producer and user
Access to Technology	Mastering elements of ICT through routine use Providing wireless access to the campus network Providing the means to modify teaching methods/course presentations

Managing campus ICT, whether from the library perspective or that of any other campus unit, presents managers with some interesting challenges. Just maintaining current technology seems to require large amounts of time. There is the challenge of maintaining technological currency while worrying about what is happening on the constantly changing horizon. Technology generates collaboration challenges as it increases the interdependency of all of the campus units. Finding the funding to stay current is a problem at most institutions. Another issue is the fact that various campus units have different needs, wants, and expectations that are difficult to resolve—for example, something as basic as support for PCs and Macs. Academic libraries are generally not technologically self-sufficient except for the largest libraries; rather their needs form part of the overall provision of communications and information technology within a campus. Table 9.2 summarizes some of the most common issues associated with campus ICT.

Table 9.2. Summary of Campus ICT Issues
Issues Common to Campus ICT
Constant pressure for more and different information/instructional technology
Challenges in determining what the priorities du jour are, especially during the busiest times of the year
Need/requirement to replace or upgrade existing technology
Users requiring support with an ever-growing diversity of hardware and software
Demands for increasing ICT functionality and network capability
Questions regarding who pays for what and from what sources

ACADEMIC LIBRARIES AND INFORMATION AND COMMUNICATION TECHNOLOGY

Libraries have a long history of using computer technology. The Library of Congress developed work applications for the first generation systems (approximately 1951–1958), which moved into other large libraries in the early 1960s. Libraries, of all types, are an example of an organizational environment that shifted quite rapidly from dependence on manual systems to an almost total dependence on technology. They have employed most of the major computer systems starting in the 1960s with mainframes, shifting to minicomputers in the late 1970s, the client/server model in the 1980s, then moving to Web-based technology in the 1990s. Librarians demanded ever-growing functionality in the systems they acquired, and by the mid-1980s the terms "integrated library system" and "turnkey system" were filling the professional literature, and more holdings were acquired in a digital format. What started in "the back room" (technical services) now is center stage in all aspects of academic library daily operations.

Check This Out

The American Library Association's TechSource Online (www.techsource.ala.org) is a site for keeping in touch with developments in library technology. Another option is the Online Insider (www.onlineinsider.net), a blog associated with Information Today's Online magazine and geared toward technology issues.

ICT impacts every library staff member and user. The administrative activities from frontline staff to the most senior managers revolve around the use of technology. Acquisitions and cataloging activities have been computer based for years. Users remotely access services ranging from having reference questions answered to document delivery along with having 24/7 real-time access to databases. Having access to and using technology effectively and efficiently allows libraries to anticipate and quickly adjust to changing circumstances to meet the emerging needs of its stakeholders.

PLANNING AND CONTROLLING COSTS

Long-Term Technology Planning

A key factor in maintaining a successful ICT program is careful long-range planning. Accurately predicting future changes in technology direction and the timing of those changes is almost impossible beyond 18 to 24 months. Nevertheless, the best insurance for handling technology in as cost-effective a manner as possible is developing at least a five-year plan.

By treating the process as a rolling plan, the benefits of long-term planning can be gained while maintaining the flexibility to adjust the plan to address a changing environment. (A rolling plan is one that is reviewed and revised each year.) All of the planning and management elements discussed in Chapter 8 apply in this context. What makes long-term technology planning somewhat different from other planning is the almost certain knowledge that the plan will probably never be carried out exactly the way presented, that each year will result in modifications as circumstances and technologies change.

Library and IT managers must think about and plan for ICT from at least four viewpoints. Most important are the following strategic considerations:

- Factors such as competitive differentiation
- Overall improvement in decision making
- Improved operational processes

Thinking about technology both offensively and defensively are also useful exercises. From an offensive perspective, considering how to achieve or realize maximum benefit from the use of ICT is vital. Defensively, think in terms of controlled growth and what is happening in similar libraries. The fourth point of view that underlies most of the other aspects is cost justification.

Critical success factors (CSFs) are the five or six areas where "things *have* to go right" or "failure will hurt performance the most." CSFs are very useful in technology planning, and in many ways they are easier to identify than organization-wide CSFs. From an academic library point of view, one of the technology CSFs is network reliability—both local and external connections to the Web. Another CSF is the reliability of the integrated library system (ILS). One last example would be the integrity of the customer database. These factors become useful in planning the architecture and long-term needs of information service technology in a library setting.

There are a number of models for technology planning; we favor Emberton's (1987) holistic approach. The following presents the holistic planning mode for information technology. The first step is to gain agreement on, or verify, that the current statement of the library's mission and goals reflect the actual

> **Try This**
>
> Some examples of the critical success factors for information technology planning have been given. Can you add four more?

desires of top management and any other approving body. If this agreement exists and the library has been conscientious about its planning activities relating to function and to specific goals and objectives, the next step is to review those functions and activities in terms of which ones might benefit from some technology application.

One obvious advantage of starting with mission and goals is that they are both general in character, which means the uncertainty about future directions of technology is less of an issue. Using objectives that are more specific and that reflect the purposes of current functions and activities allows the manager to plan this and next years' technology requirements in a realistic manner.

Another step is to examine each goal, objective, function, and activity and ask the question: Could ICT assist in its performance or achievement? Related questions are the following: What type and how much technology would, or could, be appropriate? What problem does the technology address? One example of a goal would be: To provide 24-hour access to its resources for its primary service population. By using such a general statement and assuming that the library decides technology is a factor in achieving or maintaining such a goal, managers can develop a long-range plan with a long-term direction without too much concern about unexpected technological change. This approach does not necessarily lock the library into a particular technology solution for the long term. It also makes it easier for the decision makers to look at today's state-of-the-art technology and consider experts' opinions about future trends when deciding what do during the next 12 to 18 months.

Basic technical issues also play a key role in a successful planning process. It becomes important to have answers to questions such as the following:

- Do any organizational policies influence decision making?
- What types of data are required to reach an informed decision?
- Which technology offers the greatest payoff in relation to service goals and objectives?
- What are the functional advantages, if any, of the new technology?
- What are the technical prerequisites for using a specific technology?
- If different objectives require different technologies, what are the compatibility issues?
- Does the library have the infrastructure to support the new technology?
- Is the technology an open system or proprietary? If proprietary, how difficult would it be to migrate to another system in the future?
- Which technical strategy will be most effective: network or stand alone?
- How will staff and users be affected?
- What are the staffing and training requirements?
- What are the user education requirements?
- What are the short- and long-term implications of the use of this technology?

Beyond technical considerations, there are political and end user issues to technology planning that take many forms. The following are some of the more typical questions to ask:

- What is the campuswide attitude toward expenditures on technology? Is it a long-term or short-term view?
- Does organizational policy centralize ICT services or are they decentralized?
- Will the expenditure and implementation of the technology create relationship problems with other units in the parent institution or collaborating libraries?

- What is the library's track record with funding authorities when it comes to implementing technology?
- Will all end users be able to access or benefit from the proposed technology?
- Is there an issue regarding differing end user platforms or average users' system capability?
- Does the proposed technology relate/meet immediate and long-term needs of end users?
- Does the proposed technology restrict or constrain end user creativity in using technology?
- Is the system flexible enough to meet all end user needs?
- Are there any training implications for end users?

The planning must involve functional, institutional, usage, risk, and staffing analysis as well as take into account implementation and hardware assessment. Library managers must remember that technology planning is more than developing hardware and software systems; it requires understanding of the organization, its purpose(s), and its customers. What library managers' goal should be is to create an information environment appropriate for the library while meeting the parent organization's needs, not to add technology for technology's sake or to "prove" it is up to date. In essence, technology development follows a four-stage process: problem definition and data collecting, conceptual design, detailed design, and implementation. Table 9.3 summarizes some of the key ICT planning issues.

Table 9.3. Summary of ICT Planning Issues
Key Issues in ICT Planning
Long- and short-range plans are essential.
In-depth needs assessment is a key to success.
Establishing and implementing a maintenance schedule maximizes return on investment in technology.
Developing a regular upgrading plan assists in determining long-term costs.
Building a replacement fund over time is essential to reduce "sticker shock" over price increases.
Investing in training and developing a knowledgeable staff is another key to gaining the best from technology.

Mary Alice Ball (2008) made an important observation for any of today's librarians regarding technology:

> When the talk turns to telecommunications infrastructure and broad band, most librarians leave the room or sit politely, eyes glazing over. Librarians often view Internet and telecommunication connectivity issues in the same way as technology of interest to a few, but not entirely central to our mission and services. Still, now that we exist in the highly wired world of the Internet, we can recognize that this attitude hurts the patrons and communities we serve. If we are to do our jobs effectively, then we are compelled to stay awake during these discussions and learn something new. (p. 52)

Controlling Technology Costs

Controlling technology costs are a constant challenge and a budget officer's nightmare. Taking the example of libraries, traditionally they have two categories of expense that are ongoing and always increasing in size: salaries and journal subscription costs. Both present challenges for the library and its institution. Some techniques for controlling salary expenses include not granting/creating additional staff positions, limiting annual salary increases, imposing hiring freezes, and, occasionally, furloughing employees or at worst cutting existing positions. Options for controlling subscription price increases are generally fewer: drop some subscriptions, delay access by waiting until the title is available on a microformat, or curtail other expenditures in order to cover the journal costs. In today's environment, a library may be able to acquire online access to titles at a price that is ever so slightly lower through consortial purchases.

When it comes to the cost of migrating from one generation of equipment to another, there is no option other than not doing so. Unlike some other capital expenditures, the useful life span of digital technology has been dropping, so managers must view the financial investments in this area as being short term. The payoff comes from the more efficient use of staff time and an enhanced service to users. While managers at all levels understand that the useful life of equipment is getting shorter and shorter, funding officials in some organizations may not yet accept this fact. They often think, "If we provided X amount of money for technology equipment this year, we will not have to deal with this for four or five years." Managers face several challenges: planning for technology purchases, controlling costs, and ensuring that funding authorities understand the nature of ICT costs and rates of change. Vaughan (2005) has described the challenges associated with maintaining the technology at a showcase academic research library, the Lied Library at Nevada University at Las Vegas. It provides a case study of the situation four years after opening.

Dugan (2002) identified three types of costs in the introduction of ICT: (1) one-time/extraordinary costs, (2) initial costs, and (3) recurring costs. He then described a model designed to identify and model costs. In order to minimize the risk of making a wrong purchasing decision, Marshall University introduced a decision-making governance model by merging the Office of Computing with the University Libraries both administratively and financially (Prisk and Brooks, 2005). Their strategy took account of expectations, the sales pitch, why the product was chosen, what went wrong and what was learned.

Funding concerns underlie all aspects of managing a library. However, ICT can, if not properly controlled, use all of the available equipment moneys and still require additional funds. And a warning—anyone who has not experienced a system migration may well underestimate the overall cost of the project. In addition to the obvious hardware and new software costs, there are often reprogramming and/or reformatting expenses and always staff and user training expenses.

Technology costs are the third component in the ongoing, ever-increasing cost category for many libraries. They are also beyond the control of the library managers. Unlike journals, managers are not as able to decide

From the Authors

Alire experienced this when investigating migration to another ILS. The migrating costs as a single institution were exorbitant and undoable. However, because her library was a member of the Colorado Alliance for Research Libraries and because two other Alliance member libraries wanted to migrate to the same system but couldn't financially, the three member libraries worked with Alliance personnel and the ILS vendor and developed a cost model that allowed all three libraries to jointly purchase the ILS system at half the cost.

to "cancel" technology, but like journals it is sometimes possible to join consortia to gain better deals from vendors.

Since libraries are almost totally dependent on technology to carry out their daily activities, although they may be able to delay expenditure for a time, eventually the upgrading must occur. When a vendor no longer supports the older technology, either a new version has to be acquired or the cost and frustration of attempting to maintain the existing technology on one's own has to take place.

For the less-experienced managers, the obvious costs are the hardware expenses, and perhaps some software expenses. More experienced managers would add possible programming or reprogramming expenses if the new equipment is from a different vendor. Staff training costs are always more than anticipated. One nightmare for managers is the prospect of the system vendor going out of business. In the early days of proprietary systems, libraries had to almost begin automating from square one, with the entire investment in the old system being lost. With the introduction of "open systems" in the 1980s, the situation improved.

These factors are important cost concerns, but the one that makes ICT increasingly expensive is the demand for even greater functionality. Functionality requires development by the vendor, the cost of which is incorporated into the price of the new models. Academic librarians who have been involved in several acquisitions of an automation system liken the process to buying a new automobile. It seems as if everything is an "option at an additional cost." Establishing a set of system requirements prior to starting a search is very useful in controlling the costs.

Owning a home computer demonstrates the problem of the constant need to upgrade memory and storage capacity. Just when you think the computer is up to standard and you go to buy a new software program, the package lists system requirements that exceed your computer's capability. In the institutional setting this scenario repeats itself over and over again with every employee who has a workstation. End users request additional features and functionality; software producers create a new product meeting those desires; and system requirements escalate along with costs. Given this reality, we do not feel that academic libraries should attempt to be on the forward slope of the technology curve. Too often, significant problems exist in "leading-edge" products—they are also on the "bleeding edge" and some never do mature. We suggest that the prudent library should aim to stay only near the top of the curve or just slightly behind. Someone else can work through the inevitable bugs. In most cases, securing equipment funding is difficult, and spending it on unproven products is risky. Working with staff to keep technology expectations at a reasonable level is essential in managing technology.

In addition to hardware and software costs, there are also systems costs, which primarily revolve around the people costs. Gaining approval for additional staff is a challenge, and most libraries find that they need to devote more staff effort to administering the system. One aspect of this process for libraries in education or used by the public at large is creating and maintaining equal access to electronic services for all end users who have a wide range of computing equipment.

Personnel assigned to system administration are often not additional staff but reassigned existing staff. Technology may not reduce workloads—it assists staff to accomplish more work and often creates unexpected new opportunities and activities. Hence managers

> **Try This**
>
> List six areas of expenditure on information and communications technology. Which do you expect to increase in the next five years, and which may decrease?

face the challenge of balancing traditional activities and newer systems-administration responsibilities with few, if any, additional personnel.

A trend in many colleges and universities is to outsource services to control costs. Providers of specialist services are able to employ a wide range of expertise and amortize costs over a number of customers, and perhaps move some tasks off-shore, and *may* reduce overall ICT costs for an institution. Outsourcing requires a clear understanding of expectations on the part of the customer and supplier, a consideration of what would happen if the supplier fails, a careful examination of internal costs and outsourcing, a legal contract, and close monitoring of the quality of service provided. Table 9.4 summarizes key ICT cost considerations.

Check These Out

Joseph R. Matthews, *Internet Outsourcing Using an Application Service Provider: A How-To-Do-It Manual for Librarians* (New York: Neal-Schuman, 2002).
Sheila Pantry and Peter Griffiths, *Managing Outsourcing in Library and Information Services* (New York: Neal-Schuman, 2004).

Table 9.4. Summary of ICT Cost Issues

Key ICT Cost Considerations	
Acquisition of basic hardware and software	Upgrade costs for equipment and software
Annual equipment maintenance	Replacement costs
Annual software license fees	Use/copyright fees
Network connectivity costs	

From the Authors

Evans worked at an institution that struggled with controlling institutional ICT costs. At one point, the university president made a surprise announcement on a Friday that all of the ICT services were to be outsourced the following Monday. ICT staff had the weekend to decide if they would accept a position with the outsourcing firm. In any event, they would cease being university employees at 5:00 p.m. that day. The president also announced that he had signed a seven-year contract with the company.

The turmoil that followed did not end the following Monday. After four years, and with much higher ICT costs, the contract was cancelled. Many of the former staff members once again became university employees. The notion of achieving cost saving through outsourcing any activity needs long and careful thought, especially when it comes to technology.

SECURITY

Computers and related technology are capable of doing several things faster and more accurately than humans can; however, they are prone to certain faults that can cancel out their advantages. The saying "garbage in, garbage out" perhaps started with the first computer. Human input error is a problem, and given the invisible nature of electronic circuitry, an input error can cause serious problems before anyone notices the error. More rare, but still a reality and even harder to identify, are errors within the system, such as a programming conflict. Other difficulties arise when one or more individuals begin to manipulate the system for personal reasons, such as changing or canceling a change or trying to gain access to information. There is also the accidental or malicious destruction of a database, software, or entire system.

These and other reasons are why managers must have a concern for security. There are two aspects: system security and quality assurance. Broadly speaking there are three types of control that will help ensure quality and security: (1) information system controls, (2) procedural controls, and (3) physical facility controls.

Information system controls attempt to ensure accuracy, validity, and propriety of system activities. Many relate to input as well as output data. Some of the data entry controls are passwording (or codes) for different levels of staff, formatted data entry screens, and audible error signals. Another type of information system control is control logs, which preserve evidence of all system input.

Processing controls help ensure that correctly entered data goes through processing properly—identifying errors in arithmetic, calculations, or logical operations and in data not processed or data lost are examples of processing control areas. These controls exist for both hardware and software. For hardware, such controls include malfunction detection circuitry, circuitry for remote diagnostics, and redundant components. In terms of software, checks for internal file labels, "check points" within a program to assist in building an audit trail, and system security monitors are examples of processing control.

System output is another area of concern for procedural controls. One example is logging of output documents and reports and where those reports went. Control listings are a means of providing hard-copy evidence of all output produced. Distribution lists help control personnel and ensure that only authorized users receive output.

Storage control is also important. Someone must be responsible for maintaining and controlling access to databases. Access may be controlled through passwords/codes, which the person assigns to end users, or through identification verification. The typical system has a three-level security procedure: user log-on, user password, and unique file name. One essential security measure for storage is file backup of data and programs and storage of backup material in another location.

Physical facility controls involve a variety of security measures, ranging from simply a locked room out of the public area to a high-security facility with elaborate environmental controls. In a distributed technology environment, physical security of equipment becomes more difficult and complex, but library managers must attempt to provide some security if nothing more than equipment "lockdowns."

Another important security element in the Internet environment is firewalls, which protect the network from unwanted access/intrusion by serving as a safe transfer point to and from other networks. Firewalls function to screen network activity and allow "in or out only" transmissions that are authorized. Unfortunately, firewalls are able only to deter, not completely prevent, unauthorized access. Problems of hacking will continue for the foreseeable future, and one security solution will be in the growing area of biometrics. Security systems using biometrics assess physical traits that make a person unique: voice verification, fingerprints, hand shape, keystroke analysis, and eye/retina scanning are some examples. A digitized biometrics profile is created for each user, and then special sensors measure the person wanting access and, if there is a match, allow access.

Any library with public-access computers must expect to deal with viruses, worms, malware, and other issues that follow hand-in-hand with more or less open accessibility. While the potential exists for these problems to occur with staff machines, they are an almost certain issue for public machines. Some malicious programs are just a nuisance while others can destroy contents of memory and hard disks. They often migrate from one computer to another by means of the Internet, e-mail, or through the intranet. Having effective and up-to-date virus checking/cleaning software is important, as is using it on a regular basis. A virus-checking program that automatically scans any file downloaded from the Internet or an intranet is highly desirable. Like the other aspects of managing technology, maintaining security is a never-ending but essential task.

STAFF BACKGROUND AND TRAINING

One aspect of managing technology involves making certain staff at every level have the necessary background and training to handle the technology in place as well as the technology it plans to acquire. Funding for staff development opportunities for the professional side of information work is usually limited. In the case of technology, such opportunities are *essential*. The challenge is to decide how to allocate the funding available.

> **Check These Out**
>
> Sarah Houghton-Jan, "Conducting Technology Training," *Library Technology Reports* 43, no. 2 (2007): 59-63.
> Anna Jennings, "Determining and Meeting Personnel Training Needs," *Computers in Libraries* 25 (September 2005): 13-15.

When introducing new applications or when implementing a major upgrade, having staff members update their skills on their own with a user manual is generally not a good use of their time. Vendors of integrated systems almost always offer training in the use of their systems, and so it is easier to build training costs into the price of acquiring the system than to secure funds for training. Some software vendors offer training packages that are built into the application as a "tutoring" program, either accessed online or provided as a CD-ROM or training video.

Managers must plan for three types of training: (1) of the entire staff for a new application or system, (2) for new or replacement staff, and (3) of end users. With this in mind, it is evident why training costs must be a line item in the annual technology budget. One aspect of technology training is the need to demonstrate, not just tell, how something is done. Sometimes it is possible to use a mentor approach for servicewide training. One advantage is the mentor is better able to relate to the special needs of her or his coworker than a general trainer. Training in groups is more cost-effective than the one-on-one approach—this is true for both staff and end users.

Training in ICT is influenced by networking in general and the Internet in particular. Two widely used training technologies are multicasting and video-on-demand, which can be implemented on either local area networks, corporate wide area networks (intranet), or the Internet.

Multicasting permits large numbers of users to simultaneously receive the same video. This sharing of a single video stream promotes efficient use of network bandwidth while permitting organizations to provide informational video or new application training for large numbers of simultaneous users. For instance, if a new version of a database interface is implemented, an entire staff can be trained simultaneously while they remain seated at their own desktops. Moreover, since this technology can be implemented across the Internet and intranets, its distribution center can be centralized while the receiving nodes can be distributed across multiple sites (e.g., at branch libraries) or to an entire wireless access network. One server sends the same single video file to a set or a range of IP addresses.

The primary advantage of multicasting is also one of its major liabilities. It forces individuals to work at a specific time and place. Video-on-demand, in some ways a mirror image of multicasting, addresses this lack of scheduling flexibility. Each user can access the same, or different, multimedia materials at any given moment, permitting hundreds of training lessons to be stored on a video server for ad hoc access by users. However, one of the disadvantages for both multicasting and video on demand is that these training modes may not allow for hands-on practice, user questions, or feedback.

While multicasting and video on demand have their individual strengths, in combination they provide a rich environment for delivering training. Despite the disadvantages indicated, the ability to implement these across networks makes them easy to manage, provides economies of scale, and permits personnel savings. Many libraries now create a physical space for training usage that is private and is equipped with necessary technology. Cell phones, RSS feeds, screencasts, and podcasts can be used to deliver instruction to individuals and are cost-effective ways of helping students use services and resources with which they are not familiar.

Another training cost is the help desk function staff provides. With remote access, users will ask both information-related questions and will need solutions for problems they have accessing the system. Staff members answering such calls need to understand ICT, especially if the user has their own PC and Internet service provider for remote access. Bell and Shank (2004) have described the role of the "blended librarian." There is a need for specialists who can handle the traditional requests for information and also "walk through" the technical problems with the user. It requires subject knowledge, awareness of the many technical problems the user may encounter, and the communication skills of a call center operator, with the communication skills being paramount. However, managers must establish clear guidelines for user expectations concerning the level of technical support that can be expected.

Today the education of the information professional provides a good background in the basic components of technology: database management, spreadsheets, word processing, online searching, presentation graphics, and developing Internet pages. Some will go on to gain a qualification in ICT. Support staff are less likely to have an educational background in ICT, so managers need to ensure that this is provided for them.

A manager cannot always predict when, or if, resistance to change will occur. However, among the types of change that have a very high potential for resistance is technology. Introducing new technology almost always generates some staff resistance; replacing a system or a major upgrade has less potential for resistance but still is relatively high. There are several areas of staff concern or reasons for resisting technology. These areas are the following:

> **For Further Thought**
>
> Reflect on the issues that a manager will encounter in developing a staff training program for information technology. Select the three most important issues.

- Threats to economic security
- Threats to status or power
- Increased job complexity
- Uncertainty or unfamiliarity
- Changed superior–subordinate relationships
- Increased rigidity or time pressure
- Role ambiguity
- Feelings of insecurity

Often professional staff are the least likely to resist technology change. When they do, it is usually because of concerns about job complexity, lack of familiarity, and time pressure.

Top management shares the first two concerns of the nonclerical staff but not the last, while also having concerns about role ambiguity and feeling insecure. Those in the middle levels generally express all of these concerns. Some of the resistance can be overcome through training. However, communication is the key to success for those planning and implementing technology changes. Encouraging staff input concerning their technology needs and when the best time is to make the changes will also help overcome resistance.

Table 9.5 summarizes some of the most prevalent ICT training issues of which managers should be aware. However, there is one other technology-related staff issue for managers: "technostress." One element is physical, as staff members spend more and more time using a workstation looking at a display screen. Poor posture, equipment, lighting, and physical arrangement can lead to a variety of physical or health problems, ranging from mild headaches and eyestrain to carpal tunnel syndrome. Managers must take ergonomic factors into account, and a number of countries, as in the United States, have legal requirements regarding this that must be met. Staff need information about posture and exercises to release tension and how to plan their work so that they do not spend long uninterrupted hours at a workstation. Getting away, even for a few minutes every hour, reduces technostress. One helpful technique is to build into daily tasks a mix of technology- and non-technology-based activities so that staff can take a break.

> **From the Authors**
>
> At Colorado State University Libraries, this was a very important issue such that the head of Human Resources developed an early expertise in ergonomics in the library and computer workstations that resulted in many presentations, articles, and a bibliography published as a book.

Table 9.5. Summary of ICT Training Issues
Common ICT Training Issues
Basic instruction for new users—staff and users
Advanced training for staff and users with existing equipment/software
Training in upgraded equipment/software
Converting the staff training to user training via information literacy sessions

The second aspect of technostress is mental, which can be experienced by staff, managers, and end users. Managers know that changes in technology will result in tension and/or stress, even if there is no resistance. Part of the tension/stress reduction process is having ample and adequate training for the changes. Ample lead time and written information about the change and technology usage also reduces stress when the change actually occurs. Providing ergonomic equipment/furniture reduces physical discomfort and reduces stress.

Working with vendors to produce user-friendly paper documentation and online manuals in the local language can also reduce technostress. Vendors offer their products internationally and do not always make allowances for different forms of the English language, for example. (Nothing builds stress more quickly than facing some deadline that requires the use of a new technology or software and not being able to make it work, even when every step in the vendor-supplied documentation has been followed.) Talking with managers currently using the product is always a good practice. Ask them, "How good is the documentation?" and "How good is the vendor training or support?"

This is a critical issue for libraries in geographically remote areas where local support may be limited or nonexistent. Knowing what to expect allows managers to anticipate and prepare solutions before the problem arises.

Managers may experience more "technostress" than others in the organization by virtue of the fact that technology makes it possible for them to be accessible 24/7. The ubiquitous nature of computers, fax machines, and cell phones can make it difficult to "disconnect." For managers some personal factors to consider are the following:

> **Check This Out**
>
> Terence K. Huwe, "Running to Stand Still?" *Computers in Libraries* 25 (September 2005): 34-36.

> **Try This**
>
> Thinking about an academic library, list all of the causes of technostress that you can think of. Then, in a second column, list ways of overcoming them.

- Is it really essential that I have the same technology and applications at home as in the office?
- Is it really essential that I do this work at home?
- Is it possible that I could make better use of office time so I do not have to take work home?
- Is it possible that this is a task that could just as effectively be delegated?
- Is it really essential that I check my office e-mail from home at night, on the weekend, at a conference, or even on vacation?
- Can I turn my cell phone off when I leave the office?
- Is it necessary that I become the "techie of techies" in my organization when this is not my area of responsibility?

Technostress may be a current buzz word, but technology job-related disabilities are a reality. It is not something managers can avoid for both staff and themselves, but it can be reduced or at least controlled.

COLLABORATION

Collaboration has always been part of the library service ethic. Having a collaborative relationship with the campus ICT service is critical to having effective user services. There are several points of potential stress in maintaining a collaborative spirit. We mentioned one earlier—open versus closed systems. The need for campus network security can, at times, create challenges for the library when it comes to collaborative efforts with other libraries. One example of where this may be a problem is with resources sharing programs such as OHIOLink or LINK+ (California based) in which the programming requires a substantial number of "holes" in the campus firewall. Working out a solution that allows the library to offer the service while maintaining an ICT acceptable level of security can take time, but the process will go faster if there is a history of close collaboration between the two units.

Another area that can cause difficulty is user support; in this case, it means those using the campus network. Academic libraries tend to have some of the longest service hours of any campus unit. If ICT user support is not available for as many hours as the library, it is almost guaranteed that library public service staff will be asked/expected to solve computer/network-related issues during ICT's off hours. Some of the questions are simple, while others are very technical. One issue is that the person calling about a non-library technical issue rarely differentiates between the library and ICT staff, especially when the person does not get a response that resolves the problem. Having a combination library/ICT support service location is a good solution. However, for many schools the cost is too high, the collaborative spirit is lacking, or the concept of "service" varies too much.

Some institutions have combined the management of ICT and libraries. Sometimes these duties fall under a person with a library background and sometimes this is not the case. Librarians have a long and successful record of developing large computer databases, collaborating with vendors, creating shared services, and handling frequent changes in technology. So perhaps it was not surprising that, when information and communication technologies merged in the 1980s and universities developed student-centered learning, some people who were librarians stepped into positions as chief information officers (CIOs). This title indicates they managed library, archives, records, learning support, and ICT services. They had professional, technical, and, probably above all, a user-centered approach to service, coupled with being decisive and good listeners. The critical and challenging role of the CIO when systems must deliver results is described by Broadbent (formerly a librarian now at Gartner Inc. and the Melbourne Business School) and Kitzis (2004).

The relationship between CIOs and academic research libraries has been examined by Snyder (2006). Hanson (2005) brought together papers describing convergence in the United Kingdom, and Wainwright (2005) discussed strategies for university academic information and delivery services in Australia.

A growing trend in collaboration is the one seen between independent software vendors in the library service sector, replacing the fierce competition that formerly existed. The aim is to lower cost and technical barriers for libraries, making it easier to share data.

KEY POINTS TO REMEMBER

- Technology provides access to information for users and generates management information to aid decision making.
- Technology improves productivity and assists in data collection, analysis, and use.
- Staff time is freed up through the implementation of some technologies, and it can make a library operate more cost-effectively.
- Managers require enhanced skills.
- The proportion of the budget spent on the initial investment and associated recurrent costs will continue to increase and dominate annual expenditures.
- A major investment is needed to train staff to work effectively and efficiently with new or updated technologies.
- Users benefit from coaching that can help them access information effectively.
- Rapid technological change will continue.
- Increasing attention is being paid to legal and security issues.
- Technology requires careful planning and control.

REFERENCES

Ball, Mary Alice. 2008. Connecting with connectivity: Why librarians need to care. *Public Libraries* 47, no. 3: 52–56.

Bell, Steven J., and John Shank. 2004. The blended librarian: A blueprint for redefining the teaching and learning role of academic librarians. *College & Research Libraries News* 65, no. 7: 372–375.

Broadbent, Marianne, and Ellen Kitzis. 2004. *The new CIO leader: Setting the agenda and delivering results.* Boston, MA: Harvard Business School Press.

Council on Library and Information Resources. 2008. *No brief candle: Reconceiving research libraries for the 21st century.* Washington, DC: Council on Library and Information Resources.

Dugan, Robert E. 2002. Information technology budget and costs: Do you know what your information technology costs each year? *Journal of Academic Librarianship* 28, no. 4: 238–243.

Emberton, John. 1987. Effective information system planning and implementation. *Information Age* 9, no. 3: 159–162.

Hanson, Terry, ed. 2005. *Managing academic support services in universities: The convergence experience.* London: Facet Publishing.

Housewright, Ross, and Roger Schonfeld. 2008. *Ithaka's 2006 studies of key stakeholders in the digital transformation in higher education.* New York: Ithaka.

Prisk, Dennis P., and Monica G. Brooks. 2005. Hip high-tech purchases don't always turn out as planned. *Computers in Libraries* 25, no. 10: 10–12, 14, 16.

Seadle, Michael. 2008. The digital library in 100 years: Damage control. *Library Hi Tech* 26, no. 1: 5–10.

Snyder, Carolyne. 2006. CIOs and academic research libraries. *Library Administration & Management* 20, no. 2: 72–74

Vaughan, Jason. 2005. Lied library @ four years: Technology never stands still. *Library Hi Tech* 23, no. 1: 34–49.

Wainwright, Eric. 2005. Strategies for university academic information and service delivery. *Library Management* 26, nos. 8/9: 439–456.

LAUNCHING PAD

Alcorn, Louise, and Maryellen Mott Allen. 2006. *Wireless networking: A how-to-do-it manual for librarians.* New York: Neal-Schuman.

Andrews, Judith, and Derek Law. 2004. *Digital libraries: Policy, planning and practice.* Burlington, VT: Ashgate.

Antelman, Kristin, Emily Lynema, and Andrew K. Pace. 2006. Towards a twenty-first century library catalog. *Information Technology and Libraries* 24, no. 3: 128–139.

Bills, David B., Stephanie Holliman, Laura Lowe, J. Evans Ochola, Su-Euk Park, Eric J. Reed, Christine Wolfe, and Laura Thudium Zieglowsky. 2006. The new mobile scholar and the effective use of information and communication technology. *First Monday* 11, no. 4: 2.

Bohle, Shannon. 2008. The new digital awareness. *Library Journal* 133, no. 12: 26–28.

Coles, Andrea A., and William Doughtery. 2009. Hang together or hang separately. *College & Research Libraries* 70, no. 2: 110–113.

Ghosh, Maitrayee. 2009. Information professionals in the open access era: The competencies, challenges and new roles. *Information Development* 25, no. 1: 33–42.

Hein, Karen K. 2006. Information uncommon: Public computing in the life of reference. *Reference Services Review* 34, no. 1: 33–42.

Knibbe-Haanstra, Marcella. 2008. Reference desk dilemmas: The impact of new demands on librarianship. *Reference & User Services Quarterly* 48, no. 1: 20–25.

McLeod, Julie, and Catharine Hare, eds. 2006. *Managing electronic records.* New York: Neal-Schuman.

Matthews, Joseph R. 2004. *Technology planning: Preparing and updating a library technology plan.* New York: Neal-Schuman.

Chapter 10

The Academy, Accreditation, and Accountability

Many of the current quality related practices of colleges and universities, in the U.S., can be traced to the practices of the accrediting bodies.

—Gary Rhoades and Barbara Sporn (2002)

Generally, academic libraries face two problems when trying to describe the impact of their services and resources on desired institutional outcomes and goals. First, they are not sufficiently strategic or externally focused when determining which measures to use as evidence of how the library affects educational outcomes. Second, they often do not organize their data and other supporting documentation in ways that are accessible or meaningful to academic administrators and accreditation teams.

—Bonnie Gratch Lindauer (1998)

Society's interest in higher education has varied over time; from a long-term perspective, it is only relatively recently (the past 100 or so years) that there has been widespread interest. At best, during the first 700 years, only the townspeople with a group of students and teachers cared much about higher education and its activities. What interest there was focused on behavior and payment of debts. During U.S. colonial times interest broadened slightly, and some people started questioning the value of a liberal arts education when the country needed economic development. As nineteenth-century colleges and universities expanded their course offerings with a "practical" focus, more and more people outside of academia took an interest in what was being taught and, to some degree, how it was taught. In an earlier chapter, we noted Melvil Dewey's role in producing an annual list of New York State colleges and universities "in good standing." Throughout the twentieth century, U.S. society has taken an ever-growing interest in higher education—what it does, how it does it, and how much it costs.

Six aspects of higher education that today's society, at least a segment of society, takes an active interest in are: what is taught, how it is taught, whether a degree is worth the time to secure it, the quality of what is taught, the value for money spent (tuition, tax payments, or donations), and whether the public actually gains anything of lasting value.

Many of these concerns appeared in some form in an "issue paper" prepared for the U.S. Department of Education's Commission on the Future of Higher Education. (We mentioned the Commission's work in Chapter 5; it issued its final report in 2007.) The paper (Miller and Malandra, n.d.) dealt with accountability and assessment in higher education in the sense of why there is a need for both. Miller and Malandra raised several problems relating to today's higher education environment. They began by noting:

Most Americans believe that higher education in the United States is the best in the world—and there is much to make us proud. . . . But, this belief and pride have led to a dangerous complacency about the real quality and impact of higher education. . . . There must be answers to the question posed by U.S. Secretary of Education Margaret Spellings in her inaugural remarks to the Commission, "What do we Americans expect from our shared investment in higher education?" (p. 1)

They continued, "despite this investment, the results are not merely disappointing— they are of grave concern. . . . There is a large and widening gap in higher education based on economic class" (p. 2). They later stated, "College standards are becoming diluted and there is fuzziness about what faculty teach and what is expected of students" (p. 3) and that "the focal point of some institutions is not on teaching and learning" (p. 5). They also expressed the concern that "faith in the quality of college outcomes masks a gaping information void, and that not much is known about a growing number of our students" (p. 5). They concluded with, "There must be accountability for the educational quality of our institutions" (p. 6).

One of the final recommendations of the Secretary of Education's Commission (U.S. Department of Education, 2006) was:

To meet the challenges of the 21st century, higher education must change from a system primarily based on reputation to one based on performance. We urge the creation of a robust culture of accountability and transparency throughout higher education. Every one of our goals from improving access and affordability to enhancing quality and innovation, will be more easily achieved if higher education embraces and implements serious accountability measures. (p. 21)

Certainly the commission's recommendation was not the first time there were calls for accountability and assessment, but it was perhaps the most prominent national call for greater efforts on the part of the academy to prove its worth.

Accountability and assessment, at least in terms of higher education, are sometimes used interchangeably, although they do have different meanings. One way to think of higher education assessment and accountability is as follows: when we, higher education, look at our performance to measure success/outcomes it is assessment; when outsiders look at our performance it is accountability.

Three of the most important "A's" for addressing performance questions are accountability, assessment, and accreditation. For the vast majority of the general public the last "A"—accreditation—is what they have heard about and may have some notion of what being accredited means. Accreditation activities involve both assessment and accountability and, in reality, the three concepts are tightly intertwined in higher education.

ACCREDITATION

We have mentioned accreditation in several of the earlier chapters; here we take a more in-depth look at the process. All of the topics we covered in the preceding chapters are also the areas of primary concern for accrediting agencies. Academic libraries and accreditation are also intertwined; almost every campus accreditation visit involves the library. The reason is that all of the institution's educational programs draw on library resources and services to some extent. Therefore, it is not surprising that visiting teams take an interest in the library's activities and programs.

There has been an evolution in the U.S. accreditation process over the past 130-plus years since the process started. During most of the first two-thirds of the twentieth century accreditation standards tended to focus on inputs (e.g., dollars spent, student GPAs, books acquired, and journal subscriptions held) with little or no concern about what the outcomes were for the inputs. Starting in the late 1970s, the focus began to shift toward what was accomplished as a result of the inputs. By the early 1990s, at least for the Western Association of Schools and Colleges (WASC), the shift toward outcome assessment was well in place. The expectation for more and better outcome data from the accredited institutions has increased with each passing year.

For the general public, accredited status serves as an indication of a college or university's quality and good standing. Accreditation has become the means for defining and assuring higher education quality. Accreditation agencies (they are nongovernmental bodies) also serve as "gatekeepers." Being accredited is a key to having access to billions of dollars in federal and state funds.

Many people are unaware of the fact that accreditation began in the United States as a method by which colleges attempted to ensure that high school graduates would be capable of doing undergraduate level work. (Today's regional accreditation agencies still accredit secondary education programs within their region.) By the early 1990s, higher education institutions were under pressure to assure their quality. Our present system of accreditation is a large complex of public and private interests. Although officially speaking undergoing the process is voluntary, the fact that having accredited status is key to receiving public funds makes it close to mandatory.

As of mid-2009, there were over 100 such agencies divided into three broad categories—regional, national, and specialized. Two bodies accredit the accreditors—the U.S. Department of Education (USDE) and the Council for Higher Education Accreditation (CHEA). Regional agencies (see Table 10.1 for the coverage of the six regional groups) accredit over 3,000 institutions of the type most people think of as being higher educational. National agencies accredit both degree and nondegree institutions (3,500 in 2009); many of these institutions are single-focus for-profit operations.

The "approved" accreditors on the USDE and CHEA lists are not identical. The primary difference between the two lists lie in the specialized category. Specialized agencies cover programs in specific fields such as education, music, and library and information studies. An example of the difference is ALA appears only on the CHEA list. This does not mean that ALA-accredited programs are unable to have access to federal funds; because they are part of an institution accredited by a regional association, which is on the USDE list, there is no problem.

USDE and CHEA have slightly different accreditation standards. USDE looks at nine criteria when deciding whether to add an agency to its approved list. In its review, the USDE (U.S. Department of Education, 2010) looks at how the agency handles the following:

- Assessment of student achievement in relation to the institutional mission
- Assessment of curriculum
- Assessment of faculty
- Assessment of facilities, equipment, and supplies
- Assessment of fiscal and administrative capacity

Table 10.1. U.S. Regional Accreditation Associations

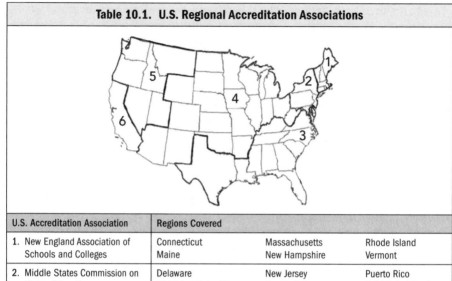

U.S. Accreditation Association	Regions Covered		
1. New England Association of Schools and Colleges	Connecticut Maine	Massachusetts New Hampshire	Rhode Island Vermont
2. Middle States Commission on Higher Education	Delaware District of Columbia Maryland	New Jersey New York Pennsylvania	Puerto Rico U.S. Virgin Islands
3. Southern Association of Schools and Colleges	Alabama Florida Georgia Kentucky	Louisiana Mississippi North Carolina South Carolina	Tennessee Texas Virginia Latin America
4. North Central Association Commission on Accreditation and School Improvement	Arkansas Arizona Colorado Iowa Illinois Indiana Kansas	Michigan Minnesota Missouri North Dakota Nebraska New Mexico	Ohio Oklahoma South Dakota West Virginia Wisconsin Wyoming
5. Northwest Association of Accredited Schools	Alaska Idaho Montana	Nevada Oregon	Utah Washington

6. Western Association of Schools and Colleges	American Samoa
	California
	Commonwealth of
	  Northern Marianas
		East Asia
		Federated States
		  of Micronesia
		Fiji
			Guam
			Hawaii
			Republic of
			  Marshall Islands

- Assessment of student support services (the place the library often lies within regional standards)
- Assessment of recruitment and admission policies
- Assessment of program length and objectives
- Assessment of student complaints
- Assessment of the institution's program compliance with Title IV (Title IV of the U.S. Higher Education Act authorizes the Pell Grant program)

CHEA employs a broader and a shorter list of standards for its approval process of accrediting agencies. The following are areas the agency reviews:

- Advancement of academic quality
- Demonstration of accountability
- Encouragement of purposeful change and innovation
- Employment of appropriate and fair decision making
- Reassessment of its accreditation process on an ongoing basis
- Possesses sufficient resources for accreditation activities (Eaton, 2009, pp. 2–3)

In addition to having access to federal and state funding, having ongoing accredited status (being accredited is not a one-time event) offers several potential benefits:

- It encourages institutional improvement through continuous self-study and evaluation.
- It provides some assurance to the public that the institution has appropriate educational objectives.
- It provides some assurance that institution *appears* to be substantially accomplishing its goals.
- It provides assurance that the institution meets *minimum* accreditation standards.
- It provides some degree of consumer protection in terms of institutional quality.

Three additional benefits, as outlined by the USDE (U.S. Department of Education, 2010), are the following:

- It protects an institution against harmful internal and external pressure.
- It creates goals for self-improvement of weaker programs and for stimulating a general raising of standards among educational institutions.
- It involves the faculty and staff comprehensively in institutional evaluation and planning.

Almost all accredited institutions view the process as time-consuming but resulting in positive institutional changes and outcomes. Three of the most common institutional areas that benefit from the process are curriculum, institutional research (data about the institution), and the library. Few institutions believe the process impacts their mission as few agencies raise questions about the mission beyond those asking about how the mission is reflected in the various accreditation standards. Essentially, accrediting agencies believe the governing board has the right to set the mission without interference; if the board says its mission is to educate students to go to Mars, then the visiting team's purpose is to see how that mission is implemented and how well that mission accomplishment meets the agency's standards.

Given there are so many agencies, is it any wonder that academic libraries always seem to be involved in one or more accreditation activities every year? There are data to be collected long before any site visit, meetings with visiting teams, and often follow-up activities after the visiting team's final report arrives.

How the Process Works

Looking at regional agencies (the only bodies to fully assess the entire institution), you will see their standards vary from one another while covering all the aspects of USDE and CHEA requirements. Also, most of them have two or more commissions that handle secondary education, community colleges, and senior colleges.

Accredited institutions pay an annual membership fee that provides the necessary operating funds for the agencies. They also pay a fee and the expenses associated with site visits.

Being accredited is an ongoing process. The longest "full" accreditation term, from a regional agency, is ten years. However, shorter periods are fairly common, as any "substantive change" at an institution may require a team visit that focuses on the change(s). You can review some of the variations and actions of WASC by going to wascsenior.org/institutions and looking at some of the institutional information such as latest action and next scheduled visit.

Check These Out

New England Association of Schools and Colleges:
www.neasc.org
Middle States Commission on Higher Education:
www.msche.org
Southern Association of Colleges and Schools:
www.sacs.org
North Central Association Commission on
Accreditation and School Improvement:
www.ncacasi.org
Northwest Commission on Colleges and Universities:
www.nwccu.org
Western Association of Schools and Colleges:
www.wascsenior.org

A typical WASC process starts with the institution developing a self-study. This process lasts from 12 to 18 months as all campus units begin writing up their responses to the standards/guidelines that apply to their area. Usually the library has its own section(s) to write while being asked to assist teaching departments in gathering library data that relates to their areas (such as library usage by their majors or books and journals in their subject area acquired since the last accreditation visit). The institution's accreditation officer takes all of the unit material and prepares a draft self-study that will eventually go the agency office to be distributed to visiting team members. Because the final self-study cannot begin to include all of the material submitted by the campus units, there is often an extended period of discussion about what should be included in the study and what material is to be made available in the "visiting team room."

The site visit may last two or three days for a special visit to a week for a comprehensive review. In Evans's experience, both as a team member and as the senior librarian at an institution being reviewed, issues not covered in the self-study and/or the supplemental materials can arise that require additional information from some department/unit. Sometimes the additional data/information is library related in some manner.

On the last day of the visit, the team usually presents an oral report to interested parties on the campus. At least with WASC, the oral report does not include recommendations the team will make to the agency.

From the Authors

An example of the supplemental information from Evans's experience was during a specialty review (electrical engineering). A member of the visiting team who was assigned to the library came from an institution that employed the same integrated library system (ILS) as did the host institution. The person had done some homework prior to his visit regarding the report capability of the ILS. Upon his arrival at the host library he requested we produce a report of not just library usage by majors but also by the student's year (freshmen, sophomore, etc.). He knew the system could produce the information and that the engineering department had not included this information in their self-study. Librarians must be ready to field one or more such surprise request during a site visit.

Visiting teams submit their written reports and recommendation(s) to the accrediting agency. For WASC institutions, there are ten possible outcomes depending on the type of visit and what the teams found (Note: the other regional agencies have similar categories although the labels vary):

- Grant candidacy or initial accreditation
- Deny candidacy or initial accreditation
- Defer action
- Continue accreditation between capacity and educational effectiveness reviews
- Reaffirm accreditation
- Issue a formal notice of concern
- Issue a warning
- Impose probation
- Issue an order to show cause
- Terminate accreditation

> **From the Authors**
>
> In 1989 Evans was involved in a WASC internal study of 20 years of negative visits and what the factors were that led to the recommendations or actions. The top four factors were, in rank order: educational programs (lack of quality), governance/administration (too little sharing of decision making), institutional finances (serious concerns about institutional viability), and library resources (insufficient support). Also, all of the negative outcomes were at private institutions. Most were small colleges, who were relatively new, had limited resources, and, occasionally, were experimenting with the curriculum. A quick review of the WASC institutional directory material, referenced earlier, suggests that the same pattern still exists.

On occasion, library support, especially for distance learning activities, comes up in an action where the visiting team recommends a shorter reaccreditation term with specific areas of concern. Rarely is it just a library concern than one of several concerns.

Before the agency makes its final decision regarding the recommendations, the institution has an opportunity to correct any errors of fact. Again, this is often a place where the library is called upon to supply data.

INFORMATION LITERACY AND ACCREDITATION

Academic libraries have two challenges when their institutions undergo a regional/comprehensive review. They must address both the campuswide support of educational programs and research as well as demonstrate the outcomes of their instructional activities such as teaching information literacy courses.

Kenneth Smith (2000), in a presentation to the Association of Research Libraries, made the following point:

> How does the focus on learning outcomes affect the mission of the library? Like other communities at the University, the library must move from a content view (books, subject knowledge) to a competency view (what students will be able to do). Within the new environment, we need to measure the ways in which the library is contributing to the learning that the university values. . . . What is important is how the library's capabilities can provide solutions that measurably impact the quality of learning. It will require a significant period of learning new ways to participate and new roles for the library professionals. (pp. 32, 36)

He presented some sample outcomes that could be library relevant, such as students becoming self-reliant in the search for information, being able to assess bias and credibility of information in its various forms, and having a grasp of intellectual property in terms social, ethical, political, and economic issues/concerns.

The challenge is how to develop meaningful measures to assess the factors that Smith (2000) outlined and become more actively involved in the overall educational process. Laura Saunders (2007), in an article examining regional accreditation agencies' approach to assessing information literacy, concluded her essay by saying:

> By getting involved in curriculum development and assessment, the library can raise its profile on campus and increase its perceived value to the institution, which will be invaluable at a time when libraries nationwide are facing increased competition and tight budgets in the face of continued questions about the importance of a physical library to campus life.... In order to accomplish these important tasks, librarians must first be aware of accreditation standards, and how the library can partner with faculty and administrators in support of the goal of its parent institution. (p. 325)

Megan Oakleaf and Neal Kaske (2009) suggest that, if the librarians teaching information literacy courses think of assessing course work as a continuous cycle, then they have the means of breaking down a large challenge into small manageable pieces. Their cycle consists of the following seven elements:

- Identifying desired learning outcomes
- Creating appropriate learning activities
- Implementing the learning activities
- Gathering data to gauge learning outcomes
- Interpreting data and identifying the issues that require addressing
- Taking action/decisions to address the issues
- Reviewing learning goals (p. 283)

Perhaps there is an eighth element that fits between creating and implementing learning activities: designing methods to collect appropriate data regarding the outcomes. Oakleaf and Kaske conclude their article with the following:

> When selecting an assessment approach, librarians should strive to follow best practices whenever possible. Using multiple methods and practicing continuous assessments are among the best practices to consider.... By using multiple methods, librarians gain a variety of assessment feedback.... Practicing continuous assessment allows librarians to "get started" with assessment rather than waiting to "get it perfect." (p. 283)

When formulating learning activities and collecting data, it is wise to keep in mind some of the types of questions accreditation visiting teams like to ask, such as:

- Are your learning outcomes linked to the library and institutional missions? How well?
- What evidence do you have of student outcomes?
- What method(s) do you employ to assess the outcomes? Why do you use those methods?
- Do you assess your assessment process?
- How do you communicate the outcome results to the various interested stakeholders?

What are some of the options commonly employed to gather assessment data? There are the long-standing pre- and posttests as well as in class performance tests. Self-reporting techniques include surveys, focus groups, and interviews. Some other options are portfolios and concept mapping.

Laura Saunders (2009) raised some serious questions regarding today's information literacy courses. "Although generally optimistic in their assessment of the continued importance of information literacy and the role librarians will play in its future, these experts acknowledged a number of obstacles academic librarians will face in fully realizing these possibilities" (p. 99). She suggested that ongoing enhancements in hardware and software that, for example, simplify the search process and ranking search results make "many of the skills currently equated with information literacy, particularly questions of access and evaluation . . . unnecessary as searching becomes more easy and intuitive" (p. 113).

Saunders's thoughts are likely to result in Association of College and Research Libraries (2000) reviewing and reassessing its "Information Literacy Competency Standards for Higher Education." The existing five standards are as follows:

> **Check These Out**
>
> An older but still very useful book on classroom assessment is Thomas Angelo and K. Patricia Cross's *Classroom Assessment Techniques: A Handbook for College Teachers* (San Francisco: Jossey-Bass, 1993). Also from Jossey-Bass is *Integrating Information Literacy into the Higher Education Curriculum* (2005) edited by Ilene Rockman. Theresa Neely's *Information Literacy Assessment: Standards-Based Tools and Assignments* (Chicago, IL: American Library Association, 2006) is a fine source of information.

1. The information literate student determines the nature and extent of information needed.
2. The information literate student accesses information effectively and efficiently.
3. The information literate student evaluates information and its sources critically and incorporates selected information into his or her knowledge base and value system.
4. The information literate student, individually or as a member of a group, uses information effectively to accomplish a specific purpose.
5. The information literate student understands many of the economic, legal, and social issues surrounding the use of information and accesses and uses information ethically and legally.

BEYOND ACCREDITATION

Accountability goes well beyond accreditation, as there are stakeholders who have an interest in holding higher education institutions accountable for actions taken or not taken. One obvious stakeholder is the funding body of the institution. Taxpayers and state legislatures both are vitally concerned about use of the funds they give to higher education. In the case of the private institution, the parents and students have expectations that the money they pay for an education will be properly and effectively expended. From a management point of view, each managerial level is accountable for what it does or does not do all the way up to the governing board. As we noted in the opening section of this chapter, society, in the broadest sense, has an interest in what does and does not take place in higher education. There are some individuals with no direct connection with an academic institution who may be highly interested in the curriculum. For example, how institutions (both private and public) teach evolution (this topic also comes up in high school biology courses and can impact students when they take college science courses). Another common concern is about the degree to which personal political/

social views influence how a course is presented. Still others may be concerned about the amount of indirect support given schools, such as tax exemptions, for example.

It is not only accountability issues that drives or ought to drive efforts to assess library programs and services. Providing the highest quality service is a key component in demonstrating value for money and of gaining user support. Some years ago, Brian Quinn (1997) wrote:

> The concept of service quality is somewhat elusive and resists easy definition, but essentially it emphasizes gap reduction—reducing any gap that may exist between a customer's expectations and the customer's perception of the quality of service provided. More traditional measures of academic library quality such as collection size are considered to be of secondary importance. (p. 359)

Today, the ever-growing competition with other information providers impacts the user's perception. Ease of access and speed of responses, for example, create challenges for the user who views "traditional library service" as quality.

Perceptions of quality will vary from person to person and even by geographic region. Having some national means of addressing library user perceptions of service quality has led to such efforts as LibQUAL+. There are generational differences as well. Table 10.2 lists some general attributes regarding quality and how younger people often view those elements, especially in terms of technology.

John B. Harer and Bryan R. Cole (2005) discussed the importance of stakeholders' interest in measuring performance/service. They engaged in a Delphi study "to determine

Table 10.2. Points to Ponder Regarding Quality Service and Millennials

Service Assumptions	Millennials' Perspectives
Service exists only at the point of delivery.	Millennials expect instantaneous results.
Quality exists during the delivery process; it cannot be assured prior to that time.	Millennials expect consistent performance.
If service of poor quality, it cannot be called back.	Millennials are used to "what you see is what you get" and make judgments accordingly.
Quality service is a one-on-one process.	Millennials expect high touch rather than high tech.
Quality service is not something you can put on display like a book or video; it does or does not happen during the delivery process.	Millennials have high expectations and don't revisit disappointing sites very often.
Service is intangible; it is an experience.	Millennials are comfortable with virtuality.
Service cannot be traded, sold, shared, or experienced by anyone but the recipient.	Millennials are fans of trading and sharing.
Service cannot be stored for future use.	Millennials expect to come back to a service time and time again and experience the same results.
Service is highly subjective, "in the eye of the beholder."	Millennials are into sharing their views on matters with the world (using social networking websites).
Service quality declines as additional people become involved in its delivery.	Millennials are no more fond of being shifted from one person to another when seeking service than any other generation.

the importance of a list of critical processes and performance measures relevant to measuring quality in academic libraries" (p. 149). Their results suggested that student, faculty, and other stakeholders' interests were the most significant to ensuring quality.

LibQUAL+ is a set of tools for soliciting, tracking, understanding, and acting "upon users opinions of service quality" (www.libqual.org) of libraries. The survey is an outgrowth of a joint effort by ARL and Texas A&M University and based on work done by Zeithaml, Parasurman, and Berry (1990) on measuring for-profit organization service quality (SERVQUAL). Although some people (e.g., Edgar, 2006) have raised questions about the adequacy of LibQUAL+ as the sole assessment method, it is useful. Conducting such a study can provide data that is both local and comparative with other libraries. It is, in essence, a gap measurement process of the type Quinn (1997) mentioned. Individuals filling out a survey form are asked to indicate, using a nine-point scale, three responses to each question: the person's minimal expectation for a service, the person's desired expectation, and, last, the perceived level of service. A "gap" is present when there are differences between expectations and perceptions.

Few, if any, libraries participate in the survey every year. In 2009, 161 libraries participated; in 2006, 298 took part. See the LibQUAL+ website (www.libqual.org) for annual participation rates and institutional names. The survey is also used internationally. The service is not inexpensive—$3,200 to participate in the 2009 survey. Each year ARL creates norm tables based on that year's responses so a library can compare its data with a broader base. The participating libraries, of course, receive both a summary of their data and the raw data so they can engage in further analysis. Thus, a library gains insights into its service quality both locally and nationally (a form of benchmarking).

> **Check These Out**
>
> Five examples of the use of LibQUAL+ in a variety of academic library settings are:
>
> William J. Hubbard and Donald E. Walter, "Assessing Library Services with LibQUAL+: A Case Study," *Southeastern Librarian* 53, no. 1 (2005): 35–45.
>
> Riadh Ladhari and Miguel Morales, "Perceived Service Quality, Perceived Value, and Recommendation: A Study Among Canadian Public Library Users," *Library Management* 29, nos. 4/5 (2008): 352–366.
>
> Jessica Kayongo and Sherri Jones, "Faculty Perception of Information Control Using LibQUAL+ Indicators," *Journal of Academic Librarianship* 34, no. 2 (2008): 130–138.
>
> Bruce Thompson, Martha Kyrillidou, and Colleen Cook, "How You Can Evaluate the Integrity of Your Library Service Quality Assessment Data: Intercontinental LibQUAL+ Analyses Used as Concrete Heuristic Examples," *Performance Measurement and Metrics* 9, no. 3 (2008): 202–215.
>
> Dominique Wolf, "LibQUAL+ en France: Un Outil pour L'Evaluation de la Qualité de Services en Bibliothèque," *Bulletin des Bibliothèques de France* 53, no. 3 (2008): 39–47.

Some libraries have recently started employing another service similar to LibQUAL+, called Counting Opinion, for assessment purposes. The organization's statement of purpose/service is "comprehensive, cost-effective, real-time solutions designed for libraries, in support of customer insight, operational improvements and advocacy efforts" (www.countingopinions.com). Their list of customers includes both academic and public libraries. Two of the company's products are LibSat ("the means to measure customer satisfaction") and LibPAS (library performance assessment).

Benchmarking

To some degree, LibQUAL+ offers a limited form of benchmarking capability; however, the technique is generally a stand-alone process. Benchmarking, at least in U.S. libraries, is a relatively recent phenomenon as jurisdictions and organizations have become increasingly concerned about operating costs. Benchmarking is basically a tool for either internal or external comparisons. The National Association of College and University Business Officers (NACUBO) has been conducting a number of benchmarking studies of various areas in academic institutions since the mid-1990s. These were large-scale efforts involving various member institutions in the United States and Canada. There have been several such projects relating to libraries over the years; the data have not been published as they were/are viewed as confidential. In 2007, NACUBO introduced an online tool to assist member organizations with their benchmarking processes (www.nacubo.org/Research/NACUBO_Benchmarking_Tool.html).

The goal of benchmarking is to provide data that can help managers answer the following questions:

- How well are we doing compared to others?
- How good do we want to be?
- Who is doing the best?
- How do they do it?
- How can we adapt what they do to our organization?
- How can we be better than the best?

There are four basic types of benchmarking—internal, competitive, industry, and best in class. As the label suggests, *internal benchmarking* looks at internal practices within an organization. An example is what it costs to create a purchase order in various departments across a campus. A *competitive benchmarking* project might collect data on the cost of creating purchase orders in various departments in a number of institutions. *Industry benchmarking* would collect data from all or a representative sample of all organizations within an "industry." (The NACUBO benchmarks are essentially an industry effort.) *Best-in-class benchmarking* collects information across industries, essentially seeking the most effective practices.

Internal benchmarking may also vary between vertical and horizontal projects. A *vertical project* seeks to quantify the costs, workloads, and productivity of a defined functional area; for example, handling accounts payable. A *horizontal study* analyzes the cost and productivity of a single process that crosses two or more functional areas; an example is database searching in acquisitions, cataloging, and document delivery.

The NACUBO studies had/have several objectives:

- To assist participating institutions to identify best practices
- To provide data that may allow participants to identify areas for improvement
- To provide data to assess relationships between inputs (primarily resource costs) and outputs (generally the quantity and quality of products and services)
- To introduce the concepts of "process improvement" and awareness of the value of benchmarking

When developing a benchmarking project, a key issue is establishing for each benchmark a clear understanding by all of the participants of what it will measure and what to include in the data collected for that benchmark. Understanding what will and will not be included—time, staff salaries, equipment costs, staff benefits—is essential if the data are to be useful. (A common problem in first-time projects is not making it clear what to include in staff costs: just salary, salary and directed benefits such as health insurance, or all of those plus vacation and sick leave costs.) If several approaches are used, the data will be essentially useless for comparative purposes.

One of the problems for the first NACUBO library project was the failure to establish clear guidelines for handling multiple campuses and libraries where the entities have separate operating budgets. For the Loyola Marymount University (LMU) library, there were two problems. The first was the fact that Loyola Law School has a separate campus as well as name but shares the same governing board as LMU. Rarely does the institution issue data combining the LMU library with the law school library; however, at many other institutions such combined reporting is common. The second issue was the fact that the LMU library also functions as the university's official archives and records management unit. Although the holdings are not included in the library's statistics, the staffing costs and other operating costs are part of the overall operating budget. Issues such as these should be thoughtfully addressed at the outset.

Table 10.3 is a sample from a library that participated in a 2003 NACUBO benchmark project. Data supplied after the completion of the study included the individual institutional results, the total average results (also the high and low amounts), and "cohorts" based on the Carnegie Classification System for academic institutions. The system also differentiates between public and privately funded institutions. The second column in Table 10.3 shows the "cost per library holding"—essentially the total library operating budget divided by total library holdings. The final column represents the total materials acquisition cost as a percentage of library cost. In the first instance, the assumption was that the lower the number the more efficient, if not necessarily effective,

Table 10.3. Benchmarking Analysis		
	Cost Per Library Holding (low number desirable)	Total Acquisitions Budget ÷ Total Library Holdings (high number desirable)
Library X's data	$7.51	$38.19
All participants mean	$5.62	$33.68
Semiquartile range	$4.10 to $6.51	$27.06 to $39.47
Assessment	Significantly above the mean but near midpoint of range. Two-year colleges a factor in range.	Higher percent than average. Public institutions had lower percent.
Private comprehensive mean	$6.33	$34.39
Semiquartile range	$4.25 to $8.72	$31.66 to $39.09
Assessment	Above primary cohort and near top of range. Need to check with other libraries about their data/practices.	Significantly higher than cohort average. We have increased percent each year for past nine years.
Public comprehensive mean	$5.10	$32.39
Semiquartile range	$4.10 to $5.65	$25.51 to $38.86
Assessment	Even greater difference. It is function of public universities' budget problems over the past ten years.	Well above cohort average. Usage of library X by local state university students reflects a stronger acquisitions program.

the library's collection building program was. For the second set of data, a high number was assumed to be desirable; that is, more of the operating budget went toward building the collections.

Quality Management

Defining quality in a library setting is more difficult when the outcome is not a physical product. How can "quality service" be defined? Can it be just user satisfaction? But doing so leaves one with a conundrum, as someone may be satisfied with information provided by a librarian but not know that information is incomplete or even inaccurate or out of date. Should the user discover such "errors," they are likely to judge the information/service as less than satisfactory. Such issues give rise to the question of when and/or how often to measure customer satisfaction.

Parasuraman, Zeithaml, and Berry (1985) identified the following ten dimensions that, to a greater or lesser degree, determine the quality of a service:

1. Reliability or consistency
2. Responsiveness or timeliness
3. Competence
4. Access or approachability
5. Courtesy
6. Communication
7. Credibility
8. Security (including confidentiality)
9. Understanding the customer needs
10. Tangibles (such as physical facilities, appearance of personnel, and tools or equipment) (p. 47)

All of these elements apply to the academic library environment and can form a starting point for defining quality in a given environment. The following sections address the issues of quality, efficiency, and effectiveness.

Sigma Six–Lean Six Sigma

Sigma Six was created from statistical and quality management modeling tools developed by Joseph Juran (1964). The goal of the Sigma Six process is to improve quality by eliminating manufacturing operations. Likewise Lean, another concept, originally was a quality control process developed for the automotive industry. Since their inception, the two tools have been modified to work in any situation in which quality is a primary interest. Essentially Lean Six Sigma tries to achieve a balance between doing just quality or just speed of operations.

One example of an academic library employing the Lean Six Sigma method is in Sarah Murphy's (2009) article. She discussed the applicability of the concept to one service element at the Ohio State University (OSU) libraries. Library service is a fleeting event and presents challenges as to when and how often to assess such transactions. As she stated, "Services are both intangible and heterogeneous, inviting variability in processes as customers and providers contribute to the inputs and outputs of the service product" (p. 216). The focus of her project was OSU library's process for managing and answering users' e-mail questions. She concluded her article with this statement:

Libraries can customize and borrow a number of quality management systems and tools from the business community to both assess their service process and continuously improve their operations. By adopting an approach like Lean Six Sigma, a library can respond better to changing customer needs and desires by creating an infrastructure that supports, nurtures, and sustains a culture of assessment and change. (p. 224)

Balanced Scorecard

Yet another technique for improving performance began in the early 1990s with Robert Kaplan and David Norton's (1992) article in the *Harvard Business Review*. Their technique—Balanced Scorecard—is a way to organize and present large quantities of complex interrelated data in a manner that fosters better managerial decision making. The approach views the service from four perspectives for which metrics are developed and data are collected and analyzed (www.balancedscorecard.org):

- Learning and growth perspective
- Business process perspective
- Customer perspective
- Financial perspective

Alfred Willis (2004) published an article based on interviews with two key University of Virginia library administrators who were lead figures in using of the balanced scorecard at the library. Jim Self, in responding to a question regarding the value of the technique said, "It can focus the library. It makes the library as an organization decide what is important. It can be used to improve organizational performance. It broadens our perspective in a structured way, and gives us a more balanced view of our work" (p. 66). Lynda White's response to the question was, "Our balanced scorecard is so user-oriented, it fits really well with what we value. Many of our metrics focus on the results for our users whether or not they are technically in the user perspective" (p. 66).

Cost Analysis

Another factor that drives assessment is the increasingly dire economic conditions for higher education. As funding shrinks, libraries must become more efficient as well as effective. Old-fashioned operations research can play a role in demonstrating a library's focus on effectiveness, efficiency, quality, and accountability.

Conducting internal cost studies provides useful data and occasionally reveals unexpected insights. Three of the most common reasons for engaging in such projects are to identify possible cost reduction areas and tasks, to provide data for cost recovery programs, and to evaluate alternatives for carrying out a task or activity. Such studies can, and in most cases should, take a pragmatic approach to data collecting. That is, one should not worry too much about using complex models or statistical analysis; "rules of thumb" are generally satisfactory, and basic statistics work well for local projects. A good starting point for engaging in such a project is *Cost Effective Technical Services: How to Track, Manage, and Justify Internal Operations* (Pitkin, 1989). Not everyone believes in the value of such studies, in part because they apparently associate the projects with some of the worst aspects of "scientific management" of the early twentieth century. A balanced discussion touching on the pros and cons of cost studies (although it is essentially pro) is Joseph Hewitt's (1989) "Using Cost Data Judiciously." Hewitt makes a point with which the authors of this book strongly agree:

Cost studies are a useful, at times necessary, tool of management in libraries. They tend to be used selectively for specific purposes. In decision making, they are used with sensitivity as data illuminating a single (albeit important) factor involved in complex decisions.... On the whole, librarians using cost studies are aware of their limitations and dangers and are attempting to make use of cost studies as tools of rational, humane management (pp. 50–51).

Work Analysis

What some individuals might refer to as old-fashioned scientific management or operations research also has a place in a library demonstrating that it is accountable and concerned with cost containment and assessment. As is true of all of the preceding assessment methods, this book can provide only a little background and suggest some sources for gaining in-depth information.

> **Check This Out**
>
> Recently, a classic source on library work analysis—*Scientific Management of Library Operations* (1982)—has been revised and updated. Richard Dougherty's *Streamlining Library Services: What We Do, How Much Time It Takes, What It Costs, and How We Can Do It Better* (Lanham, MD: Scarecrow Press, 2008) provides detailed information on how to plan work analysis projects.

Work analysis assessment normally begins with asking the standard work analysis questions. The questions are easy to ask but sometimes painful for staff to answer. The basic questions follow:

- What is done?
- Where is it done?
- Who does it?
- Why is it done?
- When is it done?
- How is it done?

Richard Dougherty (2008) made a concise case for engaging in work analysis:

Library administrators have been faced with many difficult and painful choices in recent years as budgets have remained persistently tight, and society and governments demand greater accountability among social institutions such as libraries.... One way to free up staff time and dollar resources is to streamline processes and procedures, or better yet, get rid of existing operations that are redundant or unnecessary. I was particularly taken by a recent comment attributed to a Hewlett Packard official who observed: "If a thing is not worth doing, it is not worth doing well. (p. ix)

The first sentence in this quotation also provides an excellent summary of why this chapter was essential in a book about academic librarianship.

KEY POINTS TO REMEMBER

- Today's society has a vested interest in higher education about such matters as what is taught, how it is taught, whether a degree worth the time to secure it, the quality of what is taught, if there is value for money spent (tuition, tax payments, or donations), and whether the public actually gains anything of lasting value.
- Assessment and accountability are intertwined concepts. Assessment is looking at our own performance, and accountability is when outsiders/stakeholders look at our performance.
- For higher education, the accreditation process is a means of engaging in assessment (self-study) and demonstrating accountability to stakeholders.

- Accreditation is one of the key elements in higher education's efforts to demonstrate quality and accountability.
- Although going through the accreditation process is voluntary because being accredited is a requirement for receiving federal and state funds, reputable institutions undertake the work and costs associated with gaining and keeping accredited status.
- With more than 100 accrediting bodies in existence, academic libraries in medium and larger institutions can expect to have some accreditation activities each year, from supplying self-study data to addressing concerns raised by a visiting team.
- Academic libraries often face dual responsibilities during a comprehensive accreditation visit, such as providing general data regarding curriculum and research support and demonstrating the learning outcomes of their information literacy programs.
- Accountability goes far beyond the accreditation process. The number of stakeholders expecting to have a say in what takes place within the academy is large and diverse. Academic institutions and their libraries employ a variety of techniques to demonstrate their accountability.
- LibQUAL+ is one process that assists in demonstrating accountability.
- There are a wide variety of assessment techniques available to academic libraries that will assist them in demonstrating their commitment to ongoing assessment, accountability, and cost containment.

REFERENCES

Association of College and Research Libraries. 2000. Information literacy competency standards for higher education. Available www.ala.org/ala/mgrps/divs/acrl/standards/informationliteracy competency.cfm (accessed April 7, 2010).

Dougherty, Richard. 2008. *Streamlining library services: What we do, how much time it takes, what it costs, and how we can do it better*. Lanham, MD: Scarecrow Press.

Eaton, Judith S. 2009. *An overview of U.S. accreditation*. Washington, DC: Council for Higher Education Accreditation. Available: www.chea.org/pdf/2009.06_Overview_of_US_Accreditation.pdf (accessed April 7, 2010).

Edgar, William B. 2006. Questioning LibQUAL+: Expanding its assessment of academic library effectiveness. *portal: Libraries and the Academy* 6, no. 4: 445–465.

Harer, John B., and Bryan R. Cole. 2005. The importance of the stakeholder in performance measurement: Critical processes and performance measures for assessing and improving academic library services and programs. *College & Research Libraries* 66, no. 2: 149–170.

Hewitt, Joseph. 1989. Using cost data judiciously. In *Cost effective technical services: How to track, manage, and justify internal operations*, ed. Gary Pitkin, 50–55. New York: Neal-Schuman.

Juran, Joseph M. 1964. *Managerial breakthrough*. New York: McGraw-Hill.

Kaplan, Robert S., and David P. Norton. 1992. The balanced scorecard: Measures that drive performance. *Harvard Business Review* 70, no. 1: 71–79.

Lindauer, Bonnie Gratch. 1998. Defining and measuring the library's impact on campus-wide outcomes. *College & Research Libraries* 59, no. 6: 546–570.

Miller, Charles, and Geri Malandra. n.d. Accountability/assessment. Issue Paper no. 2. Commission on the Future of Higher Education. Washington, DC: U.S. Department of Education. Available: www.ed.gov/about/bdscomm/list/hiedfuture/reports/miller-malandra.pdf.

Murphy, Sarah Anne. 2009. Leveraging lean six sigma to culture, nurture, and sustain assessment and change in the academic library environment. *College & Research Libraries* 70, no. 3: 215–225.

Oakleaf, Megan, and Neal Kaske. 2009. Guiding questions for assessing information literacy in higher education. *portal: Libraries and the Academy* 9, no. 2: 273–286.

Parasuraman, A., Valaria A. Zeithaml, and Leonard L. Berry. 1985. A conceptual model of service quality and its implications for future research. *Journal of Marketing* 49, no. 4: 41–50.

Pitkin, Gary, ed. 1989. *Cost effective technical services: How to track, manage, and justify internal operations.* New York: Neal-Schuman.

Quinn, Brian. 1997. Adapting service quality concepts to academic libraries. *Journal of Academic Librarianship* 23, no. 5: 359–369.

Rhoades, Gary, and Barbara Sporn. 2002. Quality assurance in Europe and the U.S. *Higher Education* 43, no. 3: 355–390.

Saunders, Laura. 2007. Regional accreditation organizations' treatment of information literacy: Definitions, collaboration, and assessment. *Journal of Academic Librarianship* 33, no. 3: 317–326.

———. 2009. The future of information literacy in academic libraries: A Delphi study. *portal: Libraries and the Academy* 9, no. 1: 99–114.

Smith, Kenneth R. 2000. New roles and responsibilities for the university library: Advancing student learning through outcome assessment. Paper presented to the Association of Research Libraries, May 4, University of Arizona. Reprinted 2001 in the *Journal of Library Administration* 35, no. 4: 29–36.

U. S. Department of Education. 2006. *A test of leadership: Charting the future of U.S. higher education.* Washington, DC: U. S. Department of Education. Available: www.ed.gov/about/bdscomm/list/hiedfuture/reports/final-report.pdf (accessed April 7, 2010).

U.S. Department of Education. 2010. Financial aid for postsecondary students. Available: www.ed.gov/admins/finaid/accred/index.html (accessed March 21, 2010).

Willis, Alfred. 2004. Using the balanced scorecard at the University of Virginia Library. *Library Administration and Management* 18, no. 2: 64–67.

Zeithaml, Valarie A., A. Parasuraman, and Leonard L. Berry. 1990. *Delivering quality service: Balancing customer perceptions and expectations.* New York: Free Press.

LAUNCHING PAD

Applegate, Rachel. 2006. Student learning outcomes assessment and ILS program presentations. *Journal of Education f Library and Information Science* 47, no. 4: 324–336.

Askew Waller, Consuella, and Kaylyn Hipps. 2002. Using LibQUAL+(tm) and developing a culture of assessment in libraries. *ARL* 221: 10–11. Available: www.arl.org/resources/pubs/br/br221/br221libqarl.shtml (accessed April 7, 2010).

Block, Judy. 2008. Distance education library assessment. *Electronic Journal of Academic and Special Librarianship* 9, no. 3. Available: southernlibrarianship.icaap.org/content/v09n03/block_j01.html (accessed April 7, 2010).

Burke, Joseph C., and Henrik P. Minassians. 2004. Implications of state performance indicators for community college assessment. *New Directions for Community Colleges* 126: 53–64.

Cook, Colleen, Fred Heath, Bruce Thompson, and Russell Thompson. 2001. The search for new measures: The ARL LibQUAL+ project—A preliminary report. *portal: Libraries and the Academy* 1, no. 1: 65–74.

Gilstrap, Donald L., and Jason Dupree. 2008. Assessing learning, critical reflection, and quality educational outcomes: The critical incident questionnaire. *College & Research Libraries* 69, no. 5: 407–426.

Hernon, Peter, and Robert E. Dugan. 2009. Assessment and evaluation: What do the terms really mean? *College & Research Libraries News* 70, no. 3: 146–149.

Hernon, Peter, Robert E. Dugan, and Candy Schwartz. 2006. *Revisiting outcomes assessment in higher education.* Westport, CT: Libraries Unlimited.

Jannetta, Victoria. 2008. Prove your worth: Measuring the performance of library and information centres. *Legal Information Management* 8, no. 2: 123–126.

Jones, Sherri, and Jessica Kayongo. 2008. Identifying student and faculty needs through LibQUAL+: An analysis of qualitative survey comments. *College & Research Libraries* 69, no. 6: 493–509.

Julien, Heidi. 2005. Education for information literacy instruction: A global perspective. *Journal of Education for Library and Information Science* 46, no. 3: 210–216.

Juran, Joseph M., and A. Blanton Godfrey. 1999. *Juran's quality handbook.* 5th ed. New York: McGraw Hill.

Laeven, Hubert, and Anja Smit. 2003. A project to benchmark university libraries in the Netherlands. *Library Management* 24, nos. 6/7: 291–304.

Mark, Amy E., and Polly D. Boruff-Jones. 2003. Information literacy and student engagement: What the national survey of student engagement reveals about your campus. *College & Research Libraries* 64, no. 6: 480–493.

Matthews, Joseph R. 2008. *Scorecards for results: A guide for developing a library balanced scorecard.* Westport, CT: Libraries Unlimited.

Oakleaf, Megan. 2008. Dangers and opportunities: A conceptual map of information literacy assessment approaches. *portal: Libraries and the Academy* 8, no. 3: 233–253.

Parrish, Darlene Ann, Malka Schyndel, and Jacquelyn Marie Erdman. 2009. Using a database as an assessment reporting tool. *Technical Services Quarterly* 26, no. 3: 207–216.

Pinto, Maria. 2008. Developing a checklist for qualitative evaluation of service charters in academic libraries. *Journal of Librarianship & Information Science* 40, no. 2: 111–121.

Saunders, E. Stewart. 2007. The LibQUAL+ phenomenon: Who judges quality? *Reference and User Services Quarterly* 47, no. 1: 21–24.

Saunders, Laura. 2008. Perspectives on accreditation and information literacy as reflected in the literature of library and information science. *Journal of Academic Librarianship* 34, no. 4: 305–313.

Seybert, Jeffrey A. 2002. Assessing student learning outcomes. *New Directions for Community Colleges* 117: 55–66.

Shephard, Kerry. 2009. E is for exploration: Assessing hard-to-measure learning outcomes. *British Journal of Educational Technology* 40, no. 2: 386–398.

Somerville, Mary A., Lynn D. Lampert, Katherine S. Dabbour, Sallie Harlan, and Barbara Schader. 2007. Toward large scale assessment of information and communication technology literacy. *Reference Services Review* 35, no. 1: 8–20.

Thompson, Bruce, Colleen Cook, and Martha Kyrillidou. 2005. Concurrent validity of LibQUAL+ scores: What do LibQUAL+ scores measure? *Journal of Academic Librarianship* 31, no. 6: 517–522.

———. 2008. library users' service desires: A LibQUAL+ study. *Library Quarterly* 78, no. 1: 1–18.

Part IV

The Academic Library Today

The chapters in this section cover specific academic library issues. Chapter 11, "Collections," addresses the background in which academic librarian collection development personnel find themselves, the hows and whys of the process, as well as print and digital issues. Chapter 12, "Services," explores the public services issues facing today's academic libraries. Chapter 13, "Staffing," discusses the issues of staffing an academic library and the pros and cons of faculty status for librarians. Chapter 14, "Current Themes and Issues," examines a number of academic library concerns such as effective communication, marketing, teams, institutional repositories, collaboration, and Google's Book Project. Chapter 15, "Career Development," as the title indicates, covers career issues from finding the first position to the need for lifelong learning. Chapter 16, "Leaders Look Toward the Future," presents the views of 22 academic library directors about what is required to ensure a future for academic libraries.

Chapter 11

Collections

The transition from graduate school to a professional academic library position is a challenging one, especially when facing the initial journey into collection development. Many librarians experience the stress of this move because in most instances recent graduates do not have the necessary skills, simply due to lack of applied experience and education.

—James Cory Tucker and Matt Torrence (2004)

New librarians in their first professional position reported relatively low pre-existing knowledge in a number of aspects of their jobs. They reported especially low pre-existing knowledge in two areas: dealing with workplace politics and selecting resources for the library collections.

—Joanne Oud (2008)

Collections, whether physical or digital, are the cornerstones of academic library services. In a real sense, higher education is built on the knowledge of humankind contained in the collections. Almost all academics acknowledge the importance of the intellectual content of library collections, even those who believe in digital formats only. While on the abstract/philosophical level there is agreement, recently the focus has been on the "gee-whiz" of this or that technology rather than on content. This is true of academic librarians as well as other academics. Looking at the recent academic library literature, it seems as though we have forgotten that it is content that truly matters, not its format. Junk is junk no matter how one dresses it up with technology.

Technology is changing higher education's environment just as it is changing the way academic libraries operate. As Karen Schmidt (2004) wrote, "It is important to reflect that the organization of knowledge and the ways in which libraries cull and prioritize for its users are a premium asset regardless of the format of the material" (p. 370). At times academic librarians do not emphasize the importance of the content side of their collections, often because the discussion with others focuses on costs and technology. Perhaps everyone assumes "content" will always be there, and there is no need to openly address the idea of content. It may be time to bring collection content out from the background and make it more center stage along with costs and technology.

Many years ago, Gordon Williams (1964) wrote:

Written records are usually desirable because of the meanings the words can communicate to anyone who can read them; what is wanted is what we may call, for lack of a better term, the intellectual content of words. Fundamentally, the written record itself is merely a carrier, a vehicle; and it is what is carried, not the carrier, that is usually of primary importance. (p. 374)

More recently Robert Darnton (2009) made a very important point when he wrote, "When businesses like Google look at libraries, they do not merely see temples of learning.

They see potential assets or what they call 'content,' ready to be mined" (p. 4). (We will explore the Google and libraries issue in Chapter 14.)

One of the more theoretical writers on academic library collection issues was the late Ross Atkinson (2001). He made the following point:

> The library is unavoidably part of the universal discussion by which knowledge is advanced—and, therefore, must always take a position, regardless of how much we try to insinuate a 'veil of ignorance' into our services. This being the case, then what generally should the library's position be? For libraries serving societies that have embraced basic liberal views and the (admittedly sometimes tacit) acceptance of contingency, taking no position (to play on Sartre) is unquestionably the best position to take. (p. 5)

In one of his last publications, Atkinson (2006) suggested that academic library collections serve three basic purposes. The first is that collections provide institutional capital: "Collections attract scholars, graduate students, government support, and donor funding—and add prestige to the institution" (p. 245). A second purpose for having library collections is to provide long-term preservation of the items: "The collection of material, in order to ensure their long-term access, remains the primary challenge and responsibility of research libraries, regardless of changes in technology or ideology" (p. 245). His final suggestion has been a matter of debate within the profession and academy for many years. This purpose "is to privilege [select] particular objects as more useful or reliable than others" (p. 245). In essence, who has, or should have, the power to determine what is good and not so good for long-term preservation? We will come back to this debate later in this chapter.

PAST AND PRESENT PRACTICE

Collection development/management is a relatively new concept for librarianship, at least in terms of using a single term to describe a group of activities relating to both the collections and as a role of librarians. (While many people use the terms interchangeably they have different meanings—collection *development* relates just to the building of collections, while collection *management* covers everything from building to preservation. We cover the full spectrum of activities in this chapter.) It was not until the 1970s and early 1980s that the term *collection development* appeared in the literature and in job announcements as a position responsibility. Until then, the focus had been on acquiring items for the collection and trying to secure the maximum number that were likely to be of interest to the faculty and students with the available funds.

You may recall from Chapter 2 that until well into the nineteenth century, U.S. academic library collections grew slowly, primarily from donations rather than purchases. Also, the collections were small, as the institutional mission and curriculum did not require significant library support—the focus was on mastering a limited number of approved texts that fit the liberal arts concept and the religious beliefs of the religious denomination that supported the college.

During the nineteenth century collections grew substantially as the curriculum expanded and teaching methods changed. From the earliest times until today, at least in smaller institutions with limited funding, the power to select books resided with the faculty. To some extent the view expressed by Pierce Butler (1945) would still be supported by a number of teaching faculty across the country: "The Librarian may be a technical specialist—in the technologies of book preservation and use—but he is never a subject specialist" (p. 10). The notion of subject specialists/bibliographers as library staff would not come about for many years after Butler wrote his book. Even when it did come to pass, it was primarily in the Association of Research Libraries (ARL) institutions.

The shift to allow academic librarians to make the most of the selection decisions was partially a function of time and money. After World War II teaching faculties saw their class sizes increase because of the GI Bill (P.L. 78-348). Teaching larger classes coupled with having to engage in some scholarly activity resulted in faculty having less time for book selection activities except in those institutions where there was no pressure to engage in research. At this point, librarians stepped in to handle the selection process. The trend toward librarian selection got a significant boost not only from post–World War II demands on university faculty but also through several national cooperative acquisitions projects undertaken by ARL institutions through which institutional selection responsibilities became national in scope and thus greatly increased.

As collections grew in size and an increasing emphasis was placed on evaluating existing collections, librarians began to note some of the drawbacks of faculty selection. Perhaps John Ryland (1982) put the case against faculty selection most concisely: "Faculty selection leads to major problems: the wrong books selected because of lack of time, unbalanced collections, and a tendency to overbuy in periodicals" (p. 14). Today, when there is a departmental faculty member assigned to work with the librarian(s) selecting in a subject area, that person is often a junior faculty member, not infrequently the most recent department hire. This extra time commitment seems unfair to individuals who will be under pressure to prove their worth as a teacher and researcher in order to gain tenure.

From the Authors

Evans experienced the shift from faculty to librarian selection of collection in the 1990s. When he took over the directorship of a medium-sized academic library (1988) the faculty had total control over expenditures for library materials and the budget for collections was $450,000. As the institutional fiscal health became stronger, so did funding for acquisitions. Also during this time the institution increased its emphasis on the notion that all faculty members should be "productive scholars" as well as exemplary teachers. Through a slow process, the library staff was able to demonstrate their collection development skills, and by the mid-1990s the faculty library committee and faculty senate agreed to drop the faculty handbook statement that the faculty had sole responsibility for selection. Certainly the fact that by then collection funds were over $2 million also assisted in the shift in responsibility.

Alire, on the other hand, led good-sized university libraries where the selection was done primarily by the subject specialists relying on approval plans and on some interested faculty spending time in the approval room reviewing the materials.

IMPACT OF WORLD WAR II AND ARL COOPERATIVE PROJECTS

Academic libraries in the early twentieth century had modest amounts of money with which to acquire items for their collections. The stock market crash in 1929 and ensuing Great Depression caused serious reductions in acquisitions funds. The result was a sharp decline in purchases of materials from other countries, which were generally modest in the best of times and rather minimal for non–Western European countries. When World War II military and government officials turned to research libraries for information about areas of actual and potential conflict, the results were disappointing. There was a recognition well before the United States entered the war that perhaps a reasonable goal for research libraries would be to have one copy of everything of research interest published anywhere in the world in at least one U.S. library. The expectation was all such material would be cataloged within 30 days and reported to the National Union Catalog. That monumental goal was agreed to at a meeting held in Farmington, Connecticut, in late 1942 and became known as the Farmington Plan. Obviously not too much could be accomplished during the war; however, afterward the plan served as an underlying base for research library collection development. The plan broadened the collecting scope during the Korean War by adding the word "intelligence"— one copy of everything of research and intelligence interest.

> **Check This Out**
>
> Anyone interested in learning more about the role of World War II in academic libraries should read Luther H. Evans's "Research Libraries in the War Period—1939-1945," *The Library Quarterly* 17, no. 4 (1947): 241-262.

A very large percentage of today's research library collections are a direct result of the Farmington Plan, as are other post–World War II cooperative acquisition programs. How did the Farmington Plan address the ambitious goal of having at least one copy of research or intelligence interest in a U.S. research library? The basic structure was developed using the model that the Library of Congress (LC) and research libraries created to distribute the books gathered in postwar Germany. If there was only one copy available, LC retained it; additional copies were allocated on the basis of having a widespread regional distribution and existing collection strengths. Essentially, long term, the plan distributed collection/subject responsibility among libraries based on their institutional research interests and collection strength. The plan operated until 1972, when it became too complex, costly, and operationally difficult for libraries to manage.

The demise of the Farmington Plan was a slow process. ARL collection development personnel had growing doubts about the quality and value of the material their overseas agents were shipping. Also, some other cooperative efforts appeared to provide more focused shipments. Shifting institutional interests also played a role, and libraries dropped some of their subject responsibilities. An ongoing problem was the expectation for quick cataloging of the material. Not every library was able to find a qualified cataloger to process materials in all of the languages in which it was collecting. It is also likely that new cooperative projects played a role in ending the plan.

One such cooperative program was the Latin American Cooperative Acquisition Program (LACAP) that began in 1959. This was a somewhat unusual project in that it was initially a combination of a few research libraries and a commercial vendor (Stechert-Hafner). The vendor agreed to send a representative to Latin America to gather items that would be covered by blanket orders from the participating libraries. The notion was that someone well versed in the book trade would be able to make better judgments about what was appropriate for libraries than would local agents with only minimal understanding of the libraries' needs. In fact, the first representative was a librarian.

Another factor is an ongoing issue for collection librarians attempting to acquire materials from countries with poorly developed book trades, where press runs tend to be small and books are frequently sold out before anything has been printed, and where bibliographic control is almost nonexistent. All of which means having someone locally available is the best way to ensure securing a copy of a publication. Eventually the program grew from the original seven libraries to between 30 and 40 during the 1970s.

Another program during the same time frame as the Farmington Plan was LC's PL-480 (Public Law 480) effort. This program started in 1960 with LC acquiring books and newspapers from Egypt, India, and Pakistan using "excess currencies." (Excess currencies arose from the sale of surplus agricultural products in countries in which payment was made in the local currency and could not be converted into U.S. dollars.) Unlike some of the other cooperative acquisition projects, this one was not limited to research libraries; many academic libraries benefited (it was viewed as a benefit at the time, perhaps not so much so now) from a growing inflow of English language materials from overseas. The ARL libraries also received indigenous language materials that were viewed as supplementing the Farmington Plan responsibilities. (Needless to say, there were challenges in finding catalogers who could handle all of the languages of materials that arrived as part of the project.) Later the program expanded its coverage to include Israel (1965), Nepal (1966), Ceylon (1967), Yugoslavia (1968), and Poland (1972).

A variant program that continues today as the Center for Research Libraries (CRL, www.crl.edu) started out as the Midwestern Inter-Library Center (MILC). MILC began in 1949 as a regional cooperative remote storage facility. (Research libraries have been remotely storing collections for many years and had discussed the concept for even longer.) From the outset, MILC/CRL acquired some low-use materials (e.g., college catalogs and state government publications) on behalf of its membership. Rather quickly, CRL became a national library asset that continues to acquire and lend a variety of low-use materials. It often picked up Farmington Plan subject responsibilities when a library wished to drop the subject. Today, membership is open to any library willing to pay the annual membership fee.

Our final example is the National Program for Acquisition and Cataloging (NPAC). The project focused on the Library of Congress and was not really cooperative except that research libraries were encouraged to report their foreign acquisitions and note any items for which no cataloging was available in LC's depository card sets. From the outset of the Farmington Plan, a major stumbling block had been in knowing who actually had what. The various overseas acquisition programs led to a flood of materials in languages that were beyond the capability of the local cataloging staff to handle. One outcome was that more and more material was put into the processing backlog with very minimal local records. NPAC was designed to help address this shortcoming. Looking back, it seems clear that less thought was given to handling the material than to its acquisition.

As a result of these initiatives, what some in the field call collecting for "just in case" rather than "just in time" became firmly embedded in research library collecting programs. Many of the collections in today's research libraries are a direct result of the Farmington Plan and other cooperative acquisition programs and constitute a significant portion of today's "legacy collections." Some of today's commentators about academic librarianship deride "just in case" collecting. There is seldom even a nod to why such collecting was undertaken.

In today's digital world, how would "just in time" function in a world conflict? As Evans (1947) noted, "War investigation has demonstrated that while much in a library may belong in the 'little used' category, librarians as a group can ignore nothing which

Check This Out

For readers interested in better understanding the true legacy of the Farmington Plan and later cooperative efforts, see Ralph Wagner's detailed monograph *A History of the Farmington Plan* (Lanham, MD: Scarecrow Press, 2002).

may conceivably be needed for present or future research" (p. 243). Certainly how research libraries might address such a concept in a digital environment is an open question, as is whether they should even be concerned. Ralph Wagner (2002) perhaps made the best case for recalling the reason behind the Farmington Plan and other large-scale cooperative efforts post–World War II on the part of research libraries:

> The Farmington Plan was conceived in the information crisis of World War II and extended outside the Western world in the information crisis of the Korean War. The question posed at the time of crisis remains: who will acquire the publications that are of little or no current research value, but may prove to be essential in the future.... Yet the Farmington Plan's failure was almost certainly dictated by the nature of its central concern. Marginal library materials are and will remain politically marginal. They are the concern of scholars working in obscure fields, who are unlikely to unite in support of the concept of collecting the marginal. They are also today's legacy to tomorrow's scholars... but who have no voice in today's decisions. (pp. 402–403)

DEVELOPING ACADEMIC LIBRARY COLLECTIONS

The opening quotations for this chapter make the point that, for many beginning academic librarians, one of the daunting early tasks is gaining an understanding of how collection development actually works in their library. Although some beginning academic librarians have had a course in collection development/management during their professional degree program, such courses usually cover all types of libraries was well as the basics; thus, there is little emphasis on the academic library environment. They also often find in their first professional position that collection development is only one of several job responsibilities assigned to them. Thinking broadly, academic library collection development consists of learning and working on the following areas:

- Differentiating the responsibilities of librarians and faculty in the collection development process
- Assessment of campus users' needs
- The local collection development policy
- Selection sources (reviews, publishers, and any consortial arrangements)
- How the library balances collections between print, other media and digital resources
- Collection development fiscal issues/allocations
- The local acquisitions system(s), existing approval plans, and standing or blanket order plans
- The local standards for assessing the collections
- Issues of storage/deselection
- Preservation issues

Gaining an understanding of all of these areas while also trying to master all of the aspects of a new position is a challenge for anyone, not just the recent graduate. Thus, it is no wonder that collection development is often viewed by newcomers with a certain amount of apprehension.

Learning the nature of the collection development duties is the first task for the newcomer. It is likely that collection development was mentioned in the position advertisement and during the job interview. However, unless the position is solely devoted to collection development, it is unlikely that the responsibilities and local collection development practices were given much more time and attention in the interview than the other duties of the position. Perhaps the most important issue to grasp initially is the role of the faculty in collection development.

Assessing Needs

Part of the challenge for those involved in collection development/management lies in understanding the needs of users as well as in what already exists in the collection. Understanding campus users' needs is a never-ending learning process for effective librarian selectors. They are always on the alert for news, and even rumors, of changes in the subject areas for which they are responsible. Each year they review the institution's new general catalog looking for changes in course descriptions, degree requirements, and any departmental faculty changes in their areas. If there is a faculty–staff dining room on campus, they make a point to have lunch there several times a week. They serve on campus curriculum committees and also make it a practice to join any faculty from their area of responsibilities whenever it will not cause interference (such as at new faculty orientations, departmental meetings, or symposia). This is an excellent way to develop solid working relationships with the faculty as well as perhaps hear about any changes being discussed in the department(s). Certainly it is an opportunity to learn about faculty research interests. In addition, effective selectors make one-on-one appointments with each faculty member every year or two to discuss library resources and gain feedback. (This activity may have been the antecedent to what is today's more complex liaison concept, which we will cover in Chapter 12.) If the person has only one or two subject areas to cover, finding time regularly to read one or two of the more general journals in those subjects provides potential conversation openers at lunches as well as early warning of potential shifts in research interests. Spending time in the collections looking at what is available also allows one to learn what the institutional interests are and have been.

Collection Policy

One of the first collection development documents a new selector ought to spend time studying is the library's collection policy. The reality is that in most libraries, not just academic, such policies are not "living" documents, even when they are online, in the sense that they are consulted and revised on a regular basis. However, such policies will provide a broad overview of the relationship between the library mission and collection development as well as a general sense of the depth of collecting across disciplines. They generally spell out responsibilities—faculty/student role in selection, who handles gifts and gift policies, how complaints are handled (yes, academic libraries do get occasional challenges about items in the collection), and similar matters. The policy usually describes the fund allocation model the library uses. What the selector gains from spending a few hours perusing the policy is a sense of the library's approach to collection development. The remaining learning tasks are about how the collection development program actually operates. It is not unusual to find that there are some marked differences between the policy and practice—policies are guides to thinking and acting; they are not rules.

Selection Resources

Learning selection sources can be challenging for beginners. The majority of the time, the person filling a position does so because the former incumbent has left the institution. In such cases, the other selectors will be able to provide some guidance about the general resources that they all use and perhaps offer a few suggestions. The first month or two will be something of a trial-and-error period. If the position was vacant for some time (a likely situation—see Chapter 15 for a discussion of search committees), one or more of the other selectors probably filled in to some degree. This person(s) will be able to provide valuable information about selection resources and perhaps some insights about the department(s) the new person is to work with. In rare cases, the former incumbent will have been promoted and is still on campus. Often such individuals are pleased to serve as mentors, at least for a while, and provide critical knowledge regarding the campus and the library.

For beginners, learning who are the reliable publishers and editors takes time, and making some errors along the way is to be expected. Keep in mind the old saying that "no library of a million volumes can be all bad." In today's environment of "just in time" collecting, many items will be judged a mistake if immediate usage is the measure of good and bad. With time, the number of "mistakes" will drop and some of the early "mistakes" will prove worthwhile after all. While the goal should be to make as few poor selections as possible, all selectors have this happen from time to time.

> **Check This Out**
>
> One resource worth consulting is the "Toolkit for Bibliographers" developed by the University of Colorado at Boulder Libraries (ucblibraries.colorado.edu/collectiondevelopment/index.htm). This site includes links to several well-known review sources as well as suggestions for developing subject expertise and a "Bibliographer's Training Checklist."

Consortial arrangements primarily affect digital materials; however, many large libraries have long-standing cooperative agreements whose antecedents reflect the ideas embedded in the Farmington Plan. While existing plans may not be as extensive as the earlier ARL efforts, they are often designed to reduce duplication while expanding the total resources available to students and scholars. On an informal level, many selectors, when their library is part of consortia such as OHIOLink or LINK+ (California), check the consortium database to determine who already holds the item before making the final purchase decision. It is not uncommon for nearby academic libraries to formally agree to share areas of collection building when they are part of a larger consortium database system.

Many ARL libraries have multiple branches across the campus. Learning who collects what in a multiple library environment takes time and effort. Few books today are truly single-topic works. When there is an economics, a botany, an anthropology library on campus, which one should purchase a book about the economic impact of coffee growing by indigenous people? In times of ample funding, buying multiple copies might be acceptable, but this is certainly not so in difficult economic times. Even with a shared database, knowing which selector may be considering such a purchase may not forestall unintended duplications. Face-to-face meetings to discuss and develop some basic working principles regarding cross discipline acquisitions is essential.

Collection Balance

The previous paragraph relates to another learning task—the overall balance that the library strives to achieve among print, other media, and digital resources as well as among subjects. Often this is straightforward in terms of broad categories, but when it comes to what the balance ought to be within various subject areas, the task is more complex. Often there are differences of opinion regarding the desirable levels among the library staff, between the library and the faculty, and even between faculty members in the same subject area. Sorting out these differences and reaching an acceptable compromise takes time and patience. For the newcomer just learning the organizational culture and power structures, it can be something of a minefield.

From the Authors

Evans faced a challenge regarding what were the appropriate materials to collect soon after becoming the director of a subject library at a large university. In the course of assessing library needs in one-on-one meetings with the entire departmental faculty, it became clear there was an almost universal desire for the library to build a video collection. The collection would be for class reserves to supplement in-class material as well as for student projects. Upon requesting funds for such purchases he was informed that the library system did not collect nonprint materials. After several somewhat testy sessions with the campuswide library collection development committee, his library was reluctantly given permission to add such material—if he could raise all of the necessary funds for equipment, videos, and processing costs. A brief meeting with several key faculty members led to a donation of $100,000 to start building the video collection and the attendant costs. (Note: The library system no longer has a print-only policy.)

Many collection development units, especially in larger libraries, have generated a "conspectus" that lists by subject at least three aspects of the collection—existing collection strength, current collecting level, and desired level of collection strength. If nothing else, engaging in the creation of a conspectus helps selectors focus long-term goals. It is very easy, even if selection is a person's only responsibility—and this is rarely the case—to get caught up in the details of daily activities and forget the long-term goals. Building a conspectus, when thoughtfully done, also gets selectors into the stacks to actually review the items on the shelf.

Collection Funding

Acquiring knowledge of how collection development funding is handled takes time, especially learning how the funds are allocated, as the process can and does vary from year to year. The broad issues are straightforward, but learning when and how funds may be transferred from one category to another is more involved. Also, what was/is possible to do in one year may not be so in later years as overall budget conditions change. In tight budget situations, the senior library administrators may limit transfers and even freeze purchases altogether because of the possibility of having funds taken back by the institution. An all too common experience for academic libraries has been being asked to return several percentages of their operating budget during a fiscal year. Given that the vast majority of a library's operating budget consists of salary and collection development funds, it is not surprising that the monies needed to meet the requisite recall amount comes from the collection funds rather than any other category.

At many smaller institutions, faculty members still retain the sole responsibility for collection development. There may be a small amount of funding set aside for the library staff to select items for the reference collection, but all remaining funds are allocated to teaching departments, which can generate some heated interdepartmental debates. Even where librarians have full responsibility for collection development, allocation arguments can arise. In general, scientists are dependent on journal titles (often costing tens of thousand of dollars per title) and use few books. On the other hand, humanists tend to be dependent on books and much less so on journals. Achieving some balance between costly scientific journal needs and less expensive per title costs for the humanists' books is often a contentious process. Add in class sizes and numbers of majors and minors in a subject area and you have the ingredients for endless hours of debate about how to fairly allocate the funds.

If all of the debate involved only this, the allocation process would be complex; however, it does not end there. There are other funding needs to consider such as reference materials, document delivery (per item charges for example), replacement items, and retrospective materials and the ever-growing area of digital collections that cut across disciplines as well as those that are single-subject oriented. Librarian subject selectors should be advocates for their area(s) of responsibility, and thus even when faculty are not directly involved the contentious nature of the process is not reduced by much. It takes time to learn how and who makes the final allocation decisions.

As mentioned previously, perhaps the least pleasant collection development task is handling the all too common need to address budget shortfalls, unexpected funding recalls, and inadequate budget increases for collections. The challenge is in deciding which ox or oxen to gore. Questions such as the following are becoming all too common: Do we make an across-the-board cut (some percentage) in all acquisition funds? Do we just cut the book budget in the hope that there will be enough left to cover our journal subscriptions? Do we try to preserve our funds that support reference activities?

Check These Out

William Walters's article "A Regression-Based Approach to Library Fund Allocation," *Library Resources & Technical Services* 51, no. 4 (2007): 263-278, provides a sound overview of the many factors academic libraries must weigh when attempting to develop a satisfactory allocation formula.

Three other articles worth looking at related to allocation decisions are:

Kitt Canepi, "Fund Allocation Formula Analysis: Determining Elements for Best Practices in Libraries," *Library Collections, Acquisitions, and Technical Services* 31, no. 1 (2007): 12-24.

Gayle R. Y. C. Chan, "Aligning Collection Budgets With Program Priorities: A Modified Zero-Based Approach." *Library Collections, Acquisitions, and Technical Services* 32, no.1 (2008): 46-52.

Eric FuLong Wu and Katherine M. Shelfer, "Materials Budget Allocation: A Formula Fitness Review," *Library Collections, Acquisitions, and Technical Services* 31, nos 3/4 (2007): 171-183.

Every answer will have some intended and some unintended consequences. For example, the decision to maintain journals will not impact the science faculty but will have an impact on the humanists who are book dependent. An across-the-board cut will mean some subscriptions will need to lapse; how does one decide which titles to drop, and will all departments have to lose a title or two? Dropping one chemistry title will usually "save" a substantial amount but may have more serious consequences for the department than cutting ten titles that faculty in the English department consult. An interesting article addressing the issue of journal cancellation is Carey, Elfstrand, and Hijleh's (2005) "An Evidenced-Based Approach for Gaining Faculty Acceptance in a Serials Cancellation Project."

Acquisition Procedures

Local acquisition procedures are usually reasonably easy to grasp. One area that does take some experience to understand is how vendors are selected. The larger the library, the greater the number of vendors the library is likely to use. No single vendor, regardless of what the sales representative says, is able to effectively supply all of the items a library will acquire, subscribe to, or lease. Thus, even modest-sized libraries employ a number of vendors. The usual practice is for the acquisitions department to select the vendor of choice for an order; however, the person selecting the item should pass on any special information about a request, such as a rush order for a class reserve, for example. Such information may impact which vendor gets the order.

There are several categories of acquisitions that new selectors must quickly master. Learning what standing orders and blanket orders, if any, are in place for the selector's subject areas for will save everyone time and trouble. The two orders are similar in character. The term *standing order* usually applies to serial titles such as transactions, conference proceedings, and other series that appear on an irregular basis and often in very small press runs. Having a standing order with the publisher to automatically ship a copy upon publication saves the library staff time and assures that it secures a copy. A *blanket order* usually applies to books and again calls for the automatic shipment of a class of publication as items appear. Both systems also assure payment to the publisher without having to process individual orders. (An order form/purchase order is a legal contract that obligates the library to pay for the item(s) listed upon delivery. In the case of standing and blanket orders, there is no such list/contract.) Essentially the process saves both the library and vendor time and effort.

Approval plans are a variation of these approaches and are widely employed in medium- and large-sized academic libraries. Like the blanket order, approved books arrive automatically and on a regular basis. Unlike the other automatic plans, the library has no commitment to purchase any of the items in the shipment. Rather the selectors can examine the items and decide if the items should be acquired or not. Selectors have a limited amount of time in which to review each shipment; generally unwanted items must be returned within a certain time frame, and all nonreturned items will be billed to the library. The decision to keep or not must be made in a timely manner, because none of the approval materials have any ownership indication on them (they could not be returned if they did) and, thus, what retail outlets refer to as "shrinkage" (items missing for no known reason) can occur. The risk of loss increases the longer the items remain on the approval shelves. In some cases, approval plans may be negotiated with the vendor so that items come precatalogued for the collection. In such cases, returns are generally not permitted.

There are several keys to having a successful approval plan. First and foremost is having a

> **Check This Out**
>
> An excellent review regarding the nature of approval plans and their use by academic libraries is Beth E. Jacoby's article "Status of Approval Plans in College Libraries," *College & Research Libraries* 69, no. 3 (2008): 227–240.

detailed "profile" that the vendor uses to select the items to ship automatically. Such profiles must be reviewed on a regular basis.

Assessment

Assessment of collections is a part of the library's ongoing obligation to demonstrate accountability and efforts to improve its operational activities and services. Libraries often engage in major collection assessment project; however, good selectors engage in ongoing assessments of their area(s) of responsibility on their own. Major assessment projects are frequently the result of the need to send items to a storage facility or as a preliminary step for a cooperative project.

One assessment tool that many academic libraries use is OCLC's WorldCat Collection Analysis package (www.oclc.org/collectionanalysis/about). This is a tool that has gone through many revisions and has a proven track record. With this service, a library is able to select a peer group to have comparative data drawn from OCLC's database. (One common peer group that libraries select for such comparisons is identical to the group its institution employs for comparative purposes. One might also think of the peer group as competitors for students, faculty, and support.) OCLC lists the following benefits for the Collection Analysis service:

> **From the Authors**
>
> Both authors have had very successful experiences using this type of assessment tool for such purposes as learning what weakness exist in the collection in an area where the institution is considering starting a new degree program or for demonstrating existing strengths in that area. It also is helpful in developing reasonable collecting areas for libraries in a consortium.

- Identify your unique holdings
- Compare with peer institutions
- Assess your collection (identify overlaps and gaps)
- Support decisions for both print and electronic acquisitions

- Assess collection usage
- Leverage your investment in WorldCat
- Demonstrate fiscal responsibility
- Support accreditation
- Contribute to consortia activities

Another, relatively recent assessment tool that some academic as well as public libraries are using is Bowker Book Analysis System. The service combines material from

---

Check These Out

The following are several references that provide an insight into how some academic libraries have employed WorldCat Collection Analysis:

Jennifer Benedetto Beals and Ron Gilmour, "Assessing Collections Using Brief Tests and WorldCat Collection Analysis," *Collection Building* 26, no. 4 (2007): 104–107. (Used for cooperative collection development.)

Michael Culbertson and Michelle Wilde, "Collection Analysis to Enhance Funding for Research Materials," *Collection Building* 28, no. 1 (2009): 9–17.

Elizabeth Henry, Rachel Longstaff, and Doris Van Kampen, "Collection Analysis Outcomes in an Academic Library," *Collection Building* 27, no. 3 (2008): 113–117. (Comparison with a peer group to determine collection gaps.)

Virginia Vesper, "WorldCat Collection Analysis," *Tennessee Libraries* 57, no. 2 (2007): 1–16. Available: www.tnla.org/displaycommon.cfm?an=1&subarticlenbr=146&printpage=true. (Discusses use of the service to assess support for new doctoral programs.)

Howard D White, "Better Than Brief Tests: Coverage Power Tests of Collection Strength," *College & Research Libraries* 69, no. 2 (2008): 155–174. (A discussion of the benefits and shortcomings of "brief tests" and WorldCat Collection Analysis.)

Choice and *H. W. Wilson Standard Catalogs* as the basis for the assessment. The system assists in identifying gaps and duplication in the collection:

> Spend more time focusing on selection decisions and create a custom core collection with confidence. Maintain your collection on an ongoing basis so you can provide the most current and appropriate titles to your library patrons.
>
> Using four matching methods (ISBN, LCCN & Title & Author, Title & Author, or LCCN & Title), the comparison between your collection and the core list you choose allows you to instantly recognize by subject area where the strengths and weaknesses lie in your collection. Depending on the core list selected, reports are grouped either Dewey Decimal classification, LC classification or RCL taxonomy. (R. R. Bowker, 2010)

From the Authors

One of the individuals who kindly agreed to read all of the chapters of this book prior to its printing, John Stemmer, director of the library at Bellarmine University in Louisville, Kentucky, provided the following first-hand account of using the system:

> This is a newer product but is based on the Resources for College Libraries database. We are using it to try and address faculty concerns about weaknesses in the collection. It is too soon to know how it will work in the end, but I am hopeful it will provide a good starting point. I know one library that is using it more defensively, to make sure they don't weed anything that is/was considered a "standard" resource.
>
> You asked about how we are using BBAS. One thing I did was review the overall percentages for titles held. Our percentage of Core titles held is about 14.5 percent. It provides a breakdown by call number range 000s–900s, and I can see if everything is around 14.5 percent or if there are stronger and weaker areas. We are strong in Philosophy and Religion (19–20 percent). We are weak in Technology and Arts and Recreation (6.7 percent & 9.5 percent)—not surprising results for what started as a Catholic liberal arts college, I think. So I have a sense that the collection, while small, has been consistently built up.
>
> Aside from the overview, I am using it to provide lists of current materials (post 2000) that we don't have to faculty. My plan is that it will generate a response on what they believe we need to add to the collection to support the curriculum. The faculty have consistently responded to library surveys that the collection is weak and has gaps. In terms of support the numbers have actually gone down since I got here even though we are buying more books. (I think this might be influenced by a large number of new faculty as we try to grow and who are used to larger research libraries from their PhD programs.) Generally, it will be a point of departure for conversations between the library and faculty on what needs to be added. More specifically, as the university is trying to grow from 2,500 FTEs to 4,000–6,000 FTEs, we are adding new programs both undergraduate and graduate. We have used this tool to identify appropriate materials for new programs, again focusing on the most recent, often the new programs are in areas where we have not have traditionally collected (e.g., exercise science, environmental studies).

As mentioned previously, good collection development personnel usually engage in small-scale assessment projects on an ongoing basis just as a check on how they are doing. For example, a selector might every year or two compare the reviews found in a publication such as *Choice: Current Reviews for Academic Libraries* (American Library Association, available both as a magazine and an e-publication) for her or his subject area(s) responsibilities. *Choice* also publishes an annual list of the "best of the best." Checking the major journals in the subject responsibility area(s) may also identify similar lists of core/best titles. One-on-one meetings with faculty can provide excellent opportunities to learn about their individual views about collection quality and needs.

When it comes to assessing the collection for storage or withdrawal purposes, integrated library system (ILS) reports can be major time savers. Probably the best predictor of future usage is past usage, and the goal of most remote storage or withdrawal/weeding efforts is to pull items from the shelves that will have the lowest possible use. Clearly usage will be a factor in deciding what to withdraw/weed from the collection. Almost all of the current ILS systems can produce circulation usage data for items in the collection. In the past, selecting items for storage meant spending hours and hours in the stacks looking at the date due slip in each book and pulling those that met the storage parameters. The items still must be pulled, but today the judgment calls can be made from the reports. Many systems also have the capability of including data about in-house use as well, if the library has elected to activate that module and has committed staff to inputting data. One common faculty complaint about storage efforts is that they use items in the library and thus circulated usage data fails to reflect the actual use of "important" titles. Some faculty members even suggest that not only do they use items in the library but also return them to the shelf, so their usage is not reflected in any database.

Other criteria for selecting items for storage are age and availability in an e-format. Age can be a useful criterion in the hard sciences where new information supersedes older data—for example, a book on cancer treatments published in the 1980s is a good candidate for remote storage or perhaps even withdrawal. Paper-based journals occupy a very large amount of shelf space in most academic libraries. With so many journal titles available in an electronic database, remote storage of such titles is a good option. Furthermore, today's students tend to want only e-access. However, there are some reasons to store the paper issues that are in the collection. One reason is that in the early days of "full-text" online, there was no color, and often complex charts that originally appeared in color were lost as they appeared only in black, white, and shades of gray. Another reason is that many journals and magazines carry (or once carried) advertisements that were and in some cases still are not part of the e-databases. For marketing courses as well as graphic design courses, such material is vital.

When it comes to cooperative resource sharing efforts, the likely assessment process will be based on a random sample of the collection areas under consideration for sharing

---

Check These Out

Three articles that address the broad issues of collection evaluation and faculty involvement in collection development decisions are the following:

Jim Agee, "Collection Evaluation: A Foundation for Collection Development," *Collection Building* 24, no. 3 (2005): 92-95.

Jacqueline Borin and Hua Li, "Indicators for Collection Evaluation: A New Dimensional Framework," *Collection Building* 27, no. 4 (2008): 136-143.

Sandhya D. Srivastava and Pamela Harpel-Burke, "The Library and Faculty Senate: Legitimizing the Serials Evaluation Process Using the Department of Biology Subscriptions," *Acquisitions Librarian* 18, nos. 35/36 (2006): 149-159.

The following are examples of ongoing collection assessment in Florida community college libraries.

Anna H. Perrault, with Jeannie Dixon and Barbara Cardinale, "Florida Community College Collection Assessment Report, 2007" (Tallahassee, FL: Community College Center for Library Automation, 2007). Available: www.cclaflorida.org/docs/2007_collection_assessment.pdf.

Anna H. Perrault, with Jeannie Dixon and Heather Thuotte-Pierson, "Florida Community College Collection Assessment Report, 2002" (Tallahassee, FL: Community College Center for Library Automation, 2002). Available: www.ccla.lib.fl.us/docs/2002collassess/2002_state_rpt.pdf.

Anna H. Perrault, Richard Madaus, Ann Armbrister, Jeannie Dixon, and Rhonda Smith, "Florida Community College Library Collections Assessment: A Study of Florida Community College Library/Learning Resources Collections" (Tallahassee, FL: College Center for Library Automation, 1998).

as well as on looking at general usage of the items in the sample. Even in statewide efforts, such as OhioLINK and Link+, individual libraries can decide to have some classes of material (e.g., audiovisual materials, special collection items, or a classification number) not represented in the sharing aspect.

Remote Storage

Academic libraries have faced collection storage challenges for more than 100 years. As we noted in Chapter 2, Harvard President Charles Eliot suggested in 1901 that rather than build additional library space on campus the university should store "dead books" away from campus (Carpenter, 1986, p. 122). Scott Seaman (2005) opened his essay on remote storage with the following: "The Association of Research Libraries (ARL) estimates that member libraries added 9,480,045 volumes to their collections in 2001–2002. Given a conservative estimate, one would expect such magnitude of materials to occupy 1,185,000 linear feet of shelving space or 225 miles of shelves annually" (p. 20). We may be in the digital age, but academic libraries are still (2010) acquiring vast numbers of volumes that require storage space.

Planners of new academic library facilities may occasionally be able to include space for 20 years of collection growth and remain within budget. Such a feat is rare today as the issue goes beyond dollars needed. There are two issues that campus senior administrators are likely to raise: digitization and some variation of "We can't open the new building with empty shelf after empty shelf. It would look terrible and our donors would raise questions. We told them we have run out of space for the library." Making the case for growth space for collections can be challenging.

Even in the best of times there is likely to be a substantial lapse in time between when the library staff raises the issue of needing growth space and when such space becomes available. Some years ago, Evans was involved in a nationwide study of academic library building projects. The study team found that on average the time between a library first making the case for additional space and the space becoming available was 8.9 years.

Librarians have had to be creative in order to manage collection growth and not negatively impact service too much. Even when the staff is aware that it will take time to get space and begin to raise the issue in advance of crisis situations, users will begin to notice changes. Easy steps, such as withdrawing superseded items or low-use duplicate copies, only buy a small amount of growth space. ("The library is planning on discarding some of its collections" is a rumor that will get the attention of some faculty who will be unhappy. Addressing such rumors will take staff time and not always placate the faculty.) At times the library may be able to reduce stack aisle width to the minimum allowed under Americans with Disabilities Act regulations and gain a year or two of space. Another possibility is to reduce reader space in order to add stacks, which is not usually a popular option for anyone.

In some cases, where the floor loading will allow it, a library can install compact shelving units. (Compact shelving units are mounted on rails so a person can open an aisle where needed. In an area where the library may have had ten open access aisles, compact shelving would reduce that to one aisle and add one or two extra stack ranges.) Such shelving is not cheap, but it is less costly than acquiring additional square footage and increases stack capacity by between 25 and 30 percent. One advantage of such shelving is that it can be redeployed in a new facility, thus adding collection storage space without adding to the square footage. A number of libraries have successfully employed compact shelving, with several safety features added, and have maintained the open stack concept. Some staff and users are at first reluctant to go into a compact shelving aisle, but with few exceptions they eventually become used to the system.

For many libraries, a remote storage facility for low-use items some distance from the campus has become a norm. Such facilities are usually located in areas where the cost of land is low—normally whatever vacant land exists on campus is too valuable to use for a storage unit. There are a several models for such units, such as an institutionally owned and operated system and several variations of joint use or shared facilities. Earlier in the chapter we mentioned the Center for Research Libraries, which began as a shared storage facility and has now both a storage operation and more importantly an organization that acquires a variety of low-use materials that might otherwise occupy valuable shelf space in a number of academic libraries around the country. Another example of cooperative storage is from the University of California system, which built two "regional storage" units, one in northern and the other in southern California. These units accept items from both public and private academic libraries and employ high density storage techniques, such as compact shelving, shelving by size, and double or triple shelving of items.

> **Check These Out**
>
> The following references provide more detail about off-site storage issues and indicate that storage of academic library collections is a worldwide concern:
>
> Jim Agee and Sarah Naper, "Off-Site Storage: An Analysis," *Collection Building* 26, no. 1 (2007): 20–25.
>
> Paul Genoni, "Current and Future Print Storage for Australian Libraries: Results of a Study," *Library Collections, Acquisitions, & Technical Services* 32, no. 1 (2008): 31–41.
>
> Steve O'Connor and Cathie Jilovsky, "Approaches to the Storage of Low Use and Last Copy Research Materials," *Library Collections, Acquisitions, & Technical Services* 32, nos. 3/4 (2009): 121–126.

Some libraries have had to employ third-party vendors for low use storage (Vargas, 2005; Evans, personal experience). There are commercial firms that specialize in storing records for companies and allow the organization to both add new material and retrieve material. Some such facilities have a better storage environment (temperature and humidity control) than the library. Needless to say those places charge more for their services. One stores items in the standard 1.2 cubic foot records boxes for which there is a monthly fee. There are also charges per box for intake and retrieval. Although a rather expensive approach, it does work for relatively short-term storage while awaiting a new building.

Some institutions planning a new library building have included high-density storage capability into the design plan (University of Nevada, Las Vegas, and Santa Clara University, for example). The systems are a modified version of automated warehousing retrieval systems. They are costly, but they maximize the storage capacity of the building's footprint.

J. P. McCarty (2005) raised a significant question about the storage of low-use materials. He wrote, "Why invest in housing and servicing an activity which information systems will probably make either totally or partially redundant in the not too distant future?" (p. 90). Many outside academic librarianship may indeed wonder what the answer ought to be. Google's Library Book Project makes this question even more pertinent in

2010 and beyond. One response might well draw on the issues raised earlier in the chapter regarding "just in case" collecting. The following section on preservation also holds part of a meaningful response.

Preservation Issues

Even in large research libraries with a conservation/preservation department, everyone on the library staff should take some interest in protecting the well-being of the collections, especially those with responsibility for purchasing items for the collection in the first place. Academic libraries have spent billions of dollars on the selection, acquisition, processing, and storage of their collections over the years. Allowing such investments to deteriorate due to neglect, poor housekeeping, and various other hazards (water and insects for example) is unacceptable.

At its most basic level, preservation begins with everyone on the staff knowing accepted housekeeping procedures such as how to remove and reshelve materials from shelves. What may at first appear to be stereotypical picky library practices can over the years save a library much needed funds by reducing the number of items that need some type of preservation treatment, such as rebinding or special boxing, for example.

A long-standing question for all libraries is, "who dusts the shelves in the stacks?" The most common answer is: Not the janitorial staff. Is it really necessary to be concerned about such a "small matter"? Yes it is, for two reasons. One reason is that it is a health issue for some people who are allergic to book dust. The second reason is a preservation concern. The longer the dust remains on the shelving surface, the more damage it will do to bound materials as the items are removed and replaced on the shelf. Certainly it takes time for such wear to become a problem, but academic library collections are expected to exist indefinitely. There are many other "small" stack maintence issues that if ignored will cause preservation problems. When full-time staff engage in proper housekeeping, it will set an example for the student employees who do most of the stack maintenance work, as well as for users.

Two other library housekeeping issues that relate to both preservation and health are insects and mold. Knowing what to look for when working in the stacks can keep down insect problems such as book lice, silverfish, and cockroaches. If such insects are actually seen, there is probably a serious infestation occurring as they tend to be active in the dark. The notion of the musty-smelling bookshop/library being a sign of scholarship is really a sign of possible mold problems. Mold has on occasion become so widespread and significant that libraries have had to close while the mold is cleaned up—at significant expense. With both issues, the more quickly the library addresses the problem, the less costly it will be for people, the collection, and the library.

When working in the stacks, collection development personnel should be looking also for items in need of attention. One major problem is acidic/brittle paper that, over time, can turn a book into "cornflakes" when handled. Preserving such material is a challenge. If the title is of less interest to the library and if a copy can be identified in a deacidified collection, perhaps withdrawing the local copy is the best option. Another option is encasing the item in a protective container (phase box) and/or sending it to a storage facility, which reduces the handling risks. Another possibility is purchasing a replacement copy; however, the replacement is not likely to be in much better condition as the cause of the brittleness started at the time the paper was manufactured (wood pulp paper). The most costly option is having the item deacidified (this only stops the chemical process causing the brittleness) and perhaps having the pages strengthened. This option is usually undertaken only for very important items. Selection officers are directly involved in making the decision of how to handle such items.

Paper-based preservation is not the only challenge. While acid-free paper can last for hundreds and even a thousand years, we have little solid information about the life span of digital formats. We do know that, at present, the digital records are not stable over time. Kevin Bradley (2007) made the point regarding the need to preserve all cultural heritage items and how the field has addressed that need:

Check This Out

For more information on deacidification projects as well as other preservation issues, see Conservation OnLine's "Mass Deacidification" page: cool .conservation-us.org/bytopic/massdeac/.

> Digital preservation has, at the least, a lexical link to preservation, and, at best, a philosophical and conceptual base embedded in the aspirations of traditional conservators. The profession of preservation and conservation matured both technically and philosophically in response to the 1966 disaster that saw the River Arno in Florence break its banks and wreak disaster upon a store of priceless cultural heritage objects. Practitioners and thinkers in the conservation field rallied in the salvage effort, and, in the aftermath of the flood, participated in a long reevaluation of traditional practices. (p. 151)

His article goes on to explore the complex issues related to digital preservation.

Scholars today can read the Dead Sea Scrolls written thousands of years ago as well as provide interpretations of their meaning. On the other hand it is difficult—perhaps impossible—to read digital data we stored not all that long ago. Libraries and society face two broad challenges when it comes to the data people create and store digitally in terms of long-term access. First there is the issue of how that information/data is stored (tape, CD, server, etc.) and just how long that particular media will last and remain error-free. Second, there are the issues related to hardware, operating systems, and software capable of retrieving the information/data.

Libraries have serious concerns around both of these issues. Many academic libraries house a special collections department and perhaps also the institutional archives. In addition, libraries have to wonder about the long-term commitment of commercial vendors of databases after the older materials cease to provide an adequate income stream. Who will indefinitely archive such material and at what cost? As more academic libraries create institutional repositories, thoughtful consideration needs to be given to long-term preservation and how to maintain document integrity. Yaniv Levi (2008) stated:

> While many libraries and information centers have digital asset management systems or digital repositories for managing and storing digital objects, these systems are not designed with the preservation of the digital knowledge in mind. Rather they focus on access management, or facilitating the day-to-day use of digital content by users. On the other hand, digital preservation is about guaranteeing the future usability of accessibility to digital content. (p. 22)

The following are a few examples of the types of problems libraries and others face in terms of digital longevity. Daniel Cohen (2005) noted that "the Library of Congress, which holds roughly 150,000 audio CDs in conditions almost certainly far better than those in personal collections, it estimates that between 1 and 10 percent of the discs in their collections already contain serious data errors" (p. 14). Another example of lost data was reported in an article (Tangley, 1998) that described NASA's frustration when, in 1996, they tried to read magnetic tape data from the 1976 Viking Mars mission. What they found was that 10 to 20 percent of the data were missing—this in spite of the fact that the laboratory had tried to main-tain the tapes according to "standard guidelines." Danny Bradbury (2007) related the story of how the BBC in the early 2000s decided to try to reissue a 1950s television series for which they had discarded the original tapes. BBC eventually recovered all of the episodes primarily from private individuals who had taped the show off the air. A major challenge was most of the tapes came from the United States, which employs a different television standard than the UK. As Bradbury noted, "the BBC did a lot of work building hardware that would intelligently convert NTSC [National Television Standards Committee, the U.S. broadcast system] recording back into PAL [Phase Alternating Line system, used in Europe]" (p. 42).

> ### Check These Out
>
> For more information on the issue of digitization, sharing of digital data, as well as preserving such material, visit the Digital Library Foundation website at www.diglib.org. The Digital Library Federation is a consortium of libraries and other organizations that "are pioneering the use of electronic information technologies to extend library collections and services." One of its more broad-based reports is *Electronic Resource Management* (2004) by Timothy D. Jewell and colleagues (www.diglib.org/pubs/dlf102/).
>
> An excellent article on the subject of digital preservation is Trudi Bellardo Han's "Mass Digitization: Implications for Preserving the Scholarly Record," *Library Resources & Technical Services* 52, no. 1 (2008): 18–26.

E-RESOURCES

E-collections are becoming an ever-increasing percentage of an academic library's collections. Selection of these resources builds on the criteria employed when selecting paper-based titles. One of the major differences between the two processes is that many, if not most, libraries employ a team/committee to select e-materials. This approach is necessary as there are both technical and content issues to think about as well as the fact that often the product under consideration contains multiple titles that frequently cut across disciplines. Brian Quinn (2008) made this point:

> Decisions regarding titles that represent a substantial investment, such as databases, or that involve an ongoing investment, such as subscriptions to journals, are commonly made in a group context. Important collection development decisions are made by groups whose members often consist of various stakeholders...all of whom are involved in developing the collection. (p. 10)

Having an understanding of the library and campus cultures can be vital for the newcomer to the process in order to be an effective advocate for a position on whether or not to acquire a product/title.

What are some of the most significant differences between electronic and paper-based selection decisions? Unlike paper-based acquisitions, many of the e-resources products are available only through a license. The "standard" license for a product often contains some limitations regarding access and usage of the material that may be problematic for the library. Some of the issues that may arise in the license are restrictions that may limit or forbid the use of the content for interlibrary lending; caps on the number of individuals who may access the material at the same time (simultaneous users); limits on use of the material by nonstudent, faculty, and staff (outside users); conditions relating to remote access (proxy server issues as well as in-library usage); and holding the library liable for how an individual makes use of the information gathered.

Depending on the content of the license, the library may wish to negotiate with the vendor regarding limitations. The license is a legal document, and institutional attorneys may become involved in the negotiations. Some libraries spend funds on having the campus counsel draw up a basic license that reflects the institution's needs as a starting point for the library's negotiating position. Mark Watson (2008) explored the question of whether a library needs a legal consultant to address licensing issues. He suggested:

> It is simply a fact of licensing life that where librarians care about the content, interface, or ability to perform interlibrary loan, the lawyers are looking for assurance that the university will not be subject to unlimited indemnification provisions, or that obligations for attorney fees will be subject to the limitations and conditions of the state constitution.... To sum up, I think the forces shaping our libraries today make employing a library lawyer a good, forward thinking idea. (p. 13)

Another factor to consider is that, when a library cancels a paper-based subscription, it still has the paper copies it paid for and may retain those items indefinitely. When a library cancels a subscription to e-resources, however, there is a question regarding what, if any, rights it has to long-term access to the content published during the time it paid for access. A related question that may arise in terms of cancellations is whether the library should cancel subscriptions to paper journals if the titles are in the e-package and/or withdraw the books when they become available online. Especially with journals, the issue may be more complex than it might appear. Some publishers link the cost of the e-journal to maintaining a paper subscription; they raise the price of the e-only subscription if the library drops the paper subscription.

Check This Out

The number of resources that have become available electronically has grown exponentially over the past few years. However, the time may not yet be right for an "e-only" library. For a discussion of an e-only initiative attempted by the Stanford University Meyer Library, see Johanna Drucker's "Blind Spots" article in the April 3, 2009, issue of the *Chronicle of Higher Education* (55, no. 30: B6–B7).

Ease of use is another consideration regarding e-resources. Will the new product/service require staff training? How easy would it be for the public to use, or would it require staff assistance? In terms of websites, there is also an issue of selecting and maintaining links and how to handle that ongoing task. (There is some evidence that a Web address remains active for only 18 to 24 months before the owner makes some changes to the address as he or she updates the site. See Carlson, 2004; Fisher, 2003.) A source for reviews of potential websites that a library may wish to provide links to is Internet Reviews Archive (www.bowdoin.edu/~samato/IRA/), which is the archive for College and Research Library News that provides websites for various subject areas.

If an e-product/service under consideration would replace paper-based items, it is reasonable to conduct an assessment of how great an improvement the e-version would be. Almost always the e-product will cost more than its paper-based version; thus, some form of cost-benefit analysis is in order, especially in times of tight budgets.

Related to the cost-benefit analysis is the possibility of canceling the paper-based titles in order to reduce the overall cost of the e-title in terms of the library's budget. As we noted earlier, some libraries in the early days of e-journal databases thought about and did cancel the paper subscriptions in order to keep within their budget, only to find there were problems. For example, full-text databases generally only include advertisements if there are both text and ads on the same page. For some departments the ads within the publication are important to their research and teaching. A more critical problem is that some publishers place an embargo on when an e-version of a journal issue may appear. The publisher's goal is to maintain its paper subscription base and may hold off on an e-version for as much as one year. For many scholars such a delay means the library must maintain the paper version in addition to the electronic copy or pay interlibrary loan fees for a requested article that falls within the embargo period.

When it comes to large database products, often they are available through one or more consortia to which the library belongs. Generally, a library will have a free trial period during which to assess the product/service and then decide whether or not to acquire the package. The question then becomes what will the package cost? It is not uncommon for the cost of the product/service to vary from consortium to consortium. This is due to that fact the consortium's price is often based on how many of its members take part in "the deal." Many of the e-products vendors base their academic pricing on the basis of institutional student full-time equivalent (FTE). The rate is XX cents per student FTE, and as the total number of FTE at institutions in the consortium increases the rate drops. Thus, determining what the final cost would be for each library can take some time, perhaps a month or more.

Considering all of these factors, academic library collection development may be a challenge for newcomers to handle. However, it can be one of the most satisfying/rewarding work activities as time passes. Keys to successfully mastering collection development duties are to learn as much as possible about the existing policies and user needs, take advantage of institutional knowledge (including colleagues, the predecessor, and campus faculty), and use review sources during the selection process.

KEY POINTS TO REMEMBER

- Collection development decisions ought to focus primarily on the content rather than the medium.
- A very large proportion of today's "legacy collections" arose from a national security need and not some misguided desire to build the biggest academic library.
- Effective academic library collection development is a shared effort between library staff, faculty, students, and other academic libraries.
- Collection development duties, while challenging, can also be enjoyable, satisfying, and rewarding.
- Newcomers to academic library collection development should focus on learning:
  - the responsibilities of both librarians and faculty in the collection development process;
  - the methods for assessing campus users' needs;
  - the local collection development policy;

- the selection sources (reviews, publishers, and any consortial arrangements) employed by the library;
  - the library's practices in balancing collections between print, other media, and digital resources;
  - the manner in which the library handles collection development fiscal issues and allocations;
  - the local acquisitions system(s) and understanding existing approval plans, standing plans, and blanket order plans;
  - the local standards for assessing the collections;
  - the manner in which the library handles issues of storage/deselection; and
  - the local issues related to preservation.
- The basics of selecting e-resources are the same as printed materials, with some additional issues such as technology, staff and end user training, and licensing.

REFERENCES

Atkinson, Ross. 2001. Contingency and contradictions: The place(s) of the library at the dawn of the new millennium. *Journal of the American Society for Information Science and Technology* 52, no. 1: 3–11.

———. 2006. Six key challenges for the future of collection development. *Library Resources & Technical Services* 50, no. 4: 244–251.

Bradbury, Danny. 2007. See you in 2050. *Engineering & Technology* 2, no. 11: 42–44.

Bradley, Kevin. 2007. Defining digital sustainability. *Library Trends* 56, no. 1: 148–163.

Butler, Pierce. 1945. *Books and libraries in wartime.* Chicago, IL: University of Chicago Press.

Carey, Ronadin, Stephen Elfstrand, and Renee Hijleh's. 2005. An evidenced-based approach for gaining faculty acceptance in a serials cancellation project. *Collection Management* 30, no. 2: 59–72.

Carlson, Scott. 2004. Here today, gone tomorrow: Studying how online footnotes vanish. *Chronicle of Higher Education* 51, April 30: A33.

Carpenter, Kenneth E. 1986. *The first 350 years of the Harvard University Library.* Cambridge, MA: Harvard University Library.

Cohen, Daniel J. 2005. The future of preserving the past. *CRM Journal* 2, no. 2: 6–19.

Darnton, Robert. 2009. Google and the future of books. *New York Review of Books* 56, no. 2: 9–11. Available: www.nybooks.com/articles/22281 (accessed April 7, 2010).

Evans, Luther H. 1947. Research libraries in the war period, 1939–1945. *The Library Quarterly* 17, no. 4: 241–262.

Fisher, William. 2003. Now you see it: Now you don't: Elusive nature of electronic information. *Library Collections, Acquisitions & Technical Service* 27, no. 4: 463–472.

Levi, Yaniv. 2008. Digital preservation: An ever-growing challenge. *Information Today* 25, no. 8: 22.

McCarty, J. P. 2005. The print block and the digital cylinder. *Library Management* 26, nos. 1/2: 89–96.

Oud, Joanne. 2008. Adjusting to the workplace: Transitions faced by new academic librarians. *College & Research Libraries* 69, no. 3: 252–266.

Quinn, Brian. 2008. The psychology of group decision making in collection development. *Library Collections, Acquisitions, & Technical Services* 32, no. 1: 10–18.

R. R. Bowker. 2010. Bowker's Book Analysis System. Available: www.bbanalysis.com/bbas/ (accessed March 21, 2010).

Ryland, John. 1982. Collection development and selection: Who should do it? *Library Acquisitions: Practice and Theory* 6, no. 1: 13–17.

Schmidt, Karen. 2004. Past perfect, future tense: A survey of issues in collection development. *Library Collections, Acquisitions, & Technical Services* 28, no. 4: 360–372.

Seaman, Scott. 2005. Collaborative collection management in a high-density storage facility. *College & Research Libraries* 66, no. 1: 20–27.

Tangley Laura. 1998. Whoops, there goes another CD-ROM, *U.S. News & World Report*, February 16: 67–68.

Tucker, James Cory, and Matt Torrence. 2004. Collection development for new librarians: advice from the trenches. *Library Collections, Acquisitions, & Technical Services* 28, no. 4: 397–409.

Vargas, Mark A. 2005. Using a third-party vendor for off-site storage of library materials. *Library Administration & Management* 19, no. 1: 26–30.

Wagner, Ralph. 2002. *A history of the Farmington Plan*. Lanham, MD: Scarecrow Press.

Watson, Mark. 2008. Licensing electronic resources: Is a lawyer in your future? *Technicalities* 28, no. 4: 1, 11–13.

Williams, Gordon. 1964. The librarians role in the development of library book collections. *The Library Quarterly* 34, no. 4: 374–386.

LAUNCHING PAD

Adams, Wright R. 2009. Archiving digital materials: An overview of the issues. *Journal of Interlibrary Loan, Document Delivery & Electronic Reserve* 19, No. 4: 325–335.

Austenfeld, Anne Marie. 2009. Building the college library collection to support curriculum growth. *Collection Management* 34, no. 3: 209–227.

Chadwell, Faye A. 2009. What's next for collection management and managers? Successful collaboration. *Collection Management* 34, no. 3: 151–156.

Chelin, Jacqueline Ann, Jason Briddon, Elspeth Williams, Jane Redman, Alastair Sleat, and Greg Ince. 2009. E-books are good if there are no copies left: A survey of e-book usage at UWE library services. *Library and Information Research* 33, no. 104: 45–65.

Day, Michael. 2009. Preserving the outputs of scholarly communication for the long term: A review of recent developments in digital preservation for electronic journal content. In *E-journals access and management*, ed. Wayne Jones, 39–66. New York: Routledge.

Forte, Eric, Cathy Chiu, Sherri Barnes, Sherry DeDecker, Gary Colmenar, Carmelita Pickett, Sandy Lewis, and Cecily Johns. 2002. Developing a training program for collection managers. *Library Collections, Acquisitions, & Technical Services* 26, no. 3: 299–306.

Gordon, Ian D. 2000. Asserting our collection development role: Academic librarians must take responsibility for the collection. *College & Research Libraries News* 61, no. 8: 687–689.

Grover, Mark L. 2008. Library area studies organizations and multidisciplinary collection and research: The Latin American experience. Paper presented at the International Federation of Library Associations, Social Science Libraries Section, Satellite Conference, Toronto, Canada. Available: www.ideals.uiuc.edu/handle/2142/8845 (accessed April 7, 2010).

Kinner, Laura, and Alice Crosetto. 2009. Balancing act for the future: How the academic library engages in collection development at the local and consortial levels. *Journal of Library Administration* 49, no. 4: 419–437.

Kusik, James P., and Mark A. Vargas. 2009. Implementing a "holistic" approach to collection development. *Library Leadership & Management* 23, no. 4: 186–192.

McCargar, Victoria. 2007. Kiss your assets goodbye: Best practices and digital archiving in the publishing industry. *The Seybold Report* 7, no. 16: 5–7.

McKiel, Allen. 2008. Academic libraries after print. *Oregon Library Association Quarterly* 14, no. 3: 26–29.

McSean, Tony. 2005. Research libraries and journal publishers: A marriage in trouble which both sides would like to save. *Logos* 16, no. 1: 27–31.

Munro, Bruce, and Peter Philips. 2008. A collection of importance: The role of selection in academic libraries. *Australian Academic & Research Libraries* 39, no. 3: 149–170.

Perrault, Anna H. 2008. *Florida University Libraries collection analysis project.* With the assistance of Diana Loper. Gainesville, FL: Florida Center for Library Automation. Available: shell.cas.usf.edu/~perrault/ (accessed April 7, 2010).

Perrault, Anna H., Tina Adams, Jeannie Dixon, and Rhonda Smith. 2002. The Florida Community College statewide collection assessment project: Outcomes and impact. *College & Research Libraries* 63, no. 3: 240–249.

Perrault, Anna H., and Jeannie Dixon. 2007. Collection assessment: The Florida Community College experience. *Community & Junior College Libraries* 14, no. 1: 7–20.

Perrault, Anna H., Richard Madaus, Ann Armbrister, Jeannie Dixon, and Rhonda Smith. 1999. The effects of high median age on currency of resources in community college library collections. *College & Research Libraries* 60, no. 4: 316–339.

Pochoda, Phil. 2008. Scholarly publication at a digital tipping point. *Journal of Electronic Publishing* 11, no. 2. Available: dx.doi.org/10.3998/3336451.0011.202 (accessed April 7, 2010).

Portico. 2008. Digital preservation of e-journals in 2008: Urgent action revisited. Results from a Portico/Ithaka Survey of U.S. Library Directors. Available: www.portico.org/digital-preservation/wp-content/uploads/2010/02/porticosurveyondigitalpreservation.pdf (accessed April 7, 2010).

Pymm, Bob. 2006. Building collections for all times: The issue of significance. *Australian Academic & Research Libraries* 37, no. 1: 61–73.

Rabinovici-Cohen, S, M. E. Factor, D. Naor, L. Ramati, P. Reshef, S. Satran, and D. L. Giaretta. 2008. Preservation data stores: New storage paradigm for preservation environments. *IBM Journal of Research and Development* 52, nos. 4/5: 389–399.

Soules, Aline. 2009. The shifting landscape of e-books. *New Library World* 110, nos. 1/2: 7–21.

Spires, Todd. 2006. Using OCLC's WorldCat collection analysis to evaluate peer institutions. *Illinois Libraries* 86, no. 2: 11–19.

Teel, Linda M. 2008. Applying the basics to improve the collection. *Collection Building* 27, no. 3: 96–103.

Ward, Judit H. 2009. Acquisitions globalized: The foreign language acquisitions experience in a research library. *Library Resources & Technical Services* 53, no. 2: 86–93.

Wolf, Martin. 2007. Going e-only: A feasible option in the current UK journals marketplace? *Acquisition Librarian* 19, nos. 1/2: 63–74.

Chapter 12

Services

Personal attention is at the very heart of the reference interview, and the goal of information literacy is to create confident information consumers. To reverse the decline in the use of reference services, academic reference librarians must transform their approach.

—Pamela N. Martin (2009)

The difficulty in narrowing down a definition of electronic reserves and the lack of any single methodology that carries the equivalent of a Good House-keeping Seal of Approval are intrinsic to the nature of reserve service in general. Since faculty play a key role in defining the nature and scope of course reserve materials...

—Jeff Rosendale (2002)

Liaison positions exist at nearly every research library, and a recent ARL member survey documented a substantial broadening of liaison roles. Many believe that liaison librarian functions are becoming more central to fulfilling the library's mission in a digital age.

—Karla Hahn (2009)

Librarians who have social network connections with students must be aware that the method of communication within Facebook also matters. If a student asks a reference question via a personal message, it is not appropriate to respond by posting a response to that student's wall. The wall is a public means of communication.

—Ruth Sara Connell (2009)

Services and collections are the cornerstones of academic library operations. Most of their services are similar to those of other types of libraries, with a few exceptions (reserve services and liaison activities, for example). Certainly public and technical services are more complex than in other library types, due in part to the size of academic libraries. Library school courses help prepare a person for engaging in one or more functional areas of an academic library; however, like collection management there is much to learn on the job. Since the 1990s there has been a strong movement among libraries to improve service quality by borrowing customer service techniques developed by the business community.

Although, in theory, an academic library should have no problem in attracting and retaining users, in today's Internet world, students, faculty, and staff have a variety of choices in where to go to secure information for course work, research, and institutional duties. Thus, the library needs to generate a satisfied loyal "customer" base, a base that is extremely satisfied with the service and collection quality and is supportive of library programs and its fiscal needs. If the services and collections do not measure up to expectations or keep pace with changing user preferences or needs, then repeat use cannot be ensured (Hernon, Nitecki, and Altman, 1999). As Jurewicz and Cutler (2003) observed:

> We have seen it in our own lives that as customer habits have changed, savvy businesses have changed their service strategies in an attempt to anticipate customer needs.... Too busy to go the mall? Buy from a catalog online and we'll send it to your door. Need to know when to update your online auction bid? Sign up for our service and we'll notify you. Want to know where your package is? Check our website and we'll track it for you. (p. 2)

The issue of attracting and keeping campus users along with the need for academic libraries emerged during 2001 and 2002, when an article with the words "Deserted Library" in the title (Carlson, 2001) generated a debate about the need for academic libraries both within and outside of the profession. The debate led to at least some campus senior administrators making serious attempts to cancel library building projects.

From the Authors

One example of how a debate on Carlson's article in the *Chronicle of Higher Education* took place in mid-2002 at the institution where Evans was the associate academic vice president for learning resources. The library and the university had been working on plans for a new library for over ten years. There had even been a design through working drawings and a request for construction bids issued as well as a ground-breaking ceremony in 1998. Unfortunately, the major donor encountered serious financial problems and the project was put on hold. Throughout that process the vice president for business and finance fought the concept of a new library. His position was that all that a student needed was available on the Internet, thus there was no need for a new facility.

The vice president for business and finance distributed copies of Carlson's article to all of the senior campus administrators along with a memo stating that this material "proved" his case that the university did not need to invest in a new library. Although it took the better part of a year to counteract the effort, the support of students, faculty, alumni, and several of the vice presidents put the planning process back on track. In 2009, a new library was opened at the university. The success is attributable to great service by the library staff, some careful marketing, and strong advocacy by library staff and their supporters.

The notion of a deserted library had not yet fully dissipated by 2010. Charles Martell (2008) wrote about the decline in circulation and reference transactions using data from Association of Research Libraries (ARL) statistical reports from 1995–2006. Martell concluded his article by stating:

> In mystery stories and political thrillers the advice is often "follow the money." In the library setting one might do better to "follow the user." Clearly today's users have substituted virtual use for in-person use. While they may be absent, they are not inactive. Networked electronic resources via library portals and the Internet have provided users with benefits that go far beyond anything available when physical use was the only alternative. (p. 406)

Rachel Applegate (2008) also looked at reference transactions, employing a broader data set than just ARL reports. She found that from 2002–2004 there were differences in transactions based on the Carnegie Institutional Classification (see Chapter 1 for a review of the Carnegie Classes). While ARL institutions showed a decline in reference transactions, master's institutions showed an increase. She concluded her article with the following:

A fruitful approach to understanding the future of reference in academic libraries can include the following: studying a wider range of in-library and out-of-library information-seeking activities; broadening and deepening—and in some cases abandoning—the definition of "transaction"; and incorporating a sensitivity to the differing missions, cultures, and activities of the variety of academic institutions for which the American system of higher education is justifiably famous. (p. 187)

Perhaps the internal (librarianship) view of the "situation" (declines in gate counts, circulation, and reference transactions) is still somewhat tied to the profession's long standing method of collecting input data as measures of worth. Perhaps we need to rethink that approach and develop other measures of worth. New library facilities appear to actually increase gate counts substantially, and various service transactions have an impact well beyond their former levels (Dotson and Garris, 2008; Freeman, 2005; Gayton, 2008; Shill and Tonner, 2004).

> **Something to Ponder**
>
> We know that a large majority of people turn to the Web to find an answer—the Law of Least Effort. Might it be that this law has impacted the quality of the answers? Might it be that it has impacted the quality of students' work that requires fact gathering? If so, in what way? Better? Worse? No change?

Sinwell and Stemmer (two of the reviewers of this text as we prepared it) commented that they and colleagues at other libraries have had to address increasing demand for seating space from faculty and students since 2006.

CUSTOMER SERVICE

Many businesses adopted customer service programs to attract and retain customers during the last half of the twentieth century—airline "frequent flyer miles," grocery store "rewards programs," and the like. Examples of such practices in the college and university environment are the "heritage/legacies" programs through which children of alumni have a degree of preference in the admission process.

Beside the overall service ethic of academic libraries, economics is another motivator for looking to improve customer services. Academic funding authorities are facing tighter financial situations, and evidence of good customer service helps libraries argue more effectively for support when budget priorities are decided. As Debbie Schachter (2006) noted, "Excellence in customer service leads to greater use of library services, better coordination with other departments, and a greater chance of ensuring the security of library funding" (pp. 8–9). Another driving force, also influenced by economics, is the increased pressure accountability on the part of funding authorities. Libraries may address accountability with documentation of the outcomes of service programs, how they contribute to the mission of their parent institutions, and evidence of good customer service at a minimum based on users' level of satisfaction.

Wehmeyer, Auchter, and Hirshon (1996) distilled from library literature the following items of consensus about customer service plans:

- *Frontline staff are vital to the plan's success.* Public service personnel generally are the only library staff users encounter. Thus, their attitudes and actions during their interactions with users become a key, if not *the* key, factor in public perceptions regarding the library and its services.

- *Service is a product.* Service quality is a significant element in the library's value added process in relationship with competitor information services.
- *Understand your customer.* Assessing users' information wants and needs is essential to developing excellent service programs.
- *There is no quick fix.* Quality service requires ongoing review and adjustments as users' interests are constantly changing. (p. 174)

It is possible to view customer service interactions as either transaction-based or relationship-based. "Transaction-based" service occurs at point of need, such as when a student checks out a book. This is the type of service on which most organizations, including libraries, typically focus. However, the realization that building loyalty is the best way to retain customers has caused many organizations to focus on "relationship-based" service. This is most clearly reflected in the relationship that the public services' staff members develop with their users. Academic librarians often develop collegial relationships with faculty and are able to offer specialized assistance with their research and teaching. Many Web 2.0 initiatives, described later in this chapter, are aimed at personalizing library services in an effort to make them more useful and attractive to users. Doing so increases the library's usefulness to its service community and enhances the users' perception of the value of library services.

Very few library users pay for more than a portion of the services and resources they utilize, at least not as directly, as in a commercial transaction. For example, students often have their tuition paid for by their parents (who are rarely campus library users) and, at least in the too-distant past, did not think of themselves as "customers" of the library. However, lately there is a growing tendency, especially at private institutions, for students to think of themselves as customers and act accordingly. Faculty members rarely pay for use of the library (the exception may be the need to include requests for library funding when they make grant requests). Rather, they are paid, in part, by the institution to use library resources for their teaching and research.

However, libraries do charge for some services such as photocopies. It is rare for such charges to fully cover the cost of the service; however, in large research institutions revenue from photocopies as well as overdue fines and fees for lost items do generate a substantial amount of money. The fees for "special services" (for example, borrowing privileges for nonstudent/faculty individuals) are increasing in libraries as the pressure to engage in cost recovery mounts, thus blurring the distinction between free and fee and "patron" and "customer."

The idea that libraries have a business function is anathema to many library staff members as well as to some users. It implies a paradigm shift. Businesses exist for the bottom line, to make a profit, and libraries, at least in the past, were not in the income-generating business. Today, there are increasing pressures on libraries to recover some of the costs of their services, and some libraries may even have target income levels for the fiscal year. People who dislike the notion of "libraries in business" believe libraries provide intellectual value to their users. This intellectual value, they argue, is a public good that enriches their communities beyond dollars and cents. Equating (or reducing) libraries to the level of a capitalist enterprise transforms libraries from cultural icons to something like transitory storefronts. However, it is also true that libraries are under enormous pressures today to demonstrate evidence of accountability. As Weingand (1997) stated:

Librarians who flinch at the word *customer* are operating out of an outmoded paradigm. This older paradigm portrays the library as a "public good," with as high a ranking on the "goodness" scale as the national flag, parenthood, and apple pie. As a public good, the library "should" receive public support. However, today's library is in increasingly tight competition for declining resources, and unless it adopts and masters the language and techniques of its competitors, it faces a future of declining support and significance. (p. 3)

Whether one agrees or not with Weingand's perspective, the fact remains there is an ever-growing challenge from competitors such as Google and Amazon. It is also a fact that borrowing and adapting the principles of customer satisfaction from the corporate world is a pragmatic way to improve library services and better serve our customers. It is also a way to demonstrate to those demanding accountability the value of the library to its organization and community.

In their "Top Ten Assumptions for the Future of Academic Libraries and Librarians," (Association of College and Research Libraries, 2008) the ACRL Research Committee listed as number 7 "As part of the 'business of higher education,' students will increasingly view themselves as 'customers' of the academic library and will demand high-quality facilities, resources, and services attuned to their needs and concerns" (p. 17).

The remainder of this chapter covers some of the basic public services one encounters in most academic libraries—reference, instruction, circulation, document delivery, and reserve—as well as some less widespread services such as liaison work and "embedded librarians." The discussions assume a general knowledge of the fundamentals of the basic services.

> **From the Authors**
>
> Marketing of the academic library is using a basic business concept to serve its customers/users base. The first principle of marketing is finding out what the customer wants and needs. This can be done through focus groups, surveys, interviews, etc. Once an academic library learns what the students, faculty, and staff needs and wants are, then the library has to deliver. Strategic planning plays a key role here. When the service or resource is provided by the library, then the library needs to let its customers know what it has to offer through promotion and public relations. In other words, "We asked you what you want. You told us. We've got it; here it is."

> **Check This Out**
>
> A more detailed discussion of library public services can be found in such books as *Introduction to Library Public Services*, 7th ed., by G. Edward Evans and Thomas Carter (Westport, CT: Libraries Unlimited, 2009) and Lynn Jurewicz and Todd Cutler's *High Tech, High Touch: Library Customer Service Through Technology* (Chicago: American Library Association, 2003).

REFERENCE SERVICES

Reference service in academic libraries is a relatively recent activity, as you may recall from Chapter 2.

Today, reference is no longer solely face to face with campus students and faculty as it once was. It is now a highly technologically driven activity with options for 24/7 service. Even in the past, with substantially fewer service hours to cover, providing reference service presented staffing challenges, and those challenges are even greater today. One of the challenges continues to be accurately predicting assistance demand. Yes, one can conduct studies regarding past demand and employ statistical models to predict future demands. However, there still are periods with no requests to handle to times with a queue of people waiting for help, the telephone ringing, beeps of incoming e-mail requests sounding, and only one person is on duty. During weekdays, heavy loads are relatively easy to handle. The situation is more difficult at night, on weekends, and during holidays.

Another challenge is the breadth of questions that arise. There is never enough staffing in any library to have experts on all subjects available at all times. Great reference librarians are very good at games such as *Trivial Pursuit*, as they have had to field hundreds of questions in a host of subjects. For the novice librarian, seeing a person heading toward the reference desk can start butterflies moving in the stomach; will it be an easy transaction in an area the librarian knows well or will it be so difficult the person has no clue as to where to start? There are some questions for which library resources simply cannot provide an answer. (An example of such a question that one of this book's authors has been trying to answer for over four years is what the design of the tattoo that a White Mountain Apache male receives behind the left ear upon becoming an elder is.) Many novices have difficulty in telling a user, after a diligent search, "I'm sorry, but I can not find the answer. Perhaps ___ can assist you. This person comes on duty at ___." Learning when to pass a request on or asking a colleague for assistance takes time and an understanding that doing so is not a sign of incompetence. Rather, it is recognition of the library's goal of providing the best possible service to its users.

To some extent, the library can address these challenges by making use of a collaborative approach to reference service such as OCLC's QuestionPoint. Some of the features of QuestionPoint are the following:

- Refer questions to a network of subject specialists with access to extensive resources, available throughout the world and in many languages.
- Keep the door to reference services open around the clock by participating in the 24/7 Reference Cooperative, with only a modest contribution of staffing.
- Gain better control over reference. QuestionPoint tools give deeper insights into user needs and staffing requirements.
- QuestionPoint is much less expensive and easier to implement than building your own around-the-clock staffing solution from scratch. (www.oclc.org/questionpoint/overview/default.htm)

Check These Out

Public service personnel with even modest experience are aware that some users have difficulty asking for assistance, especially at the reference desk. Heather Carlile (2007) published a very good summary of the literature related to this phenomenon, often referred to as library anxiety: "The Implication of Library Anxiety for Academic Reference Services: A Review of the Literature," *Australian Academic Research Libraries* 38, no. 2: 129-147.

Virtual reference calls for new approaches, especially in a collaborative environment. An article that looks at the issue of "chat" reference is Deborah L. Meert and Lisa M. Given's article "Measuring Quality in Chat reference Consortia: A Comparative Analysis of Responses to User's Queries," *College & Research Libraries* 70, no. 1 (2009): 71-84.

Craig Anderson (2009) provides some tips on becoming a more effective reference librarian in a virtual environment in "How to Be a Person: Tips and Tricks for Virtual Reference," *College & Research Libraries News* 70, no. 10: 577-579.

Reference service, like all other library services, must be evaluated on an ongoing basis. Pali U. Kuruppu (2007) published a literature review article about such activities: "Evaluation of Reference Services—A Review," *Journal of Academic Librarianship* 33, no. 3: 368-381.

Although such services are not the sole answer to staffing and expertise issues, they do go a long way toward creating an environment that generates loyal support from users. They also can help reduce reference staff stress regarding handling those really challenging questions that seem to arise when one is all alone at the reference desk.

Organization of Reference Services

The organization of reference services can take several forms. The three most common forms in academic libraries are *central* or general reference, *divisional* reference, and *departmental* reference. The organization of reference service depends on many factors, the more important ones being philosophy of the library, physical layout of the building, size of the library's collection, abilities of the staff, type of library and type(s) of user, and financial resources.

A central or general reference department organization brings together all reference materials in one physical location. Some arguments for this organization are:

1. Reference materials are easier to locate because they are shelved together.
2. Because knowledge is interrelated and interdisciplinary, it is easier to do reference work if all of the material is kept together.
3. It is not necessary to purchase duplicate materials or to duplicate services.
4. It is possible to make more economical use of staff at one service point rather than staffing several service points.

Nearly all small libraries and many medium-sized libraries use a central or general type organization.

Divisional reference organization is found in larger academic libraries. It brings together the reference materials for a group of related subjects within a section or floor of the library. A rather common divisional approach is to divide the collection into social sciences, humanities, and natural sciences. Whatever the divisional arrangement, it should be suited for the building floor plan and institutional focus. Some of the arguments in favor of divisional reference organization are the following:

1. A smaller reference collection is easier to use.
2. The reference materials and the general collection on a particular subject are often closer together in a divisional arrangement, allowing easier access to both types of materials.
3. Reference staff members who are subject specialists can utilize their talents and provide better service for specialized reference inquiries when they work in their area of expertise.

Many ARL libraries employ both centralized and departmental approaches. Collections in the departmental libraries, as one would expect, are usually restricted to a single subject (e.g., geology) or a broader discipline or profession such as engineering or medicine. Having a dual arrangement allows the library and users to reap the benefits of both the centralized and divisional reference formats. General reference inquiries are handled by the general reference department (main library). This arrangement, in the past, did cause confusion for newcomers as to where to go for assistance. Today, the ability to get online assistance has reduced the confusion and frustration. Users may still be a challenged, however, in selecting the best online source toward which to direct their questions.

There seems to be a trend, however, among larger university libraries to combine divisional reference areas into a central reference area. There are several reasons for this, such as budget cuts that include less reference staff available, and new or renovated designs of libraries are allowing for better central desk locations.

Access to Reference Services

Users have a variety of methods for securing remote reference assistance today: telephone, letter, fax, webform, e-mail, chat, text messages, and instant messaging (IM). Many colleges and universities have sizable distance education programs and student populations who depend on the library's off-site services. In most libraries, the users who are physically present have first priority. Staff should contact remote requestors who submit complex inquiries (those that take a substantial amount of research staff time) immediately, indicating there may be a delay in providing a full answer, offering whenever possible a realistic time frame.

Most academic libraries develop a set of reference policies addressing various issues; however, a very necessary policy covers how to handle conflicting priorities regarding off-site versus in-person requests. For example, staff will look up no more than X number of books in the OPAC or spend no more than Y number of minutes looking for an elusive statistic. During hectic periods, such as term paper and examination periods, it may be necessary for staff to log the question or save it to be answered later. Some libraries have a separate telephone line or e-mail reference address or an instant messaging account with a staff member dedicated to answering such queries as well as someone handling directional questions.

Distance education offerings by universities around the country often generate questions from local people enrolled in a program from a different institution. Handling this can be a thorny issue for both the library and its institution. Some of these institutions contract with other libraries to supply services to their students in particular areas, but this is not always the case. The library's reference service policy should address the level of service that is appropriate to deliver in support of distance education programs. (We explore the issue of external users further in the circulation section of this chapter.)

Long-standing questions in academic and public libraries have been about the cost of providing reference services as well as about who should provide those services (see Rettig, 1993; Courtois and Goetsch's, 1984). Virtual reference has added a further dimension to the issue of cost and staffing as libraries experience pressure to provide online services to their patrons, and very little is currently known about the cost structures of these services (Eakin and Pomerantz, 2009).

On the positive side of maintaining a physical reference desk, Granfield and Robertson (2008) reported on a survey that indicated that in-person reference service remains a popular method of service for academic library users. They concluded, "The reference desk continues to be the most popular method of getting help in the library, but our findings confirm that VR [virtual reference] satisfies a niche for some users.... Our results suggest that VR services seem to have a special appeal to graduate students" (p. 51). On the other hand, Susan Ryan (2008) concluded her article on reference staffing cost-effectiveness with: "The following findings should lead library administrators to reconsider staffing a traditional reference desk with librarians" (p. 398). Her finding were that only 11 percent of the reference transactions in her study fell into the "research" category, 89 percent of the questions could be addressed by "trained students and staff members," and 59 percent of the interactions were handled using the librarians knowledge of the building. Her article was reviewed by Merkley (2009). Merkley concluded, among other things, that "Ryan rightly emphasizes that individual libraries should assess their

> **Check This Out**
>
> Julie Banks and Carl Pracht (2008) conducted a survey of reference desk staffing patterns that provides some solid information about the issue of who and how to handle reference transactions: "Reference Desk Staffing Trends," *Reference & User Services Quarterly* 48, no. 1: 54–59.

current reference models to see if new staffing complements or even new methods of service would provide more value for their user communities" (p. 147).

WEB/LIBRARY 2.0

In today's virtual library service environment, it is increasingly difficult to distinguish reference, instruction, building user relationships, and quality service. It appears as though the activities are interwoven, especially when the service(s) are interactive. Virtual reference in its many manifestations, social networking, efforts to make OPACs and webpages more user friendly for the young students, and information commons are radically changing the notion of academic library public services. One can think of Web 2.0 as offering academic libraries at least six methods for attracting and holding the attention of the young students:

- A means of sharing content—blogs, wikis, podcasts, vlogs (video), and Twitter
- A means of self-sharing—social networking in its various forms
- A means of enhancing existing content—for example, user-tagging
- A means of engaging a wide range of users in discussions of library issues—user forms, blogs, and chat, for example
- A means of tailoring information for users—for example, RSS feeds and e-mail alerts
- A means of building relationships between users and library staff—Facebook and MySpace

Everyone in higher education is well aware that the vast majority of today's students are technologically oriented, although they may well be less proficient in evaluating the information they see on the web. Our professional literature is full of articles pushing Web/Library 2.0 as essential to creating the "new library." There is much less written about the need to assist the less technologically oriented faculty and staff to handle the changing information environment or how to balance our services between past and virtual services until the user community is more homogenous technologically. Sarah Faye Cohen (2008) noted:

> However, as excitement and opportunities abound, it seems we have neglected and possibly lost one of the most important constituents of our academic libraries: our faculty. As academic librarians we need to continue our efforts to embrace technology in our libraries and with our students. However, educating, encouraging, and empowering our faculties about the power, the possibility, and pedagogical opportunities of Web 2.0 is just as vital to library, student and institutional success. (p. 472)

While academic libraries have moved into many areas of Web 2.0, we have little evidence regarding how accepting students are of those efforts. One article (Connell, 2009) reported on a survey of students' views about academic library use of Facebook and MySpace pages as a means to build relationships with them. Connell reported that "the vast majority of respondents had online social network profiles. Most indicated that they would be accepting of library contact through those websites, but a sizable minority reacted negatively to the concept. Because of the potential to infringe on students' sense of personal privacy, it is recommended that librarians proceed with caution when implementing online social network profiles" (p. 25). Some readers may wonder about how much "personal privacy" a person should rationally expect when having a presence on a social networking site. However, it apparently is an issue for some individuals when the contact is institutional in character.

Although some students may object to one or more of a library's web activities/services, most do not; thus, it is incumbent for libraries to strive for highly effective sites. Darlene Fichter (2007) offered five tips for how libraries might optimize their social media activities:

- "Be friendly and mean it offline and online." (p. 59)
- "Be link-worthy" (that is, keep the sites "fresh"). (p.59)
- "Make bookmarking and sharing your content easy." (p. 59)
- "Let library Web 'stuff' circulate." (p. 59)
- "Participate and join the conversation wherever your users are." (p. 60)

Check These Out

For a good survey about academic libraries use of Web 2.0 in other parts of the world, see Nguyen Cuong Linh's 2008 article "A Survey of the Application of Web 2.0 in Australasian University Libraries," *Library High Tech* 26, no. 4: 630-653.

A 2009 article by Debra Riley-Huff, "Web Services as Public Services: Are We Supporting Our Busiest Service Point? *Journal of Academic Librarianship* 35, no. 1: 65-74, explores staff attitudes, practices, and support of Web activities in academic libraries.

For additional ideas regarding creating and maintaining solid websites, see NewPR/Wiki (2007).

The goal for social networking sites is building relationship between users and the library. Essentially Library 2.0 is about not only knowing the campus users' information needs but also seeking out and trusting users in a collaborative effort to redefine library services. Interactive web services are part of the "new" services of academic libraries. As Stephen Abram (2008) noted, "It is essential that we start preparing to become Librarian 2.0 now. The Web 2.0 movement is laying the ground work for exponential business growth and another major shift in the way our users live, work and play. We

---

Check These Out

Federated searching is one of many library attempts to attract and hold students interest in library services. A sound article about the concept and things to look for in such a tool is Alexis Linoski and Tine Walczyk's "Federated Search 101," *Library Journal Net Connect* (Summer 2008): 2-5.

A good book discussing various aspects of Web 2.0 and the library is Nancy Courtney's *Library 2.0 and Beyond* (Westport, CT: Libraries Unlimited, 2007).

Engaging in Library 2.0 activities requires library resources, so assessing the effectiveness of those activities is important. A good article that provides information about some less obvious assessment tools is Jonathan Alzen, Daniel Huttenlocher, and Jon Kleinberg's "Traffic-Based Feedback on the Web," *Proceedings of the National Academy of Sciences of the United States of America* 101, no. 14 (2004): 5254-5260.

have the ability, insight, and knowledge to influence the creation of this new dynamic—and guarantee the future of our profession" (p. 22).

CIRCULATION SERVICES

John Moorman (2006) defined library circulation as "the process by which items in a collection are taken out of the library by a user and returned to the library" (p. 263). This relatively straightforward definition, while accurate, belies the complexity of the activities encompassed by the term *circulation activities*. For example, circulation staff must know (1) the rules for what materials people may borrow and they must enforce those rules, (2) rules for who may borrow items and the loan periods for different classes of users, (3) what to do when materials are not returned on time, (4) how to maintain "the stacks," and (5) perhaps most important, how to handle upset/angry people. Julie Todaro and Mark Smith (2006) noted that for circulation staff, "Beyond basic skills, directional reference, and specialized training in customer interactions dealing with money, circulation staff need training in handling difficult customers as well as advanced conflict resolution" (p. 23). They also mentioned that when staff members must collect money, especially fines or special fees, public relations become critical. For example, some institutions have rules regarding how much money a borrower may owe and still be allowed to borrow additional materials. A student who is over the fine limit and thus "blocked" from further borrowing may become very upset by the blockage, especially if it happens during term paper periods.

Circulation department staff members are the true "front line" of the library, as they are the staff members most likely to be contacted by users regarding services. Indeed, they are often the only staff members with whom the public interacts. The circulation desk is also the point at which service quality must start, if for no other reason than because of the unit's physical location—close to the entrance/exit, which means the circulation staff are the first staff members a person sees on entering the library. This is usually where users' first and most important impressions of the library are formed.

It is not uncommon for circulation personnel to believe that they are the least appreciated staff and misunderstood by both the public and their colleagues. Part of this sense can arise from circulation staff not being fully aware of the importance their work provides in terms of quality service. It can also arise from insufficient support/praise from library managers. Managers who understand and communicate the value of the circulation staff's activities can make all of the difference between quality and lackluster service as well as good morale. It can also arise from insufficient support/praise from library managers.

Circulation units are often supervised by a support staff member rather than a librarian. Whoever has the supervisory responsibilities, if the operation is to be successful, must train unit personnel (the largest number of whom will likely be study students) in (1) proper stack maintenance activities and (2) diplomatic relationships with users in what are occasionally somewhat confrontational situations. We addressed some of the most significant stack maintenance issues in Chapter 11.

Handling Confrontational Situations

A circulation unit is not the only public service point at which difficult-user behavior occurs, but it is the most frequent point of trouble. Training for the inevitable problem situation consists of three key components: reducing tensions, maintaining control, and defusing the situation. Why the "inevitable" in the preceding sentence? Enforcing rules, imposing limits, and collecting fines all carry a high risk of having to face someone who is upset, annoyed, or even angry. The emotional response can range from mild sarcastic comments to physical violence (such violence ranges from throwing a book or other object at an employee to physically harming the employee). Needless to say, the goal of training is to provide staff with techniques/knowledge that will assist them in keeping the situation to the lowest level possible.

Reducing tensions begins by reducing one's own tension(s). Anyone with even modest experience in public service activities will have developed a sense for when trouble may arise. "Taking a deep breath" may seem like a trite statement, but doing so when the possibility of trouble arises actually does help keep tension down. When a problem does occur, being ready is a step in overall tension reduction. While it may be difficult, try not to take complainers' comments personally, even when they point at you and demand "you" change something. Having a good understanding of your own "trigger" issues/words is another aspect of maintaining your composure. Remember, working in public service requires one to tolerate some rudeness; however, it does not mean accepting abusive behavior. Having the ability to differentiate between the two behaviors and what to do when it becomes the latter (who to call for backup) is a valuable skill. Essentially, the first principle of handling a problem situation is to know that we can control ourselves, that we may be able to control the situation, and that we cannot control others.

Step two is to try to keep the situation as low key as possible. One of the most important aspects of controlling is to utilize one's most effective listening skills. Proper listening helps in better understanding what the actual issue(s) is, and it also conveys respect for the speaker. The better one understands the issue(s), the better the chance of controlling the situation. Making it clear one recognizes/respects the person's view/feelings/emotions, without suggesting those views are justified, assists in keeping the situation from escalating. Understanding nonverbal signals is also part of maintaining control of the situation; for example, an arms-crossed speaker may well be signaling increasing difficulty in controlling one's emotions. Keeping the focus on the library issue(s) is essential to keeping as much control as possible.

Defusing the situation depends on understanding the issue(s). With such an understanding one will know if one has the authority to address it or not. If not, calling the supervisor will do several things; most importantly, it will indicate to the person that the concern is being actively looked into as well as extracting one's self from the situation. Given academic libraries' long service hours, there may not be anyone on duty who has the authority to handle the complaint. In such cases, having the person write out the concern(s) will also help defuse tensions. By indicating that the purpose in having the person do the writing is to ensure that the position is accurately conveyed to those who can resolve the issue(s) can make the individual feel empowered.

Check These Out

A good text about handling problem library situations is Mark Willis's *Dealing with Difficult People in the Library* (Chicago, IL: American Library Association, 1999).

Another title with a broader scope is Warren Graham's *Black Belt Librarians: A Handbook to a Safer Workplace* (Charlotte, NC: Pure Heart Press, 2006).

A book, still broader in scope but related, is *Academic Librarians as Emotionally Intelligent Leaders*, by Peter Hernon, Joan Giesecke, and Camila Alire (Westport, CT: Libraries Unlimited, 2007).

Occasionally, just the act of writing reduces the person's emotions, just as writing a blustering memo to one's boss and filing it in the desk for a few days before sending it reduces one's own frustration and results in a rewritten document that is much less confrontational when it actually gets sent.

Confidentiality

One very rare circulation issue, but one of major importance, especially in research libraries, relates to user confidentiality. To be consistent with American Library Association's (ALA) Library Bill of Rights (www.ala.org/ala/aboutala/offices/oif/statement spols/statementsif/librarybillrights.cfm), circulation personnel are ethically bound not to reveal the reading habits of borrowers under the principle of intellectual freedom (the right to read and think whatever one wishes). The ALA Code of Ethics (www.ala .org/ala/aboutala/offices/oif/statementspols/codeofethics/codeethics.cfm) states, "We protect each library user's right to privacy and confidentiality with respect to information sought or received, and resources consulted, borrowed, acquired or transmitted." Only the reader and the circulation staff, in the legitimate performance of their duties, have a right to know what information sources the user consulted or checked out, and circulation staff have an obligation to prevent others from obtaining this information.

Probably as long as libraries have existed, police, government officials, ministers, parents, spouses, and others have asked library staff about the reading habits of borrowers. Only during the past 70 years, however, has the library profession expressed a desire to keep circulation records confidential. In 1938, the American Library Association's Code of Ethics specified the confidentiality of library records, the first formal acknowledgment of this issue in the United States. Since 1970, the profession's stand on confidentiality has become stronger. There is currently, for example, a movement to keep users' records confidential from warrantless searches by government officials pursuant to the USA PATRIOT Act.

The current status of confidentiality laws leaves several issues unclear. Under current legislation, library staff may be liable for civil or criminal liability for wrongful disclosure of records. There is no federal law regarding confidentiality of library records, and federal legislation like the USA PATRIOT Act overrides state statutes. First enacted in October 2001, the USA PATRIOT Act has been a concern for libraries. An outgrowth of the events of 9/11, the acronym stands for Uniting and Strengthening America by Providing Appropriate Tools Required to Intercept and Obstruct Terrorism Act of 2001. Section 215 of the act allows the government to secure secret warrants to obtain "business records"—this includes library records, including those from library database vendors. The act also authorizes the issuance of National Security Letters (NSLs), which do not require a judge's review, that require organizations to secretly provide information. At the time this book was prepared, the USA PATRIOT Act was being reconsidered for reauthorization in Congress in 2010. At least one library has been on the receiving end of such a letter. Between 2003 and 2006, the FBI issued over 140,000 NSLs (Pike, 2007). If one is on duty when the FBI arrives, just direct the person to the administrative office and let that office handle the situation. Do not offer assistance, even if the administrative office is closed and you are pressed to assist. One should *not* provide information until directed to do so by the senior library administrator or the campus legal counsel.

Document Delivery

With the tremendous increase in the amount of information available on the open Web and in the licensed databases available to users, one may be surprised to learn that there is still a significant demand for interlibrary loans (ILLs). We include in this category all of the titles borrowed by users from other libraries through programs such as OhioLINK and Link+. The amount of interlibrary lending continues to increase (see OCLC annual reports for interlibrary loan data), and obtaining information not available locally is an important library service.

Document delivery has several different meanings in the context of interlibrary loan. One definition involves purchasing information (especially periodical articles) from commercial document suppliers when access from other libraries is either unavailable or too slow. People sometimes prefer document delivery over traditional interlibrary loan because of its speed. Some commercial suppliers can deliver requested items within 24 hours or less, a turnaround time that is more rapid than most traditional interlibrary loan systems can achieve. Needless to say there is a higher cost for such service.

Another version of document delivery is delivering library-owned materials, via mail or the Internet, directly to library clientele. Staff members frequently do this to assist users who live at a distance or are otherwise unable to come to the library. It may also be offered as a service enhancement, for example, by academic libraries for faculty.

An active interlibrary loan program is a significant commitment of library resources. A 2002 study of mediated ILL costs for research libraries revealed average borrowing costs of $17.50 per item and lending costs of $9.27 per item. Approximately two-thirds of the cost of ILL is staff time (Jackson, Kingma, and Delaney, 2004). This same study revealed that user-initiated interlibrary loans (also known as unmediated loans) have lower unit costs, primarily due to the lack of staff involvement. A typical user-initiated loan takes place in cooperative programs such as LINK+ where, if the user does not find that the local library owns the desired title and some other library in the cooperative has the title available, the user can request the book without having local staff involved in the request process.

RESERVE SERVICES

Reserve services are exclusively characteristic of colleges and universities. Instructors sometimes wish to supplement the library collection in order to support their teaching. Instructors assign various types of material; for example, copies of journal articles, their own personal copies of books or other instructional materials, videos, copies of quizzes and answers, and so on. Libraries support this instructional endeavor by establishing policies and procedures to make these "reserved" materials available to students. The concept goes back to the late nineteenth century and until relatively recently, was a means of limiting borrowing periods for print materials so that all of the students in a class would have fair access to the material. Rather than a month or even an academic term borrowing period, reserve items could be limited to a few hours or days per circulation. Traditional reserve service guaranteed that assigned course materials were available on a first come, first served basis.

Today, reserve service is primarily electronic in nature, although it may include a small number of paper-based materials such as a faculty member's personal items, print material not suitable for scanning, sample term papers, and research reports. As the volume of digitized material "on reserve" has grown, the nature of the work has changed. In the past, the reserve desk was probably the service point with the highest rate of unhappy people (students, faculty, and library staff). Students complained that material was not put on reserve fast enough, that service was poor and waiting times too long. Teachers sometimes complained about the time it takes to process assigned material, about the amount of work they had to do before material went on reserve, and about copyright limitations. Library staff complained about the amount of time it took to process materials and that faculty did not give them sufficient time to process reserve items before assigning them, did not appreciate or adhere to copyright restrictions, placed excessive quantities of material on reserve which students never looked at, and were slow to remove items when they were no longer assigned.

Electronic reserve systems have changed most of those complaints; perhaps the major issue now is between copyright holders and academic libraries and their home institutions. This is because most e-reserve systems involve the library scanning documents or images and placing them into a database that allows users to retrieve the material at their convenience 24/7. Such systems are popular with libraries as they are a labor saving means of distributing reserve readings around the clock.

Today's reserve room operates like a mini library within the larger institution. Staff members accept reserve requests from teachers and faculty, remove books and periodicals from the stacks, and make photocopies of or scan requested items. Digitized documents are placed in files created for each instructor and course. Staff also make sure there is copyright compliance, prepare online and print bibliographic aids to facilitate access to the collection, create links to requested articles if they are contained in licensed databases, create links to digitized reserve items in the institution's course management system (such as Blackboard), check items in and out, administer fines and billing for overdue and lost items, remove material from reserve or disable electronic access when it is no longer needed, and troubleshoot the equipment. In large libraries, the reserve collection may contain thousands of items for hundreds of courses. The items are usually divided between library-owned and teachers' personal materials. The composition of the collection changes each term, and the maintenance of this service requires a significant library commitment of staff, time, and space, although e-reserve is reducing the need for extensive study/reading space for its service.

There are serious questions regarding the value of reserve services. Writers have commented on the low use of some reserve items as well as on the high cost of adminis-tration (for example, Bradley, 2007, and De Jager, 2001). In addition, there are pedagogic arguments against reserve services. There is evidence that using assigned reserve materials has no significant influence on academic performance. A study at the University of Virginia measured the correlation between over 8,000 students' use of reserve materials and the grades they received in their courses. The study revealed only a weak connection between reserve use and grades. The study also revealed that depending on reserve readings may even obstruct the educational process. Relying on reserve services to provide library materials may discourage students from using the rest of the library and learning necessary library use skills. It also prevents the serendipitous discovery of information that occurs through normal library use (Self, 1987).

Recent studies of electronic reserve systems reveal that students tend to prefer digital reserves to traditional reserve services. Freedom from the restrictions of limited numbers of copies and short circulation periods results in greater use of digital reserves than their print counterparts and greater satisfaction with the service (Jacoby and Laskowski, 2004; Pilston and Hart, 2002; Isenberg, 2006).

Staff diplomacy is key to having good working relationships with the faculty. Faculty members probably take a greater personal interest in the reserve room than in any other service, except perhaps document delivery. This is because they believe reserve services play an important role in supporting their day-to-day classroom instruction. They often have the majority of their contact with library personnel at the reserve desk. Consequently, they will form their opinion of the importance and value of the library and its service quality though those interactions.

The principle guaranteeing the confidentiality of circulation records is the same in reserve and circulation units. Although the reading is required and assigned by a teacher, no one has a right to know what anyone else reads without that person's permission. Faculty wishing to find out which students have done the required reading for their class may find it difficult to understand this principle. Revealing circulation records, however, violates the library's responsibility to guard the intellectual freedom of the students. The question may arise whether faculty have the right to see the circulation records for personally owned items placed on reserve: the answer is that they do not. While the materials are in the custody of the library, the principle of confidentiality applies to all materials issued and controlled by the library, even if only temporarily held. What a library may furnish that does not violate borrower confidentiality are data about the number of times an item circulated. Information can also be furnished on the number of individual students who checked out reserve material. Essentially, any information that does not identify an individual will not violate confidentiality.

The most vexing legal consideration in reserve operations is adherence to copyright law. Copyright law permits the copyright holder exclusive rights to reproduce, distribute, adapt, perform, and display one's creations. However, federal law recognizes that the public should also have some access to copyrighted information without having to ask permission or pay royalties. The law's "fair use" exemption is the most applicable provision for libraries:

> Fair use of a copyrighted work, including such use by reproduction in copies ... for purposes such as criticism, comment, news reporting, teaching (including multiple copies for classroom use), scholarship, or research, is not an infringement of copyright. (17 USC § 107)

With traditional reserve collections, only original book or journal volumes were on reserve, so there were no copyright concerns.

The criteria libraries use to determine whether use or reproduction of a copyrighted work qualifies as fair use includes four factors:

1. *The purpose and character of the use.* Is the use for a commercial or educational purpose?
2. *The nature of the work.* Is the copyrighted item a work of fiction (more restrictions) or nonfiction (fewer limitations)?
3. *The amount and substantiality of the portion copied.* Copying a limited portion points more toward fair use.
4. *The effect on the market value.* Will use affect the publisher's sales?

Each of these factors carries the same weight, and library policies attempt to create the greatest amount of fair use.

To help guide libraries with respect to requests for photocopies, the ALA adopted the Model Policy Concerning College and University Photocopying for Classroom, Research and Library Reserve (www.ala.org/ala/aboutala/offices/publishing/sundry/rightspermissions/reprintguidelines.cfm). Among the restrictions recommended for materials photocopied for reserve are the following:

1. The distribution of the same material should not occur every semester.
2. Only one copy per X number of students.
3. The material should include a copyright notice.
4. The students are not assessed any fee beyond photocopying costs.

For multiple copies placed on reserve the Model Policy specifies that the amount and number of copies should be "reasonable" given the nature of the course and the assignments, that the copies should contain a copyright notice, and that the photocopying should not be detrimental to the market for the work.

However difficult and confusing copyright is in terms of print-based materials, it is even more so for digital items. Growing up in a Google world, students today expect rapid and seamless access to digital information resources. Digitizing copyrighted works involves copying and distribution so must conform to copyright law. Libraries are in the difficult position of trying to provide access to digital resources while remaining in copyright compliance. While copyright law offers no clear and direct answers about the scope of fair use for electronic reserves, a number of different interpretations of the law may be found in the literature.

Higher education and its libraries faced and still are facing at the time this chapter was prepared some serious challenges regarding fair use. There have always been issues between educators and copyright holders over the concept of fair use and just how much material can be used under the concept. The digital age and its associated technologies that allow for easy file-sharing and the relatively easy generation of digital copies that are indistinguishable from the original has raised the stakes in the minds of copyright holders. Melanie Schlosser (2006) noted that "copyright law is famously difficult to understand and apply with precision" (p. 12).

During the recent past, universities and their libraries have learned that the answer to the question "is this fair use" is all too often "it depends." The Association of American Publishers (AAP) lawyers have approached a number of universities (for example, University of California, Cornell, Hofstra, Marquette, and Syracuse) regarding "alleged infringement" activities of their e-reserve activities. Andrew R. Albanese (2007) discussed the differing opinions about how friendly the dialogue was between AAP and institutional attorneys actually was. Starting from the position of alleged infringements the prospect of a lawsuit was never off the table. An interesting sidelight is most of the "discussions" were with private institutions which, unlike public institutions who have sovereign immunity, would be liable for any damages awarded to AAP. As Albanese noted, "For now, in today's world, managing e-reserves is about managing risk" (p. 38). A library's policy on copying will generally reflect the institution's risk tolerance for litigation, and libraries should seek legal counsel before adopting an electronic reserve policy.

Check These Out

Previously mentioned, one book that provides details regarding the services covered as well as other public service activities and functions is G. Edward Evans and Thomas L. Carter's *Introduction to Library Public Services*, 7th ed. (Westport, CT: Libraries Unlimited, 2009).

A 2008 article by Andrea Foster, "Despite Skeptics, Publishers Tout New 'Fair Use' Agreement with Universities," *Chronicle of Higher Education* 54, no. 20: A10, provides a good discussion of just how complex fair use has become or if the concept still exists.

An earlier article by Thomas Gould, Tomas Lipinski, and Elizabeth Buchanan (2005) provides a sound discussion of the library/higher education view of fair use and reserve services: "Copyright Policies and the Deciphering of Fair Use in the Creation of Reserves at University Libraries," *Journal of Academic Librarianship* 31, no. 3: 182–197.

LIAISON PROGRAMS

Liaison duties are becoming increasingly common in academic libraries, not just in ARL institutions. ACRL data (Dempsey, 2008) indicate that the concept is in place or under serious consideration/planning in all types of academic libraries. Just what constitutes liaison duties is evolving and varies from institution to institution. To some degree the concept has its roots in several other concepts, such as collection development liaison work with teaching departments, subject specialists/bibliographers, and a movement to have librarians work with faculty in handling "independent study" students (library college movement).

Perhaps the most comprehensive list of possible liaison roles appeared in Karen Williams (2009) article in which she outlined ten areas of work:

- Campus engagement
- Content/collection development and management
- Teaching and learning
- Scholarly communication
- E-scholarship and digital tools
- Reference/help services
- Outreach (to the local community)
- Fund-raising
- Exhibit and event planning
- Leadership (pp. 4–5)

In the same issue as the Williams article, Elizabeth A. Dupuis (2009) noted:

Responding strategically to economic pressures, many libraries are taking a fresh look at the changing needs of faculty and students and realigning the library's priorities. . . . [T]he librarian's role as an educational partner is recognized as one area of strategic importance for the long-term vitality of research libraries and the effectiveness of campus teaching and learning initiatives. (p. 9)

In order for librarians to take on liaison roles, a number of skills would need to be learned or developed, and LIS schools might need to add some coursework in the new areas. Some of the skill sets that the liaison positions require are high order communication and presentation ability, flexibility and comfort with ambiguity, project management, and promotion and marketing skills. John Rodwell and Linden Fairburn (2008) discussed this and many other skills and needs for having effective liaison programs. Some of the specific duties might include performing mediated search for a defined class of users, providing course integrated instruction throughout the term of the course, developing appropriate SDI/alerting services for faculty and graduate students, and developing and offering stand-alone courses that link information service and a subject area.

A related, or perhaps another variation of the liaison concept, is the "embedded" librarian. David Shumaker (2009) identified four distinguishing aspects of embedded librarian positions: office location (outside of the library), who funds the salary (solely from the library or shared with another department), who handles an individuals performance review (conducted solely or jointly by a nonlibrarian), and participation in both library and "customer" group meetings. Certainly the concept has gained wide acceptance in the special library environment (Shumaker, 2009). In the case of academic libraries, it appears as if some liaison positions would fit the special library definition of an embedded librarian (Shumaker, 2009), although most would not.

> **Check These Out**
>
> A case study of a liaison program is Onda Bennett and Karen Gilbert's "Extending Liaison Collaboration: Partnering With Faculty in Support of a Student Learning Community," *Reference Services Review* 37, no. 2 (2009): 131–142.
>
> Another example of the varied approach one sees in liaison programs appears in Amy Hoseth's "Library Participation in a Campus-Wide Teaching Program," *Reference Services Review* 37, no. 4 (2009): 371–385.
>
> James Thull and Mary Anne Hansen prepared a general review of U.S. liaison programs in "Academic Library Liaison Programs in US Libraries: Methods and Benefits," *New Library World* 110, no. 11/12 (2009): 529–540.

> **Check These Out**
>
> The following articles suggest the wide-ranging scope of the concept of embedded librarian.
>
> David Schumaker, "Who Let the Librarians Out? Embedded Librarianship and the Library Manager," *Reference & User Services Quarterly* 48, no. 3 (2009): 239–242.
>
> Dee Bozeman and Rachel Owens, "Providing Services to Online Students: Embedded Librarians and Access to Resources," *Mississippi Libraries* 72, no. 3 (2008): 57–59.
>
> Russell A. Hall, "The 'Embedded' Librarian in a Freshmen Speech Class: Information Literacy Instruction in Action," *College & Research Libraries News* 69, no. 1 (2008): 28–30.
>
> Linda Bartnik, "The Embedded Academic Librarian: The Subject Specialists Moves into the Discipline College," *Kentucky Libraries* 71, no. 3 (2007): 4–9.
>
> Veronica Dawn Stewart, "Embedded in the Blackboard Jungle: The Embedded Librarian Program at Pulaski Technical College," *Arkansas Libraries* 64, no. 3 (2007): 29–32.

KEY POINTS TO REMEMBER

- Quality services are essential to ongoing institutional support.
- Quality services arise out of a team effort on the part of the entire staff, including student employees.
- Customer service models from the commercial world have proven useful in academic library environments.
- Reference service, like collection management, takes time to understand and master. Unlike collection management activities, reference work carries the added pressure of working directly with users in rather hectic circumstances. Developing stress management skills will help improve a novice's comfort level with the work.

- Web/Library 2.0 has allowed libraries to expand their services; however, there are costs and trade-offs associated with that expansion.
- Keeping the library's webpages updated and looking "fresh" is important for holding young students' attention and encouraging repeat visits.
- Circulation is more important to quality library service and also more complex than many people realize. It also is the unit where staff are often called on to handle challenging/difficult situations ranging from minor confrontations with a user over a fine to having major confrontation with an emotionally upset person who has to be removed from the premises.
- Circulation units are a key element in maintaining user confidentiality regarding library usage.
- Reserve services have changed markedly in the recent past, with electronic reserve making the concept much more acceptable to students. However, e-reserves has increased the need to have some library staff conversant with all aspects of copyright laws, especially what "fair use" is in terms of the most recent court decisions.
- Liaison work to academic departments is one of the special aspects of academic library service that does not exist in other types of libraries. Just what being a library liaison means varies from library to library; however, as the concept spreads across academic libraries it will likely become more consistent from library to library.

REFERENCES

Albanese, Andrew R. 2007. Down with e-reserve. *Library Journal* 132, no.16: 36–38.

Abram, Stephen. 2008. Social libraries: Librarian 2.0 phenomenon. *Library Resources and Technical Services* 52, no. 2: 19–22.

Applegate, Rachel. 2008. Whose decline? Which academic libraries are "deserted" in terms of reference transactions? *Reference & User Services Quarterly* 48, no. 2: 176–189.

Association of College and Research Libraries. 2008. *Environmental scan 2007*. Chicago: American Library Association. Available: www.ala.org/ala/mgrps/divs/acrl/publications/whitepapers/Environmental_Scan_2007%20FINAL.pdf (accessed July 7, 2010).

Bradley, Karen. 2007. Reading noncompliance: A case study and reflection, *Mountainrise: The International Journal of the Scholarship of Teaching and Learning* 4, no. 1: 1–16.

Carlson, Scott. 2001. The deserted library: As students work online reading rooms empty—Leading some campuses to add Starbucks. *Chronicle of Higher Education*, November 16, pp. A1, A35.

Cohen, Sarah Faye. 2008. Taking 2.0 to the faculty: Why, who, and how. *College Research Libraries News* 69, no. 5: 472–475.

Connell, Ruth Sara. 2009. Academic libraries, Facebook and MySpace, and student outreach: A survey of student opinion. *portal: Libraries and the Academy* 9, no. 1: 25–36.

Courtois, Martin, and Lori Goetsch. 1984. Use of nonprofessionals at reference desks. *College & Research Libraries* 45, no. 5: 385–391.

De Jager, Karin. 2001. Impacts and outcomes: Searching for the most elusive indicators of academic library performance. In *Meaningful measures for emerging realities, proceedings of the 4th Northumbria International Conference on Performance Measurement in Libraries and Information Services*, 291–297. Washington, DC: Association of Research Libraries.

Dempsey, Lorcan. 2008. Reconfiguring the library systems environment. *portal: Library and the Academy* 8, no. 8: 111–120.

Dotson, Daniel S., and Joshua B. Garris. 2008. Counting more than the gate: Developing building use statistics to create better facilities for today's academic library users. *Library Philosophy and Practice* (September): 1–13.

Dupuis, Elizabeth A. 2009. Amplifying the educational role of librarians. *Research Library Issues* 265 (August): 9–14. Available: www.arl.org/resources/pubs/rli/archive/rli265.shtml (accessed April 7, 2010).

Eakin, Lori, and Jeffery Pomerantz. 2009. Virtual reference, real money: Modeling costs in virtual reference services. *portal: Libraries and the Academy* 9, no. 1: 133–164.

Fichter, Darlene. 2007. How social is your web site? Top five tips for social media optimization. *Online* 31, no. 3: 57–60.

Freeman, Geoffrey T. 2005. *Library as place: Rethinking roles, rethinking space.* CLIR pub. 129. Washington, DC: Council on Library and Information Resources.

Gayton, Jeffrey. 2008. Academic libraries: "social" or "communal?" The nature and future of academic libraries. *Journal of Academic Librarianship* 34, no. 1: 60–66.

Granfield, Diane, and Mark Robertson. 2008. Preferences for reference: New options and choices for academic library users. *Reference & User Services Quarterly* 488, no. 1: 44–53.

Hahn Karla. 2009. Introduction: Positioning liaison librarians for the 21st century. *Research Library Issues* 265 (August): 1–2. Available: www.arl.org/resources/pubs/rli/archive/rli265 .shtml (accessed April 7, 2010).

Hernon, Peter, Danuta A. Nitecki, and Ellen Altman. 1999. Service quality and customer satisfaction: An assessment and future directions, *The Journal of Academic Librarianship* 25, no. 1: 9–17.

Isenberg, Laurie. 2006. Online course reserves and graduate student satisfaction. *Journal of Academic Librarianship* 32, no. 2: 166–172.

Jackson, Mary E., Bruce Kingma, and Tom Delaney. 2004. *Assessing ILL/DD services: New cost-effective alternatives.* Washington, DC: Association of Research Libraries.

Jacoby, JoAnn, and Mary S. Laskowski. 2004. Measurement and analysis of electronic reserve usage. *portal: Libraries and the Academy* 4, no. 2: 219–232.

Jurewicz, Lynn, and Todd Cutler. 2003. *High tech high touch: Library customer service through technology.* Chicago: American Library Association.

Martell, Charles. 2008. The absent user: Physical use of the academic library collections and services continues to decline 1995–2006. *Journal of Academic Librarianship* 34, no. 5: 400–407.

Martin, Pamela N. 2009. Societal transformation and reference services in the academic library: Theoretical foundations for re-envisioning reference. *Library Philosophy and Practice* (May): 1–8.

Merkley, Cari. 2009. Staffing an academic reference desk with librarians is not cost-effective. *Evidence Based Library and Information Practice* 4, no. 2: 143–147.

Moorman, John A. 2006. *Running a small library.* New York: Neal-Schuman.

NewPR/Wiki. 2007. SocialMediaOptimization/homepage. Available: www.thenewpr.com/wiki/pmwiki.php?pagename=SocialMediaOptimization.HomePage (accessed March 22, 2010).

Pike, George. 2007. The PATRIOT Act illuminated. *Information Today* 24, no. 5: 17–18.

Pilston, Anna Klump, and Richard L. Hart. 2002. Student response to a new electronic reserves system. *Journal of Academic Librarianship* 28, no. 3: 147–151.

Rettig, James. 1993. From the president of RASD. *RQ* 32, no. 3: 310–314.

Rodwell, John, and Linden Fairburn. 2008. Dangerous liaisons? Defining the faculty liaison librarian service model, its effectiveness and sustainability. *Library Management* 29, no. 1/2: 116–124.

Rosendale, Jeff. 2002. *Managing electronic reserves.* Chicago, American Library Association.

Ryan, Susan. 2008. Reference transaction analysis: The cost-effectiveness of staffing a traditional academic reference desk. *Journal of Academic Librarianship* 34, no. 5: 389–399.

Schachter, Debbie. 2006. The true value of customer service. *Information Outlook* 10, no. 8: 8–9.

Schlosser, Melanie. 2006. Fair use in the digital environment: A research guide. *Reference & User Services Quarterly* 46, no. 1: 11–17.

Self, James. 1987. Reserve readings and student grades: Analysis of a case study. *Library and Information Science Reports* 9, no. 1: 29–40.

Shill, Harold B., and Shawn Tonner. 2004. Does the building still matter? Usage patterns in new, expanded, and renovates libraries. *College and Research Libraries* 65, no. 2: 123–150.

Shumaker, David 2009. *Models of embedded librarianship: Final report.* Washington, DC: School of Library and Information Science, Catholic University of America. Available: www.sla.org/pdfs/EmbeddedLibrarianshipFinalRptRev.pdf (accessed March 22, 2010).

Todaro, Julie, and Mark Smith. 2006. *Training library staff and volunteers to provide extraordinary customer service.* New York: Neal-Schuman.

Wehmeyer, Susan, Dorothy Auchter, and Arnold Hirshon. 1996. Saying what we will do, and doing what we say: Implementing a customer service plan. *The Journal of Academic Librarianship* 22, no. 3: 173–80.

Weingand, Darlene E. 1997. *Customer service excellence: A concise guide for librarians.* Chicago: American Library Association.

Williams, Karen. 2009. A framework for articulating new library roles. *Research Library Issues* 265 (August): 3–8. Available: www.arl.org/resources/pubs/rli/archive/rli265.shtml (accessed April 7, 2010).

LAUNCHING PAD

Attebury, Ramirose Ilene, and Joshua Finnell. 2009. What do LIS students in the United States know about liaison duties. *New Library World* 110, no. 7/8: 325–340.

Backe, William. 2009. How we failed the Net generation. *Online* 33, no. 3: 47–49.

Barclay. Donald A. 2007. Creating an academic library for the twenty-first century. *New Direction in Higher Education* 139: 103–115.

Belliston, C. Jeffrey, Jared L. Howland, and Brian C. Roberts. 2007. Undergraduate use of federated searching: A survey of preferences and perceptions of value-added functionality. *College & Research Libraries* 68, no. 6: 472–486.

Charnigo, Laurie, and Paula Barnett-Ellis. 2007. Checking out Facebook.com: The impact of a digital trend in academic libraries. *Information Technology and Libraries* 26, no. 1: 23–34.

Foster, Marg. 2008. Diversity—Serving all students @ your library. *Learning and Media* 36, no. 2: 3–4.

Hastings, Robin. 2009. *Collaboration 2.0: Library technology reports.* Chicago, IL: American Library Association.

Isbell, Dennis. 2008. What happens to your research assignment at the library? *College Teaching* 56, no. 1: 3–6.

Joint, Nicholas. 2009a. Managing the implementation of a federated search tool in an academic library. *Library Review* 58, no. 1: 10–16.

———. 2009b. The Web 2.0 challenge to libraries. *Library Review* 58, no. 3: 167–175.

King, David Lee, and Stephanie Willen Brown. 2009. Emerging trends, 2.0, and libraries. *Serial Librarian* 56, no. 1: 32–43.

Knibbe-Haanstra, Marcella. 2008. Reference desk dilemmas: The impact of new demands on librarianship. *Reference & User Services Quarterly* 48, no. 1: 20–25.

Kelly, Lynda. 2009. Web 2.0 and organisational change: The Australian Museum's new website. WestMuse. Available: westmuse.wordpress.com/?s=Web+2.0+and+Organisational+change (accessed April 7, 2010).

Lee, Hur-Li. 2008. Information structure and undergraduate students. *Journal of Academic Librarianship* 34, no. 3: 211–219.

ljnews: Georgia State sued over e-reserves. 2008. *Library Journal* 133, no. 9: 16–17.

Maness, Jack M. 2008. A linguistic analysis of chat reference conversations with 18–24 year-old college students. *Journal of Academic Librarianship* 34, no. 1: 31–38.

O'Connor, Steve, and Lai-chong Au. 2009. Steering a future through scenarios: Into the academic library of the future. *Journal of Academic Librarianship* 35, no. 1: 57–64.

Online catalogs: What user and librarians want. An OCLC Report. 2009. Dublin, OH: OCLC.

Ralph, Jaya, and Sonja Olsen. 2007. Podcasting as an educational building block in academic libraries. *Australian Academic & Research Libraries* 38, no. 4: 270–279.

Shih, Win, and Martha Allen. 2007. Working with Generation-D: Adopting and adapting to cultural learning and change. *Library Management* 18, no. 1/2: 89–100.

Singh, Jagtar. 2008. Sense-making: Information literacy for lifelong learning and knowledge management. *DESIDOC Journal of Library & Information Technology* 28, no. 2: 13–17.

Stein, Merrill, Teresa Edge, John M. Kelly, Dave Hewlett, and James F. Trainer. 2008. Using continuous quality improvement methods to evaluate library service points. *Reference & User Services Quarterly* 48, no. 1: 78–85.

Taylor, Stephanie. 2007. Google Scholar—Friend or foe. *Interlending & Document Supply* 35, no. 1: 4–6.

Chapter 13

Staffing

The dynamics and structure of the academic library within the higher education community create complex environments for the library administrator attempting to navigate the myriad rules and regulations (state, federal, and institutional) that affect staff recruiting, hiring, processing, compensating and related functions for library personnel.

—Dennis R. Defa (2008)

Issues regarding classification status for academic librarians have made fodder for scholarly articles, books, and theses for a long time. A quick glance through the literature reveals a decidedly higher percentage of authors favoring some form of faculty classification for academic librarians (with corresponding pay and benefits). However, there are a number of alternative positions rationally and eloquently expressed in the myriad of topical journal articles as well.

—Alan Bernstein (2009)

Teams began playing an important role in academic libraries more than ten years ago as institutions recognized the need to keep pace with a rapidly changing information environment.

—M. Sue Baughman (2008)

An academic library that is fortunate enough to have solid funding, a new building, and an outstanding service plan still may not have high-quality service. It is its staff that is the key to service success, not the technology, not the collections, and not its physical environment. Certainly all of the latter factors are important, but it is how well the staff members perform their duties that make users think "their" library is one of the best. Gaining the services of the best and brightest people is a process that requires thoughtful planning. When it comes to hiring people who will provide outstanding service, you must think and plan carefully.

Our first quotation for this chapter references library administrators and makes valid points. However, the complexities Defa mentions apply to almost everyone on the library's staff. In actuality, almost every full-time staff member has some supervisory responsibilities that include almost all aspects of human resources (HR) management activities. If nothing more, a staff member may be responsible for a part-time work study assistant. It is common for people not to think of such responsibility as involving any HR issues. Even having an intern or volunteer can and does have some HR implications. In this chapter, we explore many of major issues in handling HR in an academic library setting.

STAFFING CATEGORIES

Academic libraries utilize several categories of employees. The labels for the categories vary from library to library; however, there are four basic groups:

- Full-time individuals who have a master's degree in library and information science and/or a subject graduate degree (librarians/professionals/subject specialists)
- Full-time individuals with degrees ranging from bachelor's to postgraduate (information technologist and other specialists such human resources, development, or public relations)
- Full-time individuals with an academic degree or high school diploma (paraprofessional, nonprofessional, support staff, library assistant, technical assistant, and clerical staff are some of the more common titles)
- Part-time individuals with or without a degree (shelving assistants, interns, student/ graduate assistants, volunteers)

As the size of the academic library increases, so does the variety of staff categories it employs and the complexity of its human resources (HR) functions. Having a basic knowledge of the hows and whys of HR activities and their potential impact on service quality is beneficial for all staff members, the library, and its parent institution.

Our opening quotation from Baughman (2008) reflects another issue that is taking place within the field and that adds additional complexity to working with and for people. Budget reductions, downsizing, technology, and changing staffing patterns all create an environment of uncertainty, tension, and often fear. These concerns/worries arise as organizations make changes to their structure in order to do more without having additional resources. Teams became one of the favored methods for gaining productivity without gaining personnel. (We discuss team building and their role in academic libraries in Chapter 14.) The way HR needs to respond to such changes has been somewhat slower than the pace of change. Thus, some HR practices from a past environment remain in place often creating tensions in the workplace (an example is performance appraisal, addressed later in this chapter).

Some years ago, Paula T. Kaufman (1992) noted that the categories used to classify library employees "can create problems, tensions, and conflicts between library non-professional and professional staffs" (p. 214). Part of these tensions arise from a host of variable beliefs or understandings about the types of library work and who should do what, when, and how as what were once thought of as librarians' responsibilities get assigned to individuals lacking a library degree. Liz Lane and Barbara Stewart (1998) wisely noted that "many staff members are being assigned higher-level work which then requires an upward reclassification of jobs.... Work previously done at lower levels has either become automated, outsourced to a library vendor, or is not done anymore" (p. 156). There have been occasions when the tensions between academic librarians and library support staff over who should have what role have interfered with service quality as resentments become entwined with overall work attitudes.

One area where tension can arise relates to the question of librarian status on the campus. It is likely that the environment where librarian and support staff tensions are most pronounced are those where the librarians are seeking to move from a nonfaculty status to having such status. In such a situation, some of the support staff can harbor doubts about why the librarians should gain "special treatment" when everyone on the staff is important to providing quality service. Many of them do not understand the responsibilities of the professional position and look only at "desk time." That is, they do not see the evening and occasional weekend time librarians have to put in to do their jobs. This is particularly true for librarians who have information literacy teaching responsibilities or service or scholarship requirements. Libraries with well-established librarian status categories experience fewer intrastaff issues.

Perhaps one of today's greatest sources of tension in any organization is generational differences. Naturally there have always been different generations in the workplace; however, there are at least three factors today that make the situation somewhat unusual. First, there are rather different work values between the generations now working—see Table 13.1 for some examples. Second, work today is highly dependent on technology, and the youngest workers grew up with technology (digital natives) while the older employees must learn how to handle technology (digital immigrants). Third, the deep recession of 2008–2009 has changed the plans of older employees about when they can afford to retire. Many are staying on the job far longer than they had expected prior to the great economic downturn of 2008. This means the opportunities for advancement for younger people are less due to fewer retirement vacancies than were predicted. It also means the challenges of handling differing work values last longer.

Certainly one needs to recognize the generational differences regarding work expectations and the workplace when adding students to the staffing mix. There are only a few "Traditionalists" (born before 1945) still working in libraries, and most who are working are volunteers rather than paid staff. Such individuals worked in highly structured workplaces for almost all of their careers and are comfortable with a hierarchical system. They believe in hard work, commitment, and loyalty.

"Boomers" (1946–1964) are the largest of the generations in the workplace as well as in the population. They are now mostly in the senior positions in libraries. When they entered the workforce, there was great competition for available jobs; furthermore, they faced a highly competitive work environment for much of their careers. Generally they are less inclined to teamwork, in the sense of the term today. They were also the first generation to experience significant layoffs, which often reinforced their need to be competitive and independent.

Generation X (1965–1980) is a much smaller cohort. These are the people who will begin to fill the senior positions in libraries as Boomers retire—a process that is now under way. They grew up pretty much on their own, with two working parents or in a single-parent home. They were sometimes referred to as latchkey children. Generally,

Table 13.1. Generational Workplace Values

Value	Boomers	GenX	Millennials
Trust of authority	Low	Modest	Rather high
Loyalty to workplace	Cynical	Some	Modest
Career goals	Single focus	Portable career	Multiple careers
Compensation	Title/"corner office"	Freedom	Meaningful work
Position of authority	Strive for	Need early on	Not as important
Evaluation of work	Once a year	Structured/frequent	Whenever I want it
Reaction to changes	What's the purpose?	Will it work?	How do we do it?
Work/family life	Not balanced	Balanced	Balanced
Gratification	Work for it	Expected	Need instantly

they are very independent and have strong doubts about authority and loyalty. Often they value their "free" time more highly than doing extra work to earn more money, even when that work might lead to a promotion. They are much more comfortable with self-managed teams than are the Boomers.

Millennials (1981–1999), the most recent group to enter the workforce, are even fewer in number than Generation X. This generation will not face strong competition for positions given their small numbers; in fact, it is likely the employers will be the ones facing competition. They were the first generation to grow up in a technology-filled world—it was not new; it was just the way the world was. Technology is something they are comfortable with, and they expect it to work properly and on demand. Their expectation of a quick response often carries over into their workplace expectations. Employers are finding that Millennial generation employees have little patience when it comes to waiting for promotions and are quick to leave organizations. Teams have been a natural part of their growing up in school via highly structured group activities, so work teams do not seem unnatural to them.

When you have a mix of generations in the workplace, as do most libraries, there are motivation challenges to address. With large numbers of student workers, you add to the complexity. You will probably need to employ different approaches for the students than you do with the older full-time staff.

Several trends impact full-time academic library employees. Workloads continue to increase and generally do not generate additional staffing, even in the form of extra work study student assistance. Existing staff find themselves called on to undertake tasks and learn new skill sets they never dreamed would arise during their working life. Job postings for both librarians and support staff frequently call for broad-based skills in both public and technical services, a change from past practice. As Kennan and colleagues (2007) noted in an article comparing U.S. and Australian academic job advertisements, "The content of LIS jobs in both countries appears to be changing, almost certainly in response to changing environmental and technological demands. There appears to be a move towards job ads specifying more generic skills and competencies, including management and supervisory skills" (p. 124). Additionally, more job ads indicate preferring experience in some aspect of diversity and/or cultural competencies.

Check These Out

John D. Shank's article "The Blended Librarian: A Job Announcement Analysis of the Newly Emerging Position of Instructional Design Librarian. *College & Research Libraries* 67, no. 6 (2006): 515–524. describes both a new academic librarian role and some of the factors generally that are changing all the roles librarians play.

Jo Williams' article "MARC Data, the OPAC, and Library Professionals," *Program: Electronic Library and Information Systems* 43, no. 1 (2009): 7–17, sets forth the reasons why academic library staff, regardless of their primary job responsibilities, ought to have a sound grounding in the MARC format.

LIBRARIANS

In today's world, the difference between a librarian and other staff categories is probably most apparent in the human resources (HR) department rather than within the library and least apparent in terms of users' perceptions. The reason for HR's ability to differentiate between the categories is that it maintains the job descriptions, position holder's name, and salary classifications. None of these attributes are apparent on a daily basis in the library. "On the floor," especially for the users, it is almost impossible to know who holds what job title.

Individuals holding positions designated as "librarian" generally have a master's degree in library science (MLS) or information science (MLIS). More and more large research libraries have bibliographic/subject librarians or administrators who may hold a graduate degree in their assigned subject area rather than an MLS/MLIS. Some institutions may require or prefer someone holding a teaching certificate as well. Finally, some librarians are hired without an MLS or MLIS because they satisfy a frequent phrase in position advertisements: "MLS/MLIS or equivalent required." Just what is "equivalent" varies from institution to institution. However, the vast majority of academic librarians do in fact have an MLS/MLIS degree. Academic libraries, more than other library types, occasionally must work through the issue of how acceptable a library degree earned in another country is. A number of government regulations must be resolved when the person is not a U.S. citizen beyond the question of the degree's origin. However, what if the person is a citizen but her or his degree is from an Australian program? There are many other scenarios, but the point is how to assess the degree and the need for the skills the person may bring to the position. It can be and is done, but it takes time and effort.

Faculty Status

A few years ago, Catherine Murray-Rust (2005) wrote:

> For over a century librarians and others in academe have debated the issue of faculty status for librarians. Do librarians play the same role as teaching or research faculty members? Is academic freedom a problem for librarians? Do librarians have real faculty status if they do not earn tenure the way other faculty members do? Although some librarians now have faculty status, the pros and cons continue to be argued passionately. (p. B10)

Indeed the issue has been argued passionately. However, in spite of the passion and volume of ink spilled over the issue, it still is a matter very much up in the air at many academic institutions.

The Association of College and Research Libraries (ACRL) has taken a strong interest in the topic for the better part of forty years and produced a number of documents on the subject. In 2007, ACRL put forward new guidelines regarding faculty status (www.ala.org/ala/mgrps/divs/acrl/standards/guidelinesacademic.cfm). The guidelines cover nine topics: professional responsibilities, governance, contracts, compensation, promotion/salary increases, leaves and research funds, academic freedom, dismissal/nonreappointment, and grievance.

In terms of governance, the guidelines state, "librarians should participate in the development of the institution's mission, curriculum, and governance." The typical way in which academic librarians, regardless of status, generally get to participate in such activities is through committee assignments. At some institutions where librarians do not have faculty status, librarians still serve on the campus faculty senate/council. As we noted in the chapter on curriculum, having a library presence on the committee that handles new courses and programs is of great benefit in terms of library planning.

Employment contracts are frequently a fact of academic librarianship, regardless of status. However, the guidelines call for those holding such status to have a written contract with at least a one-year term. It also states that after no more than seven years, following a process of peer review, the person should be granted "continuing employment" (tenure), assuming the person has met the other requirements for tenure.

ACRL also has developed a set of guidelines (2005) for appointment, promotion, and tenure of academic librarians (www.ala.org/ala/mgrps/divs/acrl/standards/promotion tenure.cfm). One of the provisions that relates to the requirements for tenure is relatively brief, but it is significant in terms of implications for librarians:

> All activities shall be judged by professional colleagues on and/or off the campus on the basis of their contribution to scholarship, the profession of librarianship, and library service. The basic criterion for promotion in academic rank is to perform professional level tasks that contribute to the educational and research mission of the institution.
>
> Evidence of this level of performance may be judged by colleagues on the library faculty, members of the academic community outside the library, and/or professional colleagues outside the academic institution.

One of the challenges for librarians gaining tenure, especially at institutions with relatively recently established programs, is the impact of having performance judged by "members of the academic community outside of the library." It is rather common to have some teaching faculty who strongly doubt librarians should have faculty status. When such a person is part of the review process, there can be painful issues to resolve.

The area that usually presents the largest challenge for librarians seeking to gain faculty status revolves around the scholarly and/or creative activity. This is true whether they are attempting to get their institutions to institute a faculty status program for them or they are on the staff of libraries where such a program exists.

Just as faculty members on "the tenure track" face the challenge of convincing their peers she or he is worthy of tenure, so do librarians. The seven-year window for achieving that goal—a rather firm standard at most academic institutions that have a tenure program—seems to fly by in an instant. Being able to meet requirements of librarianship, service, and scholarship can seem daunting, if not impossible, to a new librarian. If anything, the teaching faculty may have a slightly easier time as they are better able to control their working time and are generally on an academic year (nine- or ten-month contract). Librarians on the other hand have a host of job responsibilities that are generally not all that flexible, and there is an expectation that a standard workweek (35 or 40 hours is common) will be put in year round. Even when the library makes some provision for research time, there are staffing challenges. We have noted in several chapters how difficult it is to secure additional staff positions, even in relatively "good times." While the libraries with faculty status programs attempt to build some research time into their librarian positions, they rarely are able to succeed as much they would like. Thus, "research time" may result in more work for other staff members who must take up the slack. When it comes to formal leaves/sabbaticals, the staffing challenge can be even more significant.

Another challenge for many new graduates is that they often do not have a strong research background from either their undergraduate or graduate education, unlike the teaching faculty. Identifying a reasonable research topic to tackle can be a daunting task, as is developing a sound research methodology. Their library school may or may not have had a required research methods course. Even if the person had such a course, she or he can benefit from some serious mentoring (we cover mentoring in Chapter 15). Nikhat Ghouse and Jennifer Church-Duran (2008) succinctly stated the issue when they wrote about a newcomer's transition to the academy:

These challenges are heightened for academic librarians, who often do not have the same transitional experiences as teaching faculty. The developmental challenges specific to academic librarianship are diverse and include navigating the transition into the profession, comprehending the complexity of the academic library culture, and appreciating the demands of research and scholarship. In exploring ways to successfully address these challenges, mentoring relationships are a consistently popular option for library faculty and staff. (p. 373)

How many institutions do have faculty status programs for librarians? Mary K. Bolin (2008a,b) looked at faculty status in land grant and all Association of Research Libraries (ARL) institutions and found that there is some overlap in the two samples. She employed four categories of status: professional ranks (assistant professor, associate professor, and professor), parallel ranks (assistant librarian, associate librarian, and librarian), librarian ranks (librarian I, II, III, IV), and "other." She also used four tenure types: professional, other ranks with tenure, other ranks without tenure, and nonfaculty (institutional staff). Her findings for the libraries were that 27.7 percent had professional status for librarians, 23.5 percent had other ranks with tenure, 10.9 percent had other ranks without tenure, and 37.8 were nonfaculty (2008b, p. 418). Thus just over 50 percent of the libraries surveyed had some type of tenure program in place for librarians.

Bolger and Smith (2006) reported on a study they conducted regarding faculty status and rank in liberal arts colleges. Their findings showed that just 22.4 percent "of the institutions surveyed indicated that librarians have exactly the same rights and responsibilities as other faculty on their campus" (p. 225). Clearly the debate about the appropriate status for academic librarians, even in large research institutions, is ongoing and perhaps strongly contested at times.

> **Check This Out**
>
> A highly readable essay about the process of preparing the material that goes forward to the group that will make the tenure decision is Kathleen A. Hanna, Ann O'Bryan, and Kevin F. Petsche's "Our Excellent Adventure: A Somewhat Irreverent Look at How Three Tenure Track Librarians Prepared Their Dossiers and Lived to Tell About It," *College & Research Libraries News* 69, no. 9 (2008): 554–556.

Jacalyn Bryan (2007) concluded her article about faculty status with the following:

> The positive effects of faculty status for academic librarians seem to outweigh the negative effects and are preferable to no faculty status.... Academic librarians in each college and university should seek the model that works best for them in their individual situation. (p. 785)

PARAPROFESSIONAL/SUPPORT STAFF

Deciding on a label and required background of those holding nonprofessional positions in academic libraries is not easy. Years ago, Elin Christianson (1973) reported on the various labels used to designate library personnel who did not hold an MLS as well as on the attitudes about those labels. The list included clerk/clerical, library aide, library associate, library assistant, library clerk, library technician, nonprofessional, paraprofessional, supportive/support staff, and subprofessional. The only label that did not elicit at least a few negative responses from those holding such positions at the time was *library technician. Paraprofessional* had only a few negative comments, and today there would probably be none given the rise of groups such as paralegals, paramedics, etc.

A journal for people in these ranks was *Library Mosaics*, and its editorial staff consistently used the label *paraprofessional*. (The journal ceased publication at the end of 2005. However, its back files have a wealth of information for anyone interested in this field.) Perhaps the Council on Library/Media Technicians (COLT; colt.ucr.edu) and/or the American Library Association's Library Support Staff Interests Round Table (LSSIRT; www.ala.org/ala/lssirt) will fill in the void left by the passing of *Library Mosaics*. There is still no consensus as to what the label should be. This is probably due to a lack of agreement about what training/education is required to hold such positions. We personally prefer either *paraprofessional* or *support staff*.

One reason for the confusion about labels and the use of the phrase "library degree" is because there are community college programs that offer courses and certificates in librarianship. One example is the "Library Information Technician" program (www.mesacc.edu/ library/lbt/) at Mesa (Arizona) Community College (MCC). As noted on the MCC website, library technicians "Learn and engage with new and emerging information resources & technologies. Library information technician/assistant positions are classified as professional/technical occupations. Those trained in this field are important team members of a library or information organization." The program offers 26 different courses in library and information technology, ranging from a "foundations" course to one on management.

There are many such programs across the country. The Bureau of Labor Statistics has an online publication ("Occupational Outlook Handbook, 2008–09") with information about "library technicians" (www.bls.gov/oco/ocos113.htm), which begins by noting:

- Increasing use of electronic resources enables library technicians to perform tasks once done by librarians.
- Training requirements range from a high school diploma to an associate degree, but computer skills are necessary for all workers.
- Employment should grow more rapidly in special libraries because increasing numbers of professionals and other workers use those libraries.
- Opportunities will be best for those with specialized postsecondary library training.

Given the advanced skills requirements for these positions, is it any wonder that there is some confusion in the minds of individuals who complete such programs as well as in the minds of some HR departments regarding the qualifications necessary for working in a library and what educational background qualifies a person to be a "librarian" as opposed to "library technician?"

Support staff members are the backbone of library services. Without them, few libraries could offer the variety and quality of services that they do. As noted on the ALA–APA website, "According to the 2004 statistics from the National Center for Education Statistics (NCES) 230,843 workers are employed in U.S. academic and public libraries. Of these, 160,150 (69%) are library support staff" (American Library Association Allied Professional Association, 2005). Rachel Applegate (2008) made the point, "There are more 'other staff' per librarian in doctoral institutions than in master's (that is, a smaller percentage of a doctoral institution library staff are librarians)" (p. 177).

People usually think of their work in one of two ways—as a job or as a career. Job-oriented individuals focus only on the assigned duties. They often perform those responsibilities at an extremely high level and are a very valuable organizational resource.

However, when their work shift ends, so does their interest in the organization. They have other interests. Career-oriented people, on the other hand, have a strong interest in their organization as well as an interest in the field in general. They are quick to volunteer to take on new tasks, especially those that offer an opportunity to learn a new skill or gain new knowledge. Because of their interest in the organization, they offer suggestions for improvements and accept committee assignments willingly. It is our opinion that the career-oriented individuals form the core of paraprofessional ranks. We also must note that career-oriented individuals, when overworked and undersupported, can quickly become job-oriented. This is something that all good supervisors should attempt to avoid and try to point out to more senior managers when they observe such mistreatment.

For the career-oriented person, the LSSIRT, described earlier, has created the "Task Force on Career Ladders" (American Library Association Support Staff Interests Roundtable, 1999). This document, as well as its companion publication "Continuing Education and Training Opportunities" (American Library Association Support Staff Interests Roundtable, 2000) are useful to review and should be thoughtfully considered. As the Career Ladders work indicates, "career development shifts the responsibility to the individual and away from the organization" (p. 4). It goes on to point out that libraries have an obligation in this area as well, such as providing opportunities for skill development, promotions, and the chance to put new skills to use.

A key point was made in the LSSIRT statement (2000): "Although there has been rapid deployment of electronic databases, the Internet, and other resources, there has not been nearly enough training for the staff who use these resources" (p. 4). It goes on to suggest one need is that "there should be standard core competences for all levels of support staff" (p. 5). The Support Staff Section of the Connecticut Library Association developed a competency list, both for all staff and for some areas of service such as public services (ctlibraryassociation.org/archive/class.html). Many of their general staff competencies are ones you would expect to find in any list of desirable staff traits: positive attitude toward users, being open to change, having good communication skills, and being willing and able to work independently. The following are the 11 competencies for public service staff:

- Ability to introduce users to all library services
- Ability to use the entire library collection to satisfy user requests
- Knowledge of the library's circulation system and public access catalog
- Knowledge of fine and fee policies and cash and security procedures
- Knowledge of basic reference and information resources and referral procedures
- Knowledge of available community resources
- Knowledge of library copyright requirements
- Knowledge of library classification systems with the ability to do shelving and shelf reading
- Familiarity with the reader's advisory issues and resources
- Familiarity with ILL procedures
- Ability to deal with disruptive patrons and emergency situations.

ALA is undertaking, as of 2009, a certification program for support staff. You can learn more about this program at the Library Support Staff Certification Program website (www.ala-apa.org/certification/certification.html).

OTHER FULL-TIME STAFF

There are a variety of full-time employees who work in academic libraries, especially in ARL libraries, who do not fall into the previous categories. The most obvious are clerical staff such as administrative assistants, receptionists, and secretaries. These are job categories that require only general office skills—a person does not need to have any prior background in library operations to carry out the job functions. Other clerical positions might include processing and mailing notices to users (overdue and document delivery information, for example) or monitoring/providing security at library exits.

Beyond the clerical staff there are several job categories that one may think of as non-librarian professionals. We will briefly discuss six of the most common categories that a person is likely to encounter in ARL and increasingly in other academic libraries. Furthermore, we touch on some of the issues that may arise from the presence of such categories.

The most common category is ICT (information communication technologies) personnel. Almost all academic libraries have one or more staff members who have technology-related job responsibilities, some with an MLS and many without. When large research libraries first began to computerize their activities in the 1960s/1970s many of them developed in-house systems that were the forerunners of today's ILS packages, and this work required personnel with computer expertise. As late as the early 1990s, when an academic library purchased an integrated library system (ILS), a computer specialist FTE (full-time equivalent) was part of the expected project cost package. By the mid-1990s most vendor-supplied ILSs did not require more than the type of support that existing library staff could provide. Existing ICT staff shifted their focus from the ILS to the many other technologies of growing interest to academic libraries such as the Internet and the telecommunication needs related to distance education programs. Some ICT personnel do become involved in evaluating and/or designing various commercial and in-house systems as well as digitization projects. The vast majority of people holding such a position in a library have an undergraduate or graduate degree in computer science rather than an MLS.

Probably the second most common category of professional nonlibrarians in ARL and other large libraries is the subject/area bibliographer specialist. Almost all individuals holding such position titles have at least a master's degree in a subject field and many have a doctorate. We touched on subject specialists and their responsibilities in Chapter 11. In many ARL libraries, their duties have expanded beyond collection management into such areas as providing in-depth research assistance.

A rather recent nonlibrarian staffing category is the development officer. The need for such officers has been growing and appears likely to increase across all sizes of academic libraries as the library must seek more noninstitutional funding to support its programs and services. Individuals holding a development officer position support the senior library managers in their fund-raising activities. In the authors' experience, people in this category are equally divided between those with an MLS and those who have other fund-raising experience and education. There are situations where the campus development office assigns one its staff to assist the library in fund-raising. In the authors' experience, the library is only one of several campus units the person is responsible for and, initially, has little real understanding of library operations. The authors encourage library development officers to become involved in the Academic Library Advancement and Development

Network (ALADN), which is an academic fund-raising community of peers and holds a special conference annually. Another category, which goes well beyond large research libraries, is the business/financial officer. Job responsibilities for such individuals, as the job title suggests, are to assist senior administrators in the myriad of business/financial activities of the library. Few people in this category have an MLS, rather they have either an undergraduate or graduate degree in business or public administration.

Personnel work is rather complicated, and in large research libraries the variety of job categories makes the process more complex. For this reason, some ARL libraries have in-house HR officers or even a department. As is the case with development officers, about 50 percent of such officers have an MLS. Also, like the development officer, the library HR officer/department must work closely and cooperatively with their campus counterpart.

Our last category—public relations/information officer—is primarily in ARL libraries. This position helps the library market the academic library or "tell the library's story." Many academic libraries are now involved in systematic marketing of their services and resources. This officer works closely with academic library administrators, librarians, and the development officer to market the library to the rest of the college or university. Academic libraries who employ PR people also have official marketing plans in place. The person is also the point person at times of academic library disaster or crisis. Some of the PR people are librarians who move into the position; others are not.

As one might expect, such a wide variety of job categories with differing educational and skill requirements can lead to several staffing concerns/issues. One such issue that may create staff tensions is situations in which librarians have or may attain faculty status/tenure. How to handle other professional categories in this case can be challenging, especially when there are individuals with similar backgrounds and job titles in other campus units that do not offer such opportunities.

Check These Out

ALA has interest sections related to the previously mentioned categories, and membership in the sections is open to anyone (no degree requirements) if one joins the association.

The Library and Information Technology Association (LITA) has several interest groups, such as distance education, digital library technology, and Imagineering: www.ala.org/ala/mgrps/divs/lita/litahome.cfm.

The division Library Leadership, Administration, and Management Association (www.ala.org/ala/mgrps/divs/llama/index.cfm) has sections devoted to the nontechnology areas:

· Fund Raising and Financial Development Section
· Human Resources Section
· Library Organization and Management Section
· Public Relations and Marketing Section

Perhaps the most common concern is salary differentials. Libraries, just as are their campuses, are not exempt from the need to match the local "market rates" for nonlibrarian skills. A high local rate for some job categories may require paying a similar high rate in order to attract and retain people with those skill sets. This in turn can upset efforts to maintain salary equity, both on the campus and in the library. In addition to the local rate, there are often campus issues of salary equity. (Later in this chapter we cover the factors in developing job descriptions. For now, it is important to understand that a group of related tasks constitute a *position*; that is, a grouping of tasks performed by one person. Every staff member occupies a position. *Job* is a grouping of related positions. Only in the smallest academic libraries will there be a one-to-one relationship between positions and jobs. In most cases, there will be several people in a job category. Campus HR officers employ job categories to create a classification/salary system. The purpose of such plans is to group together jobs that require the same skill sets and provide similar compensation to people in a given class. Such systems can create some staff tension in large research libraries.)

One significant challenge related to the previous job categories is how much, if any, familiarity people holding a position have about academic libraries and their activities. If beginning academic librarians who have at least some classroom exposure to the academic library environment need time to gain a level of comfort in their first full-time position (see Chapter 15 for a discussion of the adjusting to the first position), how much more challenging must it be for those without that background? On occasion there are individuals holding nonlibrarian positions who initially do not see the need to understand the library environment/operations because of the belief that an organization is an organization in terms of their job responsibilities. Two areas where this type of situation may arise include development and business/financial positions. Success comes when both librarians and nonlibrarians recognize the need for both to make an effort to understand the values and commitment of everyone to achieving the library's missions and goals.

Our last factor relates to the concept of customer service. All professions discuss and value this concept. However, there are differences in just what customer service means. The beginning point for librarianship's service concept is gaining an understanding of end user demands, needs, wants, and desires. Once there is some understanding of these factors, libraries attempt to create services to effectively address those factors within their available resources. This is not always the case for some professional groups. For example, medical doctors base their service on their professional judgment of what is wrong and how to best address it, not on what the patient thinks she or he needs or wants. Often it takes some time for nonlibrarian professionals in the library to fully grasp what library customer service is and what factors are keys to providing such service.

PART-TIME STAFF

The literature of our field pays little attention to part-time library staff. We think this is unfortunate, as often the work of part-timers is critical to quality public service—just think about the many part-time employees who reshelve collections materials or handle physical processing of materials duties for the collections and their impact on quality of service.

Students

Although one is likely to encounter part-time employees in almost any job category, one common and important part-time group in academic libraries is student assistants. Student workers are a significant portion of the library staff in most academic libraries. For example, the ARL statistics for 2007–2008 (Kyrillidou and Bland, 2009) indicated that students, on an FTE basis, represented 20.7 percent of the total FTE reported as working in the ARL universities. For many libraries, quality service would be impossible without the aid of students workers. The work such individuals perform should receive the same attention and thought given to the work of full-time employees.

Employment in the library is normally a means to help pay the high cost of getting a degree; few students view such work as a test of a possible career. Classes and social activities are their top priorities. Thus, student worker motivation and supervision are larger challenges than with full- or part-time staff. Looking at the early literature about using students as employees, you probably would come away with the view that "student workers are too much trouble and not worth the effort." The focus then was on the limitations/problems of employing students. Such an emphasis at that time may have been necessary to work out the issues employing students for ongoing library activities. We believe part of the problem did and can lie in not spending enough time on pre-planning and developing true job descriptions for what the students will do. What is clear today is that academic libraries are utterly dependent on such labor.

Beyond the obvious benefit of having valuable work accomplished at a modest cost, students bring several benefits to the library. (We addressed the issue of work study funding in the chapter on students.) One benefit, in our view, is that as peers/classmates they are often viewed as more approachable than the full-time staff. This is especially true when the student body's cultural composition and that of the full-time staff is markedly different. Student employees are more likely to have a sound idea of what technologies students use and how and when they use the technologies. Such information can be of great value when planning a new service or a different approach to an old one. Yet another benefit is that students can assist full-time staff in understanding "where the students are coming from"—they relate more effectively to the primary service population. Finally, they are the pool from which to recruit individuals to our field.

Just as you want to retain full-time staff, you want to retain student workers for as long as possible. There is an obvious built-in student turnover; nevertheless, keeping the best workers for as long as possible lowers training costs as well as supervision costs. One step to take, even if it is not well implemented with the full-time staff, is to create student work teams. As noted previously, Millennials are team-oriented and need little assistance fitting into team duties and responsibilities. Consider building teams around a set of duties rather than scheduled work times. In the past, a duties approach was difficult at best and often impossible. With constant "texting" on cell phones, monitoring and updating Facebook profiles, checking e-mail and the like, students are "in touch" all of the time. Even a team that seldom has more than one member on duty at any time can still be effective in today's technological environment.

Teams need leaders, and this provides opportunities for promotion and rewards. With multiple work schedules, there may be opportunities for assistant leaders. Such a structure may also allow for the creation of a "student career ladder" with appropriate pay differentials. Regardless of what the work structure is, students should be held just as accountable for the quality of their work as full-time staff. Having different standards of accountability can and probably will lead to major morale problems and low-quality overall performance for the library.

Sound mentoring is effective in recruiting people to our field. Students tend to be open to mentoring when it focuses on issues they perceive as relevant. If for nothing more than helping them to learn appropriate work behavior and dress, this is a useful activity. We

> **Check This Out**
>
> We highly recommend you spend time reviewing Kimberly B. Sweetman's *Managing Student Assistants* (New York: Neal-Schuman, 2007). It will pay dividends in the long run regardless of how new to or "seasoned" a librarian one is. The exercises she has at the end of each chapter are particularly useful.

have only touched on a few of the benefits of using student workers. Kimberly Sweetman (2007) summed up the need for and challenges of student workers:

Although students can execute a variety of jobs, they all require a special kind of attention. Novice librarians often receive supervisory responsibility over these workers, but few have experience managing them. Likewise, seasoned professionals often find the challenge posed by this group to be daunting. (p. xiii)

STAFFING PROCESS

Selecting appropriate staff, regardless of category—full-time, part-time, and even volunteers—requires significant time, planning, and effort. Although few libraries have an HR unit, library staff do become involved in the HR process on an operational level. Because of this, we have included a short discussion of the major HR issues. During your career, you are likely to be involved from time to time in all of the issues we cover, from selection to retirement. Understanding some of the key points of the recruitment and selection process is useful when you are looking for a job as well as when you are asked to serve on a search committee. When you become a supervisor, you will need to have a sense of what goes into a job description, how to orient and train new people, and how to handle the inevitable performance appraisal process.

HR departments expect and require library staff involvement, to some degree, in a number of key steps in the staffing process. Those steps are some variation of the following:

- Determining needs/succession planning
- Job design
- Recruitment (covered in more detail in Chapter 15)
- Selection (covered in more detail in Chapter 15)
- Orientation and training
- Evaluation
- Coaching and discipline
- Resignation and termination

Determining staffing needs is usually the responsibility of senior managers and consists of two lists. One is a wish list of positions that would be wonderful to have, if only funding were available; it is often a long list and it is a special occasion when a new FTE is finally funded. The second, and shorter, list covers expected vacancies—retirements, promotions, and resignations. It is up to the library to keep HR informed of expected vacancies. Knowing in advance what positions may become vacant and the timing may assist HR in doing some combination recruiting for several units, which should stretch limited advertising dollars and generate a stronger pool of candidates.

The job design/description (JD) is the foundation for getting the best and brightest people. The U.S. Department of Labor suggests a process for developing job descriptions and deciding on the proper selection of instruments. The suggested process starts with the library's organizational goals that a particular job is to assist in fulfilling. (Note: every staff member holds a separate "position"; however, several people may hold the same "job," such as document delivery assistant.) Designing a job requires answering questions such as "What activities are necessary to accomplish organizational goals?" Answering this apparently simple question is usually more complex than a person might expect. It requires detailed information in order to be useful. The goal is to be as comprehensive as possible in listing the tasks. Being too brief or broad only creates more work later in the process. For example, a response for a circulation service point should be more than "check out materials." It should cover all aspects of the work, such as checking the user's borrowing status, providing answers to questions about item availability or items the person could not locate, and deactivating security tags. Such detail is essential for developing sound job descriptions as it helps you identify the necessary skills and knowledge to successfully perform the work.

Another step is establishing job success criteria (JSC). JSC are the keys to selecting the right person for the right position. This is also the most difficult and subjective of the steps in the model. While the goal of the process is simple to state—What distinguishes successful from unsuccessful performance in the position?—it is difficult to carry out. What constitutes success will vary from library to library and from time to time as the work changes. For example, being courteous to users is always important, but what if a person is courteous while providing incorrect information? What about a person who is great with users but is unwilling or unable to work well with other staff members? Thinking through the JSC for a job makes it much easier to select the right person for the position and allows one to develop the best questions to ask the candidates—those that most accurately reflect the skills, knowledge and service attitude needed for success.

Job specifications (JS) are the skills, traits, knowledge, and experience that, when combined, results in successful performance. The JS are what one sees in job descriptions and advertisements, such as educational background or degree required, years of experience, and a list of the specific skills sought. From a legal point of view, these items must be BFOQ (bona fide occupational qualifications). Merely saying they are will not satisfy a court if you are challenged. You might be able to prove that they are the skills, knowledge, and experience a person ought to possess to succeed. You might like to have someone with a high school diploma, but can you prove that it is *essential* to succeed in the work? If you cannot, do not make it a requirement; make it "desirable."

Having completed these steps, you can decide what "instruments" you should use to assist in deciding which applicants to call in for an interview. Some instruments are ones that you know well—application forms, names of references, and letters of interest. Others that are less common are various tests of basic required skills, such as a certain level of error-free keyboarding. Library skills tests such as alphabetizing or putting call numbers in order are handled by the library. Whatever instruments you select, you must have a clear link back to the JSC and JS in the event that you are challenged in court.

RETENTION, DIVERSITY, TRAINING, AND STAFF DEVELOPMENT

Once a person has been selected and has accepted the position, creating a sound orientation program is critical for the new person as well as the library. Sometimes people forget that the first few days on the job set a pattern for the new person that can be either negative or positive. These first few days are critical to fitting in, retention, and the person's views about the library as well as its long-term training/development program. A well-thought-out orientation, including the training required for the position, will make it more likely that the person will stay on. Too often the first days focus only on the activities of the position; this is natural, as in most cases the position has been vacant for several months or more and work has stacked up. Falling into this trap is likely to cause a higher turnover rate than anyone would like.

Generally, the first week should be equally divided between position training and learning about the library and its parent organization. For most people, the first days on a new job are stressful and confusing. The common practice of taking new people around to meet everyone, assuming there are more than a dozen people to meet, leaves them with a blur of faces, a few names (rarely connected to the right faces), and a vague sense of what others do. Breaking the process up over several days gives new people a better chance to absorb information and make meaningful connections. Starting with the "home" unit and working out through units that feed into and receive output from the "home" unit allows them to gain a sense of where their position fits in the scheme of things and how it is important to library operations. After this, one can move on to other units to allow them to gain an overall picture of operations. Linking a new person to someone at her or his level in the workgroup (a mentor) provides a personal connection for clarification or for questions that the person may be afraid to ask the supervisor, lest she or he be thought of as silly. It also helps the mentors by giving them recognition and the motivation to check over those points that are often taken for granted. One institution with a well-thought-out orientation program is the University of Washington (www.washington.edu/admin/hr/roles/newee/index.html).

Retention

A major concern for today's organizations is retaining their best people. Nora Spinks (2005) offered some interesting thoughts about generational differences and impacts on retention:

> If you were a child in the 50s (a Boomer), you saw that working hard was a strategy that led to success. Loyalty was rewarded with long-term employment through to retirement. However, if you were a child in the 70s or 80s (a Nexus), you saw adults working hard and getting laid off, downsized or reengineered out of a job anyway. Employment tenure was out of your control, employers offered you a job as long as they felt you were of value, then let you go. (p. 11)

For many employers, their lack of loyalty to long-term staff is coming back to haunt them. "Why should I have any loyalty to the organization if it has none for me?" is a question in the minds of many workers today. For many of them, all it takes is a hint of staffing changes—real or imagined—or something perceived to be a threat and people start looking for other employment and in many cases actually leaving. They have experienced or heard of organizations that announce staff reductions and say in effect to the staff, "We don't need you but fully expect you to give a 100 percent work effort until the day you are terminated." When that happens, the outcome is what one would expect: performance decline and people leaving as quickly as possible. Although the pattern is primarily seen in for-profit organizations, staff reductions in force (RIFs) or furloughs (temporary leave without pay) are not unheard of in libraries.

Another retention factor that is just gaining the attention of researchers is "new-job regrets." This is something that about 25 percent of newly hired people experience (Gardner, 2007). All too often the regrets arise from the employer overselling the nature of the position or some other aspect of the environment. If one properly follows the steps we outlined previously regarding job descriptions and the individual had a copy of the job description prior to accepting the offer, there should be few problems related to the nature of the work. Where an employer may unknowingly oversell is when there is a critical need to fill the position and the recruiter falls into the trap of making the institution, opportunities, benefits, and so forth as better than they actually are. In the long run, overselling or misrepresenting the position makes for very unhappy people—both the new hire and yourself. When the remorse is strong, the probability that the person will quit is extremely high.

Maria Bagshaw (2006) suggested some ways to help with the retention of student workers in particular:

> Of course, more money would be nice. But we are not permitted to give our student workers raises—they receive the minimum wage. So, we use little things to let them know they are important to us: a candy bowl for finals week, or a pizza party at the end of the year.
>
> Above all, treat your student workers like the adults they are. Take their education as seriously as they do. In return, they will offer great service with minimal professional staff input and financial resources. (p. 44)

Retention of student w orkers is just as important as retaining any other category of library employee. A supervisor may have a number of applicants at the beginning of the academic year, but finding students becomes more difficult as the year progresses. Finding the right mix of Bagshaw's "little things" throughout the year, not just during finals or end of year celebrations, is one element in long-term student retention.

Diversity

A complex staffing issue is the concept of diversity. Many, if not most, of today's academic institutions strive for diversity in both the student body and in the staff (faculty included). Just what "diversity" means in a particular institution may be somewhat vague—the individual, contextual (defined through societal constructs), or both. As Patricia Kreitz (2008) wrote about institutional diversity:

> Single-threaded diversity solutions such as focusing only on recruitment, or single-approach management techniques, such as requiring every employee to take diversity training, do not create lasting change. Implementing the changes needed to build and sustain diversity requires commitment, strategy, communication, and concrete changes in organizational structure and processes. (p. 101)

Diversity is a complex topic and has been defined in a number of ways. Some writers and organizations take a narrow view, relating it mainly to racial or sexual discrimination, but how an organization addresses diversity issues can impact staff relations and retention efforts.

Hofstede (1997), in writing about culture and organizations, indicated why it is a complex issue:

> Every person carries within him or herself patterns of thinking, feeling, and potential acting which were learned throughout their lifetime.... As soon as certain patterns...have established themselves...he must unlearn these...and unlearning is more difficult than learning for the first time. (p. 4)

Check This Out

A book that will help any manager/supervisor become a more effective leader is *Academic Librarians as Emotionally Intelligent Leaders* by Peter Hernon, Joan Giesecke, and Camila A. Alire (Westport, CT: Libraries Unlimited, 2008).

Check These Out

Hofstede provides a readable and informative introduction to cultural diversity in his work *Cultures and Organizations: Software of the Mind* (New York: McGraw-Hill, 2005) and also on his website: www.geert-hofstede.com.

By drawing attention to the way in which beliefs are formed and the crucial issue of "unlearning," it becomes easier to understand why the subject is so complex and sensitive. The range of issues that are influenced by diversity are easier to identify when one employs Hofstede's (1997) method, which distinguishes between the several layers of culture that people carry within them as "mental programming." They are the following:

- A national level according to one's country
- A regional and/or ethnic and/or religious and/or linguistic affiliation level
- A gender level
- A generation level
- A social class level
- For those who are employed, an organizational or corporate level (p. 10)

The Government Accountability Office (2005) issued a report that identified nine "best practices" regarding diversity:

- Top leadership commitment—a vision of diversity demonstrated and communicated throughout an organization by top-level management
- Diversity as part of an organization's strategic plan—a diversity strategy and plan that are developed and aligned with the organization's strategic plan
- Diversity linked to performance—the understanding that a more diverse and inclusive environment can yield greater productivity and help improve individual and organizational performance
- Measurement—a set of quantitative and qualitative measures of the impact of various aspects of an overall diversity program
- Accountability—the means to ensure that leaders are responsible for diversity by linking their performance assessment and compensation to the progress of diversity initiatives
- Succession planning—an ongoing, strategic process for identifying and developing a diverse pool of talent for an organization's potential future leaders
- Recruitment—the process of attracting a supply of qualified, diverse applicants for employment
- Employee involvement—the contribution of employees in driving diversity throughout an organization
- Diversity training—organizational effort to inform and educate management and staff about diversity (p. 4)

Managers have the responsibility to create an organizational culture that values diversity in all of its manifestations and ensures that everyone has and shows respect for the views and experiences of others. Good practices based on sound policies ensure that diversity brings benefits to the library. The key to success is to make flexibility a central component that will both support and retain staff and users.

Normally the organization will have a vision statement concerning diversity written in operational terms that guides strategic planning. In addition it should have committed funding for implementing the policies that will have been derived from the planning process. Goals will be monitored at the organizational level, such as by monitoring the outcomes of recruitment and promotion programs.

One point that may be overlooked in the planning process is the state of readiness of the library to engage in a comprehensive diversity initiative. Royse, Conner, and Miller (2006) discussed the design, methodology, and outcomes of a climate assessment survey at the University of Tennessee (UT) Libraries.

> **Try This**
>
> Think about the ways that society is changing; for example, the nuclear family is not the norm. There are female heads of households, unmarried couples, dual-income families, same-sex partners, and single parents who have children at school. Add to the list and consider how each of these affects both staff and users.

This provided the UT Libraries with benchmarks for measuring the progress and success of its diversity programs. The authors encouraged other institutions undergoing similar diversity studies to share their results, noting, "Libraries who undertake diversity climate assessments need to share their efforts with the profession, for it is critical that we learn from each other as we chart courses for diversity in our libraries" (p. 44).

By working within the organizational framework, and in consultation with the staff and users, one can develop appropriate policies as well as monitor progress within the library. The important factor is to embed them into the organizational plan and ensure their implementation.

If a diversity plan is being developed from scratch, the American Library Association provides examples of plans from large and small libraries that may be consulted (www.ala.org/

> **Check This Out**
>
> A comprehensive title on diversity in the workplace is Barbara I. Dewey and Loretta Parham's *Achieving Diversity: A How-To-Do-It Manual for Librarians* (New York: Neal-Schuman, 2006).

ala/aboutala/offices/diversity/diversityplanning.cfm). Plans are not only essential for setting policies and practices but also provide the benchmarks against which progress is monitored.

Training and Staff Development

One key method for gaining and retaining staff "loyalty" is to have programs in place that give ample opportunities for staff to grow and develop. Without a doubt, this will help with the long-term retention of the best and brightest people. You have two basic training/development areas to consider—specific job-related skills and career development competencies and opportunities.

We know that libraries face a rapidly changing technological environment. Keeping staff current with the changes related to their activities is a major challenge, especially when budgets are static. It is also crystal clear that failing to maintain staff skills will result in users receiving poorer service, which in turn leads to user dissatisfaction. Technology carries with it two financial challenges—acquiring and upgrading requisite technology and funding staff training.

Certainly training and development goes beyond technological issues. Other major areas include training for individuals moving into supervisory positions and keeping staff up to date on changing professional standards. In technical services, for example, staying current with standards is critical, and too often limited travel funds for staff leads to long-term performance problems for both the staff and the library.

Professional associations can and do provide excellent training opportunities. Annual conventions often have workshops and other continuing education programs as part of their overall program. Unfortunately, there are few such organizational opportunities for support staff. This seems to be changing, at least with the ALA, where the annual conference has started to include a "conference within a conference" for support staff. (The primary reason is that there is limited financial assistance for support staff travel. In addition, their salaries are substantially lower, making it difficult for many of them to pay for such opportunities on their own. Thus, groups such as COLT have difficulty attracting enough people to a workshop to make the effort worthwhile.) As more educational institutions and professional bodies extend the range of distance education programs, training opportunities are increasing for support staff, particularly via "webinars" and video conferencing. Notable examples of these training opportunities are the SirsiDynix Institutes (www.sirsidynixinstitute.com), offerings from the College of DuPage's "Library Learning Network," including the "Soaring to Excellence" series (www.dupagepress.com/library_learning_network), or the programs available through the Online Computer Library Center's WebJunction (www.webjunction.org).

In addition to funding struggles, libraries face the problem of limited staffing, at least in most libraries. When staff is limited, it becomes difficult to have employees away at training programs for any length of time. Some jurisdictions are so shortsighted that they refuse to give time off to attend training programs even when the staff member is willing to pay for the program—shortsighted because in time the staff member's services become less and less effective.

Singer and Goodrich (2006) outlined five critical factors for retaining and motivating library staff. The following are principles for a supervisor to exemplify to help employees perform as well:

- Focus: employees know what they need to do and what is expected of them.
- Involvement: people support most what they help to create.
- Development: opportunities for learning and growth are encouraged.
- Gratitude: recognition of good performance (formal and informal).
- Accountability: employees are responsible for their performance or lack thereof. (p. 62)

PERFORMANCE APPRAISAL

Singer and Goodrich's fifth point regarding accountability directly links to performance appraisal. Performance assessment takes two forms: ongoing daily review with occasional corrective action and an annual overall assessment. After all, "Employees have a right to know what their managers expect from them, and they're entitled to learn how to meet those expectations" (Armstrong and Mitchell, 2008, p. 63).

In terms of corrective action, you should discuss poor performance as situations arise. Trying to avoid unpleasant interactions regarding performance and letting problems "slide" only hurts everyone in the long-run. Being told that something was/is amiss during the annual performance review when it is too late to take corrective action causes anger, frustration, and poorer performance down the road. Furthermore, other employees will notice the lack of any corrective action and they are likely to conclude that you don't really care about quality performance. When this happens, they are likely to let their work performance slide as well. By the time this happens, you face a highly complex situation that will be difficult to resolve. Finally, service to users also suffers, and this in turn can lead to a serious lack of user support.

Some steps to follow when corrective action is necessary can help make the process as effective as possible. Start by stating the purpose of the session. Even if the situation has the potential for confrontation, speak calmly. Plan on letting the employee talk as much as possible. *Listening* is the key to having a successful session. Too often, there is a tendency to start planning one's response rather than listening and trying to *hear* what the person is saying. Silence, even a long one, although uncomfortable, serves a good purpose—it lets both parties think about what is taking place. Setting a time limit for the session can defeat the purpose of the session; it may take time to get to the central issue(s). Expect the employee to be unhappy, upset, and probably argumentative, and prepare for the possibility that she/he may engage in a verbal attack. It is important not to take the attack very personally. Above all do *not* respond in kind. Total resolution is not the only indication of a successful session. Sometimes it takes a series of sessions to reach a complete resolution. Try to end the session on a positive note and, if appropriate, schedule a follow-up session.

DISCIPLINE AND TERMINATION

Regardless of whether or not the assessment is positive or negative of an employee's performance, the goal is to be as consistent as possible in the evaluations. Standards should not shift from one week to the next or, worse, vary from one employee to another. Remember, the goal should be on outcomes rather than on the appraisal process (as long as the process does not cause trouble or problems for others). In addition, one should not hold a new employee as closely accountable for an error as an older, more experienced person. This does *not* mean ignoring the newcomer's problem. A person lacking the skill to do a task needs additional training rather than criticism. If the training does not work, then other adjustments will be necessary, including the difficult but occasionally necessary step of termination.

Something to consider before taking corrective steps is to think about personal biases that might color one's judgment of people and their performance. If the matter is serious, look at prior annual appraisals before moving ahead. When it is clear something should be done, think about how soon the next appraisal will be and what is needed to show improvement (keeping in mind any and all personal biases) and then begin the counseling process. This may require further serious steps, especially if a person has a negative review for two years in succession. It is always wise to collaborate with or ask for guidance from HR in these situations.

Annual performance reviews are something that most people endure and almost never look forward to, much less enjoy. Neither the givers nor the recipients have great faith in the process or that much good will come out of the ordeal. Probably the biggest challenge, and where the difficulty lies, is in the dual nature of the review process. Although most HR departments attempt to keep it to a single purpose, performance enhancement, the reality is that there is sometimes an unofficial but real link to salary increases. The dual purpose is well documented in the literature but most clearly articulated by Saul Gellerman (1976). He makes the point that essentially the single process attempts to handle behavioral issues (work performance) and administrative issues (compensation and occasional promotions). He further states that the two purposes are almost diametrically opposed in character. To be effective in improving performance, the process should be open and candid. From an administrative perspective it should be closed and secretive. Trying to accomplish both in a single process is a challenge. Almost every employee believes the salary aspect is the dominant factor.

In spite of one's best efforts, there will be times when disciplinary action must take place. Needless to say, such action follows only after a number of counseling sessions have failed to resolve the issue. Progressive discipline is critical before any move is made toward termination. Giving an employee a chance through agreed-on goals for improvement, including a time line, demonstrates the supervisor/library's willingness to work with an employee.

What the process consists of is a series of steps that become progressively stricter and can end with termination. Although institutions employ their own stages of progressive discipline, the stages generally include the following: oral warning (one or more depending on the institution's procedure), counseling sessions (again one or more), formal reprimand (a copy of the reprimand is placed in the individual's personnel file), suspension with or without pay (the time frame varies), and, finally, release/termination. Most of the time, the process never reaches the termination stage, as the parties resolve the issue earlier. The sooner one address performance issues, the less likely it is one will have to go through the stress of a formal grievance procedure.

KEY POINTS TO REMEMBER

- Basics of library personnel management are the same for all types of libraries, with only a few but significant variations.
- Academic library staff are increasingly expected to fulfill a variety of roles, and libraries are seeking generic skill sets in order to maintain the greatest possible flexibility in job assignments.
- Faculty status for librarians is a long-standing issue and is a desired goal at many academic libraries; however, many do not have such status.
- Librarians at libraries with faculty status programs face the challenge of performing well as a librarian and demonstrating strong research/scholarship skills.
- Support staff members are increasingly being asked to assume duties that were previously librarians' responsibilities as workloads increase and economic times are difficult. Developing and maintaining solid working relationships between support and professional staff leads to quality service.
- Student workers constitute as much as one-fifth of the academic library workforce in most libraries. They may be a challenge to supervise and motivate at times, but they bring a number of benefits that more than offset the challenges.
- Academic library staffing patterns today reflect the diversity of U.S. society, based on gender, cultural background, and generational differences, for example, which creates some interesting issues for managers/supervisors and the staff in general.
- Understanding the staffing process, especially the planning and job description stages will make the first supervisory experiences less daunting.

REFERENCES

American Library Association Allied Professional Association. 2005. Library support staff certification program. Available: www.ala-apa.org/lsscp/lsscp.html (accessed March 21, 2010).

American Library Association Support Staff Interests Roundtable. 1999. Task force on career ladders. Available: www.ala.org/ala/mgrps/rts/lssirt/lssirtstratplan/taskforcereports/career.pdf (accessed April 7, 2010).

American Library Association Support Staff Interests Roundtable. 2000. Task force on access to continuing education and training opportunities. Available: www.ala.org/ala/educationcareers/education/3rdcongressonpro/ce_trainingops.pdf (accessed April 7, 2010).

Applegate, Rachel. 2008. Whose decline? Which academic libraries are "deserted" in terms of reference transactions? *Reference & User Services Quarterly* 48, 2: 176–189.

Armstrong, Sharon, and Barbara Mitchell. 2008. *The essential HR handbook*. Franklin Lakes, NJ: Career Press.

Bagshaw, Maria C. 2006. Keep your student workers. *Library Journal* 131, no. 19: 44.

Baughman, M. Sue. 2008. Assessment of teams and teamwork in the University of Maryland Libraries. *portal: Libraries and the Academy* 8, no. 3: 293–312.

Bernstein, Alan. 2009. Academic librarians and faculty status: Mountain, molehill or mesa? *Georgia Library Quarterly* 46, no. 2: 12–15.

Bolger, Dorita. F., and Erin T. Smith. 2006. Faculty status and rank at liberal arts colleges: An investigation into the correlation among faculty status, professional rights and responsibilities, and overall institutional quality. *College & Research Libraries* 67, no. 3: 217–229.

Bolin, Mary K. 2008a. Librarian status at US research universities: Extending the typology. *Journal of Academic Librarianship* 34, no. 5: 416–424.

———. 2008b. A typology of librarian status at land grant universities. *Journal of Academic Librarianship* 34, no. 3: 220–230.

Bryan, Jacalyn E. 2007. The question of faculty status for academic librarians. *Library Review* 56, no. 9: 781–787.

Christianson, Elin. 1973. *Paraprofessional and nonprofessional staff in special libraries*. New York: Special Library Association.

Defa, Dennis R. 2008. Human resource administration in the academic library. *Library Administration & Management* 22, no. 3: 138–141, 154.

Gardner, Marilyn. 2007. New-job regrets: Should you go or stay? *Arizona Daily Sun*, August 12, pp. D1, D4.

Gellerman, Saul. 1976. *Management of human resources*. New York: Holt Rinehart.

Ghouse, Nikhat, and Jennifer Church-Duran. 2008. And mentoring for all: The KU Libraries' experience. *portal: Libraries and the Academy* 8, no. 4: 373–386.

Government Accountability Office. 2005. Diversity management: Expert-identified leading practices and agency examples. GAO-05-90. Available: www.gao.gov/new.items/d0590.pdf (accessed April 7, 2010).

Hofstede, Geert. 1997. *Cultures and organizations: Software of the mind*. New York: McGraw-Hill.

Kaufman, Paula T. 1992. Professional diversity in libraries. *Library Trends* 41, no. 2: 214–230.

Kennan, Mary Anne, Patricia Willard, Concepción S. Wilson, and Fletcher Cole. 2007. Australian and US academic library jobs: A comparison. *Australian Academic & Research Libraries* 38, no. 2: 111–128.

Kreitz, Patricia A. 2008. Best practices for managing organizational diversity. *Journal of Academic Librarianship* 34, no. 2: 101–120.

Kyrillidou, Martha, and Les Bland. 2009. *ARL statistics 2007–2008*. Washington, DC: Association of Research Libraries. Available: www.arl.org/bm~doc/arlstat08.pdf (accessed April 7, 2010).

Lane, Liz A., and Barbara Stewart. 1998. The evolution of technical services to serve the digital library. In *Recreating the academic library: Breaking virtual ground*, ed. Cheryl LaGuardia, 151–168. New York: Neal-Schuman.

Murray-Rust, Catherine. 2005. Should librarians get tenure? Yes, it's critical to their jobs. *Chronicle of Higher Education*, September 30, p. B10.

Royse, Molly, Tiffani Conner, and Tamara Miller. 2006. Charting a course for diversity: An experience in climate assessment. *portal: Libraries and the Academy* 6, no. 1 (January): 23–45.

Singer, Paula, and Jeanne Goodrich. 2006. Retaining and motivating high performing employees. *Public Libraries* 45, no. 1: 58–63.

Spinks, Nora. 2005. Talking about my generation. *Canadian Healthcare Manager* 12, no. 7: 11–13.

Sweetman, Kimberly. 2007. *Managing student assistants*. New York: Neal-Schuman.

LAUNCHING PAD

Alsop, Justine, and Karen Bordonaro. 2007. Multiple roles of academic librarians. *Electronic Journal of Academic and Special Librarianship* 8, no. 1: 1. Available: southernlibrarianship.icaap.org/content/v08n01/alsop_j01.htm (accessed April 7, 2010).

Applegate, Rachel. 2007. Charting academic library staffing: Data from national surveys. *College & Research Libraries* 68, no.1: 59–68.

Baldwin, David A., and Daniel C. Barkley. 2007. *Complete guide for supervisors of student employees in today's academic libraries*. Westport, CT: Libraries Unlimited.

Cary, Shannon. 2001. Faculty rank, status, and tenure for librarians: Current trends. *College & Research Libraries News* 62, no. 5: 510–511, 520.

Crump, Michele, Carol Drum, and Colleen Seale. 2008. Establishing a pre-tenure review program in an academic library. *Library Administration & Management* 22, no. 1: 31–36.

Dewey, Barbara, and Jillian Keally. 2008. Recruiting for diversity: Strategies for twenty-first century research librarianship. *Library Hi Tech* 26, no. 4: 622–629.

Garner, June, Karen Davidson, and Becky Schwartzkopf. 2009. Images of academic librarians: How tenure-track librarians portray themselves in the promotion and tenure process. *The Serials Librarian* 56, no. 1–4: 203–208.

Gray-Little, Bernadette. 2009. Diversity in research universities. *Research Library Issues* 263: 1–9. Available: www.arl.org/bm~doc/rli-263-diversity.pdf (accessed April 7, 2010).

Hammill, Greg. 2005. Mixing and managing four generations of employees. *FDU Magazine* 12, no. 2. Available: www.fdu.edu/newspubs/magazine/05ws/generations.htm (accessed April 7, 2010).

Hill, Janet Swan. 2007. Technical services and tenure: Impediments and strategies. *Cataloging & Classification Quarterly* 44, nos. 3/4: 151–178.

Hoggan, Danielle Bodrero. 2003. Faculty status for librarians in higher education. *portal: Libraries and the Academy* 3, no. 3: 431–445.

Jennerich, Elaine Z. 2006. The long-term view of library staff development. *College & Research Libraries News* 67, no. 10: 612–614.

Kemp, Jane. 2006. Isn't being a librarian enough? Librarians as classroom teachers. *College & Undergraduate Libraries* 13, no. 3: 3–23.

Kendall, Frances E. 1994. Creating a multicultural environment in the library. In *Cultural diversity in libraries*, eds. Donald E. Riggs and Patricia A. Tarin, 76–91. New York: Neal-Schuman.

Kisby, Cynthia M., and Suzanne E. Holler. 2009 Formalizing staff development from inception to implementation at University of Central Florida Libraries. In *An introduction to staff development in academic libraries*, ed. Elizabeth Connor, 54–76. New York: Routledge.

Lemery, Linda D. 2008. Student assistant management: Using an evaluation rubric. *College & Undergraduate Libraries* 15, no. 4: 451–462.

Leonhardt, Thomas W. 2005. Holistic librarianship. *Technicalities* 25, no. 3: 1, 13–14.

Lowe, Sidney, and Susie Skarl. 2009. Talkin' 'bout my generation. *College & Research Libraries News* 70, no. 7: 400–403.

Lubans Jr., John. 2006. Coaching for results. *Library Administration & Management* 20, no. 2: 86–89.

Matheson, Heather. 2007. Promoting (for) change: New academic librarians in managerial roles. *Feliciter* 53, no. 2: 70–72.

Nixon, Judith M. 2008. Growing your own leaders: Succession planning in libraries. *Journal of Business & Finance Librarianship* 13, no. 3: 249–260.

Rumble, Juliet, and Bonnie MacEwan. 2008. The UCLA senior fellows program. *Journal of Business & Finance Librarianship* 13, no. 3: 271–286.

Saponaro, Maggie Z., M. Sue Baughman, and Jennifer Kinniff. 2009. You came for the snacks, but what have you learned? Evaluation of a staff learning program at the University of Maryland Libraries. In *An introduction to staff development in academic libraries*, ed. Elizabeth Connor, 201–219. New York: Routledge.

Walter, Scott. 2008. Librarians as teachers: A qualitative inquiry into professional identity. *College & Research Libraries* 69, no. 1: 51–71.

Chapter 14

Current Themes and Issues

Understanding organizational culture is a necessary first step in thinking about organizational change, and in reshaping organizations for effectiveness and organization success.

—Carol Shepstone and Lyn Currie (2008)

The Texas A&M University Libraries experience provides evidence that the implementation of an organized, cohesive marketing strategy can have a positive effect on the promotion of library services.

—Karen I. MacDonald, Wyoma vanDuinkerken, and Jane Stephens (2008)

In writing about the academy and academic libraries, Elizabeth Wood, Rush Miller, and Amy Knapp (2007) wrote:

> Academic libraries are in trouble too. They have been edged out of the top spot as the "go-to" place for virtually all aspiring researchers by the delicious (if deceptive) convenience and immediacy of the Web. Worse yet, some funding entities now view academic libraries more as bottomless pits than as what economists call a "self-evident good." (p. 3)

This quotation notes some of the many challenges confronting today's academic libraries, many of which are more significant than in the past. Elizabeth Hallmark, Laura Schwartz, and Loriene Roy (2007) asked some questions that further highlight the challenges: "Are today's academic libraries poised to serve as essential centers of campus activities? Will they be relegated to the background of campus life? Will libraries be, at best, ignored as collateral support services? What tools are available to help academic libraries reposition themselves to serve as new social commons?" (p. 92). Perhaps Lyman Ross and Pongracz Sennyey (2008) summed up the present academic library environment most succinctly when they wrote:

> The Internet has made a significant shift in the environment in which libraries find themselves and is making our professional assumptions seem as foreign as a medieval manuscript in chains. . . . This fact diminishes the value of local collections and services. Libraries are no longer islands of information, but one among many nodes through which information flows to the users. (p. 147)

When reviewing the recent (2005–2010) professional literature relating to academic libraries, a person might reasonably develop a list of three or four very broad categories of issues or themes about what libraries must address now and in the future. Undoubtedly, different people would have different labels for the broad groupings; however, it is likely that the topics under the headings would have a high degree of similarity. Any such list probably would identify, in some manner, the themes covered in Association of College and Research Libraries' (ACRL) *Environmental Scan—2007* (Association of College and Research Libraries, Research Committee, 2008). In our case, we have identified four broad themes/issues: change, communication, governance, and collaboration. Within those themes we will discuss issues that are and will influence what and how academic librarians perform their duties.

CHANGE

People

One truth about today's organizational environment is that change is ubiquitous and constant. Another truth is that successful organizations are those that address change head on in a proactive manner. Monitoring the operating environment is a key to anticipating what changes may surface and allows the opportunity to think about what organizational adjustments might be necessary. There are times when the organization faces a situation that calls for innovative/creative ideas that cause a sharp break with the past. (This is where we see academic libraries in today's digital world.) Libraries should foster a work environment that is accepting of change and should also create an atmosphere that promotes and encourages innovation and creative thinking.

Organizational change takes place across a continuum from incremental to radical. "New orders" (radical) change in an organization's environment, such as Google, and call for just as radical change(s) in the organization. On the other hand, every day there are small incremental changes occurring as the external and internal environments change. Staff members deal with change on a daily basis and without realizing they are doing so. The vast majority of the changes are so small as to be unnoticeable. It is change beyond the midpoint that creates the challenge.

Leslie Szamosi and Linda Duxbury (2002) explored the continuum of change and defined radical change as something that:

- interrupts the status quo;
- happens quickly or abruptly;
- is fundamental and all encompassing; and
- brings something that is dramatically different than what used to be. (p. 186)

Clearly such change does not happen often but obviously challenges the skills of the library staff. Most changes are at a lesser level. However, even at the incremental stage staff may need support during the change process. Some examples of incremental change are the resignation and hiring of a replacement staff member, an adjustment in the work schedule, a shift in the timing of work activities, and who one reports to. Such changes are natural and as important to organizational success as larger scale changes and require thought and attention to make them not appear as "a change" to the staff.

Something to Ponder

What are some of the change areas in technology, structure, and strategy for information services? Thinking about your current or recent work experience, what forces of change did you observe?

Beyond the character of change (incremental to radical), one can fit almost all organizational change into one of four broad categories: people, technology, structure, and strategy. Some changes may represent a single type while others are combinations; the more categories in a change situation, the more complex the change process becomes. A few examples of the areas where "people change" occurs are skills, activities/ performance, attitudes, perceptions, and, of course, replacement (transfer, promotion, resignation, retirement, etc.).

Looking at the total body of change literature shows it to be dominated by discussions of planned and emergent change (rate of occurrence). However, it is in the area of planned and emergent change where change management models were developed, such as Lewin's (1951) classic model—unfreezing, changing, and freezing. No one disagrees that planned change is desirable or possible using his model; however, some important limits do exist on the models' utility.

Unfreezing is the process of creating a readiness to acquire or learn new behaviors. This means assisting staff in recognizing the ineffectiveness of the current behavior in terms of the area of the planned change. It also means pointing out how the change will be more effective. Unfreezing staff may be very time-consuming, and without gaining their active participation, it is very, very difficult. Not only do people need to adjust but in many cases so does the organizational culture.

Changing is the period when staff begin to work with the new behavior pattern. There will be a testing period while they make their assessment of the new pattern. This period is when staff may begin to slip back into the old pattern. Staff may need more support than normal in order to encourage people to make the adjustments.

Refreezing takes place when the staff internalizes the new pattern and it becomes part of the organizational culture. Rewards for implementing the new pattern are a key factor in achieving refreezing.

John Kotter (1990) expanded Lewin's three-phase model by breaking each one down into smaller steps/activities. During the unfreezing process he suggested managers should establish a sense of urgency, create a "guiding" coalition, develop a vision and strategy for the change, and finally communicate the vision and strategy. His subset for the change phase is: empower a broad base for action, identify/create some short-term "wins" for people, and consolidate gains (don't declare victory too soon). The only difference for the freezing stage is that Kotter makes the point that it may take years before the change(s) are anchored in the staff and become a part of the organizational culture.

> **Something to Ponder**
> Think about successful and unsuccessful change(s) you have experienced in an organization. What factors can you identify that lead to either the success or failure? Were there elements of the change models employed by the manager(s)?

John P. Kotter and Leonard A. Schlesinger (1979) provided four realistic suggestions for managing resistance to change. In fact, the four points are good management tools for almost any purpose:

1. Education plus communication
2. Participation plus involvement
3. Facilitation plus support
4. Negotiation and agreement

If implemented, these points allow access to information that only the staff may have, commitment to a change they helped design, and acceptance of compromises that are necessary into which they had input.

Institutional

Few, if any, academic librarians doubt the need for major change within the field. In 2008, the *Harvard Business Review*'s cover story (Gottfredson, Schaubert, and Saenz,

2008) addressed how to assess the organization regarding areas of potential concern or in need of change. Although the authors' focus was on the profit sector, almost all of the points raised can apply to academic libraries. The points in the following are from the article; however, the text regarding the points is ours.

Analyzing costs and prices has always been important in terms of library performance. However, by analyzing your cost curve(s) and comparing the curve(s) with our peer group often identifies areas that may require more attention. Also, as noted in Chapter 12, expanding or starting new services will probably require reallocating existing resources, especially in weak economic circumstances. The analysis may illuminate activities that are very costly in relation to their outputs and are thus prime areas to consider for making significant changes.

Another key consideration is to determine one's *market share* (relative market share, RMS). As noted in many places in the text, academic libraries face major competition for the first time when it comes to delivering information. Knowing costs and RMS helps narrow the focus for performance improvement. For example, what are the costs and market share for reference and online reserve services? How can the cost be reduced and market share improved? Two important questions to ponder are whether we should even try to improve performance or even maintain the activity and whether we have resources to make such improvements if it is desirable.

Try This

Think about a library you know reasonably well. What are the competitors for academic library reference and online reserve services? What are the typical cost factors? What options may exist for alternative delivery systems?

A third principle is to assess the *evolving market and users*. Librarians know both are changing rapidly, but do we understand the drivers of change beyond "technology?" Gaining an understanding of the drivers of change will help in anticipating potential shifts that may impact performance, costs, and market share.

Complexity of services and structure are often barriers to making timely adjustments to changing circumstances. Both public and technical services have potential areas where simplification will improve service. Another area of concern is how complex the existing decision-making process is. If the process is too drawn out, opportunities that had existed may have disappeared.

Gottfredson, Schaubert, and Saenz (2008) concluded their article by stating, "A diagnostic template such as the one we've described here is powerful not because it contains any single new insight but because it covers the ground a management team needs to cover. By answering the questions we've provided, you can understand the gap between your current performance and your full potential" (p. 73).

Our opening quotation from Shepstone and Currie (2008) concerns understanding that organizational culture is an important component of understanding and managing organizational change. In their article they discuss the use of the concept of competing values framework (CVF; Cameron and Quinn, 2006) as a tool for assessing organizational culture, the staff's value orientation, and potential issues in implementing change. CVF is based on a vertical and horizontal axis in which the vertical axis continuum goes from "stability and control" to "flexibility and discretion" and the horizontal axis from "internal focus and integration" to "external focus and differentiation." The CVF analysis assists in assessing the organizational readiness for change and helps identify potential areas of

---

From the Authors

One of our readers, John Stemmer, contributed the following regarding change and academic libraries:

The people are changing and the organizations are changing. What is the mission of the organization? This is what the library needs to keep its eye on and then interpret how we can respond to those changes. But we need to do this in a manner that also takes into account the changing nature of the wider information environment.

We talk about digital natives and digital immigrants. While the natives may be more comfortable with screens and screen-based technologies, even the natives are not necessarily more "knowledgeable" about new technology that has come out after they grew up. Various reports have indicated that they tend to think they know more than they actually do. I wonder if this isn't especially true in the realm where they are touted as "natives."

The technology is also changing, but it is not just IT [information technology] that librarians must deal with, it is the next topic: communication. We used to know how scholarly communication would take place—journals, conferences, and books. Now? Those all still exist, but so do e-mail, blogs, webpages, wikis, and Twitter. While the state of scholarly acceptance for digital media accomplishments has been a subject of discussion for promotion and tenure, generally it has been the old standbys. Lately, I have seen some comments that indicate that perhaps blogs should be considered as part of scholarly activity for promotion and tenure processes. The library's middleman role in scholarly communication is being stressed. This is the environmental change that libraries need to be aware of and address. It is not just technology; it is what the technology does to how we are perceived. The OCLC report indicated that we are all about books. How do we explain to stakeholders what we do when there are no physical items involved?

---

resistance. Shepstone and Currie concluded, in part, "Change by its very nature requires risk-taking and letting go. . . . Implementing change is an ongoing process of discovery and it requires addressing some questions, such as, how shared is the vision, how can anchors to the past be preserved while moving to the future?" (p. 36).

COMMUNICATION

Personal

Everyone's, including the organization's, success rests, in part, on communication skills. In the workplace, working with others and delivering services to users, it is essential that meaningful, understandable, clear communication—oral, written on paper, or sent electronically—takes place.

Many of the complaints from the user community as well as the staff are the result of poor, ineffective, or nonexistent communication. Getting the right message out at the right time is essential for effective operations and quality service. What people often forget is that communication is both a complex pattern of personal behavior (influenced by each person's entire life experiences) and a two-way process (in which the receiver has as much responsibility as the sender). True communication takes place only when a person receives the identical meaning and emotion meant and felt by the person sending the message. So both sender and receiver must make the effort to verify the intended meaning and how the message has been understood. The extra time spent verifying messages results in better performance and better relations, and, in the long run, saves the service time and money.

> **Tip**
>
> Keep in mind that people from different cultures may have varying approaches to authority figures/agencies such as libraries. Some may feel it is not appropriate to question a statement made by someone who they perceive is in an "authority role."

Complicating the process is the fact that communication consists of three elements. First, there are verbal, written-on-paper, and electronic communications—it takes practice to be equally effective in all three. A second pair of elements is listening and reading. In many ways these two activities are even more difficult to master in the workplace. Third, there are the nonverbal aspects of communication. Nonverbals can often completely change the intended and/or perceived meaning of a message.

Ralph Waldo Emerson supposedly said:

> Communication is like a piece of driftwood in a sea of conflicting currents. Sometimes the shore will be littered with debris; sometimes it will be bare. The amount and direction of movement is neither aimless nor non-directional at all, but is a response to all the forces, winds and tides or current which come into play.

Academic library staff must think about both internal and external communication and the currents and tides that can become obstacles to effective communication.

Language structure also may create difficulties in communication. Most Indo-European languages employ a two-value orientation: good/bad, black/white. Yet other language families have different bases, such as the multivalue system seen in the Chinese languages. A person who is only partially conversant in another language rather than truly bilingual (especially if the second language has a different value base) will probably miss a great deal of what is meant when someone speaks or writes in that second language. In a diverse campus environment where both the staff and user community are multi-cultural and composed of several different generations, the library must take extra care in drafting messages, memos, and instructions.

If everyone in the library is careful to use job-related terms in a consistent manner, then true communication can take place. Without this consistency, the staff develops individualized meanings for words, and things become hazy. One example is the difference between "policy" and "rule"; a supervisor needs to explain these terms to new employees, making the differences clear. It is particularly important in matters of personnel action, salaries, and sick leave, where the difference between rule and policy is often critical. A newcomer may feel that policy is something that must occur rather than something that can occur. Needless to say, professional jargon may be acceptable within the staff, but care should be taken not to employ such terms/ words in communications intended for the user.

> **Try This**
>
> Archivists and librarians have a technical vocabulary. List ten terms commonly used within libraries that might baffle the user.

The way in which one says something—the emphasis, lack of emphasis, omissions, and order of presentation—also influences meaning. Only when you have had some experience working with the same people will the meanings of their word order, tone of voice, facial expressions, and other nonverbal characteristics be clear. This understanding is not always possible, so it is best to remain constantly alert to these points, no matter how well the parties involved think they know one another. It is an essential factor to consider in teamwork. From the users' perspective, all of the preceding factors will be absent, thus it is essential that staff members do their best to develop a "customer friendly" communication style.

Advocacy/Marketing

We firmly believe that in today's highly competitive information world libraries must market themselves. Furthermore, we believe that all of the communication issues discussed previously applies to these activities. Even without the competition it would still be critical for long-term success. When funding is difficult, being able to draw on a knowledgeable, satisfied user community can make all of the difference between success and failure. Market analysis and marketing programs will help build such a base. For many years, libraries and archives did not see much, if any, need to market their products and services. They expected users to know about services, but they took little action to create awareness and persuade the service community that the service could offer something of value.

Marketing and advocacy, while different, are *very* interrelated. Marketing begins with a sound strategic plan that recognizes the need to apply basic marketing principles to the plan's elements as well as to the library's overall vision. Once a library has successfully marketed its vision and services, it can and should start developing an advocacy strategy (employing users as a major source of advocates).

The opening paragraph of Hallmark, Schwartz, and Roy (2007) raised the question, "Are today's academic libraries poised to serve as essential centers of campus activities?" (p. 92). They went on to suggest, "Marketing can provide an arsenal of skills to assist academic librarians. The essential marketing document to assist librarians in designing their marketing activities is the marketing and outreach plan" (p. 92). Naturally such plans must draw on the library's strategic plan.

Most academic libraries have a strategic plan, either developed independently or as part of a campuswide planning process. What is important, rather than its mere existence, is the degree to which the library communicates, implements, and regularly reviews the plan. When those factors are in operation it has what management scholars refer to as strategic credibility. Diffenbach and Higgins (1987) define it as "how *others* view a company's overall corporate strategy and its strategic planning capability" (p. 13). Essentially, strategic credibility revolves around communicating a few concise strategic messages to the external environment and backing up those messages with observable actions that reflect the content of the messages. Gail Staines (2009) reported on a study that attempted to assess strategic credibility of Canadian and U.S. Association of Research Libraries (ARL) libraries. She concluded, "Determining the level to which ARL libraries in the U.S. and Canada have strategic credibility is difficult to surmise from this Study. This study revealed that, although libraries are planning, sharing planning accomplishments is not occurring through traditional annual reports" (p. 161).

Strategic marketing is an approach that draws on methods of strategic planning and combines them with marketing methods. Phillip Kotler has written extensively about nonprofit marketing and how it differs from profit marketing in important

> **Check This Out**
>
> A thorough review of the whats and hows of marketing an academic library can be found in Brian Mathews's *Marketing Today's Academic Library: A Bold Approach to Communicating with Students* (Chicago, IL: American Library Association, 2009).

ways. He has published six editions of his text on nonprofit marketing (Andreasen and Kotler, 2003). Starting with his fourth edition, he added the strategic planning aspects to the approach. The strategic marketing process for not-for-profit organizations, based on their model, has three major elements: analysis, strategy, and implementation. Much of their process involves the steps of strategic planning. The steps are the following:

- Generic product definition
- Target group definition
- Differential marketing analysis
- Customer behavior analysis
- Differential advantages analysis

- Multiple marketing approaches
- Integrated market planning
- Continuous market feedback
- Marketing audit

Mathews (2009) makes the point in his book that advocacy goes hand in hand with marketing and that one of key advocacy groups is the student body. "Not only do these students groups advise us, but they can help us spread information about the library. They can increase awareness about our services and lobby for our needs" (p. 74). Association of College and Research Libraries' (2006) publication *The Power of Personal Persuasion* provides the whats and hows of developing an advocacy plan/program for academic libraries.

Check These Out

Camila Alire, "Advocating to Advance Academic Libraries," *College & Research Libraries News* 68, no. 8 (2005): 590-591, 614.
Camila Alire, "Advocacy: Part I," *American Libraries* 40, no. 8/9 (2009): 8.
Camila Alire, "Advocacy: Part II," *American Libraries* 40, no. 11 (2009): 8.
American Library Association, "Eleven Library Advocacy Myths—Debunked" (Chicago: American Library Association), available: www.ala.org/ala/issuesadvocacy/advocacy/advocacyuniversity/coalitionbuilding/myths/index.cfm.
Nicholas Joint, "It Is Not All Free on the Web: Advocacy for Library Funding in the Digital Age," *Library Review* 57, no. 4 (2008): 269-275.

From the Authors

John Stemmer, one of our readers, offered the following thoughts about marketing and advocacy:

This is an extremely important aspect of what we need to address as a profession. It is partly due to the changing information environment. We need to explain to our local users and administrators what benefits we are providing. Often they think of the library as books. I think it is perhaps unconscious for many people. But we need to constantly promote the library's services and resources. The library is not just about information, it is about knowledge. We need to convince (and not just market) our users of our abilities to effectively support their research (faculty) and learning (students). We need to advocate that we are more than information (books and journals, print or digital) to our users and our administrators.

Scholarly Communication

The chapter on the faculty has a general discussion of scholarly publishing as it has been and continues, to some degree, to be practiced. Everyone in academia knows this process is changing and will continue to do so for the foreseeable future. There are many elements that need to be resolved: what to count in the promotion and tenure process, intellectual property issues, and quality control to name just three.

John Shuler (2007) perhaps summed up the situation most effectively when he wrote:

The bibliographic (and technological) monopoly fostered over the centuries of using Gutenberg's invention is being pushed from the policy stage by a shifting blend of cultural and technological liquidity (defined here as the digital ability to mingle, exchange, compare vast amounts of information regardless of its original format and/or tangibility). The information liquidity further sustains a digital network of global civic exchange and commercial interests through a broad spectrum of individual communication channels and technological choices. This liquidity demands new library organizations and policy structures. (p. 710)

In Maron and Smith (2009), ARL and Ithaka reported on the range of Web resources faculty members pay special attention to and value that fall outside the traditional scholarly works. The report identified eight major types of digital scholarly resources of interest to scholars that met the nontraditional category: e-only journal, reviews, preprints and working papers, encyclopedias/dictionaries/annotated content, data, blogs, discussion forums, and professional/scholarly hubs.

Some of the findings were that, although different disciplines made greater or lesser use of digital-only resources, all disciplines do use that type of material. Scholars still place great emphasis on peer review, and some fields were experimenting with "open peer review." (This may greatly change the views regarding peer review if the process gains traction. Anonymous reviews of anonymous papers have been a mainstay for assuming the reviews will be true assessments of content regardless of the reviewer's or author's reputation in the field.) Many of the "born-digital" publications are of interest to a very small number of scholars and do not require large operating budgets. "For

---

Check These Out

Julian Fisher, "Scholarly Publishing Re-invented: Real Costs and Real Freedoms," *Journal of Electronic Publishing* 11, no. 2 (2008), available: dx.doi.org/10.3998/3336451.0011.204.

Glenn S. McGuigan and Robert D. Russell, "The Business of Academic Publishing: A Strategic Analysis of the Academic Journal Publishing Industry and Its Impact on the Future of Scholarly Publishing," *Southern Librarianship* 9, no. 3 (2008), available: southernlibrarianship.icaap.org/content/v09n03/mcguigan_g01.html.

John Willinsky, "Toward the Design of an Open Monograph Press," *Journal of Electronic Publishing* 12, no. 1 (2009), available: http://dx.doi.org/10.3998/3336451.0012.103.

From the Authors

John Stemmer's thoughts about scholarly communication:

This struck a nerve when I read it. It is good that all of this is under communications, but it is also all about change and how communication is changing and what libraries need to do to adapt to it. People's notions of a library have been formed by what we have done in the past collecting books and journals—scholarly communication. The notion of a library as a storehouse of information is very hard to overcome. Our services in providing, preserving, and organizing information as well as in instruction are often taken for granted.

How do the changes in scholarly communication impact what we do and what we are perceived to be doing? Do we collect blog posts if this becomes a recognized scholarly activity? I think the topic of institutional repositories is directly relevant here. Libraries have always collected local materials both about the institution/region and locally produced scholarship. We need to move this to the digital environment and begin to acquire our locally produced scholarship digitally. Once we do this, it also means we need to tie it back into the marketing/advocacy. We need to preserve and promote our institutions' scholarly activity. I think faculty members are always very pleased to see that the library has acquired their publications. This will continue in the digital age, but now we need to not only provide them to the local community but allow their worldwide scholarly associates access to their work. At one conference I have heard that putting an item in an institutional repository increases the amount of citation that item gets over and above just being published in a scholarly journal. As the pace of scholarly communication speeds up through digital publication and blogs the library needs to speed up the process of providing it to the entire scholarly community. We go from bringing together resources from around the world into a local collection for our community to providing and highlighting our local resources to the world.

open access sites—the vast majority of the resources studied here—the challenges can be great, since subscription fees are not an option. Nearly all of the publications that emerged in our survey are experimenting to find economic models that will support their work" (Maron and Smith, 2009).

Institutional Repositories

The concept of institutional repository (IR) is relatively new, post-2000. Like the term *information commons*, repositories have a variety of meanings and functions depending on the institution. To some degree the term *repository* suggests one of the less positive views about academic libraries: a storehouse of little-used dusty materials. This is unfortunate as such programs are active/interactive in nature rather than a static/inactive image of a storehouse.

The purpose of a repository program is to encourage the campus community (students and faculty especially) to deposit/contribute material individuals create as part of their teaching/learning/scholarly activities that may have broader interest than the original purpose that led to the creation of the material. Furthermore, the program makes this material available, normally through open access, to anyone worldwide who has an interest in the topic.

The two major open source repository software programs are DSpace and Fedora (Flexible Extensible Digital Object Repository Architecture). Both address the needs of various disciplines and researcher/scholars, and each has it advantages and limitations. A library must decide on which will work best for the application it has planned.

Gaining the support from the campus community to contribute material can be challenging. One method assuring materials are contributed that some institutions with such programs employ is to require that all thesis and dissertations be submitted in a digital format that is compatible with the IR software. A few have expanded this to include undergraduate capstone or honors papers.

Mike Furlough (2009) made the point that "no library should implement a digital repository program without examining the role it will play in its broader strategy for collection development, stewardship, and providing access to its primary constituencies. The strategy should be based on a clear understanding of the community's needs and the requirement for long-term stewardship of the data collected" (p. 22).

Check These Out

Institutional Repository Bibliography: digital-scholarship.org/irb/irb.html.

Ronald C. Jantz and Myoung C. Wilson, "Institutional Repositories: Faculty Deposits, Marketing, and the Reform of Scholarly Communication," *Journal of Academic Librarianship* 34, no. 3 (2008): 186–195.

Mary Piorun and Lisa A. Palmer, "Digitizing Dissertations for an Institutional Repository: A Process and Cost Analysis," *Journal of the Medical Library Association* 96, no. 3 (2008): 223–229.

GOVERNANCE

Perhaps the most significant changes in academic library structure and, in a sense, governance are the flattening of the structure and ever-growing use of teams. The use of "empowered" teams certainly pushes decision making down the structure and probably also speeds up the process.

Teams in the Workplace

Teams in the workplace have been with us for a long time, in one form or another. They are not a new concept; however, they are playing an ever-greater role in how libraries operate. Over the past 20-some years, organizations including libraries have undergone a "flattening" of their structures, resulting in fewer layers of management. In many cases, they experienced downsizing, or at least received no increase in staffing even with increased workloads. As a result of these events, the staff must be more productive, be flexible, learn new skills, and take on more responsibilities. So far, the twenty-first century has only added pressure on organizations and their personnel to be adept at handling rapid change. All of these factors place a premium on flexibility and having a knowledgeable workforce that is more capable of working independently than in the past.

Some of the differences that exist between a true team environment and the traditional workplace are significant. Teams call for consensus rather than command and control. They require that team members accept the idea that conflict (both positive and negative) is a normal part of team operations and that those conflicts must be addressed in an open, honest manner. Although not every difference of opinion that occurs in a team will result in negative conflict, time will still need to be spent in meetings resolving problems or reaching decisions. Reaching decisions in a team setting tends to be more knowledge/technically based than when it is done on the basis of one person's opinion. In teams, one needs to place more emphasis on the "whys" rather than the "hows." Essentially, the team must engage in a collaborative process.

Keep in mind that there are important differences between teams and committees. John Lubans (2003) identified five significant differences:

- Team members are equals, while committees may have an implicit pecking order or hierarchy.
- Conflict in teams is normal and addressed, while committees may labor under unresolved, often historic, conflict.
- Teams seek high trust, while committee members may have turf issues and hidden agendas.
- Teams strive for open communication, while committee members may be overly cautious in discussions.
- Team members are mutually supportive, while committee members may work independently and represent factions. (p. 144)

These are factors one should keep in the back of one's mind when creating a team. Essentially, be certain it is a team and not a committee by another name.

The literature is filled with labels for teams—project teams, self-managing teams, quality circles, cross-functional teams, virtual teams, and production groups are some examples. Whatever the label, successful teams, be they permanent, temporary, or virtual share some common elements. All effective teams share a commitment to a goal or purpose. Certainly interpersonal relationships play a role in the team's success, and members work on these relationships in an open manner. Additionally, all teams should be empowered.

When a library employs teams, especially self-managing teams, it should be beneficial in several ways. First, overall performance ought to improve, especially when teams work directly with users. Being able to make a decision on the spot, beyond enforcing rules and regulations, generally results in service(s) that better meet customers' needs and time frames. Second, there ought to be more "learning" and greater flexibility for both the organization and the staff. This occurs, in part, because teams can and do experiment as well as engage in new/ innovative approaches to challenging situations. Third, staff commitment to the organization and its goals tends to be higher. Greater commitment results in higher retention of staff, which in turn reduces personnel costs (recruitment and training). Finally, more committed and motivated people are more productive as well as more willing to change as circumstances change.

Academic libraries currently make some use of teams, and such usage will likely increase over time. However, currently there are not a great many institutions where it is the primary organizational pattern. Perhaps one of the best known team-based information services with the longest operational experience in the United States is the University of Arizona Library, which has received a substantial amount of publicity. Other academic institutions that have employed the team concept include Emory (web.library.emory.edu/about/reorg), Indiana UniversityPurdue University Indianapolis (IUPUI; www.ulib.iupui.edu/libinfo/teams.html), and the University of Maryland, College Park (www.lib.umd.edu/PUB/documentation.html).

Check These Out

M. Sue Baughman, "Assessment of Teams and Teamwork in the University of Maryland Libraries," *portal: Libraries and the Academy* 8, no. 3 (2008): 293-312.

James Castiglione, "Self-Managing Work Teams and Their External Leadership: A Primer for Library Administrators," *Library Management* 28, no. 6/ 7 (2007): 379-393.

Tricia Kelly, "Where Is My Team? A Manager's Point of View on Working with a Team of Remote Information Specialists," *Quarterly Bulletin of the International Association of Agricultural Information Specialists* 50, no. 3/ 4 (2005): 119-124.

William F. Young, "Reference Team Self-Management at the University at Albany," *Library Administration & Management* 18, no. 4 (2004): 185-191.

COLLABORATION

In Chapter 9 we discussed the need for collaborative working relationship (if at "arms length") between the library and the campus IT department. What we did not mention was the ever-increasing pressure from upper-level campus administrators that such a relationship is no longer just desirable but mandated. "Turf wars" are less and less tolerated, and the library/IT struggles have been one of the longer-running campus feuds.

One important element in achieving a sound working relationship is the recognition and acceptance of the fact that the two entities both have important but different roles to play in the institution achieving its educational mission. First, in today's world is the need for an effective stable technology infrastructure (IT's role). Second, an essential component of a quality education is

---

From the Authors

John Stemmer contributed the following views about library and IT collaboration:

The need for collaboration with IT is an issue that will not go away until the library re-establishes itself as concerned with knowledge, research, and learning and not just information. We need IT to succeed, but if all we have is IT then we will not succeed. This can easily become a turf battle with a loss of focus by both groups on the functions they should be fulfilling. I think librarians need to venture more into the use of IT in order to demonstrate our mastery of what it provides and highlight the added value we bring to the learning/research process.

having access to appropriate scholarly materials, which in today's digital environment are more and more web-based (the library's role).

It is important to note that programs that educate people who become IT personnel generally do not address the issues of handling information beyond the physical aspects of moving electronic bits from one location to another. They do not learn about the nature of information, its structure, and the methods of organizing or accessing it. On the other hand, more librarians are not only learning about these issues but also a surprising amount about the technologies involved in handling information in a digital world.

Learning Commons

Robert Boyd (2008) noted, "There are quite possibly as many definitions of 'information commons' as there are potential staffing models. Even a common name for this common space proves elusive" (p. 232). Some of the name variations include information commons (IC), learning commons (LC), gateway commons (GC), knowledge commons (KC), electronic information learning center (EILC), and information arcade (IA) as well as several other labels. What takes place in this library space is equally varied.

To a large degree, Donald Beagle's (1999) article began the movement to create an environment that better links the two roles (content and technology) we mentioned in the prior section. Generally the basic skills needed to be effective in a commons setting is being very competent in the standard work application software programs (word processing, spreadsheets, presentation, etc.) and in transferring/storing data. Additional skills include troubleshooting technological issues and the use of imaging software. What is special is that those skills are combined with skills in selecting and accessing information to incorporate into the appropriate software. The essential elements in Beagle's model called for:

- research guidance and technological support,
- access to appropriate hardware and software,
- appropriate physical spaces, and
- intent to create, support, and maintain the service.

> **Check This Out**
>
> Donald Beagle's 2006 book *The Information Commons Handbook* (New York: Neal-Schuman).

In a real sense the commons is, and increasingly will be, a portal through which users can access the vast storehouse of world knowledge and information through the effective employment of technology and assistance from skilled personnel. There are, of course, some challenges for this vision of campus service. Laurie MacWhinnie (2003) noted:

However, the IC is not without its challenges. The most difficult one is the need for trained staff. With student demand for twenty-four hour access resulting in more libraries hours, an IC can be staff intensive.

> **From the Authors**
>
> John Stemmer's comment about commons labels:
>
> I prefer the term *learning commons* since I think the term *information commons* seems to continue the notion of the library as a storehouse. We are focused on the thing "information," and not on the activity "learning." Librarians need to do this to emphasize we have an educational role in the academic environment, not merely a technician's role.

Assistance must either take the form of cross-trained staff that can handle both technology and provide research assistance, or a joint staffing arrangement with experts in both information resources and technology available to provide the appropriate types of service on demand. (p. 244)

Both models are in use in U.S. academic libraries; we think that in the not too distant future it will be librarians handling both roles.

External Collaboration

Libraries have engaged in cooperative activities for a long time, well over 100 years. Thus, you would expect they would have mastered the process. Overall they know what is necessary for achieving a successful cooperative venture. They also have learned that each new effort will bring with it some new challenges. They also know that truly successful programs must change with the changing times.

You can think of the Library of Congress's distribution of cataloging information as one the very oldest of U.S. library cooperative programs. As mentioned previously, the program began late in 1901 with the distribution of catalog cards. Over the years it changed both the manner of distribution (from card stock to online as well as individual title information within the publication—"cataloging in publication") and expanded the number of libraries that contribute data. As Martha Yee (2009) wrote:

> This ingenuous scheme, by which a shared cataloging program to lower cataloging costs produced the equivalent of a national bibliography at the same time, has become the envy of the rest of the world. This approach is now very much taken for granted in the United States, but could not have happened without the conjunction of a number of economic, political, and social factors. (p. 68)

Another highly successful and long-standing endeavor is OCLC, close to 50 years old. Later efforts focused on multitype regional or statewide programs. Today we see the results of those efforts in OCLC Inc. as well as in state and regional "networks" that go well beyond offering technical service activities. The two most common academic library cooperative ventures involve statewide resource sharing programs such as OhioLINK and California's LINK+ and joint purchases of database access (SCELC and Amigos are examples).

Check These Out

G. Edward Evans, "Management Issues of Co-operative Ventures and Consortia in the USA—Part One," *Library Management* 23, nos. 4/5 (2002): 213-226.

G. Edward Evans, "Management Issues of Consortia—Part Two," *Library Management* 23, nos. 6/7 (2002): 275-286.

Lisa German, "It's All About Teamwork: Working in a Consortial Environment," *Technicalities* 28, no. 3 (2008): 1, 12-15.

From the Authors

John's thoughts regarding consortia:

Library consortia will continue to grow to take advantage of the many resources we can offer to our users through cooperation that will not be possible independently. Most academic libraries benefit tremendously from statewide consortiums. We need to provide our administrators and state stakeholders the information and knowledge to see the benefits for their continued funding. Statewide consortia are important, but I wonder if we will see some effort to expand these even further. I know FoKAL, a newly formed Kentucky consortium, has just started to work with TENN-SHARE, our Southern neighbor. Vendors seem to be resistant to this. But even working just locally, our collective resources are always better than our individual resources. Everything we can do to provide a positive experience to our users will help us. Our physical resources, as learning tools, will be in demand for many years to come. Our interlibrary cooperation will make our services that more effective for our users.

In addition to this we need to go beyond just our local institutional community. Most academic libraries benefit tremendously from statewide consortiums (or is this just an unconfirmed assumption?). We need to provide our administrators and state stakeholders the information and knowledge to see the benefits for their continued funding.

Google Book Project

The Google project had started by at least 2003 when Google approached the Library of Congress (LC) with a proposal to digitize all of the books in the library. When LC offered a counterproposal that would include only public domain (no longer covered by copyright) books, Google did not follow up. Rather, it turned to other major research libraries such as University of Michigan, Oxford University, Harvard University, and the New York Public Library with some success. Of interest to academic libraries are intellectual property issues and what types of access and their associated costs will be to the scanned material.

From the Authors

This is an additional reason for collaboration as many users will find an item that addresses their interests and not want to use it online. This will actually increase demand for library resources as more people will want us to provide the item for their use. In the long run though, this is basically a digital backfile, much like the Open Content Alliance effort. When combined with Kindle, Nook, and all the other e-book options we may finally be approaching the era of digital books—both current materials and the "accumulated knowledge" of the past will be digitally available. Will digital natives find they are as useful as learning tools as the physical counterpart? I have seen some reports indicating no. On the other hand, I expect the technology to continue to develop and our users to become ever more focused on digital media (not just text). So it may well be that libraries will need to work to provide an alternative to Google Books. The Open Content Alliance and Institutional repositories could both play a role in this. And all of this hinges on intellectual property, copyright, and digital rights management. (John Stemmer)

The notion that some company would be allowed to make digital copies of copyrighted works got the attention of many rights holders who sued Google in 2005. The case was complex and took until October 28, 2008, before a proposed settlement was reached. What Google did and still does is scan material and create an electronic index available free of charge to users to search the database. In the case of public domain items, users may view or download the entire text. Copyrighted works are available in small segments. Google offers downloadable files for a fee in the case of "orphan works" and copyrighted works that are not commercially available. The settlement was not yet given final approved by a Federal judge as of December 2009 because the judge requested some modifications (Associated Press, 2009).

Marybeth Peters (2009), U.S. Register of Copyright, in a statement to the U.S. House of Representatives on September 10, 2009, wrote:

> Under the proposed settlement, the parties have crafted a class that is not anchored to past or imminent scanning, but instead turns on the much broader question of whether a work was *published* by January 5, 2009. As defined, the class would allow Google to continue to scan entire libraries, for commercial gain, into the indefinite future. The settlement would bind authors, publishers, their heirs and successors to these rules, even though Google has not yet scanned, and may never scan their works. (p. 4)

Google's scanning project is not limited to U.S. copyrighted works. Needless to state, other countries are monitoring what U.S. courts are ruling and in at least one case have sued Google for violating their copyright laws. Greg Keller (2009) reported that not only had a French publisher sued Google for copyright infringement but a French court ruled in favor of the plaintiff and was imposing a $14,000-a-day fine. In addition, the court awarded the publisher damages in the amount $430,000. Naturally Google plans to appeal the judgment and as they "stay tuned for the latest developments"; however, given the complexity of such cases, one will probably need to stay tuned in for some years. Nevertheless, international reaction, almost uniformly negative, to Google's plans illustrates how complex intellectual property/copyright/scholarly communication issues have become in the digital world.

How does the Google project impact libraries? (A reminder, the courts hadn't yet finally ruled on the settlement when this book went to press.) On the good side, for society, is that the digitized material will be searchable using the Google search software, searching depth that is impossible in a paper version, at least not without great expense. It means that anyone who can connect to Google will, for the present, have free access to a wealth of information that has been vetted by the standard quality control process of "traditional" publishing, unlike the material anyone can post on the Web. A potential concern, for society, is the limitation built into the good side "for the present." What are the implications of a private organization with a near monopoly on these digitized materials? What if the organization changes their easy access policies in the future?

KEY POINTS TO REMEMBER

- Addressing change effectively is a major challenge for today's academic libraries.
- Effective change requires thoughtful planning and recognizing that both people and institutions often resist changing.
- Communication underlies all aspects of interactions between people as well as organizations.
- Marketing academic libraries is essential in today's environment.
- Marketing plans/programs must be based on a sound understanding of the library's mission and strategic plan.
- Advocacy is also an essential element in securing and maintaining proper library support.
- Scholarly communication is quickly changing, with less dependence on traditional formats.
- Institutional repositories and open access are two elements changing the way in which scholarly communication takes place.
- Self-managing teams and a flattening of the library's organizational structure are factors that are changing what skills a person needs to be a successful academic librarian.
- Learning/information commons are another element that is requiring new skills for academic librarians.
- Collaboration both within the campus as well as outside of the campus is changing how academic libraries go about providing services and expend their funding resources.
- Academic libraries are facing some very challenging competitors, and projects such as Google Books are likely to force serious rethinking about the nature of services.

REFERENCES

Andreasen, Alan R., and Philip Kotler. 2003. *Strategic marketing for non-profit organizations.* 7th ed. Upper Saddle River, NJ: Prentice Hall.

Associated Press. 2009. Deadline in Google Book deal extended to Friday. *Arizona Daily Sun,* November 10.

Association of College and Research Libraries. 2006. *The power of personal persuasion: Advancing the academic library agenda from the front lines.* Chicago, IL: American Library Association. Available: www.ala.org/ala/mgrps/divs/acrl/publications/booksmonographs/catalog/ppptoolkit .cfm (accessed April 7, 2010).

Association of College and Research Libraries, Research Committee. 2008. *Environmental scan—2007.* Chicago, IL: American Library Association.

Beagle, Donald. 1999. Conceptualizing an information commons. *Journal of Academic Librarianship* 25, no. 2: 82–89.

Boyd, Robert. 2008. Staffing the commons: Job analysis in the context of an information commons. *Library Hi Tech* 26, no. 2: 232–243.

Cameron, Kim S., and Robert E. Quinn. 2006. *Diagnosing and changing organizational culture: Based on the competing values framework.* Rev. ed. San Francisco, CA: Jossey-Bass.

Diffenbach, John, and Richard Higgins. 1987. Strategic credibility can make a difference. *Business Horizons* 30, no. 3: 13–18.

Furlough, Mike. 2009. What we talk about when we talk about repositories. *Reference & User Services Quarterly* 49, no. 1: 18–23, 32.

Gottfredson, Mark, Steve Schaubert, and Herman Saenz. 2008. The new leader's guide to diagnosing the business. *Harvard Business Review* 86, no. 2: 62–73.

Hallmark, Elizabeth Kennedy, Laura Schwartz, and Loriene Roy. 2007. Developing a long-range and outreach plan for your academic library. *College & Research Libraries News* 68, no. 2: 92–95.

Keller, Greg. 2009. Google fined $14,300 a day in France over book copyright issues. *USA Today* December 18. Available: www.usatoday.com/money/industries/technology/2009-12-18-google-fined-in-france_N.htm (accessed April 7, 2010).

Kotter, John. 1990. *A force of change: How leadership differs from management.* New York: Simon & Schuster.

Kotter, John, and Leonard Schlesinger. 1979. Choosing strategies for change. *Harvard Business Review* 57, no. 2 (February): 106–114.

Lewin, Kurt. 1951. *Field theory in social sciences.* New York: Harper & Row.

Lubans, John. 2003. Teams in libraries. *Library Administration & Management* 17, no. 3: 144–145.

MacDonald, Karen I., Wyoma vanDuinkerken, and Jane Stephens. 2008. It's all in the marketing: The impact of a virtual reference marketing campaign at Texas A&M University. *Reference & User Services Quarterly* 47, no. 4: 375–385.

MacWhinnie, Laurie A. 2003. The information commons: The academic library of the future. *portal: Libraries and the Academy* 3, no. 2: 241–257.

Maron, Nancy L., and K. Kirby Smith. 2009. Current models of digital scholarly communication: Results of an investigation conducted by Ithaka Strategic Services for the Association of Research Libraries. *Journal of Electronic Publishing* 12, no. 1. Available: quod.lib.umich.edu/cgi/t/text/text-idx?c=jep;view=text;rgn=main;idno=3336451.0012.105 (accessed April 7, 2010).

Mathews, Brian. 2009. *Marketing today's academic library: A bold approach to communicating with students.* Chicago, IL: American Library Association.

Peters, Marybeth. 2009. *Hearing on competition and commerce in digital books: The proposed Google Book settlement.* Available: www.copyright.gov/docs/regstat091009.html (accessed April 7, 2010).

Ross, Lyman, and Pongracz Sennyey. 2008. The library is dead, long live the library! The practice of academic librarianship and the digital revolution. *Journal of Academic Librarianship* 34, no. 2: 145–152.

Schuler, John. 2007. Academic libraries and the global information society. *Journal of Academic Librarianship* 33, no. 6: 710–773.

Shepstone, Carol, and Lyn Currie. 2008. Transforming the academic library: Creating an organizational culture that fosters staff success. *Journal of Academic Librarianship* 34, no. 4: 358–368.

Staines, Gail. 2009. Towards an assessment of strategic credibility in American libraries. *Library Management* 30, no. 3: 148–162.

Szamosi, Leslie, and Linda Duxbury. 2002. Development of a measure to assess organizational change. *Journal of Organizational Change Management* 15, no. 2: 184–201.

Wood, Elizabeth J., Rush Miller, and Amy Knapp. 2007. *Beyond survival: Managing academic libraries in transition.* Westport, CT: Libraries Unlimited.

Yee, Martha M. 2009. "Wholly visionary": The American Library Association, the Library of Congress, and the card distribution program. *Library Resources & Technical Services* 53, no. 2: 68–78.

LAUNCHING PAD

Association of College and Research Libraries. n.d. Strategic marketing for academic and research libraries. Available: www.ala.org/ala/mgrps/divs/acrl/issues/marketing/FacilitatorGuide.pdf (accessed April 7, 2010).

Bailey, Charles W. 2009. Google Book Search bibliography. Available: www.digital-scholarship .org/gbsb/gbsb.htm (accessed April 7, 2010).

Bailey, Russell, and Barbara Tierney. 2002. Information commons redux: Concept, evolution, and transcending the tragedy of the commons. *Journal of Academic Librarianship* 28, no. 5: 277–286.

Band, Jonathan. 2008. *Guide for the perplexed: Libraries and the Google Library Project settlement.* Chicago, IL: American Library Association, Association of Research Libraries. Available: www.arl.org/bm~doc/google-settlement-13nov08.pdf (accessed April 7, 2010).

Buehler, Marianne A., and Marcia S. Trauernicht. 2007. From digital library to institutional repository: A brief look at one library's path. *OCLC Systems Services International Digital Library Perspectives* 23, no. 4: 382–394.

Duke, Lynda M., Jean MacDonald, and Carrie S. Trimble. 2009. Collaboration between marketing students and library. *College & Research Libraries* 70, no. 2: 109–121.

Fitzpatrick, Elizabeth B., Anne C. Moore, and Beth W. Lang. 2008. Reference librarians at the reference desk in a learning commons: A mixed methods evaluation. *Journal of Academic Librarianship* 34, no. 3: 231–238.

Franks, Jeffery A. 2008. Introducing learning commons functionally into a traditional reference setting. *Southern Librarianship* 9, no. 2. Available: southernlibrarianship.icaap.org/content/ v09n02/franks_j01.html (accessed April 7, 2010).

Gaspar, Deborah, and Karen A. Wetzel. 2009. A case study in collaboration: Assessing academic librarian/faculty partnerships. *College & Research Libraries* 70, no. 6: 578–590.

Genoni, Paul, and Eva varga. 2009. Assessing the potential for a national print repository. *College & Research Libraries* 70, no. 6: 555–577.

Kaur, Kiran. 2009. Marketing the academic library on the Web. *Library Management* 30, no. 6/7: 454–468.

MacDonald, Karen I., Wyoma vanDuinkerken, and Jane Stephens. 2008. It's all in the marketing. *Reference & User Services Quarterly* 47, no. 4: 375–385.

Singh, Rajesh. 2009. Does your library have an attitude problem towards marketing? *Journal of Academic Librarianship* 35, no. 1: 25–32.

Tenopir, Carol. 2003. Electronic publishing: Research issues for academic librarians and users. *Library Trends* 51, no. 4: 614–635.

Xia, Jingfeng. 2008. A comparison of subject and institutional repositories in self-archiving practices. *Journal of Academic Librarianship* 34, no. 6: 489–495.

Chapter 15

Career Development

Library schools do not teach everything individuals need to know to be a good librarian; this knowledge often comes from on-the-job experience. Mentoring newly graduated librarians in the workplace is a way to gain valuable knowledge and to become a better librarian.

—Marta Lee (2009)

Many academic librarians starting down the tenure track are put off by the research requirement that is often part of such a position.

—Deborah Lee (2005)

As the opening quotation from Marta Lee states, no library school can teach everything a person will need to know to have a successful career. They do an excellent job of offering course work that will create a solid foundation for starting a career. It is also true that it is unrealistic to expect the school to provide all of the knowledge and skills a person will need during a long-term career. Career success is largely dependent on four elements: the quality of the basic education, a person's commitment to mastering the basics, the amount and frequency of training provided individuals during their career by their employers, and, perhaps most important, the individual's commitment to and investment in lifelong learning.

The immediate years after moving from being a student to "librarian status" to being an employed academic librarian can have a considerable influence on one's career development. Actions and decisions taken or not taken will shape a rewarding and enjoyable working life as well as affect a future librarian's ability to meet the challenges and opportunities that will arise. Thinking about the future has never been as important as it is today. The possibilities are enormous—information skills are transferable skills, and the work is challenging and offers great job satisfaction. Just think about how much the work environment has changed for those few members of the "Traditional" and the larger cohort of "Boomers" generation librarians still in the workforce. Even the succeeding generations have witnessed some remarkable changes in the higher education landscape.

An interesting perspective on just how quickly one's work environment may change and require a host of different skills and knowledge appeared in an article by Mary Madden DeMajo (2008). She records the challenges she faced transitioning from being a public library reference staff member at the New Orleans Public Library to joining the reference staff of Southeastern Louisiana University post-Katrina. Her opening sentence spelled out the issue: "Much has been written about teaching information literacy to library users and about in-service training for library professionals and paraprofessionals, but little has been said about mid-career librarians who must retrain when moving from an environment with only basic technology to one that's technology-rich" (p. 50). More to the point of this chapter, she took it on herself to go beyond the basic assistance her new employer could reasonably provide and as she concluded her essay, "I have developed a deep appreciation for both academic and public library environments and for the dynamic, knowledge-fostering components of each; and I continue to renew my commitment to my profession" (p. 53).

In a somewhat similar vein, Susan Kell (2007) wrote:

> Deciding what we need to learn is also tough. While professional growth is the hallmark of every good librarian, deciding what is a critical skill to learn can be daunting....Considering that I went back to school to earn a second master's degree in Instructional Technology and am continuing on with coursework toward a doctorate, it might seem that I've got a good handle on keeping current. But coursework is only part of professional growth. (p. 8)

She went on to discuss seeing learning opportunities arising from work experience and from unexpected events, commenting, "I believe that knowing your shortcomings can help you leverage them to advantage" (p. 8).

Everyone starts a new career with high hopes, expectations, and aspirations. We can dream about where we might be in the years ahead and how our careers will develop. At one time it was a case of getting a foot on the ladder in an academic library of our choice and moving upward. Careers were often based in a local large organization, and with hard work, people moved up the ladder in a hierarchical structure.

Today it is very different. People now change jobs more frequently, they expect to get to the top faster and hence younger, and they may even take a career break along the way. Continuing professional development is important, and time and money is invested in gaining the skills essential in a rapidly changing information profession. Librarians now work in organizations that are less stable, often smaller, more agile, and that have a flattened organizational structure. People are, or were until the recent economic slow down, more mobile. Technology enables teleworking. Family considerations enter into choices. There are challenges, but also more opportunities.

There is only one factor that can be accurately predicted about the future: the work environment will change. Change is expected to occur more rapidly and be fundamental. When the authors started this text, they solicited the thoughts of some current academic library leaders about the future of academic librarianship (see Chapter 16 for a summary of their insightful comments). Their number one issue regarding the challenges facing the field was the urgent need to change. Many commented that the nature of the required changes would need to be profound, not incremental in character.

Try This

Think about what you do best, like best doing, what you do not like doing or do not do so well, what you hope to accomplish from your working life, and what your long-term goals are. Try to create a first draft of what your career goals will be.

Planning your career and personal goals will assist you in having a rewarding and successful career. Such a plan will need flexibility, and it ought to be reviewed occasionally, as should organizational plans. What appears reasonable today may in a year or two be unrealistic as the field changes. Seriously thinking about long-term goals while still in school provides some direction when thinking about what your ideal first academic library position should be.

FROM STUDENT TO ACADEMIC LIBRARIAN

Many students completing their master of library science (MLS) degree will have some work experience in an archives or library as a result of internships and/or part-time employment. Such work provides not only the opportunity to gain work experience at a general level but also a "taste" of what a career in that area might be like.

Applying for your first full-time academic library position may well be influenced by the size of your student loans, the state of the job market, and geographic or family constraints. Thus, it may well be a compromise in terms of your ideal; however, when possible, seeking a position that fits your long-term plan is desirable. You can identify vacancies from a number of sources. Employers make recruiting visits to students; professional conferences hold placement fairs; and advertisements are placed in newspapers (such as the *Chronicle of Higher Education*), professional journals (*C&RL News* is a prime source), or on the websites of professional bodies.

You could also approach organizations with a résumé (or a curriculum vitae, CV) and cover letter to inquire about potential vacancies. It may pay off with larger academic libraries. Perhaps later one of them may come back to you or remember your name if you apply for an advertised vacancy at a later date. Such inquiries demonstrate an interest in and enthusiasm for the particular institution/library.

Marketing Yourself

Keep in mind that in applying for a position you are essentially marketing yourself— you are looking for a buyer. The first step of selling yourself starts with your résumé. The key factor to keep in mind is that it performs two functions. First and foremost, it is, or should be, a record of your achievements. Keeping the document current is important, as it is the foundation for job applications, for volunteer work on professional and other committees, and for applications for further study grants, travel, scholarships, etc. Second, it is, or should be, adapted for each application through the thoughtful selection of information that is appropriate and relevant to that position or grant.

Even at the start of a career you have a substantial amount of information that needs to be in your résumé, such as the following:

- Name, address, phone number, fax number, and e-mail address
- Education: high school, university degrees, and any distinctions or awards
- Special courses or workshops that developed additional skills such as information technology, languages, communication, etc.
- Work experience to date (including all that preceded your current course work— remember that any work with the public, for example in a supermarket, will have developed communication and team skills)
- Publications regardless of subject as these reflect writing skills
- Membership in relevant organizations
- Any attendance at professional conferences
- A brief note of interests and hobbies, to provide a talking point at interviews

As your career develops, the document will include such items as attendance at professional development courses, papers presented at conferences, additional or first publications, professional awards, and, of course, positions held. A mentor or librarian friends can provide sound advice on what to and not to include.

In a competitive job market, you might well turn to a professional résumé writer. They are in touch with employers, they know what the current approaches are and have the skills to design and lay out compelling documents. You can be sure that the finished product will not contain errors that a spell-checker can miss.

When applying for a position, you can tailor the résumé to reflect the information most relevant to that position. Be honest, but don't embellish your talents. Generally, especially for beginning posts, the résumé should be no more than two pages long. If it is longer, the prospective employer probably won't read it thoroughly and might even put it straight into a trash can thinking it was a fabrication. Have a mentor and/or friends proofread your application documents.

Check These Out

Richard Nelson Bolles, *What Color Is Your Parachute? 2006: A Practical Manual for Job-Hunters and Career-Changers* (Berkeley, CA: Ten Speed Press, 2006), and Richard Nelson Bolles, *What Color Is Your Parachute Workbook: How to Create a Picture of Your Ideal Job or Next Career* (Berkeley, CA: Ten Speed Press, 2006).

Dick Bolles also has a website: www.jobhuntersbible.com. It contains career and personality tests, articles, practical advice.

Most employers require that you fill out their application form. An increasing number of institutions are using software to process applications (SIEM—security, information, event management) prior to sending it on to the search committee; it looks for keywords and phrases relevant to the employers interests (such as involvement in volunteer work or certain types of teaching experience). Online forms often ask for a personal statement because they are looking for employees who can express themselves. A well-written answer can help secure an interview. Paper-based forms present something of a challenge since it is not always easy to find a typewriter, not everyone has beautiful handwriting, and fitting information on forms may not be easy. In such cases, it is wise to make several photocopies and practice getting the required information into the form in a manner that creates a positive impression.

Try This

List the factors that will influence your decision concerning job applications. Now put them in a priority order.

Generally, a cover letter or e-mail statement is part of the total application process. Reviewing the posted job description and outlining, in your letter, how you match the required and desired attributes of the position is another key to getting an interview. Your goal in the letter is to be concise while covering all of the pertinent points. Again, remember you are selling yourself, and it is likely to be a buyer's market.

SEARCH COMMITTEES

Search or screening committees for vetting candidates is a fact of academic life for almost all higher education professional positions. Two of the most relevant reasons for such committees harkens back to the concepts of shared governance and shared decision making. Another reason is the staff in the hiring unit has a much sounder understanding of the position, expectations, and organizational culture that the appointee will encounter than will a person in the Human Resources department. In Chapter 13 we outlined the process for assessing staffing needs and the elements of a proper job description. The following discussion assumes such issues were addressed prior to posting the vacancy.

One important aspect of creating a search committee is to develop a crystal clear committee charge. There is something of a continuum regarding the committee's role in the hiring process. At one end is the committee that reviews applications and interviews a small pool of "finalists." It then prepares a written assessment of each interviewee. The committee passes the assessments on to the person who will make the decision regarding the person to whom an offer will be made. The committee makes no recommendation/ ranking of the candidates. A middle ground approach is for the committee to forward the material along with its recommendations or ranking of the candidates, but the final decision remains with someone else (director, dean, vice president, for example). The other end of the continuum is where the committee makes the choice, a rather rare approach in higher education.

It is the middle ground where there are occasional campus kerfuffles occurring. If the charge is not very clear, the committee as well as others may believe the ranking or recommendation is tantamount to the final decision. When the person making the decision makes a selection that is different, people become upset, and campus politics become pointed if not ugly. One reads of one or more such events in the *Chronicle of Higher Education* every year or two.

Another fact of the academic hiring process is that it tends to be long and expensive in terms of time and money. Almost all national and even regional searches are slow moving. From the time a position becomes vacant until there is a person again performing the work can be as much as two years for a senior library administrator and take the better part of a year for a beginning librarian.

Why so long? Part of the time lag is institutional; another element is legal; an advertising deadline also can extend the time frame for the process; and last but far from least is the search committee itself (scheduling meetings is a major issue). From the applicant's perspective, the last three factors draw the process out. For the staff waiting for a new colleague, all of the factors are involved. They may begin to feel "put upon" as time passes without a decision, and they have to continue to share the workload of the vacant position. Karl Bridges (2002) wrote an opinion with the title "The Unbearable Slowness of Hiring" in which he identifies additional time factors.

Often, especially in difficult economic times, the library may have to fight to be allowed to refill the vacant FTE (full-time equivalency). Even in the best of times, there is usually a period of time spent in rethinking the position and how it might be most effectively allocated. There certainly will be some time spent in reviewing the job description with an eye to the foreseeable future needs of the position even when the FTE is not reallocated. Furthermore, there is likely to be some discussion regarding salary for the position and maintaining salary equity within the library. (A significant morale problem for existing staff is to have a newcomer receive a higher salary when doing the same work as they are.)

After all of the institutional concerns regarding a posting of a vacancy are addressed, the question of where to place the announcement comes into play. Beyond the easy posting on various Web sites, including the institution's, there may be limitations on how much money may be spent on advertisements. Deciding where best to place the ads as well as the publication deadlines for advertisements and allowing for a reasonable response time for applications add yet more time.

As applications begin to arrive, most HR departments will want to make certain the "pool" will satisfy affirmative action regulations. At some point, usually prior to the posting the position, the search committee comes into existence. One of the early committee meetings will spend time going over all of the legal pitfalls that exist for how they handle the screening of applications and conduct interviews.

We should mention one more time factor that the can slow the process. It is not all that rare that, after a considerable passage of time, an offer is made to the top candidate only to learn the person has accepted a position elsewhere or rejects the offer for some reason. Sometimes even the second choice is unavailable. This is when committee members' "agendas" almost always surface. There are several options for the committee: continue down the current rankings (there were reasons for the lower rankings), go back to the overall pool to see if there may be one or two applicants they might also interview, or reopen the search. Committee members as well as campus administrators will have strong views about the options. Whatever the decision is, the process will get just a little or substantially longer.

Given all of this, is it any wonder why the academic hiring process is so unbearably slow? Many first-time job seekers have no idea about why things move so slowly and wonder if they should contact the library. The jury is out on whether such contact is appropriate or worthwhile. Keeping in mind the discussion of the usual time frame for the process may provide some small guidance for deciding when or if to call or write.

Selecting the Pool

Most recruiting efforts usually generate a larger pool of applicants than it is feasible to interview. Deciding who to interview draws on information produced by the selection instruments the library identified (see Chapter 13 to review this concept). The most common place to begin the sorting process is the application form and cover letter (when you apply for a position keep this fact in mind; how carefully you prepare these documents often decides your chances of getting interviewed). Some of the factors the committee looks for are whether the person has the required skills, how carefully the material is presented, and whether the person supplied all of the required information. A "gross" sorting of applicants just using the basic issues will reduce the pool by a substantial number. A further reduction, if necessary, would be to review how many of the "desirable" skills/abilities the applicant possesses. Having a final interview pool of three to six people usually produces a candidate suitable for the position. Because the selection process involves a substantial amount of subjectivity, having developed sound job success criteria and job specifications will assist in keeping the process as objective as possible (again, these concepts may be reviewed in Chapter 13).

THE INTERVIEW

Being interviewed for a position is always somewhat stressful, regardless of how senior a person may be in terms of her or his career. Doing some preparation will help reduce the stress, such as doing some research about the institution, the library, and their surrounding community. Doing so will give you some background information and a basis for developing some questions you can ask when you go to the interview.

Focusing part of your preparation on how best to sell yourself to the prospective employer can also help reduce the stress. Draw up a list of potential questions that may be asked and decide how you will answer them. Some of the frequently asked questions, regardless of what the position may be, are the following:

- What interests you in this position?
- What are some of the skills you would bring to this job?
- Have you performed the work entailed in this position before? If so, when, and do you see any significant differences between then and now?
- How do you define service?
- What do you consider to be your strengths?
- What are your weaknesses?
- What do you think your current supervisor/faculty advisor would say are your strengths and weaknesses?
- Tell us about a job you've had that you did not like and what it was about that job that caused the dislike.
- Tell us about the job you liked best and why.
- What are your current career plans? Do you see them changing in the next three to five years?

Often the interview will begin with something like "tell us something about yourself." One reason for starting this way is everyone knows the interview is stressful, and starting with something the candidate knows best will help release some of the tension. Decide what is and is not appropriate to say. Sometimes minds go blank at the start of an interview, and it is easy to say the first thing that springs to mind. Do your homework about the questions that an employer shouldn't ask, and have polite ways to deflect them. Carrying out a mock interview with someone who knows you well so that he or she can offer constructive criticism to help adjust your presentation also can ease pre-interview stress.

> **Check This Out**
>
> The Association of College and Research Libraries (ACRL) issued some guidelines for screening candidates in 2009: "A Guideline for the Screening and Appointment of Academic Librarians," which can be found at www.ala.org/ala/mgrps/divs/acrl/standards screening guide.cfm.

Interviewing

We devote some space to the interview process because it will come into play when applying for a position and when you serve on a search committee. In both instances, it requires an understanding of the process as well as a good deal of practice to become effective as interviewee or interviewer. What follows applies to both sides of the interview table.

A sound interview process has six important elements. First, there is the need to plan the process. Beyond the obvious, such as timing and place, some of the key planning issues are length of the interview, whom to involve in the interview, the questions to ask, whether a tour should be given, and how much time should be devoted to answering candidate questions. As a candidate, you should also plan your questions about the position and institution.

The second element, and perhaps the most critical in a legal sense, is to carefully review the interview questions for their compliance with nondiscrimination laws. This is an area where HR staff can be of great assistance. You also want to have consistency and comparability of information about each candidate. Maintaining consistency in the questions and in the structure of the entire process for all the candidates is critical when it comes time to assessing each one and making a final selection/ranking/recommendation. Questions must be job related (the example questions provided previously are legal). If you can't link each question to the job description, don't ask it. Asking a few open-ended questions gives candidates an opportunity to respond more fully and demonstrate some of their skills.

What should you do if you are asked inappropriate questions, and is this likely to happen? Gardner (2007) indicates it happens more often than you'd expect, especially with medium- and small-sized organizations, in part because the people are not aware that they are doing anything wrong. In her article she quoted John Petrella, an employment lawyer, "It happens all the time.... It's really easy for employers to get in trouble. It's really easy to run afoul of the antidiscrimation laws" (D1). The article goes on to address what to do when asked improper questions and offers approaches for you to think about before responding to such questions. First, ask yourself and perhaps the interviewer, "Is this question related to the position I'm applying for?" Remember, the question could be appropriate if it is clearly job related. At the same time you might want to consider, "Do I really want to work for an organization that asks such questions?" You do have the choice of not answering the question knowing it might cause you not to get an offer. You can of course answer the question and then inquire as to the relevance of the question to the position. There is a reasonable chance of your having to deal with this issue at some point in your career, as an interviewee. Try not to do it when you are the interviewer.

The third element is having a segment of time where the candidate is given a clear sense of what the vacant position actually does as well as an overview of the library's operation and mission. Also, having some time to explain the relationship of the library to the campus helps candidates make an informed decision should an offer be made. It is also the time for the candidate to ask the search committee questions.

The fourth element in the process is the "personal impact" of both the candidate and the interviewers on each other. Creating a relaxed and friendly atmosphere at the outset helps candidates become less nervous and thus more effective during the formal interview. Practices such as tone of voice, eye contact, personal appearance and grooming, posture, and gestures on the part of both candidate and interviewer influence both parties. Keep in mind that in a culturally diverse community the meanings of these actions may be very different. For example, lack of eye contact does not always mean the person is the "shifty-eyed nasty character" of English novels.

Related to impact is how the interviewer responds to the applicant (the fifth element). Interviewers must be careful to control their nonverbal behavior that may encourage or discourage an applicant in an inappropriate way. Not showing an interest in what the candidate is saying will discourage the person from expanding on her or his thoughts, and this may well carry over to the remainder of the interview. Anyone with extensive experience with interviewing understands just how difficult controlling those two behaviors can be at times.

The final element is to assess the interview data fairly and equitably for all the interviewees. Some of the issues that can cause unfair processing are the following:

- Stereotyping the "right" person for the position
- Using different weights for various attributes by different members of a search committee
- Overusing visual clues about the candidate that are not job-related
- Not recognizing "contrast effects"—that is, when a strong candidate follows a very weak candidate the contrast makes the stronger applicant look even stronger than she or he may be

The following is a summary of things to keep in mind regarding the interview process as a candidate:

- Take some time to research the library and its parent organization ahead of time. Their websites can tell you a great deal about them.
- Generate a few questions about the library based on your research and your own interests.
- If you did not receive a full position description, don't be shy about asking for one; take time to think up questions about the position.
- Spend some time thinking about the answers you might give to questions that are likely to be part of the interview (e.g., What interests you about this particular position? What do you consider your strengths and your weaknesses? What does the term "service" mean to you?).
- Dress appropriately.
- Be on time.
- Be certain to have the interviewer's name and its correct pronunciation.
- Remember that your "body language" also reflects your interest and attentiveness.
- Taking time to think before answering complex questions is appropriate—thinking before speaking is always a good idea.
- With a multipart question be sure to cover all of the parts—asking for clarification or for repetition of a part of such questions is appropriate.
- Asking how any personal or potentially illegal question(s) relate to job performance is appropriate; however, be sure to ask it in a nonconfrontational manner, as the question may be job related.
- Thank the interviewer(s) for the opportunity to interview for the position.
- Asking about the anticipated time frame for deciding on who will be hired is appropriate.
- To learn from each interview experience, jot down a few postinterview notes about some of the high and low points of the interview.
- Even if you decide during the interview process that this is not the position for you, send a follow-up thank-you note to the chair of the search committee, position supervisor, or head of HR (which ever is most appropriate), thanking the person for his or her time and for giving you an opportunity to meet with him or her.

Philip C. Howze (2008) conducted a study of how well search committees do in narrowing down the pool to the interview stage. He concluded his article with:

Whether resumes, particularly for "entry-level" positions, are too long or contain too many sections headings . . . is certainly a question worthy of professional concern. . . . More studies are needed, to determine whether "qualified" applicants are being advanced in large search pools or prematurely discarded, in order to contribute to our understanding of the interface between applicants and search committees, in light of the costs associated with failed searches. (p. 352)

His study suggested that too often the search committee appears to have "determined the viability of a finalist pool based on little more than intuition" (p. 352). If nothing else, his study emphasizes how important the set of application documents are when it comes to getting an interview.

ADJUSTING TO THE POSITION

Moving into the first professional position is not easy. There is enthusiasm and desire to demonstrate one's skills and knowledge. All of these feelings are important as motivators. However, they can also generate problems. Yes, everyone wants to have a team member who is keen, talented, and committed, but sometimes new appointees go over the top in attempting to prove themselves and believing that they can use their talents to improve local practices. It is best to remember that there are usually good reasons why the procedures are the way they are, so look and listen and wait awhile before offering your advice as a newcomer. It may well be that there are newer and better ways to carry out a task—the new graduate should be at the cutting edge of developments—but understand the reasons why things are being done in a certain way before proposing a change.

One challenge of any new job is learning the organization's culture and politics. There will be the organizational chart that shows formal relationships, but not infrequently the way things are done is rather different than what the official structure would suggest. It takes time to gain a clear understanding of the culture; ignoring the culture is probably one of the factors that leads to serious job dissatisfaction.

Another factor is this is where expectations meet reality. Internships and part-time employment provide useful insights into what the field is like, but they cannot replicate full-time day-in and day-out work. Everyone experiences some degree of difference between hopes/expectations and actuality when starting a new job. However, first-time librarians experience a much higher difference than do librarians having several years of experience.

Joanne Oud (2008) wrote about the transition from student to academic librarian. The first year is critical in career planning. A good or great experience will probably lead to a long-term successful career. Less positive experience may lead to a decision to leave the field. Part of what makes for a good or not so good experience is what the expectations were for the new profession. Oud surveyed 111 "new librarians" who began work in the spring of 2004; she received 97 useable responses. Her major themes regarding the individuals' differences between expectations and reality are worth listing. There were nine "themes" drawn from the respondents' open-ended responses regarding the differences between expectations and the work:

- More flexibility/independence
- Greater variety of job responsibilities/tasks
- Bureaucracy, slow pace of change
- Negative workplace environment (politics, not collegial)
- Collegial workplace
- Busier/heavy workload
- Faculty and students attitudes to the library
- Difficult school-to-work transition
- Lack of training and time to learn (p. 256)

The first points were positive differences while the remaining seven were negative. Oud also asked about what aspects of the job were most challenging. Not too surprisingly the most difficult was "getting things done," when and how to take the initiative, followed by learning the politics/organizational culture. Also not surprising was that these new librarians with the highest degree of difference between expectations and the job had the lowest job satisfaction.

In her conclusions, Oud (2008) wrote, "First, the results confirmed that most new librarians would benefit from more assistance in their new workplace ... in many academic libraries the new librarian is left to learn much of the job informally or on his or her own initiative" (p. 263). She went on to suggest, "Given the difficulties reported by new librarians in learning the cultural aspect of their new jobs and workplaces, more effort should be made to develop ways to assist new employees in this critical area of their transition process" (p. 264).

STARTING YOUR CAREER DEVELOPMENT PLAN

Once in your first position and getting through the first year or so of transitioning to the workplace it is time to assess those long-term career plans that you thought about while in school. Hopefully there has been time to read some of the professional journals and even a little time to read something about current events in higher education, perhaps a regular scanning of the *Chronicle of Higher Education*. Such reading helps one keep current with what is happening in one's specialty as well as in the broader environment, both of which are beneficial when it is time to take the next career step.

Getting involved in professional matters through a professional association is an effective and enjoyable way to develop ideas and to network. Becoming involved professionally provides the start of networking that can pay many dividends throughout a career. It cannot be predicted which of your peers at college will later become influential people.

Networking is an essential element in career development; it applies to both the campus and the wider world. Any large institution operates rather like a series of tribes. Each unit has its own technical jargon and local shorthand, ways of organizing itself, and socializing. Moving across these boundaries provides new insights and adds to a deeper understanding of the organizational culture. Getting involved in staff associations and committees within the wider organization develops the awareness of who, and what, makes the campus tick.

> **Check This Out**
>
> For those interested in exploring networking around the world, the International Federation of Library Associations' New Professionals Discussion Group has a webpage: www.ifla.org/VII/dg/npdg/index.htm.

Mentors

Mentors and role models are another element in developing one's career. A mentor can be an asset at any stage in a career providing advice and comment, when requested, on upcoming decisions. A key factor in having a mentor is that the person needs to be able to understand/relate to the mentee and that person's goals. A mentor can offer realistic advice and provide a second opinion on a proposed course of action but cannot make decisions on behalf of the person mentored. A mentor is not a crutch but rather an informed sounding board. The mentor's role is of adviser, counselor, friend, and supporter, and he or she needs to be able to affirm decisions or provide alternative scenarios. In turn, the person being mentored needs to develop listening skills, to be able to learn from the experience of others, evaluate the offered advice, and understand as well as accept constructive criticism.

Mentors need to be chosen with care, having demonstrated a rapport and interest in you as a new professional. They could be a member of the library school faculty or an experienced practitioner. Many of the most effective mentoring arises almost without either party thinking the relationship is a mentoring one—it just happens. There are some formal programs that work at linking people into a mentoring program. In making a choice, it is important that you have respect for the would-be mentor, have good rapport, and both parties have a level of trust that enables advice to be offered and received in the spirit in which it is offered.

Mentors may be asked to provide references and comment on strengths and perhaps weaknesses. They should be able to offer advice about a position that is under consideration and should have a view about its suitability. The mentor's networks may yield advance notice of a post not yet advertised. Some professional associations have established committees that match people willing to mentor with those seeking a mentor.

In today's world much of the mentoring is virtual rather than face-to-face. Certainly, the informal mentoring relationships depend in large part on e-mail and other technologies with only occasional face-to-face mentoring such as at conferences and workshops. The formal organizationally sponsored programs that are virtual in character require a substantial amount of organizational support.

One area where academic librarianship mentoring is probably critical is for those new librarians at institutions that have faculty or similar status for their librarians, as our opening quotation from Deborah Lee (2005) suggested. Her article outlines one form of such mentoring, a library research committee. The committee she discussed had six charges:

Check This Out

One interesting website to check out regarding mentoring is Mentornet, which focuses on one-on-one higher education mentoring in engineering and science (www.mentornet.net/Documents/ About/). Having such a site for academic librarians would be great benefit for the field. A more general site is National Mentoring Center (www.nwrel.org/mentoring).

Check This Out

An article by Diana Farmer, Marcia Stockman, and Alice Trussell (2009) provides an overview of another institutional based mentoring program for new librarians seeking to meet tenure requirements: "Revitalizing a Mentoring Program for Academic Librarians," *College & Research Libraries* 70, no. 1: 8-24.

For Further Thought

Do you have a mentor? List the attributes that you think a mentor for you would need.

- Developing programs to enhance the research skills of the library faculty
- Sponsoring informal discussions of research ideas, strategies, methodologies, and opportunities
- Apprising faculty members of upcoming conference and deadlines for paper submissions
- Providing individual mentoring as needed, including editorial advice
- Recognizing faculty publications in appropriate ways
- Recommending to the dean improvements to support research (p. 711)

She ended her article by stating, "These activities can assist new academic librarians as they adjust to the expectations of a tenure track position" (p. 724).

Self-Assessment of Knowledge and Skills

Doing a self-assessment is not easy, and a mentor should be able to provide input. The points to be considered include the following:

- Degrees held
- Short courses attended
- Any study in progress
- Involvement in professional activities and committee work within the organization
- Work experience
- Level of job satisfaction
- Preferred career direction
- Preferred sector and specialization
- Areas that would not be welcomed at this stage
- Personal strengths—what you do well
- Personal weaknesses—what you do not do well
- Level of commitment to working in the field—is the current institution a long-term career goal or a shorter-term goal?
- Are there other factors that are important? Are there other activities outside of work that are important and that influence professional growth?

The last two factors are particularly important. Long-term intention to stay in the field may not be part of your career development; however, information skills are transferable skills. Taking personal circumstances into account will result in better decisions. Carrying out a regular self-assessment assists career development at any point in a working life. A preferred move may require the acquisition of new skills or the honing some that have been dormant.

Lifelong learning and developing new skills is essential for career development. Thus, education and training needs change over time. Some individuals take the option of taking a second-level master's degree in the discipline of their undergraduate degree or a new area of interest. Then there may be a shift to doctoral study to pursue research in a professional subject or academic discipline.

One long-standing question in academic librarianship has been that of additional advanced degrees: are they nice or necessary? Clearly the issue is a significant factor in terms of career development. In spite a great many informal discussions among academic librarians, there has not been very much research on the value of having advanced degrees beyond the MLS. An older article by Mary Grosch and Terry Weech (1991) reported on a study of perceptions of the value of such degrees. Occasionally you see ads that list a second advanced degree as desirable and even more often in directorship vacancies that an earned doctorate is "highly desirable." Some academic institutions, in an effort to encourage professional growth, will provide an increase in salary when an individual completes another advanced degree.

Probably one of the common benefits of such degrees, from a workplace perspective, is enhanced creditability with teaching faculty outside of the library. Having the degree indicates that you have successfully been through the process and understand the scholarly process.

Jennifer Mayer and Lori Terill (2005) revisited the issue of attitudes about graduate degrees beyond the MLS. Their methodology used a web-based survey. The survey generated 1,213 responses; the authors did not indicate how they controlled for multiple responses from an individual. They concluded their essay by stating, "The question of academic librarians and advanced-subject degrees does not have an easy answer, but it is hoped that this article has provided some valuable insights into the debate" (p. 69).

From the Authors

Both of us have advanced subject degrees and have found them to be intellectually satisfying, useful if not essential in securing one or more of our professional positions, and above all very useful in working with teaching faculty and campus administrators. Do we believe such degrees are essential for a successful career as an academic librarian? Not at all. Do we believe they can be beneficial to one's career? Absolutely.

CHANGING VIEWS OF A "CAREER"

In the past, most people's view of a career was probably one of steady progression from the bottom to the top of an organizational structure. Today's careers are more flexible, but the factors that contribute to the achievement of progress include having the appropriate qualifications, experience, attitude, and aptitude. Setting a career goal helps to sharpen the awareness of specific needs and how they can be met.

One of the frustrations that many academic librarians face is that the higher they move up the salary ladder the greater the percentage of time spent on managing. Less time is devoted to using their professional knowledge and skills. The question of the balance between the two often is a significant factor in considering whether or not to apply for a position with higher salary. Just how much management will it entail? For some people the management aspects of the workplace are not all that attractive, yet they know higher salaries are more or closely linked to how much management is involved in a position. Giving serious thought to this issue early in the career and making some personal decisions may well save some heartache, stress, and frustration down the road.

A final point to make about career goals is that they will change over time. Changes take place in one's personal life and the profession, but having goals and knowing your personal values makes better decisions when considering a change of post. Making job applications takes time, quite a considerable amount of time. It also involves an investment on the part of an employer.

To "test the water" before taking your career in a new direction, examine the range of flexible working practices available since libraries generally have very extended service hours. Most academic libraries, at least during academic terms, operate seven days a week. Part-time posts may be available at a nearby library during your off hours and can provide some insight into a new work area assuming you are thinking of staying in the field. A job-share is one way of using acquired professional expertise while moving into a new field.

The growth of the Internet has introduced another flexible way of working. Working from home on a freelance basis can be effective for an increasing number of areas of professional practice. It has been common for indexers and abstractors to work in this way for many years, and the practice now extends to handling inquiries, marketing and public relations, information brokers, consultants, editors, etc. The range of work is expanding as services outsource more of their services. Working in this way requires good organization and communication skills and close attention to customer care.

Career Breaks

Career breaks benefit both the employee and the employer. Academic librarians often have two options for a break from the daily workplace. Most with faculty status have an opportunity to apply for a sabbatical. The other method is to secure an unpaid leave. The person who enjoys a break comes back refreshed and reinvigorated. Another benefit for the staff development program is that another member of the staff can be offered the opportunity to demonstrate their skills in a different post.

For the person considering a break either as an unpaid leave or sabbatical, there is a range of opportunities. Developmental internships or fellowships, such as those organized by the Association of Research Libraries, may be available for those designated as high flyers. In the case of librarians eligible for a sabbatical, the person must have a research project to pursue during the time away from the library. Such projects usually have to have some linkage or relate to what the person does or will do. It even may be an opportunity to the test the water in a new area, such as studying how university presses select the manuscripts they publish.

Traveling overseas may be the choice at any stage in a career. Travel scholarships for short periods of time are offered by a number of organizations. Exchanges with professionals in other parts of the world can be set up with facilitators through exchange registers that list people seeking an exchange in all types of services and in a number of countries around the world. Most are for three or six months and often involve a swap of job, house, and car. Voluntary service overseas was, at one time, the province of the new graduate; but now as more people take early retirement or a career break, their skills and experience can be of value in other countries.

Breaks for family responsibilities, such as maternity or paternity leave, are becoming part of established employment policies and practices. This can help parents enjoy and more fully participate in the early stages of their child's life. An article by Graves, Xiong, and Park (2008) reported on a survey they conducted with tenured and tenure track librarians about parenthood and professorship. Their study did show that the promotion and tenure process does play a role in decisions regarding parenthood. They concluded, in part, "The study has implications for academic libraries and the larger university audience. The message is clear that there is still a sense of discrepancy between parenthood and professorhood in librarianship" (p. 209).

Work/Life Debate

Management literature demonstrates a continuing concern regarding the pressures being placed on managers and their staffs as organizations strive to cut operating costs. Much has been written about the negative effects of stress that can affect anyone within an organization, regardless of age, gender, or level. Progressing in a career can increase the susceptibility to stress. Learning a new job can mean taking work home and acquiring new knowledge, qualifications, or skills. E-mail, the Internet, and intranets can add to the pressures of daily life, resulting in a situation where it is hard to break away from work and always feeling the need to "catch up." In its most serious manifestation, excessive eating, drinking, or smoking can be the individual's answer to the problem. But stress can damage physical and psychological health and reduce the effectiveness of a person's performance, which, in turn, impacts on the work of their colleagues. Recognizing the symptoms may be unpalatable to the employee and difficult for the employer. Many universities provide in-house counseling that may help staff and themselves. The remedy lies with the individuals, and they should limit the amount of overtime they work; take all of their leave allowance; have a holiday; ensure that they have a leisure-time interest; and ensure that family and friends have a share in their life.

MOVING FORWARD

Part of moving forward is making your talents known. Success is easier to achieve if others know about you, both within and outside of the institution in which you are working. Looking for ways to do your job more effectively and presenting them to a supervisor—at the right time and in the right way—will show initiative, particularly if the thoughts have been developed as part of a team. Becoming known in the profession can come from joining committees, attending meetings, writing in the professional press, and making thoughtful contributions to discussion on the Internet.

> **For Further Thought**
>
> List four steps that you can take now to make others aware of your talents.

Membership in a professional association pays dividends. Its journal, publications, and website keep practitioners in touch with news and developments. Selecting appropriate discussion lists and contributing to discussion stimulates professional thinking and allows an exchange of viewpoints and experiences. Meetings provide an opportunity to exchange ideas and make yourself known outside of your library. Conferences provide exposure to a wide range of professional activities. Those who travel to the annual professional conference find that it is an exhilarating potpourri of meetings, exhibitors, and enthusiastic librarians and prospective employers.

Keeping in touch with change means that a range of sources will need to be consulted regularly, in both paper and electronic formats. First, reading a range of journals in the professional is essential. Clearly, the relevant national titles will be of primary importance, but there will also be international titles.

Becoming a member of a professional committee develops the essential political skills needed in career development. Giving papers and talks enhances communication skills. Involvement in the activities of international associations extends a network and provides insight into professional practices overseas. No single country has a monopoly on good practice. And for the librarian who cannot travel and is geographically isolated, the Internet provides the means of taking part in debate around the globe without leaving your desk.

The direction a career may take will, to an extent, be conditioned by factors outside of the control of the individual and will include economic, political, social, and technological change and the state of the labor market. But there is a range of opportunities, and individuals have choices in selecting the direction in which they would prefer to move. Career development depends on staying well informed. Information-handling skills are transferable skills, and they can be used in many occupations outside of the mainstream of the information professions.

KEY POINTS TO REMEMBER

- Know yourself, both the strengths and the weaknesses.
- Have high standards, both personal and professional, and demonstrate them in your daily work.
- Demonstrate commitment to whatever job you have.
- Cultivate clear thinking and maintain an objective viewpoint.
- Be reliable.
- Be adaptable.
- Cultivate and never lose your sense of humor.
- Understand the way that others think.
- Show a concern for others in your professional and personal life, but in unobtrusive ways.
- Keep at the cutting edge of change.
- Develop good communication and influencing skills.
- Acquire political skills.
- Extend managerial knowledge and know what is best practice in management thinking.
- Ensure that you are working effectively as a member of a team at all stages in a career.
- Know how to make decisions and change them if the situation demands.
- Delegate.
- Maintain control over your own time.
- Recognize mistakes that you have made and learn from them.
- Believe in yourself.
- Understand the career development requires an investment of time and money.
- Enjoy the job you are doing—if you don't enjoy the one you are in, find another.

REFERENCES

Bridges, Karl. 2002. The unbearable slowness of hiring. *American Libraries* (November): 43–44.

DeMajo, Mary Madden. 2008. It's never too late to retool. *American Libraries* 39, no. 10: 50–53.

Gardner, Marilyn. 2007. Job interviewers: What can they legally ask? *Arizona Daily Sun*, July 29, pp. D1, D4. (Also printed as: What you need know about what they can ask. *Christian Science Monitor* July 23, 2007.)

Graves, Stephanie J., Jian Anna Xiong, and Ji-Hye Park. 2008. Parenthood, professorship, and librarianship: Are they mutually exclusive? *Journal of Academic Librarianship* 34, no. 3: 202–210.

Grosch, Mary, and Terry L. Weech. 1991. Perceived value of advanced subject degrees by librarians who hold such degrees. *Library Information Science Research* 13, no. 2: 173–199.

Howze, Philip C. 2008. Search committee effectiveness in determining a finalist pool: A case study. *Journal of Academic Librarianship* 34, no. 4: 340–353.

Kell, Susan E. 2007. Technically speaking: Professional growth is essential for librarians. *Learning Media* 35, no. 2: 8–10.

Lee, Deborah. 2005. Mentoring the untenured librarian. *College & Research Library News* 66, no. 10: 711–713, 724.

Lee, Marta. 2009. Growing librarians: Mentorship in an academic library. *Library Leadership & Management* 23, no. 1: 31–37.

Mayer, Jennifer, and Lori J. Terill. 2005. Academic librarians' attitudes about advanced-subject degrees. *College & Research Libraries* 66, no. 1: 59–70.

Oud, Joanne. 2008. Adjusting to the workplace: Transition faced by new academic librarians. *College & Research Libraries* 69, no. 3: 252–266.

LAUNCHING PAD

Doolittle, Elizabeth M., John-Bauer Graham, Alyssa Martin, Hal Mendelsohn, Kent Snowden, and Amada Stone. 2009. Creating a culture of mentoring @ your library. *Southeastern Librarian* 57, no. 1: 29–38.

Englert, Tracy. 2009. Toastmasters: Boost your resume without breaking the bank. *Mississippi Libraries* 73, no. 2: 35–37.

Farkas, Meredith. 2007. A roadmap to learning 2.0. *American Libraries* 38, no. 2: 26.

Fietzer, William. 1993. World enough, and time: Using search and screen committees to select personnel in academic libraries. *Journal of Academic Librarianship* 19, no. 3: 149–153.

Holley, Robert P. 2003. The ivory tower as preparation for the trenches. *College and Research Libraries News* 64, no. 3: 172–175.

Kong, Chris Evin, and Rachel Applegate. 2008. Bridging the gap in digital library continuing education. *Library Administration & Management* 22, no. 4: 172–182.

Lehner, John A. 1992. Reconsidering the personnel selection practices of academic libraries. *Journal of Academic Librarianship* 23, no. 3: 199–204.

Murphy, Sarah Anne. 2008. Developmental relationships in the dynamic library environment: Re-conceptualizing mentoring for the future. *Journal of Academic Librarianship* 34, no. 5: 434–437.

Seiss, Judith. 2005. It's your career: What are you doing about it? *One-Person Library* 22, no. 6: 1–2.

Spencer, Brett, and Allyson R. Ard. 2006. Nurturing new careers. *Electronic Journal of Academic and Special Librarianship* 7, no. 2. Available: southernlibrarianship.icaap.org/content/v07n02/spencer_b01.htm (accessed April 7, 2010).

Templeton, Mary Ellen. 1997. *Help! My job interview is tomorrow! How to use the library to research an employer.* 2nd ed. New York: Neal-Schuman.

Wilkinson, Frances C., and Linda K. Lewis. 2006. Training programs in academic libraries. *C&RL News* 67, no. 6: 356–358, 365.

Womack, Kay. 1997. Applying for professional positions in academic libraries. *Journal of Academic Librarianship* 23, no. 3: 205–209.

Chapter 16

Leaders Look Toward the Future

Yet while waves of change will come our way, one thing is certain and sure. The future of the academic library will be dependent on the future of learning. As the premier supporting service to learning, the library must chart its future in alignment with the direction of learning.

—Susan C. Curzon (2010)

The challenges facing academic libraries are intrinsically different to that which we have been taught and which we have experienced. The challenges need to be imagined; they need to be totally reconceptualized; they need to be seen from the outside-in rather than inside-out perspective.

—Steve O'Connor (2010)

Is there a viable future for academic libraries and their staffs, and for that matter what is the future of the academy? More than a few individuals have declared that the library, higher education, or both are in their death throes. (One example was Don Tapscott's [2009] essay about the demise of universities appearing in *Edge: The Third Culture*.) Looking at catchy titles of articles or newspaper headlines, you might think there was some merit to such views. However, the material following the provocative titles makes it clear the authors are focusing on how technology and Web are, or should be, forcing changes in the status quo rather than causing the demise of the institution(s).

In Chapter 1 we wrote the following regarding the future of both postsecondary education and academic libraries:

There are pointed and valid concerns about academia's viability, just as there are about libraries. Tom Abeles (2006) wrote, "The direction of the university today must be seen, first as an enterprise that is different from the idea of university as seen by Newman, Kant, and von Humboldt. Secondly, it must be seen as a problem for faculty and not that of the institution" (p. 36). The technological challenges facing the academy appear to be just as great as those facing libraries. Abeles also suggested that "the time has come for institutions and the academics to understand that the caterpillar must transform into a butterfly" (p. 42). A few years earlier, Snyder and Edwards (2003), in writing about the context of education in the United States in the year 2020, wrote, "We found little evidence of significant innovation or change in the social technologies by which we formally organize and deliver education. Nor did we find any serious movement to assess alternatives to teacher mediated classroom-based learning" (p. 5). One fact is crystal clear: higher education and its libraries must change together. Without a joint process, there is little chance of long-term viability for either entity.

Academic libraries provide open and generally free access to the entire world of knowledge, not just to some segment of it. Furthermore, we agree with the following quotation from an article about e-government and print versus electronic distribution of information:

> Reports of the death of paper, rampant in the 1990s, were evidently greatly exaggerated. The paperless office never materialized; nor, yet, have e-books. People still print letters and flip through pages of magazines. ("Flat Prospects," 2007, p. 72)

A few years ago, Okerson (2003) offered her thoughts about the digital library. Her view was that eight "eternal verities" about library collections and services remain valid today and will continue to do so into the future. Most of the truths relate to services in some manner. These truths were the following:

- Content is selectable.
- Content is collectable.
- Libraries retain information for the long term.
- Collections grow and require some type of space.
- Long-term retention requires preservation of some type.
- Libraries expect to be around for a very long time.
- Libraries exist to meet users' information needs.
- Today's information is worldwide and so are libraries, helping ensure worldwide preservation of information/knowledge.

She concluded by writing, "May we all go boldly together where no libraries have gone before" (p. 285). We believe her views are accurate and to the point—libraries will indeed go successfully and boldly forward into the future.

We also agree with Lewis's (2007) assumptions about twenty-first-century academic libraries:

- Libraries are a means not an end.
- Disruptive technologies can and will disrupt libraries.
- A small change here and there will not result in real change.
- There is time to make effective changes, if we do not wait too long. (pp. 419–420)

We think a fifth assumption is necessary to complete the picture: If libraries do not change, they will join the dinosaurs.

Everyone is in agreement that academic institutions, libraries, and librarians have changed, dramatically so when looking back over just the past 20 years. Even a cursory look at the history of the academy makes it clear that the institution and its various components are adaptable to changing circumstances and societal needs. Admittedly, the pace of change has often been rather slow, but it does change.

Check This Out

A good book to read about where libraries and librarianship are and should be in the future is John M. Budd's *Self-Examination: The Present and Future of Librarianship* (Westport, CT: Libraries Unlimited, 2008).

Successful organizational transformations are seldom neither quick nor painless. Thinking back to discussions in basic management courses about change and the change process—at its most basic level the process of unfreezing, change, freezing (Lewin, 1951)—it is clear that time is a key factor in moving from one organizational state to another. Another factor is that some organizations change more quickly than others. The agile ones tend to be the most successful in the long term.

FUTURE OF ACADEMIC LIBRARIES: LIBRARY DIRECTORS' PERSPECTIVES

Early in our planning for writing this book, we decided to ask some director colleagues if they would contribute a short essay about what they saw as the future of academic libraries and librarianship. Twenty-one people graciously contributed. The individuals

Table 16.1. Institutional Types Represented by Essay Contributors	
Type of Institution	# of Essay Contributors
Research Libraries (ARLs)	4
University Libraries	4 (two international)
College Libraries	3
Community College Libraries	3
Academic Health Science Libraries	2
Academic Law Libraries	2
Special Collections	1
Library Education	1
Academic Library Consortia	1

reflect something of a cross-section of the field from the largest institutions to specialized libraries. Table 16.1 provides a breakdown of the coverage.

One interesting fact about the essays is that they all reflected an optimistic view about the future. They almost all do so with some serious caveats or necessary conditions for there to be a viable future, as we will discuss. Unfortunately, several individuals who suggested they might contribute a less positive view of the future were unable to do so due to work commitments. We had looked forward to reading such views, if for no other reason than to gain some insight into what factors were identified as beyond addressing.

An analysis of the essays identified 48 "topics" mentioned by one or more individuals. Tables 16.2–16.4 provide an overview of the issues raised by the essayists.

The balance of this chapter focuses on the 12 double-digit topics from Table 16.2. We will also briefly touch on some of the topics in Tables 16.3 and 16.4. You can read the full text of all the essays by going to www.nealschuman.org/academic.

Table 16.2. Double-Digit Topics Discussed by Essay Contributors	
Topic Discussed	# of Essay Contributors
Radical change necessary	19
Effective adaptation of technology	18
Increase role in digitization	17
Library as place	13
Addressing financial challenges	13
Creating a positive user experience	13
Developing new skills for librarians and staff	13
Enhance/build better cross-institutional collaboration	12
More and better library advocacy	12
Build better connections with students	12
Strengthen mission focus	11
Essential to balance digital and print resources	10

Table 16.3. Topics with Two or More Listings

Topics Mentioned 2+ Times	# of Essay Contributors
Address the necessary and growing diversity on staff and student body	9
Improve students' research skills	9
Address the storage of legacy print collections	9
Engage in better collaboration with faculty	8
Take on greater campus leadership roles	8
Stay current with learning trends	8
Engage in deeper research into user needs	7
Become a campus agency of change	5
Disseminate campus research	4
Improve library distance education interface	4
Engage in efforts to truly become campus core	4
Vastly improve our business models	4
Be willing to change our organizational structure quickly	3
Be more supportive of faculty research	3
Help address need to make degrees more affordable	2
Increase awareness of librarians as teachers	2
Recognize and support the concept of the social side of libraries	2
Effectively address the changing relationship with information producers	2
Recognize the important role of the community colleges play in higher education	2
Recognize the role of academic health science libraries	2
Recognize the value of archives	2

Table 16.4. Topics Mentioned Once

Topics Mentioned 1 Time	
Need for more staff	Information haves and have-nots
Cross-cultural challenges	Becoming a campus publisher
Censorship	Loaning equipment
Librarian activism	Migrating U.S. academic library model to others
Collection size	Increasing diversity of academic library work
Accreditation	Necessary changes in cataloging practices
Copyright	Library of Congress versus Dewey as academic
LIS degree	classification system

CHALLENGES TO CHANGE

The most frequently mentioned issue (19 of 21 essays) for academic libraries to address in terms of their long-term viability was *change*. Not the incremental change libraries have always undergone but rather dramatic or radical change. For the majority of contributors this was the most important factor in terms of the survival for the field. Perhaps the most pointed statement regarding this need came from Jim Neal (Columbia University) who noted in the opening paragraph of his essay, "The two things we must advance are primal innovation, a basic commitment to risk and experimentation, and radical collaboration, deep and unprecedented partnerships. Renovation is grossly inadequate. Deconstruction is totally essential."

Joan Giesecke (University of Nebraska, Lincoln), while slightly less pointedly, closed her essay by stating, "Can academic libraries survive and thrive in the future? I believe they can if they are willing to make the tough choices to let go of the past, seriously review sacred cows, and build the partnerships that are needed to cement the role of the library as more than the symbol of the heart of the campus."

A voice from the college library environment echoed these views. Thomas Carter (St. Mary's College of California) wrote, "In order for libraries to continue to perform the vital functions of making information available to students and faculty, libraries need to adapt to the changing information landscape and our changing user's needs. Our challenge is to remain relevant to teaching and learning by doing the following: (1) continuing to adapt new technologies and existing spaces to serve our students and faculty, (2) continuing to juggle support for both analog and digital resources, and (3) publicizing and marketing to our campus communities what we are doing and why it is still important."

Lynne King (Schenectady County Community College) concluded her essay by noting:

> Community colleges have long specialized in rapid adoption of new programs to support the retraining of workers throughout their careers and in ever-changing economic conditions. As a result, their libraries are nimble in the regular changes necessary to support this need. In addition, community college librarians may be less set in their ways than many of their peers in other academic and research libraries, many more of whom serve in tenured positions, which can reduce incentive for change.... These libraries are perhaps the best prepared among those across all sectors of higher education to apply the rapid cycle change skills necessary to develop libraries of the future. And these libraries will be all the better for being defined by the real world needs of their students and by an institutional mission to provide opportunity to all who choose to enroll at their campuses.

Specialized academic libraries are equally vulnerable if they fail to adjust to the changing environment. Law libraries, whose primary clientele are highly dependent on information for their daily work activities, face some particular challenges, as Barbara Bintliff (University of Colorado, Boulder, William A. Wise Law Library) noted in her concluding paragraph:

> We may not be entirely clear on what the future will hold for academic law libraries, but academic law library administrators will, to a great extent, make their libraries' own futures by actions taken today. If academic law libraries are to remain relevant in the educational

---

From the Authors

We believe the challenges for academic libraries to respond to twenty-first century developments are profoundly different from past pressures to adjust to new environmental circumstances. First, unlike in the past, slow incremental modifications are unlikely to work in time to assure viability. Second, the current set of circumstances impact every academic library regardless of their parent institutional type. Third, the breadth of the challenges means there ought to be an almost simultaneous commitment by all academic libraries to address the requisite changes. Fourth, there must be regional, national, and international efforts to identify the areas of critical importance for long-term survival as well as to suggest priorities for where to start in order to assist individual libraries to begin to address change(s).

program of the law school, the future must include recognition of the research expertise of the law librarians as well as incorporation of librarians into the formal teaching mission. For this to happen, law library administrators will need to be active politically, in the law school and even across campus. To do anything less will confine the academic law library to an increasingly marginal role in legal education.

TECHNOLOGY CHALLENGES

The second most frequently discussed concern regarding the future of academic libraries was *technology*. Certainly this was not surprising, nor is it a very new challenge for libraries of all types. As we noted in Chapter 9, libraries have been adopting and adapting computer and related technologies for some time. Time and speed are two variables that generate more pressing challenges today. New developments in technology seem to occur faster than we have time to even begin to assimilate much less determine how or if they will be useful to adopt or adapt into our information services. Clearly the top three "issues" (change, technology, and digitization) that our essayists discussed most frequently are tightly intertwined.

Loretta Parham's (Atlanta University Center, one of the historically black colleges and universities) concluding paragraph illustrates the interrelated nature of the three issues:

> There is a future for the academic library, although not for all libraries. Those that are on pause for too long, waiting for the perfect moment and the absolute best solution, or failing to partner with faculty and other organizations in the absence of plentiful resources, simply won't last. The future, I believe, is promised to those whose adoption and rapid deployment of new ideas are guided by a leadership that is willing to risk and able to innovate, for these times, they are certainly changing.

A comment that linked current practice to education, technology, and the globalization of higher education appeared in Patricia Wand's (Zayed University, United Arab Emirates) essay.

> Information literacy is so fundamental to the Zayed University curriculum that it forms one of the six learning outcomes for all undergraduates. It is an educational value espoused by everyone in the university and is uniformly promoted by the library, faculty, and administration as a key deliverable. The founding librarians worked closely with faculty in developing a curriculum that integrates information literacy skills development into general education and in specific courses in the majors. Information literacy at Zayed University serves as a model and is the envy of librarians working in many North American academic libraries.

Chapter 12 and Chapter 10 explored information literacy and its importance in the education of today's students as well as in the general public, which is beyond the scope of academic librarianship to address. Obviously the content of such course work and informal instruction will be changing as technology evolves.

One ARL library director (Catherine Murray-Rust, Georgia Institute of Technology) noted that technology is a mixed blessing:

> The rapid growth of digital technology challenges libraries in positive and negative ways. Librarians have always been early adopters of new technologies to enhance services, and digital technologies are no exception. The university community has far better discovery

tools—catalog records, abstracts, and indexes—than ever before. They have commercially available search tools, most of which work better for personal retail activities than complex scholarly queries, but they are nevertheless increasingly used. Users have embraced digital technologies and tools for a wide variety of academic purposes, and librarians have been happy to assist.... Yet, the new tools and technologies, and the services they support, such as data curation services, institutional repositories, and multimedia presentation centers, are both marvelous and terrifying. For librarians to be able to support the campus in taking full advantage of these services, robust infrastructure, funds for adding and replacing hardware and software, and constant updating of faculty and staff skills are required. All of these demands put more pressure on the library's finances and constrain its ability to act in support of its user communities.

Susan C. Curzon (California State University, Northridge) noted how some of the technological changes will impact library operations:

> Ironically, the preservation role of libraries will increase. The lifespan of digital resources is not yet known, so libraries must continue to preserve physical resources as a guarantee that important resources survive into the future.
>
> The online catalog, already under fire for being too cumbersome, will be radically reconceptualized. Two trends will take hold. First, users will expect a catalog that has the capability to display full-text resources, sound, and images. Second, libraries will collectively venture onto a single unified catalog easily accessible to search engines. Once this occurs, libraries will connect more and more, forming a vast national and eventually international library. This connection may have powerful consequences in terms of creating large buying consortiums and true cooperative collection development as the resources of other libraries are more fully displayed and accessible.

Our last two examples of technology concerns are from specialized academic libraries—special collections/archives and health sciences. Michael Kelly (University of New Mexico Libraries) described the technological evolution in terms of special collections:

> What brought us to this crossroads? For many years special collections enjoyed a privileged existence. We had limited but mostly adequate funding; our offices and reading rooms occupied premium spaces; we came to work clearly knowing our jobs were important.... With our unique and valuable collections, special collections gave prestige and uniqueness to the whole institution.... Then sometime in the 1980s, I can't remember exactly when, this all began to change. The opportunities of the Web, scanning technologies, and a better understanding of how our collections could be discovered converged. We embraced these technological changes with a vengeance, seeing in them the promise of finally exposing our rich materials to the world. Over the next 20 years we scanned, we developed EAD (Encoded Archival Description) documents, we cooperated with other institutions to create shared finding aids and subject-based collections of images and documents, and we adapted our processing procedures to incorporate various forms of metadata....
>
> Today we can no longer rely solely on the magic we worked in the dark days before the explosion of electronic resources. We remain confronted with the challenge—the expense—of traditional ways of processing and preserving collections, but we are also faced with more and more digitized materials, better discovery tools, and the need to preserve digital collections and born-digital documents. Bringing the old ways and the new together offers us a road to survival. How we do this will determine the new role for special collections in this ever expanding, rapidly changing, new world we find ourselves inhabiting.

Almost everyone acknowledges that adopting and adapting technology will cause academic librarians' roles to morph into something very different. Holly Shipp Buchanan and Brian Bunnett (University of New Mexico Health Sciences Center) speculated about what some of the role changes may be for health science librarians:

> The centrality of information technology to all types of health sciences librarianship has led to another new role for today's librarian. The emergent technologies librarian or digital research and development librarian is responsible for investigating new technologies that promise to be of special benefit to health sciences libraries. UCLA and the Mayo Clinic are two examples of health science campuses employing emergent technologies librarians.
>
> The close linkage between technology and libraries can also be seen in the development of educational or instructional technology centers within health sciences libraries (e.g., University of Cincinnati's Donald C. Harrison Health Sciences Library).

DIGITIZATION CHALLENGES

The line between "technology" and "digitization" is almost so fine as to be invisible. Our contributors discussed both terms often in the same essay. As we did in earlier chapters, they used *technology* in a broad sense and *digitization* as a specific application of technology.

Glenda Thornton (Cleveland State University) described how the convergence of various technologies led to a merger of campus services:

> In my own organization, the university's independent instructional media services department (which shared walls and access points with the library) experienced the retirement of a director at just the same time that the library was fast expanding its utilization of digital technologies in electronic course reserves and was creating a digital image database. With the increasing utilization of digital technologies in multimedia design, the move of interactive video distance learning to voice- and video-over IP, and the similarities between equipment checkout and library materials circulation, this service was placed under the library. Today, it is very difficult to say exactly what is library and what is instructional media. These two areas are increasingly merging and taking advantage of the synergies that have developed, sometimes rather unexpectedly. However, not every library would necessarily have the technology talent on hand to make this kind of merger successful. They will, however, have different talents that the institution can exploit for the overall benefit of the campus.

Preservation activities of libraries is one area where digitization has played and will play an ever greater role. Carol Parker (University of New Mexico School of Law) identified some preservation projects related to digital data:

> Several recent preservation initiatives seek to establish repositories of this material to ensure the continued existence of legacy print primary law collections. The Legal Information Preservation Alliance (LIPA) seeks to preserve legal information in both print and digital formats that are at risk of loss. Under the LIPA model, various law libraries throughout the United States will inventory and pledge to maintain their print primary law collections to serve as repositories. Other smaller, regional initiatives are also springing up. The Desert States Law Library Consortium set out recently to inventory and preserve territorial- and statehood-era print primary legal materials in their respective home states. Under the Desert States model, a library would pledge to maintain a repository of its home state's legal material, to preserve it and make it available to other member libraries within the consortium. Other member libraries can then rely on electronic access in most instances and safely discard print from all but their home states.

The extended quotation from Michael Kelly's essay provides still more examples of how libraries are employing digitization to preserve and protect our cultural patrimony.

One area where digitization has played a large part in the general press is in terms of books. Two examples are Amazon's Kindle and the Google Books project. One of James Neal's (Columbia University) points about what academic libraries must do to remain viable was, "Build the digital library through published/licensed content, primary and unique content, open web content, and institutional content increasingly multimedia, integrated with services, and with embedded tools and functionality."

Theresa Byrd (Ohio Wesleyan University) also noted some of the challenges regarding e-books and digitization projects:

> In the digital age, the college library collection is a hybrid of books and electronic resources. However, with digitization projects underway in libraries, are we starting to see a paradigm shift? That is, as college librarians become more involved with digitizing and maintaining the institution's special collections and hidden collections, will we need to rethink collection development? It appears that we might, given the gravity of the current economic crisis and reduced library budgets.... The OWU Libraries have jumped into the new territory of digitization by hiring a digital librarian and digitizing two collections.... Will OWU Libraries need to establish a digital department? How will the liaison librarians find time to work with faculty to incorporate digital projects into the curriculum and teaching and learning? How will the liaisons handle metadata? Digital initiatives will require equipment, training, staffing, and money as well as a rethinking of work processes.

PHYSICAL SPACE CHALLENGES

It is a rare academic librarian who has not read at least one article about the predicted demise of the library as a physical space. One of our contributors (Glenda Thornton, Cleveland State University) mentioned in her essay a newspaper cartoon showing an image of a library building with its name changed: "Museum of the Internet, formerly the New York Public Library." Thirteen contributors commented about the future of the library as place, all of whom believe there will be a place, if one that offers very different services from those of today.

Cynthia L. Henderson (Morehouse School of Medicine) identified nine roles the academic health services library will continue to play in the future:

- A physical symbol of the search for knowledge
- A focal point for the campus and intellectual commons
- A haven for study and research
- A place for individuals and groups engaged in collaborative learning, teaching, or work
- An access point and interactive distribution center for print and electronic information
- A learning commons to support trends in education, research, service, and outreach
- A functional and pleasant workplace for staff
- A virtual gateway for institutional knowledge
- A signature space that is attractive, flexible, and useful

A community college perspective on the library as place was provided by Lynne King (Schenectady County Community College):

> For example, as the shift in expenditures from print to digital collections moves forward in the library of the future to include most books as well as the article-length material already

available, changes in the way library space is utilized will become more affordable and therefore more widespread. Academic libraries of all types will be able to more easily reach the goal of providing a physical learning commons space without costly building expansions.

Library space previously needed for print book collections can be used to bring together multiple campus services from separate physical locations. These services that support student learning outside of the classroom can be co-located in the interconnected manner that fits with the way in which students actually work. Colleges and universities that can afford to do so now already benefit from bringing services such as academic computing, instructional technology, and tutoring services into a library learning commons.

Carol Sinwell (Northern Virginia Community College) noted how the library as place will and has changed due to technology and very different student body expectations for what a library ought to be:

> The needs of library users continue to change at a rapid pace. Libraries struggle to predict the learning styles of the NeXt generation, which has grown up with computers. They are empowered. They are able to connect to digital sources. They are able to create and publish through the Internet. They are more likely to connect with the library remotely versus the traditional face-to-face visit inside the library. They want 24/7 access to information. More and more of them want to know how to find the answers on their own. They also want spaces for collaborative group work.
>
> Space planning is yet another challenge. Scott Bennett, Yale University Librarian Emeritus and library space planning consultant, acknowledges that colleges and universities want to get a good return on their investments in physical space. In a competitive environment, the campus and its learning spaces will be a principle asset or a chief liability....
>
> Users of the information commons require instructional support, which comes from collaboration between librarians and instructional technologists (Bennett, 2007). Community colleges are already there. For over 30 years, LRCs have blended technology resources, instructional support, and library services.

Thomas Carter (St. Mary's College of California) suggested some ways in which the physical library is important to the campus beyond holding collections:

> Library space, too, will continue to be necessary, both to house physical collections and, of increasing importance, to provide study, collaboration, and social space for students. The importance of the "library as place" has been articulated in numerous publications. Since most learning takes place outside of the classroom, students need a place to accomplish this learning. Whether studying alone, collaborating with peers and/or faculty on group projects, developing multimedia projects, or engaging in social or cultural events, students need a place to accomplish these goals, and the library fits all of these requirements like no other campus facility. Indeed, recent student surveys reaffirm the importance of library facilities in students' enrollment and retention decisions.

Another college library perspective was that of John Murray (Westmont College), where he noted:

> What space is required for student and faculty users of the library? This partly depends on what other meeting places exist on campus. We are all aware of the social nature of campus life and the increased use of group projects as a teaching tool. At one point in the existence of our library, it was the social hub of the campus. The voices that said a library should be a quiet place won the battle of noise, and over time the students went away. In the future we must readjust our vision about noise and activity. The library is already a foreboding place

to students newly arrived from high schools where libraries have no teaching role, where they are at best study halls, and where they must *be quiet!* The idea of having a coffee shop in the library will remove some of the barriers. This is being done commonly now. I don't see it diminishing in the future. The genie of the library as a social space is out of the bottle. It will not go back in. Libraries will have to accommodate it, and the spots it leaves on the rugs, and the trail of critters it attracts.

Catherine Murray-Rust (Georgia Institute of Technology) mentioned how, contrary to expectations, technology has not changed the need for physical space:

Although governing boards and trustees in the 1990s were gleeful that digital technologies would mean they never had to spend another dollar on the relentless expansion of library facilities, digital technologies often had the opposite impact on libraries than they anticipated. The use of libraries has grown dramatically with the increasing use of retail techniques, such as comfortable seating, group study rooms, and coffee bars, to bring users into library buildings and the commitment of librarians to make their spaces more lively and inviting for users. The result is a renaissance of beautiful, functional library spaces in facilities all over the country.

In her concluding paragraph, Joan Giesecke (University of Nebraska, Lincoln) made the point that failing to change leads to a useless physical facility:

Tomorrow's academic library can be the content provider for the campus, the group that connects scholars with the scholarly and cultural record regardless of format, provides access to primary source materials, and helps to disseminate the scholarship of the campus. To students and faculty, the libraries can be the partner that helps unravel the complexities of the information world and can create a positive user experience in which students and faculty feel welcomed and valued whether they enter the building or visit the library online. If academic libraries choose to not change and to not meet the challenges of today's world, they stand a chance of becoming little more than a well air-conditioned and heated landfill of unwanted materials.

FINANCIAL CHALLENGES

A major worldwide economic downturn has added still more pressure on all libraries in terms of their financial well-being. Addressing the issues our contributors raised in their essays will be disruptive and to some extent expensive. Certainly many of the ideas they suggested, such as innovative thinking, reassessing the past practices including the sacred cows, increasing collaboration, focusing more clearly on user needs and interests, will not have an initial cost associated with them. However, the outcome of such activities is likely to require funding. Certainly some of those funds may come from reallocation of existing support. The problem will be how much funding will remain after the fallout from the 2007+ economic woes is finally finished. Thirteen contributors made reference to the fiscal challenges that exist and lay ahead.

Perhaps Joan Giesecke (University of Nebraska, Lincoln), one of the essayists from an Association of Research Libraries (ARL) library, put the challenge most succinctly in her opening paragraph when she noted:

In the uncertain economic times of 2009, predicting the future has become quite a challenge. The impact of budget reductions over the next two years on higher education could change the very nature of our institutions. Major private institutions are decreasing spending as the value of their endowments decrease. Public institutions continue to struggle with less and less state funding and fewer sources for additional revenue. Tuition increases cannot resolve the economic crisis as the public protests the rising cost of education. Institutions will need to focus on their core missions and establish a few areas of excellence to retain their reputations as viable institutions. Major research libraries will also need to focus their efforts to support the core missions of the campus and will be less and less able to collect materials in a wide range of subject areas that may be of little use to the campus.

Ninfa Trejo's (Trejo Foster Foundation for Hispanic Library Education and former community college library director) essay provides an overview of community colleges and their possible future. She discussed the financial issues facing such institutions, especially in light of the demands for more services and programs:

> Despite extraordinarily large differences across the nation in proportional funding sources, particularly among tuition and state and local government funding percentages, community colleges have found ways to obtain the necessary levels of support from all sources (Tollefson, 2009, p. 391). However, funding may continue to be a serious problem for community colleges given the state of the U.S. economy. Community colleges may have to increase tuition because state and other sources of funding decrease. The lack of sustainability may not advance their mission to provide access to higher education and may not be able to support "student success programs." However, community colleges will continue to grow. They will continue to change, perhaps sharply, due to their diffused institutional missions and high responsiveness to prevailing economic, social, and political environments. Class distribution and employment stability of the U.S. population are being transformed by technology and the global economy. Businesses close or move abroad, and class inequality has been increasing. Community colleges are stepping up to the efforts at job preparation and economic development (Ballantine and Spade, 2008). Immigration, even though challenged, brings more people who require acculturation and preparation for high-skill jobs.

Lynne King (Schenectady County Community College) addressed the situation in the following terms:

> But for organizations with modest financial resources, such as community college libraries, the deal breaker early on can be costly changes to facilities or funds for expensive equipment that may take years to secure and may not be guaranteed from reallocation to institutional needs, such as the reduction of unexpected gaps caused by reductions in state or local funding. As a result, routes to major changes in such organizations need to have low out-of-pocket costs. Does that mean that big, outside-the-box thinking is unrealistic for academic libraries of modest means? Are large, well-funded libraries, possibly only those with endowments of their own, the only part of the academic library world that can lead the way to the future? Not necessarily....
>
> Once it becomes possible for digital books to actually serve in place of their print counterparts, libraries serving similar audiences—such as academic libraries supporting comparable degree programs—the promise of shared collections that achieve savings by reducing at least some of the costs of duplicative holdings, such as processing and storage, will be realized. Such savings have positive implications for other parts of academic library operations.

Holly Buchanan and Brian Bunnett (University of New Mexico Health Sciences Center) commented on the struggle to make budgets meet the current needs as the economy slows:

> A survey by AAHSL [Association of Academic Health Sciences Libraries] in early 2009 was undertaken with the realization that while its member libraries "have long been grappling

with constrained collection budgets, we face a new urgency in continuing the transformation promised by new publishing models and new technologies in an era of economic recession" (Tooey, 2009). Over 100 AAHSL members participated in this survey and indicated that two-thirds of them had experienced "recent budget reductions, cuts, or other negative fiscal impacts" averaging $388,023. Collectively, these cuts in 2008–2009 totaled almost $11 million nationally. Given that 53 percent of the libraries cut collection expenses and the majority of respondents anticipate additional cuts over the next two years, the long-term impact nationally on health sciences collections will be significant.

CREATING POSITIVE USER EXPERIENCES CHALLENGES

Service to users is a fundamental principle around which libraries design their activities and programs. Today academic libraries' service populations are increasingly diverse. The populations are a mix of young people (digital natives) and an increasing number of older students (who are at best digital immigrants), many of whom are recently unemployed and seeking an education in something that they hope will provide more job security. Values, expectations, and skills are just three of the factors that generate a resource challenge (staff, time, and funding) to create a positive user experience for all users.

With this in mind it is worthwhile pondering Patricia Wand's (Zayed University) comments regarding her experiences in transplanting the U.S. academic library model into a totally different society and culture:

> One challenge is the ideal of library service to everyone, whether they are members of the royal family or laborers from a construction site. The core value of egalitarian service to library users emerges from the democratic principle of equal treatment of all learners and equal access to information. I ask myself, "How to explain service to everyone in cultures where the tradition of extending hospitality to strangers does not include the Western notion of treating everyone equally?"
>
> The concept of service to everyone is a concept that runs contrary to many cultures that do not share the democratic principles so deeply entrenched in North America. It's easier to pay lip service to the core value "service to all library users" than to bring it into practice when you view society as appropriately stratified. And even more basic is the question, "How to explain service when the concept is interpreted as something provided by a servant?"

Carol Sinwell (Northern Virginia Community College) spelled out some of the issues facing community colleges in terms of student expectations as well as needs:

> Where are underprepared students going to learn the skills needed to be successful and productive citizens of a rapidly emerging global economy? The community college "serves as both springboard and safety net for the inevitable millions who wish to move upward as well as those who missed earlier opportunities and are now ready to try anew" (Gleazer, 1980, p. 131). According to the American Association of Community Colleges, nearly half of all students pursuing postsecondary education attend a community college. A core function of community colleges is to offer college-level course content to a broadly diverse group of students, a population growing in its diversity....
>
> Historically, the community college has provided a learning resource concept that supported a strong instructional relationship between the library and the classroom. During the late 1960s and early 1970s, when new community colleges were being established at an unprecedented rate, the concept of a comprehensive Learning Resources Center

(LRC) became fully developed. The new LRCs were designed to encompass a broad range of instructional services, including the library, audiovisual services, and tutorial services and learning assistance. In the early 1970s, the LRC responsibilities expanded to include computing and telecommunication services. The LRCs have been evolving since as they respond to institutional instructional objectives....Libraries must continue to expand this arena of innovative ideas, especially as they face the dichotomy of institutional financial constraints and expanding user needs.

The specialized ARL perspective comes from Michael Kelly (University of New Mexico, Special Collections and the Center for Southwest Research) in his description of the first of six issues he believes will shape the future of academic libraries:

> First, we need to learn more about our users and understand how they find and use our materials. As our users become more and more networked, our cyberspace navigators' research strategies, their methods for discovery of materials, and their expectations when they find them may be very different from the content we currently provide them and how we deliver it. By conducting user surveys, forming focus groups, and collaborating with our users, we will begin to better understand their needs and be able to develop the tools that deliver accessibility not just availability.

Broadening the perspective to the international scene, Patricia Wand (Zayed University) discussed aspects of culturally sensitive issues and user experience:

> Almost every conversation about libraries in the Middle East eventually touches on the issue of censorship. How can an academic library in the North American tradition deal with sensitive issues such as the human body as art, recognition of Israel as a country, and images of the Prophet? When Zayed University was founded, the rulers of the country emphasized that all subjects could be taught in the curriculum and that the Internet would be unfiltered. Nonetheless, not all students or parents desire to be exposed to sensitive issues, so the library has practices in place to respect cultural values and to avoid conflict if possible as we select materials for a collection to support the curriculum....
>
> In North America, *special collections* refers to a collection where rare or unique items are stored. At Zayed University, special collections is a locked room where items of a sensitive nature are placed and where they remain available to students if they sign a form accepting personal responsibility for viewing the material and if a faculty member signs permission for the student to use the materials.

NEW SKILLS FOR STAFF CHALLENGES

Radically changing libraries, as James Neal suggested in a quotation earlier in the chapter, will almost certainly call for some different skills and greater depth in others. Librarians still practicing when the radical changes occur will likely be hard pressed to function in the new world. They will need substantial re-education or training. It is unlikely that individual institutions will be able to undertake such training, if for no other reason than cost. Professional bodies, library schools, and perhaps consortia (more about collaboration later in the chapter) must assume the lead roles in providing the new requisite skills. Needless to state, library and information studies schools will need to further adjust their curriculums to produce individuals with what it will take to be effective in the changed environment.

Peter Hernon (Graduate School of Library and Information Science, Simmons College) outlined some of the competencies needed to address the coming challenges:

Academic libraries seek a professional workforce that is conformable with change and accepting of new roles and responsibilities. Such individuals must not want to confine themselves to the library, and they should welcome interaction with different people. The workforce provides the face of the library on a daily basis (requiring greater diversity among the staff) and needs to be problem solvers, able to engage in critical thinking, and outstanding communicators, both orally and written. As part of problem solving, they need the ability to engage in planning, evaluation, and assessment, and they need to be able to work in teams or groups to accomplish stated goals and objectives. In addition, those making a difference in the workforce must have intellectual curiosity, flexibility, adaptability, persistence, and the ability to be enterprising. To this list, I add a commitment to career development and lifelong learning as well as competencies associated with leadership and a commitment to ensuring that the workplace is a learning organization that is highly respected.

As people advance in management positions, any set of competencies expands to include, among others, effective engagement in development; effective management of people, resources, and services within a political context; the ability to implement and evaluate research for accountability and service improvement; and the possession of more leadership competencies as well as an understanding of leadership theory and practice.

Hernon continued his essay by outlining his observations as to how these competencies can be generated into library and information science (LIS) education:

Increasingly the student population in LIS schools is much younger, but they express little interest in academic librarianship, and a number of the students have never worked in libraries or at all. They might lack an understanding of the transformation through which libraries are going and what is expected of them. They also may not understand what the library of today and tomorrow is; their knowledge might be based on a view of libraries that existed 20 or more years ago. It is my assumption that the LIS schools, in cooperation with area librarians and employers, are trying to correct this image. Still, students may not understand what comprises theory, especially for research, nor the cross-disciplinary foundations of relevant theory. This adds to the educational challenge of preparing students to master student learning outcomes that LIS schools lay out for their master's program....

Such partnerships between LIS education and practice involve, for instance, the program of the Association of Research Libraries to educate those holding doctoral degrees but lacking formal knowledge of libraries about academic librarianship as a career; efforts to educate, retain, and advance people of color; and involvement in leadership institutes.

Glenda Thornton (Cleveland State University) discussed some of the issues facing existing academic library staff in terms of facing a very different future:

Library staff members are wonderfully talented individuals who often not only have specific intellectual interests but are usually generalists as well, displaying broad interest in the academic enterprise. Most value education, and many of them hold degrees in excess of what they actually need to perform their duties. Library deans and/or directors are skilled managers who are good at recognizing undeveloped talent and obtaining continuing education for staff members, following human resource rules and union contracts, staying within budgets, and figuring out how best to use space to meet campus needs. And, most important, they are usually excellent planners. Given these skills, colleges and universities will more aggressively group "orphan" departments under the management of the library director, especially if there are any synergies to be obtained. Thus, over time, libraries will acquire an ever broader range of functions just because talent that can be utilized is waiting in the library—never mind that it may be already fully utilized.... This will result in vibrant organizations for those who can market the unique skills of the library staff and remain nimble and flexible.

Several of the contributors mentioned teaching skills as something that will see greater emphasis in the future. Essentially those commenting on this aspect of skill requirements for the future noted that while teaching is something some librarians do and do well it is not one of the top priorities when seeking new staff members. Theresa Byrd (Ohio Wesleyan University) suggested some of the skills that will become ever more important:

> Not only must the college librarian teach traditional library skills and work toward incorporating digital initiatives into instruction, he or she must also teach what has been called information fluency skills, which involves teaching basic computer skills, Power-Point, Word, multimedia, scanning, etc. The librarian, if not proficient in all of these skills and the library is not a part of a merged organization (library and IT combined), may need to partner with his or her campus's information technology department to teach these skills. The "best practices" approach and ultimate goal is for the librarian to partner or team-teach with faculty members in planning and teaching a library instruction course(s).

Carol Parker (University of New Mexico, School of Law) also commented on a changing emphasis on teaching:

> Academic librarians have a long tradition of teaching in subject-specific fields and providing bibliographic instruction. More recently, this charge has expanded to librarian-taught classes in information literacy. Within academic law libraries, growing numbers of law librarians now also teach courses in legal research for credit within the law school curriculum. Previously, the academic law library director was likely to be the only librarian to teach within the law school. Now, many more rank-and-file law librarians are offering semester-long courses in general and specialized legal research instruction.
>
> The impetus for librarians to teach regularly and often comes from multiple sources. Many law librarians now hold both MLS and JD degrees, especially within the public services sector. Dual-degreed, lawyer librarians are more readily accepted as qualified to teach within a law school curriculum. Legal research has, in many ways, become more rather than less complex with the introduction of online resources. The expertise of law librarian teachers significantly increases the likelihood that law students will become proficient researchers while still in law school.

Carol Sinwell (Northern Virginia Community College) identified leadership as one area of interest and suggested one option where those interested in developing the skill could find help:

> Today's challenges create a dynamic environment in which librarians must perform unique and essential roles in shaping culture and developing citizens with democratic ideals. The knowledge needs of the twenty-first century will demand leadership that can articulate vision clearly and forcefully. Administrators will share dreams and directions that other people will want to follow.
>
> To meet this call for powerful leadership, where can librarians go to enhance their leadership skills? Professional organizations and associations provide an array of services and resources, but one outstanding opportunity is the Leadership Institute for Academic Librarians. Offered by the Association of College and Research Libraries (ACRL) and Harvard University Graduate School of Education, this institute offers professional discourse on

effective leadership techniques and *how to make librarians' voices heard*. Noted scholars engage attendees in analytical exercises that promote strategic thinking on teaching and learning, inspire innovative approaches to problem solving, encourage intellectual growth and development, and provide opportunities to expand one's collegial relationships. Graduates leave inspired to make an impact on their institutions.

COLLABORATION CHALLENGES

Based on the contributors' essays, a reader might conclude that if academic libraries do die they ought to do so as a group rather than singly. Libraries have a rather long history of developing collaborative efforts to achieve this or that objective. Many of the essayists believe we need to broaden our thinking to reach out in all directions to find new and better ways of serving our future users. Steve O'Connor (Hong Kong Polytechnic University) wrote:

> The future for academic libraries lies in addressing these three issues. The majority of academic libraries can no longer survive separate from their library confreres. They need one another to be able to provide quality services. They need to work together to find new solutions to their futures. The futures will not all be the same, but there will be common threads. There are good examples of consortia purchasing and operations, but the tough decisions regarding shared collecting and more effective service delivery to one another's clients are not always being made. Indeed many consortia are facing their own crises with major amalgamations occurring. Most libraries protect their physical collections and buildings as their own when there is a reasonable suspicion that there are significant amounts of overlap between other comparable and local collections. Their mission will easily collapse to only supporting undergraduate programs. The creation of a few collaborative storage facilities instead of many storage facilities, for example, would save enormous sums of capital expenditure for their collective institutions....
>
> A new paradigm of collaboration is desperately needed, for instance in service provision, in the collective storage of single copies of lesser used materials, and in the negotiation of wide area service agreements. Collaboration is paid only lip service at this time. Along with the development of new metrics of library value and identity will come new management styles and behaviors designed to improve performance in a collaborative rather than a single managerial environment. Work patterns will not be hierarchical but lateral; the organizational structure will need to be project focused and flexible, allowing people to work across the library and other professional communities in the university. Staff will have to be empowered by their collective directors to work on projects for the common benefit. New business models will need to be developed, but these will draw power or influence from the sum of the parts rather than from the parts only.

Catherine Murray-Rust (Georgia Institute of Technology) suggested in writing about the opportunity and challenge of invisibility:

> The challenge is increasing invisibility. The causes of our present situation are many, but three forces stand out: radical changes in the scholarly information landscape; rapid, widespread adoption of information technology; and structural changes in the economics of higher education.... There are many hopeful signs that the research library community is rising to the challenge of invisibility. Libraries are changing services, collaborating on new ways of working, getting out into the university community as partners with faculty in creating solutions to their information problems that will help them work more effectively, which is of paramount importance in this world of competition for research dollars and

recognition within research communities. Young scholars need all the help they can get, and libraries are in a perfect position to assist them.

Holly Shipp Buchanan and Brian Bunnett (University of New Mexico, Health Sciences Center) wrote about the need for more collaboration within the parent organization:

This model [library as support agency] has been replaced largely by one in which the librarian is expected to be a partner or collaborator with clinicians, scientists, and educators from all parts of the AHC [Academic Health Center]. The responsibilities of these librarians vary but typically require that they work well beyond the walls of the library. These "embedded" librarians are often called informationists (Rankin, Grefsheim, and Canto, 2008, p. 194). As biomedical information experts they participate as full members in committees and departments. This level of involvement ensures that the librarian is well placed to advocate for information services and resources that are properly integrated into the student's educational experience. The spread of curricula centered on evidence-based health care has also underlined the important role librarians play to ensure that students are skilled at searching the literature and retrieving information that is the most authoritative and relevant, properly analyzed, and evaluated. In addition, many librarians now have responsibility for pedagogical training designed to improve students' teaching abilities.

The proliferation of library liaison programs is another example of librarians collaborating outside of the library with peers in hospital departments or within educational programs such as public health or nursing. Liaisoning requires an in-depth subject knowledge of the specialty or program, an ability to establish strong relationships with key individuals within those programs and specialties, and a talent for recognizing when library services and resources can be effectively introduced into them. A librarian's liaison activities often lead to his or her appointment to the sort of committees described previously.

We end this section with an extended quote from an executive director of an academic library consortium, Rick Burke (Statewide California Electronic Library Consortium):

Library consortia promote new standards that are helping libraries better manage their usage statistics with Project Counter and SUSHI to standardize the transmission of statistics. Consortia are also promoting the utilization of new standards such as ONIX-PL for the XML transmission of licenses to ease the burden of license management and bring some order to the chaos of electronic resource management. Finally, consortia work with NISO, the National Information Standards Organization, to promote SERU, the Shared Electronic Resource Understanding, where libraries and vendors working together can eliminate the need for a signed license altogether to reduce the overhead costs of licensing.

In all of these scenarios consortia can play an important role as promoters of new paradigms. Consortia excel at promoting collaboration, and the most effective library consortia will move beyond being buying clubs for electronic resources and provide significant value in other ways. They might help libraries create institutional repositories and promote the aforementioned new models for new forms of publication that move beyond the old print model. Consortia will also help libraries collaborate in other ways, including support for digitization and preservation projects and union catalogs for patron-initiated borrowing to reduce ILL costs and to create opportunities for cooperative collection development. Innovative approaches may also include technology support activities, such as helping consolidate redundant technical services activities among member libraries. As libraries move print resources into storage to create more public services space, consortia will assist in the creation of print repositories and finding aids that will hold the copy of record for a particular work.

ADVOCACY CHALLENGES

All of the press, both public and professional, regarding the relevancy/viability of libraries makes our task of remaking the field all the more challenging. There appears to be at least a twofold challenge. First, there is the need to demonstrate that what we do best is still essential to the educational process in the emerging new world of higher education. Second, in order to make the first case, we must remake our libraries. To do either alone probably will not be adequate; the two must move forward together. An essential element in accomplishing both goals is to increase the effectiveness of our advocacy.

James Neal (Columbia University), among his 30 suggestions for effectively facing the future, outlined three dynamic steps that would assist in demonstrating that we are both essential and adapting to the changing higher education environment:

19. Advocate the information policy agenda in the critical areas of intellectual freedom, privacy, civil liberties, telecommunications, government information, and appropriations.
20. Fight the copyright wars, recognizing that international agreements, new laws and legislation, licensing of content, user guidelines, and digital rights management can undermine balance and threaten fair use.
21. Participate in the entrepreneurial academy by leveraging assets to advance new markets and new products and by building a culture of competition, risk, and innovation.

Thomas Carter (St. Mary's College of California) identified one area where we could improve our advocacy on the campus, via making users aware of what tools are available to assist them in their research:

Our vendor data and Web traffic reports tell us that use of our resources has increased, as measured by downloaded articles and hits on the website, but this use is not visible to the campus administrator or faculty member who visits the library but rarely and notices only empty seats. One of the issues libraries need to deal with is addressing the misperception that, because so much of the work we do is performed behind the scenes, libraries are no longer necessary. A continuing challenge for librarians today is to publicize and market the different ways libraries are being used. In the face of the increasing hype about freely available information on the web, like Google Books and Wikipedia, libraries need to make greater efforts to educate faculty and administrators about the information available only on the invisible web and the work we are doing to make it available. The digital tools we have available, including vendor reports of database use, weblogs of hits on our websites, and the National Center for Education Statistics website "Compare Academic Libraries" (nces.ed.gov/surveys/libraries/compare/index.asp?LibraryType=Academic) are invaluable in giving us the evidence we need to illustrate how libraries are being used today more than ever.

Likewise, Barbara Bintliff (University of Colorado, School of Law) identified another action area. Although her focus was legal research, the basic idea of addressing the political issues on the campus applies to all academic libraries:

Law librarians need to take action. Our subject expertise is legal research, but we have done little to develop a theory or pedagogy of teaching this fundamental legal skill in mandatory first-year classes. We must address this shortcoming. Law librarians have seen legal writing faculty, who teach a far different skill, incorporate legal research into their portfolios, and we allow, if not encourage, vendors' representatives to teach electronic research skills. We have not claimed the mandatory legal research instruction of first-year students as "our" territory, focusing instead on elective advanced legal research classes that reach a small portion of the student population. Research is an important subject, with full professors teaching research methods and skills in virtually every other graduate field. In law, no other doctrinal or skills faculty claim research as an expertise or a legitimate academic subject. By not "claiming" legal research as an academic subject, law librarians are contributing to their own appearance of irrelevance....

Improving legal research instruction will require curricular changes. Before they will approve a curricular change to improve legal research, the law faculty must be re-educated on the importance of legal research in the educational process and in law practice. All curricular changes are political, and the law library director and public services head must take the lead in educating faculty and advocating for this change. Ironically, the extraordinary efforts of law librarians to increase faculty service in the past 20 years have shielded law faculty from the changing nature of legal research and thereby hampered their decision making.

The political nature of a curricular change and the groundwork that must be laid by the law library director and administration illustrate what may be the second largest challenge to law libraries in the coming years. This challenge is the necessity of political involvement in the life of the law school, and maybe even in the university itself.

ARL director Joan Giesecke (University of Nebraska, Lincoln) linked advocacy and fund-raising:

Academic librarians need to learn to sell the value of libraries to the students, particularly to graduate students. These students become tomorrow's donors to the institution, and librarians need to help potential donors connect with the libraries to create an "alumni" base for the libraries. Libraries will not be able to survive without private support, and building the donor base for future support is a key role for today's librarians. This task cannot be fulfilled by a development officer alone. Each librarian who interacts with users needs to be thinking about how to create the best possible user experience so that today's users can become tomorrow's donors.

CONNECTING CHALLENGES

Joan Giesecke's quote provides one reason why connecting with students is important. There is a slight distinction between creating a positive user experience and connecting with users, as our contributors noted. Providing great service based on an understanding of user needs are certainly elements in making a connection; however, there is also the personal side. Creating such connections will call for public service staff to have strong people skills. One of the challenges for the staff to face in the near term will be the generational difference between themselves as well as those they serve. Social networking connections will work very well and in fact will be essential for reaching the young cohorts, but they probably will not reach the older students. In some cases, it may even lead to a disconnect between the groups. Thus, the staff will need to have the skills of a digital native while being able to relate to those who are less technologically oriented, many of whom will not have even started down the digital immigrant road.

John Murray (Westmont College) and Cynthia L. Henderson (Morehouse School of Medicine), although coming from very different institutional environments, share the idea of the importance of the human touch. First, John's perspective:

The academic library of the future will be a highly collaborative creature. Collaboration will include libraries from other institutions and the faculty and students of its own institution.... I don't know if the word *collaboratorium* has been invented already, but if not, then now it has.... A collaboratorium encourages a high degree of respectful involvement of the principals of any inquiry. It involves as much listening as speaking. It involves the encouragement of all participants in the projects' ends....

To develop the collaboration envisioned by this idea, staffing will be the first consideration. The sort of staffing required in this environment is heavily oriented toward serving student and faculty requirements. The ideal staffing situation would involve all library faculty, whatever their assignment, in assisting students and faculty in achieving their goals.

Cynthia looked at both the technological and people aspect of connecting with users:

The Internet has not made public physical space obsolete for people. People need and want personal contact and interaction. So even though the electronic article will be the chief unit of information and wireless access will be the primary access mode, with all library transactions being conducted online, personalized access and services to users wherever they are (campus, hospital, clinic, etc.) will continue to be a major priority....

Academic health sciences libraries remain, with all of their technology-friendly service and their diverse information formats, a cherished and utilized place where people, ideas, information, and knowledge meet and interact. It is refreshing to the soul. And there is always a future for that.

There is a need to connect with all users, not just students, as Joan Giesecke (University of Nebraska, Lincoln) noted:

Libraries in the future will need to find ways to work more closely with faculty, providing research and instructional support. Librarians who wish to spend their time in their offices avoiding face-to-face contact with faculty and avoiding promoting library services will become the dinosaurs of the profession. Future academic librarians must get out of their comfort zones and develop true partnerships with faculty, helping to put together courses and class assignments and ensuring that researchers know how to find the materials they need to be successful. Libraries need to find more interesting ways to teach information-finding skills, to move away from the idea that students need to be fantastic searchers to realizing that students need to know how to efficiently find what they need. If a student needs a few references to complete an assignment, librarians should show students the best way to find two or three key resources rather than insisting that the students learn how to do an exhaustive search every time they seek information.

Susan C. Curzon (California State University, Northridge) wrote about the need to continue some of the basic roles librarians play in assisting users:

Academic librarians will continue their major role in helping the user to find information. The development of so much online information does not mean that students have equally developed their searching skills. In the domain of information seeking, librarians have always had four major roles. First, we have been filters, making selections from a large array of knowledge resources to support learning. Second, we have been navigators, guiding the user one by one through these resources. Third, we have been educators, teaching students the core skills of information literacy. Fourth, we have been information disseminators, assertively linking the user to resources. Consider that the body of knowledge within cyberspace will grow and grow, eventually occupying a vast space. This will make our fourfold role more important than it has ever been. The dramatic increase in electronic information worldwide only increases the need for librarians.

MISSION CHALLENGES

At least ten of our contributors mentioned a requirement to sharpen our focus on the library's mission. Mission statements have been a relatively long-standing component in the planning process. In the past those statements frequently stood unchanged long after the parent institution's mission had shifted incrementally over the years. It is easy to not go back to check that the library's mission accurately reflects the parent institution's statement. All too often staff begin rolling their eyes at the suggestion that it is time to review the statement. However, as a number of our contributors stated, not doing such a review may imperil the library's future.

Catherine Murray-Rust (Georgia Institute of Technology) suggested some of the factors why closely examining the mission statement is important:

> Every academic research library shares the mission and goals of its parent institution, which can be defined broadly as social and intellectual progress through research and learning. In research libraries in the United States, the division of labor has long been that faculty conduct research, teach, and publish; students listen, read, and learn; and librarians acquire, organize, preserve, and provide access to the scholarly works mostly created by faculty.
>
> Today, the role of the library in the academy is not so straightforward. Librarians continue to enjoy the respect and regard of most of the communities they serve, but libraries are no longer the undisputed source of credible academic information on campus. The libraries' major technology in the past, the book, is no longer the dominant form of delivering information. Librarians are no longer able to supply information without the cooperation and support of a host of other specialists in information technology. Libraries are increasingly invisible in terms of collections, costs, infrastructure, and, most of all, success. Much of what librarians and libraries do is not apparent to users.

Rather similar views were expressed by Loretta Parham (Atlanta University Center):

> The library has to rethink assessment and routinize the use of redesigned instruments and then broadly blast the results. If there is to be a viable and rewarding future for the academic library, it is highly dependent on its capacity to promote the college/university mission in ways that will have a measurable impact on the business of scholarship and learning. We must influence recruitment, retention, fund-raising, and the outcomes of learning and teaching.

One of several specialized academic library directors discussed some of the opportunities for expanding the mission for the future. Among several ideas presented for academic libraries to consider as they move toward the future, Michael Kelly (University of New Mexico, Special Collections) suggested:

> ... we must seek new opportunities to expand our missions, including management of institutional repositories (IR), electronic publishing including university presses, and expertise in intellectual property issues. The role of an IR is very close to our own and could easily be folded into our portfolio of responsibilities, particularly for the archiving of born-digital institutional records. Understanding and communicating the intellectual property rights for both authors and users of our materials is growing in importance. Our ability to understand copyright issues and to advise others within our communities will become a very valued skill.

Another example came from Holly Buchanan and Brian Bunnett (University of New Mexico, Health Sciences Center):

Today's health sciences librarian's partnership in the AHC's missions requires a different type of personality or behavior than that prevalent in traditional librarianship. Today's librarian must be active, even assertive, rather than passive; capable of working independently outside of the library; quick to recognize opportunities for introducing library resources and services into the curriculum, research laboratory, or hospital department; full of initiative; and technologically proficient. These essay authors believe that even in a period of economical challenges and new technology that radically changes traditional processes, the future of academic health sciences libraries remains bright. AHC libraries have positioned themselves as integral units in the health education and delivery system. Librarians are seen as educators in the learning process, as full members of the research and clinical teams, and their libraries are viewed as providing social spaces critical to the development of collaborative and lifelong learning skills.

Patricia Wand (Zayed University) emphasized the linkage of the library mission to that of the university in her concluding paragraph:

> What will be the outcome of this truly grand educational experiment of transplanting American-style libraries in the Middle East? I predict a hybrid library, incorporating many core values of American-style libraries but modified by the flavor of local customs and mingled with the best of many cultures. The library, like the university that it serves, must keep its mission in focus yet remain agile to keep pace with the goals of the emerging knowledge society envisioned by the rulers of the United Arab Emirates.

PRINT/DIGITAL CHALLENGES

The final issue that was mentioned by ten or more contributors was the challenge of balancing print and digital resources. Regardless of what the long-term future may hold, for the near term there will be a pressure to balance print and digital resources. Certainly on the journal side the digital format is dominant. However, for scholarly monographs, the print format is still dominating the marketplace. How long this will remain the case is largely dependent on the continued developments in e-book technology. As of 2010, the e-book has not demonstrated that it is ready to displace the long-standing printed scholarly book. Another long-term resource concern is the very large "legacy" book collections that academic libraries have spent billions of dollars on acquiring, processing, and storing over the years. Whether to digitize or not will require careful thought. Where to find funding to do the work is another issue, as is long-term storage or preservation.

Thomas Carter (St. Mary's College of California) had the following to say about mission and collections:

> The traditional mission of the academic library is to serve the teaching and learning mission of its parent institution. Historically this has meant acquiring, cataloging, housing, preserving, and making information accessible to the academic community. The first reason for optimism about the future of academic libraries is that these basic functions continue today, both for "traditional" forms of information (physical books, journals, videos, recordings, maps, etc.) and for today's digital sources of information. Libraries today are in a hybrid state, retaining the familiar historic functions for analog resources while adapting them to the acquisition, preservation, and accessibility of digital sources. Many of the recent library obituaries acknowledge that libraries still play a role with regard to physical information sources, but they presume that these physical sources will soon disappear, or perhaps no longer matter. In some sense they are probably right. Particularly with regard to periodicals we are seeing

an unmistakable shift from paper to digital. Libraries are canceling paper subscriptions in favor of digital access. In many cases the cost is less, especially when acquired through an aggregator or through a purchasing consortium, and also because the use of digital journals is much greater than their print counterparts. How many of us have counseled students to journey to another level of the library to find a paper article, only to be told by the students that they would rather find something they can download or e-mail to themselves? E-books, with the exception of reference sources, are gaining much slower acceptance among readers, although the continuing improvements in e-book readers are impressive. I think we may assume that libraries will purchase an increasing percentage of monographs in digital form in the coming years.

An ARL perspective was provided by Barbara Bintliff (University of Colorado, School of Law), who further emphasized the ongoing shift to e-resources:

We can be sure that our collections will be increasingly electronic, and that changes in technologies and patron expectations will necessitate corresponding changes in physical space, resource allocation, and staffing. And we are seeing even today that less ownership and more licensing of resources will see a corresponding diminution in control over collection development, an extraordinary challenge until the day, if ever, that technological platforms are stable and new models of ownership are established.

Glenda Thornton (Cleveland State University) suggested that we will not see the end of print in our collections for the foreseeable future:

First, there is no doubt that many magnificent research libraries will continue to function primarily as the institutions that gather, store, and preserve information for scholarly research. Although many print texts have been and will continue to be digitized, unless they were "born digital," there may always be the need for some physical repositories for these materials—and maybe they will be more museum-like than I want to admit. I believe that some scholars will always want to examine the physical item, which itself may become an object of research. Perhaps this situation will change in the distant future, but I truly believe that it is distant. However, these magnificent research libraries will be relatively stable in number, if not declining, as fewer institutions of higher education seek to enhance their reputation by creating such monuments.

Institutional repositories and scholarly communication was the focus of Theresa Byrd's (Ohio Wesleyan University) discussion regarding resources:

Institutional repositories are a place where institutions can store digital archives and preserve and access their institution's instructional, research, and creative materials. While a repository may serve many schools, it does feature a local brand for each institution. As a member of OhioLINK, the OWU Libraries utilize OhioLINK's institutional repository, called the Digital Resource Commons. Digital collections and institutional repositories will reduce the size of library collections and the need for new library buildings. Moreover, if the concept of the institutional repository becomes popular with students and faculty, it has the power to become a disruptive technology for the current scholarly communication model.

New forms of scholarly communication include digitization and electronic formats. Like other college and university librarians, the OWU librarians have tried to introduce the faculty to changes in scholarly communication by inviting speakers to campus and disseminating the Scholarly Publishing and Academic Resources Coalition's (SPARC) brochures. Future plans for scholarly communication include more training for librarians about scholarly communication; formation of a faculty committee on scholarly communication; more faculty workshops about scholarly communication; and plans for an online journal to feature student honors papers, essays, and creative output such as poetry, drama, music, and images. Because the college environment places an emphasis on teaching for faculty, the OWU librarians hope to encourage faculty to include preprints, postprints, or working papers as well as other creative resources in its OhioLINK institutional repository.

Rick Burke (Statewide California Electronic Library Consortium) provided a picture of what academic library collection development depends on:

> Another way to look at this might be to take a holistic view of the current library environment, casting aside old models and looking ahead to new, more sustainable ways to provide resources to library patrons. For example, with the aforementioned example of e-journal packages, in consortial negotiations we strive to move beyond legacy print-based pricing models to a database model approach. In light of the atomization of all kinds of information into discrete subsets that users want to access (e.g., songs in iTunes instead of albums or chapters within books), perhaps it's time to move beyond thinking of journals and books as we know them in print and instead think of how this information might optimally be accessed and used in the electronic environment. With journals we see high use of articles, and metrics to measure the impact of journals persist. If faculty in the academy were to move beyond the "publish or perish" syndrome, which seems unlikely, journal impact models might become less significant. In their place might arise similar metrics to measure the value of self-publication in repositories, for example, or in other open access publishing models. In e-books or new models for e-textbooks, we will likely see new pricing models for accessing chapters of books. Pay-per-view models might in some instances supplant subscription models. Micropayment models might emerge that fit accessing microsets of information instead of entire journals or books.

He also outlined the significant services consortia can offer members. We also believe that many of these services can and will help academic libraries address the many challenges in the future. Some of the challenges are taking on a firm shape while others have not yet come over the horizon:

> Library consortia play a major role in the world of academic libraries, and have been particularly influential in the following areas:
>
> - Acquisition of electronic resources, with a particular emphasis on pricing and price models
> - Negotiation as a skill to be mastered by librarians responsible for the acquisition of library resources
> - Licensing terms and conditions that are acceptable in the higher education environment
> - The preservation and archiving of electronic journal and other e-resource information
> - The importance of usage statistics as a metric for the value of acquired information
> - Developing collaborative models of print resource sharing
> - Streamlining and consolidating technical services through a centralized (i.e., union) catalog
> - Professional development and training
> - Collaborative digitization projects, including setting standards for best practices and providing training therein
> - For those consortia that are statewide or government funded, providing advocacy for libraries and library funding...

These are but a few concrete examples where consortia will be partners with their libraries, helping libraries adapt to the rapidly changing information landscape. As commercial publishing will continue to play a major role in the mix of library resources, consortia will continue to play a key role in the negotiation and licensing of electronic resources, providing significant savings to libraries when the cost of those acquisitions would otherwise be unaffordable. As library budgets shrink and the old ways of operating become economically untenable, consortia become more important than ever.

FINAL THOUGHTS ON THE FUTURE OF ACADEMIC LIBRARIANSHIP

Again we invite the reader to review the full text of all the essays cited in this chapter. Doing so will help the reader understand the full context of each of contributor's ideas; we also apologize for any failure on our part to fully acknowledge a person's intended context. We conclude this chapter with two quotations from our contributors. Loretta Parham (Atlanta University Center) suggested:

> The future of the academic library is contingent on librarians sitting at the table where dialogue and decision making occurs—locally, regionally, and internationally. We have to do things differently and get the opinions of the very community we serve often and always. This future may not resemble our existing physical shapes, our learning commons, or our reference desks. We may not be as comfortable with the changes required, but we will need to be confident as we accept new ideas and draw nearer to the intersection and point of information need. The future is not all about technology, nor is humanities forgotten. Our future is contingent on librarians who are willing to take the risk and do things in a way that will innovate.

A quotation from Susan C. Curzon (California State University, Northridge) opened this chapter, so we believe it is only fitting her concluding thoughts should end the chapter. She noted:

> Importantly, we must remember that the true value of thinking about the future lies in helping us prepare and plan for the transition to a continually changing new environment. However, no matter what level of preparation or planning we do, academic libraries will survive only if they provide services truly valuable to learning in its evolving environment.

However, more striking to us was her following thought:

> As Confucius said, "Study the past if you would divine the future." The past of libraries was driven by the value that access to knowledge was vital for the success of society. Our past was value driven and so our future will be also.

REFERENCES

Abeles, Tom P. 2006. Do we know the future of the university? *On the Horizon* 14, no. 2: 35–42.

Ballantine, Jeanne H., and Joan Z. Spade. 2008. *Schools and society: A sociological approach to education.* 3rd ed. Los Angeles: Pine Forge Press.

Bennett, S. (2007). Designing for uncertainty: Three approaches. *Journal of Academic Librarianship* 33, no. 2: 165–179.

Flat prospects. 2007. *Economist* 382, no. 8520: 72–73.

Gleazer, Edmund J. 1980. *The community college: Values, vision & vitality.* Washington, DC: American Association of Community and Junior Colleges.

Lewin, Kurt. 1951. *Field theory in social sciences.* New York: Harper & Row.

Lewis, David W. 2007. A strategy for academic libraries in the first quarter of the 21st century, *College & Research Libraries* 68, no. 5: 418–434.

Okerson, Ann. 2003. Asteroids, Moore's Law, and the Star Alliance, *Journal of Academic Librarianship* 29, no. 5: 280–285.

Rankin Jocelyn A., Suzanne F. Grefsheim, and Candace C. Canto. 2008. The emerging informationist specialty: A systematic review of the literature. *Journal of the Medical Library Association* 96, no. 3: 194–206.

Snyder, David Pearce, and Gregg Edwards. 2003. The strategic context of education in America— 2000 to 2020, part 2. *On the Horizon* 11, no. 2: 5–18.

Tapscott, Don. 2009. The impending demise of the university. *Edge: The Third Culture* 291 (June). Available: www.edge.org/3rd_culture/tapscott09/tapscott09_index.html (accessed April 7, 2010).

Tollefson, Terrence A. 2009. Community college governance, funding, and accountability: A century of issues and trends. *Community College Journal of Research and Practice* 33, no. 3: 386–402.

Tooey, M. J. 2009. Hard times survey summary report—Winter 2009. Seattle: Association of Academic Health Sciences Libraries.

LAUNCHING PAD

Abram, Stephen. 2008. Social libraries: The Librarian 2.0 phenomenon. *Library Resources and Technical Services* 52, no. 2: 19–22.

Council on Library and Information Resources. 2008. *No brief candle: Reconceiving research libraries for the 21st century.* Washington, DC: CLIR. Available: www.clir.org/pubs/reports/pub142/pub142.pdf (accessed April 7, 2010).

Dempsey, Lorcan. 2009. Always on: Libraries in a world of permanent connectivity. *First Monday* 14, no. 1. Available: firstmonday.org/htbin/cgiwrap/bin/ojs/index.php/fm/article/v%20iew/2291/2070 (accessed April 7, 2010).

Dougherty, William C. 2009. Managing technology: Virtualization and libraries: The future is now (or virtualization: Whither libraries or libraries wither?). *Journal of Academic Librarianship* 35, no. 3: 274–276.

Hawthorne, Pat, and Nicole A. Cooke. 2008. Trendspotting and microtrends in academic libraries. *College & Research Libraries News* 69, no. 4: 214–215.

King, David Lee, and Stephanie Willen Brown. 2009. Emerging trends, 2.0, and libraries. *Serials Librarian* 56, nos.1/4: 32–43.

Long, Sarah Ann. 2007. Interview with David Bishop: A primer on staying flexible and relevant. *New Library World* 108, nos. 1/2: 83–84.

Parry, Julie. 2008. Librarians do fly: Strategies for staying aloft. *Library Management* 29, nos. 1/2: 41–50.

Pritchard, Sarah M. 2008. Deconstructing the library: Reconceptualizing collections, spaces and services. *Journal of Library Administration* 48, no. 2: 219–233.

Schachter, Debbie. 2009. Adjusting to changes in user and client expectations. *Information Outlook* 13, no. 4: 55–57.

Somerville, Mary M. 2009. *Working together: Collaborative information practices for organizational learning.* Chicago, IL: American library Association, Association of College and Research Libraries.

Storey, Colin. 2007. Treasuring our traditions and our people: Riding the wave and making a difference over the next 25 years. *Library Management* 28, nos. 8/9: 488–500.

Surprenant, Thomas T., and Claudia A. Perry. 2002. The academic cybrarian in 2012: A futuristic essay. Available: alpha.fdu.edu/~marcum/supernant_perry.doc (accessed April 7, 2010).

Xia, Jingfeng. 2009. Library publishing as a new model of scholarly communication. *Journal of Scholarly Publishing* 40, no. 4: 370–383.

CONTRIBUTORS' ESSAYS

Bintliff, Barbara. 2010. "Keeping Future Law Libraries Relevant." Available: www.neal-schuman .com/academic.

Buchanan, Holly Shipp, and Brian Bunnett. 2010. "Looking to the Future: Academic Health Care Centers and Their Libraries." Available: www.neal-schuman.com/academic.

Burke, Rick. 2010. "Library Consortia and the Future of Academic Libraries." Available: www.neal-schuman.com/academic.

Byrd, Theresa. 2010. "The Twenty-First-Century College Library." Available: www.neal-schuman .com/academic.

Carter, Thomas. 2010. "The Future of Academic Libraries, or 'The Report of My Death Was an Exaggeration.'" Available: www.neal-schuman.com/academic.

Curzon, Susan C. 2010. "'Ain't What It Used To Be': The Future of Academic Libraries." Available: www.neal-schuman.com/academic.

Giesecke, Joan. 2010. "Academic Library Futures." Available: www.neal-schuman.com/academic.

Henderson, Cynthia L. 2010. "Soul Provider: Some Thoughts on the Future of Academic Health Sciences Libraries." Available: www.neal-schuman.com/academic.

Hernon, Peter. 2010. "Academic Libraries Looking Forward: The Role of Schools of Library and Information Science." Available: www.neal-schuman.com/academic.

Kelly, Michael. 2010. "'It Was the Best of Times, It Was the Worst of Times': Special Collections at the Crossroads." Available: www.neal-schuman.com/academic.

King, Lynne. 2010. "The Future Is Now." Available: www.neal-schuman.com/academic.

Murray, John. 2010. "Toward Collaboration." Available: www.neal-schuman.com/academic.

Murray-Rust, Catherine. 2010. "The Opportunity of Invisibility." Available: www.neal-schuman .com/academic.

Neal, James G. 2010. "The Future Academic Research Library: Hope/Power/Action through Primal Innovation and Radical Collaboration." Available: www.neal-schuman.com/academic.

O'Connor, Steve. 2010. "Future Paths for Academic Libraries." Available: www.neal-schuman .com/academic.

Parham, Loretta. 2010. "Challenges for the Future of the Academic Library." Available: www.neal-schuman.com/academic.

Parker, Carol A. 2010. "Academic Law Librarianship—A Look to the Future." Available: www.neal-schuman.com/academic.

Sinwell, Carol. 2010. "Creating a Future: Community College Libraries." Available: www.neal-schuman.com/academic.

Thornton, Glenda. 2010. "Academic Libraries: A Poly-Faced Future." Available: www.neal-schuman .com/academic.

Trejo, Ninfa A. 2010. "The Future of Community Colleges in Our Country." Available: www.neal-schuman.com/academic.

Wand, Patricia A. 2010. "Core Values and Cultural Context: Reflecting on the Fundamentals." Available: www.neal-schuman.com/academic.

Index

About the Authors

Dr. G. Edward Evans is semiretired after a career of more than 50 years in academic librarianship. (Currently he looks after the Harold S. Colton Memorial Library and Archives at the Museum of Northern Arizona.) Academically, he holds graduate degrees in both anthropology and librarianship. He started his career as a student worker in the reserve room of the University of Minnesota Library and spent the past 25 years as a library director. His last full-time position was as Associate Academic Vice President for Scholarly Resources at Loyola Marymount University. He has taught librarianship courses as a practicing librarian and completed the faculty "academic ladder" (moving from assistant professor to full professor) while at the University of California, Los Angeles. Evans's practical experience was in both public and private academic library environments. He has held both National Science Foundation and Fulbright fellowships during his career and has been active in statewide and national library associations. He currently has eight books in print, covering a range of library-related topics including management, collection development, public services, and technical services.

Dr. Camila Alire is Dean Emeritus at the University of New Mexico and Colorado State University. Camila received her doctorate in Higher Education Administration from the University of Northern Colorado and her MLS from the University of Denver. She teaches in the PhD program at Simmons College in managerial leadership and at San Jose State University's executive MLS program in managerial leadership. Camila is Past-President of the American Library Association (ALA) and ALA/APA (2009/2010). She is Past-President (2005/2006) of the Association for College and Research Libraries (ACRL), and also Past-President of national REFORMA, the National Association to Promote Library and Information Services to the Spanish-speaking. Working with Neal-Schuman Publishers, Camila has co-authored books on library service to Latino communities and disaster planning and recovery. She was the first recipient of ALA's Elizabeth Futas Catalyst for Change Award and was named one year by *Hispanic Business Magazine* as one of the 100 most influential Hispanics in the United States.